Proactive Police Management

Fourth Edition

EDWARD A. THIBAULT, PH.D.
*State University of New York
College at Oswego*

LAWRENCE M. LYNCH, M.P.A.
*Onondaga Community College, Professor, Ret.
Town of DeWitt Police Department, Chief, Ret.
Syracuse Police Department, Captain, Ret.*

R. BRUCE McBRIDE, ED.D.
*State University of New York
Assistant Vice Chancellor for Student Affairs
and Public Safety*

PRENTICE HALL
Upper Saddle River, New Jersey, 07458

Library of Congress Cataloging-in-Publication Data

Thibault, Edward A., *(date)*
   Proactive Police Management / Edward A. Thibault, Lawrence M.
Lynch, R. Bruce McBride. — 4th ed.
     p.   cm.
   Includes bibliographical references and index.
   ISBN 0-13-616665-2
   1. Police administration   2. Police administration—United
States.   I. Lynch, Lawrence M., *(date)*.   II. McBride, R. Bruce.
III. Title.
HV7935.T47   1998
353.3'6—dc21   97-12969
                                          CIP

Production Supervision: *Kathryn Pavelec Kasturas*
Managing Editor: *Mary Carnis*
Director of Production and Manufacturing: *Bruce Johnson*
Manufacturing Manager: *Ed O'Dougherty*
Acquisitions Editor: *Neil Marquardt*
Editorial Assistant: *Rose Mary Florio*
Marketing Manager: *Frank Mortimer, Jr.*
Interior Design and Electronic Paging: *Kathryn Pavelec Kasturas*
Proofreading: *Bunnie Neuman*
Cover Design: *Bruce Kenselaar*
Interior Illustrations: *Mark LaSalle*

©1998, 1995, 1990, 1985 by **Prentice-Hall, Inc.**
Simon & Schuster/A Viacom Company
Upper Saddle River, New Jersey 07458

Printed in the United States of America

10 9 8 7 6 5 4

ISBN 0-13-616665-2

Prentice-Hall International (UK) Limited, *London*
Prentice-Hall of Australia Pty. Limited, *Sydney*
Prentice-Hall Canada, Inc., *Toronto*
Prentice-Hall Hispanoamericana, S.A., *Mexico*
Prentice-Hall of India Private Limited, *New Delhi*
Prentice-Hall of Japan, Inc., *Tokyo*
Simon & Schuster Asia Pte. Ltd., *Singapore*
Editoria Prentice-Hall do Brasil, Ltda., *Rio de Janeiro*

Contents

SECTION II–BASIC ORGANIZATIONAL CONCEPTS

▷ **SECTION III—OPERATIONAL CONSIDERATIONS**

SECTION IV—MANAGING THE POLICE ORGANIZATION

CHAPTER 9   ADMINISTRATIVE STAFF FUNCTIONS   **217**

CHAPTER 12 TRAINING POLICIES 313

▶ SECTION V—THE FUTURE: COLLECTIVE BARGAINING AND PROACTIVE MANAGEMENT

CHAPTER 14 COLLECTIVE BARGAINING AND POLICE MANAGEMENT   379

Introduction

Our approach to police organizational management is proactive rather than reactive, with police managers anticipating events through planning, using police personnel and resources effectively, and delivering a whole range of police services to the community.

This proactive concept is not new. In the preface of the 1829 duty manual of the recently organized London Metropolitan Police, Commissioners Rowan and Mayne wrote

> It should be understood, at the outset, that the object to be obtained is the prevention of crime. To this great end every effort of the police is to be directed. The security of person and property, the preservation of public tranquility, and all other objects of a police establishment will thus be better effected than by the detection and punishment of the offender after he has succeeded in committing the crime. This should constantly be kept in mind by every member of the police force as the guide for his own conduct. Officers and police constables should endeavor by such vigilance and activity as may render it impossible for anyone to commit a crime within that portion of the town under their charge.

Thus proactive policing is a grand and noble tradition of both the first modern police force and policing throughout the ages.

Based upon the authors' experience in teaching, policing, and management, three important considerations must be made before discussing proactive management for American policing. First, we believe that sound management is management based upon a combination of theory and practice. Practice without analysis will cause us to repeat the mistakes of history, so our theoretical analysis must be directed toward the practical for implementation into the day-to-day rigors of operating a police department.

Second, we reject complete adherence to the authoritarian as well as to purely participatory styles of management. In the authoritarian model, which indeed dominates most police organizations, important elements of planning and communications are eliminated or lost, whereas in the full participatory model, response to emergency and life-threatening situations will be hampered if too many people are involved; one person often has to be in charge—subordinates must respond to others.

Third, we rely, to a great extent, on the consultative style of management. As will be shown, the consultative style leaves room for change and "doors open" throughout all elements of the police organization. It can be an efficient and dynamic style of management, provided that the necessary elements of a well-run law enforcement agency are met. Consultation also includes discussions with the community on law enforcement and safety problems. It is one of the key ingredients for community-oriented and problem-oriented policing, which are being publicly advanced by police and community leaders.

Proactive Police Management, Fourth Edition, provides a review, analysis, and synthesis of the various approaches to police management, including traditional scientific management, the behavioral/systems approach, and the human relations approach. There is enough detail concerning basic organization and management skills that police managers and students of police management will find the text useful. At the same time, major conceptual contributions from the behavioral sciences and human relations are explored in the context of police management. Most important is the constant theme of being proactive: planning ahead, anticipating the future, and hopefully establishing some control for police managers over those future events.

Community policing is emphasized. Overall, community policing echoes the relationship between police and the community before automobiles and wireless radios. Much attention is also paid to evolving theories such as total quality management, and to new applications of computer technology—which together continue to revolutionize policing as well as other private and public services in the United States.

In our first edition, we wrote that most police departments operate on traditional organization principles as stated in Wilson's text. Since 1986, college-educated and professionally-trained managers are today concerned with communication advances and organizational theories that can be readily applied to their departments.

Policing today remains in the limelight in terms of ethics, the use of authority and force, the crime problem as related to increased drug use and trafficking, and repeated calls by state and national leaders for dealing with crime problems. Correspondingly, many police managers complain that they must do more with less under the burden of antiquated civil-service and collective-bargaining rules and reduced budgets. From the viewpoint of the general public, there is widespread support for police to contain crime. Communities, however, will no longer tolerate corruption and brutality, as shown by the riots that have been sustained in many cities. It is against this background that we present the proactive style of management.

ABOUT THE FOURTH EDITION

Proactive Police Management is widely used as both a textbook for classes in police management and a reference text for police managers in dealing with operational issues in their departments. It is also used for training police supervisors and administrators.

Section I, Historical and Police Culture Context, places the skills and concepts needed to become a professional police manager in an historical (Chapter 1) as well as a police subculture context (Chapter 2). Modern police management has a legacy from public administration, the social sciences, and traditional policing policies adapted throughout the United States and England. Basically, with few exceptions, the modern police organization is the result of an Anglo-Saxon heritage with a unique American contribution. This book concerns the American experience in modern police administration. The latest contributions owe much to the behavioral sciences, particularly psychology and sociology.

More modern police administrators have been promoted through the ranks This increases the importance of the effect of the police subculture on these managers. The police subculture will shape their everyday policies in many ways that these managers may not even comprehend, especially in the crucial areas of internal discipline, training, personnel selection, and personnel management. The increasing number of African and Latino Americans and women is having a strong impact on this subculture.

A knowledge of subcultural norms is important for police management. For the police manager, an understanding of the police subculture is more important than are all other administrative skills and knowledge combined.

Section II, Basic Organizational Concepts, provides the fundamental conceptual framework for the structure of the police agency. To have a department operate effectively, both the formal and informal goals of the department have to be made explicit (Chapter 3). There are general purposes for any department, including community service, criminal apprehension, and crime prevention. However, a small department may wish to define its purposes in terms of community service, whereas a metropolitan police agency has to have broader goals including traffic engineering, vice, organized crime, and so on. It is important for police managers to understand the specific purposes of their own departments so as to implement them effectively. Chapter 3 also includes discussions on the extended use of civilians in police agencies and the accreditation movement.

For a department to go from basic organizational conceptual models to one of high operating efficiency, certain basic operating principles have to be implemented (Chapter 4). These basic concepts, such as range and span of control, unity of command, division of work, and so on, are basic to the operational knowledge of all police managers and supervisors from the chief on down to the supervising sergeants. With these concepts in place, it becomes possible to have an efficiently operating department whose internal policies make for consistency and cost-effective operations.

A basic review of leadership styles allows us to have an understanding of how the implementation of authority by police managers can make or break a department (Chapter 5). The style of leadership in the police management team will give an indication of the type of department being managed. Elements of democracy and hierarchy that are needed to have an optimally efficient department demand a fairly complete knowledge of the styles of police leadership. Although many writers would like effective leadership to be scientific and cut and dried, it is still an art—the art of the possible. No matter how many books are written on leadership, the subject still concerns a human being leading other human beings. In this area we review the concept of reengineering, which is often associated with restructuring and downsizing in large, complex organizations.

Good communication skills are at the very center of good management (Chapter 6). It is more than having a radio, a cell phone, a beeper system, or a computerized communication center. Communication relates to how human beings understand each other. Policing and police management are human services made possible by communication between individuals. The implementation of first-class communication skills is the heart of the police organization. Chapter 6 also reviews how computers and advanced technology are revolutionizing police operations. However, we feel that the police manager has to assume leadership and allow technology to assist, not drive, policy decisions.

Once the major concepts are in place, it is necessary to operate the police agency on a daily basis to get the job done. Much of the daily work revolves around the patrol function and the various line functions related to carrying out the patrol operations (Chapter 7). These basic line functions include traffic, youth services, vice (including organized crime), and investigation. Following our earlier editions, we present a mix of new and old community relations programs that are offered by these areas.

The proactive approach is seen as a positive approach to increase the effectiveness of the delivery of line and patrol services. Advanced planning and analysis of a metropolitan or even smaller area means that patrol activity is directed activity; in other words, the patrol is sent to do specific jobs in specific areas along with the normal activity of responding to citizens' phone calls.

Traffic is seen as primarily a planning/accident investigation activity. Traffic flow is basically an engineering problem where police pressure can be helpful but not related to the core of the problem. Accident investigation is a technical function somewhat different from criminal investigation.

Vice, including organized and economic crime, is a place for specialists and officers who can work closely with a multitude of jurisdictions on the local, state, federal, and even international level. Youth services are seen as both preventive and useful for the solving of cases through youthful informants. Some specialized knowledge is needed concerning youth culture and gangs, and many departments are instituting or have instituted specialized youth officers or youth bureaus for this area. Considerable time has been spent on investigations in many departments with no criteria of when to stop them. To make investigations functionally efficient, a management control system of specific responsibilities and the ability to stop them when necessary is vitally important.

Chapter 8 deals with the heart and soul of any police department—patrol. After reviewing patrol operations trends, we focus attention on directed patrol, foot patrol, bike patrol, problem oriented policing, and community-oriented policing. At this time community policing is the subject of much debate among police administrators, since this philosophy offers so much in delivering services to citizens.

Administrative functions deal with how young uniformed police officers on the line related to the basic administrative staff (Chapter 9). Although primarily task oriented, this is also a function of two-way communication. Community relations are seen as the police being part of the community they are policing rather than simply the speech-making function of a special unit. Many departments have instituted a legal advisor, who, besides solving legal problems, can be an important link to the district attorney's office (Chapter 10).

Internal affairs and disciplinary problems are seen to be intertwined. The citizens-review-board approach is rejected as being too political, whereas having the police protecting their own and hiding bad police work and corruption is also rejected. A positive approach between these two models is recommended. A department needs an ongoing anticorruption goal with clear-cut policies and an internal affairs officer or unit that will treat everybody fairly. This is seen as one of the toughest problems in managing a police agency but one that must be met head-on with solid due process for officers but an overriding concern with eliminating corruption.

Our chapter on Human Resource Management presents a wider focus onto general personnel issues including officer recruit steps, affirmative action, Americans with Disabilities Act (ADA), sexual harassment, and police stress.

A major concern with training is quality control and an up-to-date curriculum that promotes the full range of police services, with a major emphasis on human services. Training is seen as an ongoing function. Society changes, innovations in police work come into the field every year, new police management texts are published, and a professionally trained and operational police officer has to be aware of all this. The only way to have an aware and professionally trained police officer is to have a management team that allows for ongoing training for all of the officers over the duty year.

Planning and research is the core of the proactive approach (Chapter 13). The basic idea is to plan ahead so that the police agency can deal with changing situations before they happen. Most police departments are reactive; that is, they wait for events to happen and then respond to these events. This means that many departments do not do the operational planning nor have the resources to meet emergencies and unforeseen situations. Planning is also related to fiscal affairs, and it is vital in this age of scarce resources for major police administrators to have top-flight budgeting skills.

Auxiliary functions entail a variety of administrative activities. When we examine the communication function in this chapter, we are focusing on the actual carrying out of communications in the department and how the communication unit is organized. Other concerns discussed involve (1) vehicles (maintenance, turnover, and garage considerations), (2) the maintenance of the police laboratory (either as a centralized regional laboratory or as a facility that can be operated by the department depending on its needs, size, and capabilities), (3) property rooms, and (4) records management.

One of the most important areas of police management skills concerns collective bargaining (Chapter 14). With police unions being adversarial, the collective bargaining process is important. It is vital for a chief and his or her management team to understand this process. The collective bargaining process can be an important management tool for creating innovations in the structural and personnel procedures of the department so that both management and the personnel "win" in the process. However, it has to be seen in this positive light; otherwise, collective bargaining can make enemies of management and the personnel who are being managed. Attention is paid to the Fair Labor Standards Act, which has become an issue for police managers and unions.

Finally, the model for the future and the present is seen to be the proactive police agency where there is forward planning (Chapter 15). A brief scenario of what the future might bring to police managers is offered, to give you a carefully ordered set of ideas that can be considered for implementation in present and future departments: the proactive police agency.

ACKNOWLEDGMENTS

In closing we would like to acknowledge the hundreds of students we have taught over the past two decades. Today, many former students are police and public administrators, and their comments and questions on the topics in this book have been invaluable. In similar fashion, we also thank the many faculty members who adopted this book and gave us critical comments.

We would also like to thank the many police administrators who have used this book for administrative and educational purposes. Proactive administrators who continue to give us new insights into management issues include Chief Michael Stein and Management Analyst Sandra J. Embick, Escondido Police

Department; Professor Larry L. Roberts and Chief Kevin Barrett, Palomar College; Dr. Alfred Cali, SUNY Albany; Major Fred Aron and Inspector James Young, New York State Police; the training and management staff at the Bureau for Municipal Police, State of New York; and all the public safety directors in the SUNY system.

Writing a book takes much time and so we thank Barbara, Robbie, Megan, and Brian (McBride), and Marilyn (Lynch) for their patience and apologize for the late hours.

A very special thanks goes to our skillful editor, Kathryn Kasturas, who put up with all the rough re-writes and additional last-minute materials. We would also like to thank Neil Marquardt and the staff at Prentice-Hall for their continuing support and for publishing the fourth edition of *Proactive Police Management*.

EDWARD A. THIBAULT, PH.D.
Fulton, New York

LAWRENCE LYNCH
Escondido, California

R. BRUCE MCBRIDE, ED.D.
Delmar, New York

1

Historical Perspective

The origins of the modern police force can be traced to the creation of the Metropolitan Police in London, England in the year 1829. The social and economic conditions created by the Industrial Revolution caused a great surge in the numbers of people migrating to the cities of England. And this largely uneducated and poorly trained population brought with it the chaos of poverty, unemployment, and crime. This, in turn, led to a proliferation of private and special police forces designed to serve the needs of the diverse interest groups prevalent at the time. The merchant police were hired to protect the individual store owners and shopkeepers, a parochial police protected churchgoers and church property, and special police were hired to protect the harbor front and shipping interests on the Thames, just to mention a few.

Organization of these special groups was at best haphazard and self-serving. The people of the big cities had no organized group to serve the general interests of the total population. The home secretary at the time, Sir Robert Peel, lobbied intensively in Parliament for a professional organized police force under government control. His Act for Improving the Police In and Near the Metropolis of London, commonly known as the **Metropolitan Police** Act, was approved in 1829 with the main purpose as outlined in the first duty manual to prevent crime and protect property.

Lt. Col. Charles Rowan and Richard Maynes, Esq., the authors of the first manual of instruction, adapted their text from the 1803 military manual of the Irish constabulary police, entitled *Military Training and Moral Training*. The force was organized into ranks of superintendent, inspectors, sergeants, and police constables (Reith, 1975:135–36). Some 11,000 recruits were screened to attain the final 1,000 officers to make up the semimilitary structure of the forerunner of our modern police organizations.

Before we examine the historical development of police management theory, we should trace the main stages of development of the present managerial systems of law enforcement in the United States. The history can be divided into roughly six periods. As can be seen from Table 1-1, these periods are actually cumulative; that is, many characteristics from one era persist into subsequent periods.

TABLE 1–1
PERIODS OF HISTORY IN POLICE MANAGEMENT[a]

YEARS	PERIOD	MAJOR LEADERS AND AUTHORS	MAJOR CONTRIBUTORS TO POLICE MANAGEMENT
1750–1900	Industrial revolution, traditional management model	Sir Robert Peel, Charles Rowan, Richard Maynes, John Moore, Henry and John Fielding	Economic man, centralized administration, semimilitary model, ranks, strong leadership, crime prevention objective of policing
1900 to present	Scientific management	Max Weber, O.W. Wilson, Frederick Taylor, Henry Fayol, Raymond Fosdick, Elmer D. Graper, Bruce Smith, August Vollmer, V.A. Leonard, Dwight Waldo, William Parker	Modern bureaucracy, unity of command, civil service, division of labor, specialization, one-way authority, narrow span of control, omnipresent patrol officer, hierarchy
1925 to present	Human relations and participative management	Elton Mayo, Chester I. Barnard, Leonard Fuld, Hawthorne, Frederick Herzberg, R.R. Blake and J.S. Mouton, Rensis Likert, W. Edwards Deming	Focus on personnel management, motivation techniques, morale, stress management, participatory and democratic management with team approach, communication models, TQM
1945 to present	Behavioral management	Herbert Simon, Douglas Murray McGregor	**PPBS**, organizational development, **PERT**, **STAR**
1960 to present	Systems management	Parick Murphy, James McNamara	Zero-based budgeting interfacing of subsystems
1981 to present	Proactive management	James Q. Wilson, George Kelling, Robert Trojanowicz, Herman Goldstein, Lee Brown, David Couper, Steven Bishop	Synthesis of the foregoing theories, with emphasis on forward planning and consultative management techniques, high-technology computers, and communication

[a]PERT, program evaluation and review techniques; PPBS, program, planning, budgeting system; STAR, system training and analysis of requirements.

► INDUSTRIAL REVOLUTION: THE TRADITIONAL MANAGEMENT MODEL, 1750–1900

One of the major management principles of the Metropolitan Police Act that appeared in the original 1829 duty manual was Principle 9 (Reith, 1975: 166), namely, *the test of police efficiency is the absence of crime and disorder and not the visible evidence of police action in dealing with them.* This principle should become increasingly important as police managers look toward the proactive management model and utilize more planning and research to provide a more efficient delivery of services to attain this principle.

The authorized strength of 3,295 men in 1829 was arrived at by attempting to determine, in as logical a fashion as possible, the relationship between disorder and crime in each section of London and the personnel necessary to deal with it. During the first four years of existence, this police force was not only engaged in all-night battles with rioting mobs, it was also under constant threat of being eliminated by the government. However, strong leadership coupled with an excellent command structure and semimilitary organizational model brought order to the streets of London along with diminished evidence of crime in general. This model, which continued to have a solid history of success in the later nineteenth and early twentieth centuries, was gradually extended to all parts of England.

Another important component of this fledgling force was the principle of **local control**. As Reith, in his history of police (1975: 169) points out: "In England, each separate police force in the provinces is established under local authority which in the boroughs is the Watch Committee of the town or city council and in the countries the Standing Joint Committee of the county council, comprising justices of the peace and county councillors in equal numbers....There is no central headquarters, no minister or chief of police." The British were very proud of their local control of their police forces and exported this concept to America. As a result, the selection of constables and election of sheriffs in the United States have to this day been strictly controlled and zealously guarded by their respective communities. The fear of an oppressive centralized police state has severely curtailed the creation of countywide or metropolitan police agencies in the United States. This reluctance to consolidate or combine forces in light of modern-day economics is a major factor to be considered by proactive police managers.

Today, Great Britain's police have traded local control for centralized administration and services, especially in the area of supervisory and command-level training. At present, it is the policy of most constabulatories to transfer a newly appointed officer after an appropriate training period to a different constabulary. This transfer policy of not promoting police managers to take charge in their local districts eliminates a great deal of local influence and control over the police force.

In the United States, the lack of lateral entry between agencies has created a career ladder within the agency that has had the opposite effect: increased local control. The American promotional system leads to some special management problems in both the area of training and control. The demand for local control by communities in many areas continues to hamper a more efficient delivery of services. The result is an overlapping of jurisdictional authority and duplication of services.

With the passing of the **Pendleton Act** of 1870 by the federal government, federal employees were placed under a civil service merit system governing conditions of their employment in an effort to reduce the political interference that had prevailed in the Jacksonian era. Shortly thereafter, the civil service reform spread throughout the states. The new era created by the scientific management writers and leaders after 1900 gave rise to the modern bureaucratic techniques and civil service reforms in policing.

 # SCIENTIFIC MANAGEMENT, 1900 TO PRESENT

Nigro and Nigro, in their widely used textbook on public administration, refer to **scientific management** as the machine model, where the emphasis is on efficiency, orderliness, and output. They cite Frederick Taylor as providing the four basic principles of this approach (Nigro and Nigro, 1973: 92–96).

1. Division of labor and specialization.
2. Unity of command and centralization of decision making.
3. One-way authority.
4. Narrow span of control.

This, along with the monocratically organized bureaucracy developed by Max Weber (see Chapter 3 for a discussion of Weber's principles), became the basic conceptual structure for scientific management. As Nigro and Nigro (1973: 97) point out, the emphasis was on "rationality, predictability, impersonality, technical competence, and authoritarianism." This model fit well with the already existing semimilitary model of police organization, where the manager was definitely in charge of the organizational machinery.

Blau and Meyer in their study of **bureaucracy** (1971: 34) give us three stages of developing bureaucracies that are also characteristics of police organizations. First, cash salaries replace unpaid work by family members. Then, a clerical component is added, the owners are separated from management. Finally, managers are expected to have professional qualifications. This has had further implications that are distinctly nondemocratic, namely, that "Bureaucratic authority…prevents the group itself from conferring the position of leadership upon the member of their choice" (1971: 66). If the group itself cannot pick its leaders, then a rationale has to be developed for another selection process. This is also true of the surrounding political context. One of the thrusts of scientific management is to have professional police managers replace political appointees whereby authority is then conferred by expertise and professional standards.

Other parts of this book examine specific contributions of this approach to police management in some detail. Rather than introduce material that will be examined later in a variety of contexts, let us take two major figures steeped in this tradition and examine them as typical examples of the scientific management approach: O.W. Wilson and William H. Parker.

O.W. Wilson

Orlando Winfield Wilson served as a patrol officer under August Vollmer, chief of the Berkeley, California, Police Department, from 1921 to 1925. His career included being chief of police, Fullerton, California (1925-1928) and Wichita, Kansas (1928-1939); professor of criminology, University of California at Berkeley (1939-1960); and then dean (1950-1960). In World War II, Col. Wilson served as chief public safety officer in Italy, England, and Germany (1943-1947). From 1960 to 1967 he was the reform-minded chief of police in the Chicago Police Department. His book, *Police Administration* (1950, rev. 1963, 1973, 1977), became the most influential management textbook for use by modern police managers and police management faculties in the United States.

Basically, Wilson carried on Vollmer's sound approach to police management under the main principles of encouraging

1. A professional police department divorced from politics.
2. Rigorous police personnel selection and training processes.
3. Use of the latest technological innovations available for law enforcement (for example, maximum use of patrol cars, radio systems, computerization of record keeping).

Interestingly, Wilson was both committed to the professionalization of policing and opposed to civil service. He felt that civil service tests and rules of seniority hampered the police chief in selecting the most qualified personnel for law enforcement and promotion to leadership positions.

Wilson organized his book around three basic administrative processes: (1) planning, (2) activating, and (3) controlling. In 1963 he wrote: "Wisely conceived plans are the keystones of administration; without them the entire venture may fail" (p. 89). He goes on to explain the key part planning has in his organizational scheme. Good planning, based upon the study of needs and used as a continuing process, serves to bind an organization together, to implement the policy underlying its aims and purposes, to direct its efforts into the proper channels, and to guide in both training and performance. He saw the process of activating as one primarily of organization and leadership. Accordingly (1963: 9), "The essence of leadership is the ability to obtain from each member of the force the highest quality of service that he has the capacity to render." Wilson stressed that this leadership was a positive force and that relying on punishments ultimately means a failure of leadership.

His third process control also tied to organization was accountability. He opposed the creation of civilian review boards, since police leadership should be accountable for all officers' actions. He was concerned with punishing officers who used excessive force. As Gazell states in his excellent biographical article (1974: 373), Chief Wilson was "worried about what is sometimes called lawlessness in law enforcement." He considered this to be a definite police management problem that should be handled internally. Gazell also sums up O.W. Wilson's legacy to police management (1974: 375):

> As Vollmer's most renowned pupil and disciple, he refined, extended and synthesized the former's work through multiple roles as practitioner, educator, scholar and consultant. His voluminous writings are divisible into the following basic categories: (1) the internal administrative milieu, especially the salience of organization theory, personnel and technology, and (2) the external environment, particularly the importance of foreign models and…police interactions with citizens in such disparate areas as inputs, community relations, civil liberties, accountability and organized crime.

WILLIAM H. PARKER

Between 1927 and 1939, William Henry Parker rose from police officer to captain in the Los Angeles Police Department (LAPD), earned an L.L.B. degree, and uncovered scandal in the police promotion process that resulted in a grand jury investigation and general cleanup of the department. During World War II, working under Colonel O.W. Wilson, Parker developed the police and prison plans for the invasion of Europe and organized democratic police departments in Frankfurt and Munich (Gazell, 1976: 29).

Parker shared many of the concerns of O.W. Wilson. Basically, Parker's main contribution was in the implementation of scientific management in the LAPD, one of the largest police departments in the country, during his tenure as chief from 1950 to 1968. Parker was known for his strong stand on effective law enforcement, accountability, technocratic innovations, and commitment to police professionalism. Besides the normal background investigation, Chief Parker also demanded that recruits have IQs of 110 or above, undertake a closely supervised one-year probation period, and undergo a thorough psychiatric examination. He also created an exhaustive **modus operandi**, or method of procedure, file made up of over 2 million cards, one of the finest police laboratories in the world, and a planning and research division that used and still uses state-of-the-art computer technology. Gazell sums up Parker's internal changes (1976: 33):

> organizational innovations (such as the establishment of the Internal, Intelligence, and Planning and Research Divisions, as well as the creation of rehabilitation centers for alcoholics), a procedural revamping (such as one-man patrols, intradepartmental repairs of equipment, paperwork reductions and a lower ratio of police officers

to population), and some widely acclaimed results (such as lower incidence of crime, vigorous narcotics control, inroads on organized crime and few traffic deaths).

Under Parker's leadership, the LAPD became a model for the country in terms of standards of excellence for police personnel recruitment and training, sophisticated planning, and a solid image for professional law enforcement. His willingness to take on technological and some organizational innovation in the spirit of scientific management served to encourage other departments throughout the country to accept these innovations. This became especially true when the **Law Enforcement Assistance Administration (LEAA)** was willing to provide startup costs and basic capital throughout the 1970s.

OTHER CONTRIBUTORS

Other noted works on police organization based on the scientific approach appearing throughout this period were Elmer D. Graper's *American Police Administration* (1921), August Vollmer's *The Police and Modern Society* (1936), Raymond B. Fosdick's *European Police Administration* (1915) and *American Police Systems* (1920), *Municipal Police Administration* (1943) published by the International City Managers Association, and Bruce Smith's *Police Systems in the United States* (1940). What appears in the writings of these early observers is a skepticism towards municipal police operations, and a willingness of police officials to blame immigrants and other public officials for crime problems. One theme that is most common, however, is the resistance to change by police officials. For example, Raymond Fosdick, in 1920, wrote that uniformed patrol in many cities was outdated since patrol zones had not changed over the course of 20–40 years (1920: 306). Bruce Smith, who wrote a comprehensive review of American policing after World War II, had in 1923 addressed operational and ethical problems with the New Orleans police. When he returned in 1946, he found many of the same problems he had encountered in his first study.

Nevertheless, the contributions of these early observers collectively forge the basis for present study and discussion on crime and policing. Wilson's classical approach, which emphasizes the traditional elements of the unity of action, division of labor, and centralization of authority, continues to serve as the benchmark for American police administration.

HUMAN RELATIONS AND PARTICIPATIVE MANAGEMENT MODEL, 1925 TO PRESENT

Basically, this model does not exist in any one department. It has a part of the personnel thrust of the scientific management model and part of the democratization of the team policing approach and its variations. This is enlarged upon in both the communication and leadership chapters. The current concern using this approach is called stress management.

The **human relations** approach considers the police executive to be a team leader who creates a cooperative effort among line officers through the use of a management team. In Maslow's terms, the police executive is a self-actualizing individual who helps to fulfill the social security, self-esteem, and autonomy needs of the personnel in his or her police organization. As found in McGregor's Theory X and Theory Y approach, the manager is responsible for motivating personnel and developing talent. This is done organizationally by having the manager create opportunities and provide guidance so all members can realize their potential in contributing to the organization. The theme here is that management should be group centered. According to Tannenbaum and Schmidt (1975), the manager would basically operate from two premises:

1. The manager defines limits within which the group makes decision.
2. The manager and group jointly make decision within limits defined by organizational constraints.

The team policing approach as it existed in 22 departments cited by Gay (1977) relied on the police manager acting as a *primus inter pares* (first among equals) rather than as a traditional autocratic administrator. The human-relation approach is especially germane to the participatory management model where full-service and multispecialist teams operate with strong community commitment. In other words, team policing is an adaptation of McGregor's Theory Y to the field.

When we examine the components for the production of stress among police officers, the twin Maslow needs of autonomy and security come into play. Basically, the police officer needs to feel that he or she has the prospect of a promotion along a reasonable career line and that his or her job is relatively stable and free from potentially capricious management. Personnel grievance and promotion matters play as large a role in producing stress on the job as does the work on the streets. With the strong perception of danger and the need for alertness to deal with the unexpected in the field, police officers have a special drive and a need for security on the job. Participatory management, when applied correctly, may deal with and solve these problems. Traditional, autocratic, scientific management often fails to deal with these human-relation problems in a satisfactory manner.

Departmental participatory management models, in which mid-level and line personnel have an important say on how to address local crime problems, become an essential element of community policing, which is discussed in chapter 8. What comes into play is the formation of a new working relationship between line officers and police administrators that reduces the traditional concept of centralized authority. Participatory management results in more individualized accountability in discipline and rewards. Closely allied to this is the term *empowerment*, which is commonly found in many police articles on participatory management. By definition, empowerment is a condition whereby employees have the authority to make decisions and take action in their work areas without prior approval.

In recent years, there have been a number of organizational theory books which are modern versions of the 1930s human-relations school. Based upon operations in large Japanese and Scandinavian corporations, many observers discuss the positive aspects of employee-management work teams (see the discussion of Theory Z in Chapter 5.) This includes the production of high-quality products and the creation of positive employee relations in a noncollective bargaining atmosphere. Theorists such as James March and Karl Weick have concluded that it is the informal structures that generally result in getting things done.

Most popular in this vein are a series of "prescriptions" based on Tom Peters and co-authors (*In Search of Excellence*, and *A Passion for Excellence—The Leadership Difference*) that veer away from traditional management models and recommend people-oriented, humanistic systems as the basis for future national and international competition by U.S. businesses. Key terms such as "management by wandering around," "entrepreneurship," and "client satisfaction" are in tune with the traditional concepts of planning, forecasting, and budgeting based on the author's observation of successful companies.

The successful companies discussed by the Peters group are primarily in the private sector, and some from his first book do not exist today. Among the key concepts that have application for police management is the idea of a **common culture** where the mission of the organization is culturally shared between management and employees. The concept of a corporate culture is much like the concept of the police culture that has been explored thoroughly by writers on policing.

Ten years after publishing *In Search*, Peters is still fond of customer satisfaction and the need for companies to be conscious of "fashion" in their products in order to compete on a global level. The term *fashion* applies not only to the workability of a product but also to such things as color and attractiveness of design. His case studies of successful companies in *Liberation Management* deal with the hard reality of reorganization or downsizing that has occurred in both corporate and public sector organizations who sought to decrease levels of mid-management or combine work sites to reduce operating and personnel costs. In the private sector, many multinational corporations "farmed out" or "outsourced" the production of certain units of work to countries or non-union concerns with lower wage rates. If anything, this trend has resulted in the establishment of smaller business enterprises and the demise of worker loyalty to the norms and values of common culture found in large companies.

Closely allied to the participative management model is the concept of quality teams or project teams created by management to address a certain problem. This forms the basis of total quality management (TQM) which uses the participative approach among employees to improve products or service. These concepts are also discussed in Chapter 5. It is important to note that companies using these approaches retain, for the most part, the traditional hierarchy model.

Both management and employees are brought into this corporate culture through vigorous training, constant employee recognition, and reform of organization processes that have a negative impact on employee performance. As discussed in Chapter 2, the police occupational subculture can be used in a positive manner to achieve organizational goals.

 ## BEHAVIORAL MANAGEMENT, 1945 TO PRESENT, AND SYSTEMS MANAGEMENT, 1960 TO PRESENT

These approaches have had their major impact in the area of fiscal organization, day-to-day budgeting, and short-range and long-range planning. Behavioral systems have interfered with the human relations approach in terms of developing two-way communication systems in terms of formal orders as well as the informal communication systems that serve as a framework for personnel morale systems. Although often seen as competing with the human relations approach, as both systems have evolved in the 1980s, the systems-behavioral management approach compliments much of the human relations approach, having developed mechanisms for accountability as it integrated quantitative measures for both fiscal and human behavior goals.

A behavioral goal has three major components:

1. A goal stated in an empirical manner so that any ordinary person would be able to see, hear, taste, smell, or feel something.
2. A criterion of success that is normally less than 100 percent.
3. A context in which to measure the goal developed in empirical terms.

Examples are:

The patrol officer will increase by 1 hour each shift the time spent on foot patrol from his or her radio car. The location and time is to be based on the crime situation of the community. Time is to be logged as special foot patrol and will be exclusive of routine property and business area checks. (A realistic goal is to attempt an increase in preventive patrol, apprehension, and community relations.)

The investigator shall interview an average of three to five suspects for every 40-hour tour of duty and shall document these interviews in a written report within one 8-hour tour of duty of the documented end of each interview. (This would constitute an increase in the productivity of an officer whose main duties consist of such interviews.)

Where possible, such behavioral objectives can develop into excellent tools of accountability for management. However, there is a risk of creating goals that are too detailed and involve an inordinate amount of paperwork as compared with that needed to get the job done.

Proponents of the systems-behavioral approach developed a number of systems for accountability, forward planning, and fiscal organization:

1. Management by objectives (MBO).
2. Program evaluation and review techniques (PERT).
3. Programming, planning, and budgeting (PPB).
4. Organizational development (OD).
5. Zero-based budgeting.

These various approaches will be reviewed in the appropriate chapters.

 ## PROACTIVE MANAGEMENT, 1980 TO PRESENT

The proactive approach is the focus of this book. Various aspects of this approach are discussed throughout the chapters and reviewed in detail. However, the most significant elements can be outlined here:

1. Objective of policing is crime prevention.
2. Strong commitment to community policing.
3. Modern bureaucracy, range of control techniques.
4. Full-service department with multispecialist teams.
5. Full use of modern communication models (both technological/computer and human relations techniques).
6. Modern budgeting and accounting systems in full use.
7. Great emphasis on forward planning.
8. Consultative management approach (all elements of organization consulted; management team makes final decisions and organizes the implementation of policy decisions).
9. Optimal use of modern technology.
10. Emphasis on art of the possible and operational utility of management approaches.

Scholars who advocate this approach in their work with community policing include James Q. Wilson, Robert Trojanowicz, George Kelling, and Herman Goldstein. Police managers who serve as recognized leaders in the proactive approach are Lee Brown, former head of the Houston and New York City police departments and former head of the Police Foundation; David Couper, former chief of the Madison (WI) Police Department; Steven Bishop, former chief of Kansas City; and Willie Williams, current head of the Los Angeles Police.

The history of police management is seen as an evolving field of study where some elements that did not work still exist but, by and large, are being replaced by modern management and budgeting techniques. Every approach has had something useful and of operational and theoretical utility to the modern police executive. The secret of success of the modern police organization is picking and choosing a synthesis of approaches that will work for that department given its size, jurisdiction, local problems, and political context. The proactive approach is meant to be flexible and utilitarian, yet adhere to principles that will give coherence to police management as it has to respond in the world of the 1990s. The proactive model, of course, incorporates many of the previous schools of theory presented including current discussion regarding community-oriented policing (COP), problem-oriented policing (POP) and total quality management (TQM) that are being applied to police operations today.

► CONCLUSION

Police management has evolved from the rather rigid (semimilitary) organizational model of the late nineteenth century to a more flexible approach that emphasizes human relations skills. Proactive police managers who have been professionally trained and college educated synthesize contributions from all periods of police management.

From the traditional model, these managers develop a finely honed sense of bureaucratic organization. The organization itself has to be created, and this means the creation of a hierarchical organization. The scientific management period focused on goals and the placing of these goals in organizational context. O.W. Wilson and William H. Parker adapted the basic bureaucratic model from Max Weber to make Weber's model functional in today's communication-sophisticated society. The approach depends on having a central organization along with the ability to respond rapidly to ordinary as well as unusual crises.

Regarding the human relations period, although it tended to overemphasize the importance of democratic management, the emphasis on the vital importance of human relations and personnel skills contributed significantly to modern police administration. One finding from this movement is the recognition of the need for human-relations skill training for both middle managers and supervising personnel. Besides having a good sense of leadership and organization, sergeants and lieutenants need to be able to persuade police officers to do their jobs with the utmost efficiency. Sergeants especially are important to the morale and the optimal use of personnel.

Our modern manager grounds himself or herself in behavioral reality by utilizing the contribution of the behavioral management movement. After becoming firmly grounded in achievable practical behavioral objectives, the police organization can adopt the proactive police management model of anticipation and the forward planning needed in all aspects of police management—personnel, fiscal, community, and so on.

Questions for Review

1. Discuss the basic principles of the following managerial models: scientific, traditional, human relations, system, behavioral, proactive.

2. Explain the significance of the following individuals to police management: Frederick Taylor, Sir Robert Peel, O.W. Wilson, and William H. Parker.

Key Terms

bureaucracy
common culture
empowerment
human relations
LEAA
local control

Metropolitan Police Act
modus operandi
Pendleton Act
proactive
scientific management

Bibliography

BEARD, EUGENE, "The Black Police in Washington, D.C." *Journal of Police Science and Administration*, 5, no. 1 (March 1977), pp. 48–52.

BLAU, PETER M. , and MARSHALL W. MEYER, *Bureaucracy in Modern Society* (2nd ed.). New York: Random House, 1971.

FOSDICK, RAYMOND B. , *European Police Systems*. Montclair, N.J.: Patterson Smith, 1915, reprinted 1969.

_____. *American Police Systems*. Montclair, N.J.: Patterson Smith, 1920, reprinted 1969.

GAY, WILLIAM G. , T.H. SCHELL, and S. SCHACK *Improving Patrol Productivity*, Vol. 1: *Routine Patrol*. Washington, D.C.: U.S. Government Printing Office, 1977.

GAZELL, JAMES A. , "O.W. Wilson's Essential Legacy for Police Administrators," *Journal of Police Science and Administration*, 2, no. 4 (December 1974), pp. 365–75.

_____. "William H. Parker, Police Professionalism and the Public: An Assessment." *Journal of Police Science and Administration*, 4, no. 1 (March 1976), pp. 28–37.

GELLER, WILLIAM A., ed., *Local Government Police Management*. 3rd ed. Washington, D.C.: International City Management Association, 1991.

GRAPER, ELMER D., *American Police Administration*. Montclair, N.J.: Patterson Smith, 1921, reprinted 1969.

HOY, WAYNE K., and CECIL G. MISKEL, *Educational Administration: Theory, Research and Practice*. New York: McGraw-Hill, 1991.

INTERNATIONAL CITY MANAGERS ASSOCIATION, *Municipal Police Administration*. Chicago: The Association, 1943, reprinted 1969.

NIGRO, FELIX A. , and LLOYD G. NIGRO, *Modern Public Administration*, (3rd ed.). New York: Harper & Row, 1973.

PETERS, THOMAS J. , and NANCY AUSTIN, *A Passion for Excellence: The Leadership Difference*. New York: Random House, 1985.

_____, and ROBERT H. WATERMAN, *In Search of Excellence: Lessons from America's Best Run Companies*. New York: Harper & Row, 1982.

PETERS, TOM, Liberation Management. New York: Alfred A. Knopf, 1992.

RIETH, CHARLES, *A New Study of Police History*. Edinburgh: Oliver & Boyd, 1956.

_____. *The Blind Eye of History*. Montclair, N.J.: Patterson Smith, 1952, reprinted 1975.

SHERMAN, LAWRENCE W. , "The Sociology and Social Reform of the American Police: 1950-1973," *Journal of Police Science and Administration*, 2, no. 3 (September 1974), pp. 255-62.

SHERMAN, LEWIS J. , "An Evaluation of Policewomen on Patrol in a Suburban Police Department," *Journal of Police Science and Administration*, 3, no. 4 (December 1975), pp. 434-38.

SMITH, BRUCE, *Police Systems in the United States*. New York: Harper & Row, 1940, rev. 1960.

TANNENBAUM, R. , and W.H. SCHMIDT, "How to Choose a Leadership Pattern," *Harvard Business Review* (March–April 1958), p. 36; also reprinted in *Business Classics: Fifteen Key Concepts for Managerial Success*. Cambridge, Mass.: Harvard University Press, 1975.

VOLLMER, AUGUST, *The Police and Modern Society*. Montclair, N.J.: Patterson Smith, 1936, reprinted 1970.

WILSON, O.W. , *Police Administration* (2nd ed.). New York: McGraw-Hill, 1963.

2

Police Culture

Let's face it, cops are the same no matter what agency they belong to.
Drug Enforcement Agent, San Francisco

You know, I thought the bloke was going to do me in. I was really happy when all those guys arrived on the scene.
Constable, Metropolitan Police, London

You don't manage police organizations like you would other agencies. You got to know the police mentality.
Crime Control Planner,
Cobb County, Georgia, Police Department

Police management operates within the context of one of the strongest vocational subcultures existing in American society, and all soon recognize that they are different from most of society in the eyes of others. In this chapter, we have two objectives. First, we are going to look at the police subculture and examine its effect on day-to-day business and on police managers. Then, we shall consider the informal organization that exists in all police departments and must be reckoned with by all managers. The informal organizational can be used to increase effectiveness and efficiency or it can be turned to managerial sabotage.

➤ THE CONCEPT: POLICE SUBCULTURE

According to Edward B. Tylor (1871), with whom many anthropologists seem to agree:

> Culture…is that complex whole which includes knowledge, belief, art, morals, law, custom, and any other capabilities and habits acquired by man as a member of a society.

The police, although part of the American culture, form a distinctive subculture because of characteristics of their particular vocation—law enforcement.

Subculture is "a group that shares in the overall culture of the society but also has its own distinctive values, norms, and lifestyle." (Robertson, 1987: 76). Police subculture has its own set of cultural norms. Robertson states, "norms—shared rules or guidelines that proscribe the behavior appropriate in a given situation" (1987: 62). These norms creates a lifestyle for a police office both on and off the job. The major norms of the police subculture are **secrecy**, **solidarity**, and **social isolation**. The **3 S's** define the everyday life of every police officer in the nation.

Secrecy

Police deal with people's valuable reputations that can be destroyed by routine police investigations. A school official may be a target of an investigation in which a young woman was raped in a van. Any public knowledge of the investigation can destroy the official's reputation, even if the investigation is proved to be unfounded. Many months can go into a drug investigation. Talking about the investigation, even to a spouse, means jeopardizing lives.

Solidarity

The officer is part of a police family. The children are police children. The spouse is a police wife or a police husband. Police officers stick together. They protect the brother and sister officer from a hostile public and your own brass. The operating norm is: "You are never alone."

Social Isolation

The perception of a hostile public is part of what makes police officers feel alone. (Shernock, 1988) Officers carry a gun and arrest people. They know they can trust a cop but never an outsider. Every day, officers deal with the underclass in society, people who steal, drunks and drug dealers, people who sell dope to children, or child molesters who prey on the weak and innocent. Police officers are doing *dirty work*. This is work that deals with an undesirable population. Officers in the public eye can take on the stigma of that population. As one author stated, "I guess what our job really boils down to is not letting the assholes take over the city…They're the ones that make it tough. You take the majority of what we do and it's nothing more than asshole control." (Van Maanen, 1985: 221) So your friends and family are other cops and people in the "business."

Many police officers are unaware of cultural norms that affect their daily lives. Still, all officers have to take these norms into account; for example, the role of secrecy, the norms of police unity and loyalty, and the perception of danger and suspicion that pervades this subculture.

 ## CHARACTERISTICS OF THE POLICE SUBCULTURE

A.B. Hollingshead has given us the basic definition of a vocational subculture and its major characteristics (Arnold, 1970: 22): "a group of specialists recognized by society, as well as by themselves, who possess an identifiable complex of common culture, values, communication devices (argot or other symbols), techniques, and appropriate behavior patterns." Two forces in American society have a monopoly on the use of legal force: (1) the armed forces concerning outside threats and (2) the law enforcement community concerning internal social control. The police department is a human service agency that specializes in the use of legitimate force and is recognized as such by law. The police, themselves, make a great distinction between those who have a "tin" and those who are civilians. Those who have a piece of **tin**, that is, a police badge, are sworn police officers and have the right to carry a gun.

George Kirkham, a professor who became a sworn officer, expresses the feeling of many officers in this vocational subculture when he says (1974: 19): "Every police officer understands that his ability to back up the lawful authority, which he represents, is the only thing which stands between civilization and the jungle of lawlessness." Although this seems to be a dramatic point of view, it does have meaning for police officers who really do feel that they are the **thin blue line** of legitimate authority protecting civilization. This theme is heard daily in every police department in the country. It is part of the web of common values that ties the subculture together.

ARGOT

Police officers in every region of the nation have developed an **argot** (specialized vocabulary of those in the same work) that is generally not shared by outsiders. This stems, in part, from the nature of normal communication between officers. Police officers spend considerable time riding in patrol cars or patrolling on foot with miniaturized portable radios attached to their belts. They are also continually involved with their state's penal law. Much of police argot revolves around (1) citations to the penal law, (2) words and phrases that are coded and phrased so that they can be heard without ambiguity over a radio, and (3) criminal and street jargon laced liberally with obscenities.

Examples of argot have become well known from the major police forces. In the New York City Police Department, officers may have a **rabbi** (a highly placed police official) who can help them out if they get caught **cooping** (sleeping, etc., on duty). In other departments, the *rabbi* might be called a **hook**, or a horse. Argot from the black community also creeps in such as when a *rabbi* becomes a **main man**.

Consider the following radio transmission:

> Car 56, signal 79 possible 80 at intersection of Academy Place and Stacy Place. A 78 and 75 dispatched. Driver may be 1192. You are out at 2330.

This says that police car 56 has been directed to respond to the Academy Place and Stacy Place location to investigate a vehicular accident (signal 79) with the possibility of an injury (signal 80). An ambulance (78) and a tow truck (75) are being sent to the scene. The driver may be intoxicated (1192). The patrol car was dispatched at 11:30 at night (2330) military time. Two police officers who meet in private conversation can communicate openly and yet be incomprehensible to civilians.

---

case study

The argot of the police subculture came to light in October 1993 from hearings conducted on police corruption in New York City. The Mollen Commission investigated corruption dealing with on-duty crimes including assault, burglary, and drug dealing. As reported by the Albany Times-Union (1993), this was the glossary of terms used by police officers under investigation:

"Blue wall of silence"—The unspoken agreement among the rank and file never to turn each other in for acts of corruption.

"Collars for dollars"—When officers purposely wait until the end of a shift to make an arrest. The time it takes to process a suspect can guarantee as much as 24 hours in overtime.

"Doin' doors"—Kicking in doors at known drug locations without a warrant for the sole purpose of stealing cash and drugs.

"Dumping ground"—A precinct, usually in a poor, crime-ridden neighborhood where the department dumps officers with discipline problems.

"Four to four"—The 4 p.m. to midnight shift, plus the four hours spent drinking after work with fellow officers.

"Good cop"—A police officer "who would never rat on another cop," former officer Michael Dowd said. In other words, a bad cop.

"The morgue," "the pool," and "Wally World"—In order, a meat refrigerator factory in Brooklyn, a bay inlet in Queens, and a dead-end street in the Bronx where small bands of cops would meet to plot illegal drug raids or split their haul.

"Movers," "parkers," and "red lights"—Traffic tickets, sometimes fraudulent, given to meet quotas for summonses.

"The Thirsty Third"—Nickname for the 46th Precinct's Third Squad in recognition of its members' penchant for drinking on the job.

ESOTERIC KNOWLEDGE

Hollingshead's (Arnold, 1970: 22) second major characteristic of a vocational sub-culture is an excellent description of what researchers refer to as the transition from the police academy recruit to police officer:"the acquisition by initiates of the body of esoteric knowledge and appropriate behavior patterns before the novices are accepted by the initiated." The police academy spends hundreds of hours teaching such subjects as marksmanship and safety around weapons, unarmed combat, preservation of a crime scene, and basic investigation techniques. Today, increasing time is being spent on human relations, family crisis intervention, and other human-service subjects such as child and drug abuse. The objective of the police academy, over and above teaching basic knowledge and skills, is to instill into the recruit an acceptance of the police role model. This means an acceptance of both the formal and informal codes and discipline making up a police officer.

Arthur Niederhoffer, in his classic work *Behind the Shield*, shows the stages of cynicism as the police recruit moves from the idealistic role models of the police academy to the street (1969: 104). The first stage is titled *pseudo-cynicism*, which is at the training school/recruit level and is an attitude that "barely conceals the idealism and commitment beneath the surface." The second stage, *romantic cynicism*, comes within the first five years of an officer's career. The third stage, *aggressive cynicism*, is evident at the 10-year mark where "resentment and hostility become obvious." At this stage. Niederhoffer talks about a subculture of cynicism. The end of the police officer's career is what Niederhoffer calls *resigned cynicism*, when an officer accepts the flaws of the system.

This cynicism has also been called *realism* (Wilt and Bannon, 1976: 43): "The writers are of the opinion that there is a meaningful degree of realism—at least for Detroit officers—reflected in their "cynical" responses. Objective data cause us to question Niederhoffer's operationalization of cynicism." Whether you wish to call it cynicism or realism, the recruit continues to be socialized into a role model different from that of the academy. The emphasis is on the harsh realities of street violence and internal police politics.

INTERNAL SANCTIONS

Hollingshead's final point on the characteristics of a vocational subculture focuses on the internal social control that helps describe how a police department's informal structure actually works (Arnold, 1970: 22): "appropriate sanctions applied by the membership to control members in their relations with one another and with the larger society and to control nonmembers in their relations with members." **Peer groups** pressure concerning loyalty to the police profession is enormous and overwhelming. William Westley, an earlier researcher in the sociology of the police, showed that the police in Gary, Indiana, would even be willing to perjure themselves to protect a brother officer (Westley, 1970). Although the research was done in the 1950s, the conclusions hold for today's police culture.

Westley (1970: 115) has given us a list of standard sanctions that are normally applied to officers: "the nature of sanctions that would be applied or that the men thought would be applied, should they break the group rules. These include a program in which the culprit would be an outcast, isolated from social relationships so that nobody would talk to him, so that he wouldn't know what was going on, so that the other men would go out of their way to get the man in trouble."

As we will see later, these are especially powerful sanctions in a vocational subculture that is isolated from the rest of the community. Police officers depend upon each other for both professional and private friendships and social life. These sanctions and this internal loyalty also become powerful tools for the managers of police departments.

SOLIDARITY

As has been shown, there is a great deal of pressure for conformity among police officers. Reiser (1974: 158) consider peer influence to be "one of the most profound pressures operating in police organizations." He continues on and shows how it functions: "It bolsters and supports the individual officer's esteem and confidence, which then allows him to tolerate higher levels of anger, hostility and abuse from external sources." This department psychologist for the Los Angeles Police Department (LAPD) has pointed out an important factor concerning peer pressure: It can be a positive force in the life of the individual police officer. One of the most profound statements that any police officer can make is that he or she is never alone once having become a sworn officer. On the job, the call for "officer in trouble" will mean that officers in and outside the immediate vicinity will normally drop what they are doing and rush to that officer's aid. And officers off duty will feel compelled to come to that officer's aid, even from a distance. Reiser (1974: 158) stresses the cost of this group support and that is a "loss of autonomy in the areas of values and attitudes." It seems that group values become shared while there is a great deal of rationalization created to support conformity to the police group.

Examples of this type of pressure appears in many of the novels of veteran LAPD officer, Joseph Wambaugh (especially in *The Choir Boys*). The following advice is from Wambaugh's first novel, *The New Centurions* (1970: 81):

> "I hope I can do this job," Gus blurted, surprised at the desperate tone in his own voice.
> "Police work is seventy percent common sense. That's about what makes a policeman, common sense, and the ability to make a quick decision....You'll learn to appreciate this in your fellow policeman. Pretty soon, you won't be able to feel the same way about your friends in the lodge or church or in your neighborhood because they won't measure up to policemen in these ways."

Joseph Wambaugh himself experienced another kind of pressure once his first novel had been published—jealousy from his peers because of his new fame and earning power. The dedication of his second novel, *The Blue Knight* (1972), reflects how he felt at the time: "I often remember the rookie days and those who had discovered the allure of the beat. Then I thought them just peculiar old men. Now I wish they were all still here and that they might approve this book."

The most frequent example of this feeling of unity, besides the officer-in-trouble call and the need for backup in potentially dangerous situations, is probably seen in the area of professional courtesy. Professional courtesy is normally not discussed in textbooks and articles, but it is practiced every day in police forces. When civilians are stopped for a traffic infraction, they expect a traffic citation. When police-officers are stopped, they do not expect a traffic ticket; they expect to be let go because of professional courtesy. When professional courtesy does not occur, it is a story carried from jurisdiction to jurisdiction and can lead to a feud between police officers in two different jurisdictions.

When a police officer has an automobile breakdown, he or she does not necessarily call a garage mechanic, but may, in fact, call the nearest police department or highway patrol. Help from the local officers may range from driving the officer to a good garage that will give special service and rates to police to having the police mechanic fix the private auto while the stranded officer has coffee with the other officers.

SOCIAL ISOLATION

Most researchers concerned with police culture agree that police are isolated from the rest of American society (see Banton, 1964: Clark, 1965; Skolnick, 1966; Tauber, 1967; Westley, 1970; Savitz, 1971; Ahern, 1972; Sherman, 1974). A typical response to the question, "What do you do for a living?" in a social gathering often evokes this response from a police officer (Banton, 1964: 198): "If someone asks my wife 'What does your husband do?' I've told her to say, 'He's a clerk,' and that's the way it went because she found that being a policeman's wife—well it wasn't quite a stigma, she didn't feel cut off, but that a sort of invisible wall was up for conversation purposes when a policeman was there." In the United States (the preceding was from a Scottish police officer), we have a similar situation, as reported by Skolnick (1966: 51): "I like the men I work with, but I think it's better that my family doesn't become a police family. I try to put my work into the background, and try not to let people know I'm a policeman. Once you do, you can't have normal relations with them."

These sentiments are repeated time and time again—when asked at a party what he does, the police officer says that he is a government worker. When he is pressed, he walks away. Why does he do this? As many officers have said, "If I tell them that I am a cop, they'll want to give me a hard time about some traffic ticket they got. Next will come some bull concerning police corruption and then they'll hold me personally responsible for some court letting some killer loose on the street. What do you want me to do, spoil all the parties I go to that have civilians there, spoil these parties for myself and my wife? It's really better if you stick to your own." And stick to their own, they do. There are police bars, police picnics, and police poker parties. From these and other social activities dominated by fellow officers and their family, police officers create a feeling that each one of them is part of the *blue minority*. This social isolation has made many police officers consider themselves a persecuted minority. Stan Shernock in his survey of eleven police department concludes, "As a result of police perception of public hostility toward them, police officers have assumed many of the characteristics of a minority group." (1988, 184). Shernock showed, as did Westley in the 1950s, that police socialize almost exclusively with police. Since Westley did his research there have been no changes in the fundamental police norms of secrecy, solidarity, and social isolation. There have been great communication and technical advances, women and minorities have become part of police culture, and we have educated police officers with advanced degrees throughout the country; but the police are still a blue minority with unchanging subcultural norms.

PERCEPTION OF VIOLENCE AND PSYCHOLOGICAL DISTANCE

However, there is a positive, functional aspect to this social isolation, and that is the need for psychological distance between the police officer and many of his or her clients (Tauber, 1967: 98):

> I will argue that separateness from the public leaves the policeman free to make negative moral judgments about a person's character and that without feelings of isolation a policeman's job would be untenable.

When a teacher becomes too involved emotionally with students, the job as a teacher becomes untenable because he or she is not able to make objective judgments. The same thing can happen to a police officer. Police are not always dealing with citizens of good will who are unafraid, calm, and friendly. Sometimes they have to deal with drunken drivers who throw up on their uniforms and urinate in the back seats of their patrol cars.

Picture yourself going into a low-income neighborhood on what is called "mother's day," the day when welfare checks arrive in the mail. Here is an actual incident.

Two officers answered the call for a domestic dispute. Using good police procedure, they separated the shouting husband and wife, one to the living room and one to the kitchen. The wife was shouting to the officers that her husband tried to beat her up. Her language was obscene—as was her husband's. Both had been drinking alcohol.

The officers returned to the living room and positioned themselves between the husband and wife to try to calm them down. The wife took out a small-caliber hand gun and managed to fire a shot at her husband. The wife was disarmed and taken to police headquarters. But both officers never forgot that incident.

In another case, one of the authors of this book, in responding to a domestic dispute call, approached the front door of the house and promptly encountered a loaded shotgun being thrust into his body. The homeowner explained that he didn't want the officer on his property. After a good deal of talk, the shotgun was withdrawn and the fight was dealt with. But the author too will never forget the incident.

Incidents like these engender statements like George Kirkham's, following his first months as a police officer (1974: 134):

> Some nights I would lie in bed unable to sleep, trying desperately to forget the things I had seen during a particular tour of duty: the rat-infested shacks that served as homes to those less fortunate than I; a teen-age boy dying in my arms after being struck by a car; small children clad in rags with stomachs bloated from hunger, playing in urine-splattered halls; the victim of a robbery, senselessly beaten and murdered.

Officer "Doc" Kirkham concludes: "In my role as a police officer, I found that the victims of crimes ceased to be impersonal statistics."

The Director of Psychological Services for Los Angeles County Sheriff's Office shows what happens to officers who are involved in traumatic events such as killing another human being. Roughly one-third develop major problems that affect their family, and they may leave the profession because of the trauma; about one-third have moderate problems, like waking up screaming at night, but they recover; and about one-third have minimal problems (Stoddard, 1984). Stoddard's case notes describe such major trauma for one officer (Stoddard, 1984: 228):

> Jim S. shot and killed an armed-robbery suspect who was leaving a store. The shooting was necessary and the officer did his job...He told me: "I saw you three years ago after a shooting...I lost 20 pounds. I'm divorced. I've screamed in the middle of the night and have been startled out of nightmares. I don't have the same drive, and my interest in work is lost...

Law enforcement is not just another job. After all, college professors are not expected to shoot people; but police officers do shoot people. Police culture is a total way of life.

A number of police officers have put the situation this way: "You are at the scene of a fatal auto accident on a busy high-speed highway. Spread before you is a young person with a limb cut off, blood flowing across the highway, and guts spilled out. This person is dead, and there is an auto blocking traffic. You don't have time to gag; you have to save lives, you have to make sure there is a call for help, take care of any other injured, and direct traffic so that there are no more bodies spilled out on the highway." This is not a normal experience for a civilian, but it is a normal one for a police officer. You need to have objectivity and distance if you are to be able to go home at night, love your spouse, and hug your children.

When a recruit joins the force, he or she can lose friends. The next person you arrest may be an old friend. The question is, "How are you going to keep your professional integrity and live with yourself?" The answer, more often than not, is to have few civilian friends. This is what it means to be a police officer and part of an isolated vocational subculture in America.

INFORMAL GROUP STRUCTURES IN POLICE ORGANIZATIONS

Any organization has a formal and an informal structure. The formal structure involves the organization chart and lines of authority (e.g., police chief, deputy chief, inspectors, captains, lieutenants, sergeants, police officers). Although official business is conducted by the formal organization, the informal structure often determines which decisions will be made and the manner in which these decisions will be carried out.

In informal structure, as Berger and Berger point out (1972: 202-3): "There is a general notion that every bureaucracy has an informal structure that exists…beneath its formal tables of organization…it might serve to maintain the system by smoothing difficult situations, filling in gaps left open by the formal procedures and generally giving staff members feelings of belonging and personal satisfaction." Hughes (1971: 12) adds that "an **informal organization** takes on a pattern but in a much more individual and personal way.

This is a reality that every manager has to be able to deal with if he or she is going to have a smooth, efficient police organization with high morale. This is the role of the social groups within the informal structure and the effect of these groups on the formal structure and the police manager's ability to manage. Light and Keller give us a widely accepted definition of social group (1975: 184): "A number of people who define themselves as members of a group; who expect certain behavior from members that they do not expect from outsiders; and who others (members and nonmembers) define as belonging to the group." Typical social groups that exist in and influence police in a police department include fraternal orders comprised of officers; officers who play golf, racquet ball, or cards together; and ethnic and extended kinship groups.

THE HAWTHORNE STUDY

In the early 1920s and 1930s, under the leadership of Elton Mayo, the Harvard Business School conducted a series of research projects at the Hawthorne plant of the Western Electric Company (Roethlisberger and Dickson, 1939). Nigro and Nigro, in their standard textbook, *Modern Public Administration* (1973: 97-102), also refer to this as the beginning of the human relations approach to management. The key to this approach was the discovery of the informal organization and its communication system.

Management in one part of the Hawthorne plant tried to speed up production in parts for telephone switches by placing the workers on a piece-rate system. Production did not change even though the workers could have easily increased production. Researchers discovered informal work norms within the workers' group where there were social penalties placed upon (1) "rate busters," who exceeded the work norm; (2) "chiselers," who did not fulfill the work norm; and (3) "squealers," who might have informed management of this system. This research on the informal structure has been replicated in many organizations both public and private with much the same results.

THE WORK COMMUNITY

We are going to be looking at a variety of groups within the police organization such as informal cliques, ethnic and racial groups, and fraternal societies. All these make up what Drucker calls the work community (1974: 281–84).

According to Drucker, management is interested in making necessary decisions in relation to the mission of its business. He states also that management should not be making incidental decisions related to the work community and that these decisions can clog the organization's decisionmaking machinery. Decisions on such items as vacation schedule and cafeteria and recreation facilities should be decentralized and left to the work community. Although these decisions may not have a high priority, for the worker they are important and can be a means of fostering leadership opportunities. This is not a participatory democracy, for management organizes the working teams. As Drucker concluded (1974: 228),

> The worker and his group are responsible for their own job and for the relationships between individual jobs. They are responsible for thinking through *how* the work is to be done. They are responsible for meeting performance goals and for quality as well as for quantity. And they are responsible for improving work, job, tools, and processes and their own skills.
>
> These are exacting demands. Yet whenever we have made them, they have been met—providing the planning has been done. Indeed in most cases—IBM is the typical example—workers will set higher performance goals than the industrial engineer and will tend to outdo their goals.

This is an approach that we recommend for modern, reality-based police managers. The officer on the street and his or her immediate supervisor have a great deal of responsibility. Peter Drucker's recommendation will enable modern police management to tie this commitment to discretion and responsibility to quality work. As will be discussed in later chapters, this concept has been reinvented in the 1990's for "quality circles" and work teams for community-oriented and problem-oriented policing. However, this takes a precise knowledge of the law enforcement work community and the informal norms and social groups that govern much of this community.

Social scientists, business psychologists, and personnel managers have been studying this informal group structure for many years. A basic concept that they use is that of the primary group as it operates in the secondary or formal organization. Both concepts have to be understood if we are to be able to use them to analyze police organization and how it really operates on a daily basis.

THE EFFECT OF THE PRIMARY GROUP ON POLICE BUREAUCRACY

In the primary group, communication is normally

1. Deep and extensive.
2. Face to face.
3. Intimate.
4. Relaying a sense of belonging.
5. A response to a whole person rather than to a fragmented social role.

In addition, the primary group assumes many of the characteristics of what Max Weber calls a **Gemeinschaft** group where there is a high degree of cohesion and the group is often perceived as an enlarged kinship (for example, when male officers speak of their partners in the patrol car as their wives).

As enlarged upon in Chapter 3, where bureaucracy is examined, secondary organizations are normally

1. Impersonal.
2. Formal.

Communications are formal and impersonal, and relations are based on specialized roles. This is what Max Weber calls **Gesellschaft**, and that is the modern corporate bureaucracy that is found at the core of many police structures.

Primary groups include the family, personal friends, neighborhood social groups, and people who play friendly card games on a regular basis. Examples of secondary organizations are civil service, organized religion, local government, and the military.

These secondary organizations normally operate as classical bureaucracies with hierarchical sets of offices and chains of command. As Niederhoffer (1969; 11) shows, "Large urban police departments are bureaucracies. Members of the force lose their bearings in the labyrinth of hierarchy, specialization, competitive examinations, red tape, promotions based on seniority and impersonality."

Members of the public in such instances as obtaining an accident report, or attempting to find out the status of a case in which they were a witness or the complainant, discover that they have encountered a bureaucracy. They are dealt with courteously, but impersonally, and the correct form must always be filled out. Although officers in smaller agencies tend to become generalists, offering the entire range of police services, bureaucracy occurs in the smaller setting for the same reason as in the larger urban departments.

It is in this impersonal setting that primary groups grow and have a profound influence on organizational life. To feel that he or she is a total human being, the police officer needs roots in the security of a primary group setting within the organization. Primary groups provide the following for individual members:

1. Personal development.
2. Sense of security.
3. Sense of well-being.
4. Sense of being accepted for one's self.
5. Sense of sustaining one's identity and defining that identity.

Primary groups are powerful, supportive mechanisms maintaining a sense of personal identity and security for the individual. They become of major significance for the police manager who recognizes the importance of informal police groups in sustaining morale.

The role of the primary groups in the police bureaucracy may

1. Support or undermine the formal police organization.
2. Form a powerful informal police structure.
3. Have a mediating function, binding the individual to the larger police organization.
4. Have a major role in creating social stability in the police organization and in society in general.

Generally, these primary groups form around a community of shared experience and proximity. The members of the same police academy class or those who work in the same squad may become members of the same social group. Those who grew up in the same neighborhoods form groups. In larger departments Irish, Italian, German, Jewish, and black social groups may pressure management in many subtle and not so subtle ways to have their policies promoted or their group protected or enhanced. The New York City Police Department, for example, has the Emerald Society (Irish), the Columbus Society (Italian), and an influential organization of African-American police officers.

Besides shared experiences, there is often a core of officers who plan group activities and encourage new officers to join. Finally, there are often family ties within and without the group. In relating to the secondary police organization, we must examine the group's informal ties to top management. Is the chief or deputy chief a former member of the group? Does the chief have a relative or close friend in the group? Answers to these kinds of questions often determine who will get that assignment, who will get promotions, and whose policies will be adopted by the department. This kind of information is simply not available in an organization chart. These organizations may also determine productivity. Officers do not want their colleagues to be rate busters, chiselers, or squealers to management.

In one case, a state trooper assigned to traffic duty on a major superhighway decided to be a rate buster. He issued three times the number of traffic citations that other officers were issuing at that same duty station. He was talked to by many of the other officers but said that he would not change and that he thought that the rate of citations he had was just part of doing the job. After a few months, most of his fellow officers would not talk to him. His superiors praised him officially for his work but indicated informally that he might have overdone it as a rate buster. Everyone at the station was relieved when he was transferred.

 ## POLICE PEER NORMS

Secrecy, solidarity, and social isolation are the major police norms. They are fiercely strong and have been documented time and again (Niederhoffer, 1969; Westley, 1970; Balkin, 1988; Blumberg, 1985; Dietz, 1988; Shernock, 1988; Walker, 1992; Peak, 1993). We can go from *Walking the Beat* in 1968 to Shernock's 1988 "Police Solidarity and Community Intervention." Shernock's report on 11 police department showed that secrecy "maintained group identify and supports solidarity." (Shernock, 1988: 185) He added a curious footnote—when he asked if the police officers would turn in another officer for illegal behavior, "As many respondents pointed out to the researcher, they possibily 'should' but 'would not' take the aforementioned actions against fellow officers." (Shernock, 1988: 193)

Gene Radano, in discussing internal police norms in his book, *Walking the Beat* (1968: 13), gives us a few internal police norms:

> A coop is a shelter where cops go to sit down, grab a smoke, escape the weather, or to lie down….Cops move in like the proverbial camel nosing his way into the tent, and soon squatter's rights prevail.

What is obvious from the rest of his discussion is that the **coop** is a resting place for officers shirking their duties and that the officers who know about the coop are under considerable pressure not to inform management of its existence. Upon coming into the coop, the rookie realizes that he is becoming accepted as a member of the line officer police group. As Radano indicates, the subjects of discussion are "man" talk. "Talk in coops is the usual man talk: sex, politics, hemorrhoids, the Sergeant. Not always in that order."

Savitz (1971) documents Westley's finding of strong interpersonal police loyalty in the face of citizen hostility and as a self-protection society of line officers against the brass. Westley documents these internal sanctions, giving them a human dimension (1970: 115):

> If I turned a man in everybody would be out to get me. They wouldn't talk to me. They would go out of their way to get me in trouble. When you are on the police force you can't afford to have a man against you. There are too many situations in which you have got to

depend on him....If a man would turn you in for one thing he will turn you in for another. This is what I figure.

Interviewer: How serious would a crime have to be before you would turn a fellow officer in?

Answer: I wouldn't turn him in for anything. When you are on the job, police stick together.

POLICE CORRUPTION AND INTERNAL NORMS

Another source of information about internal police norms and pressure are those involving police corruption and police abuses. Some of the better known of these reports and studies are the Wickersham Commission's *Lawlessness in Law Enforcement* (National Commission, 1931); *The Tarnished Badge* by Smith (1965); the report on that famous organized crime town in Pennsylvania, Wincanton (Gardiner, 1967); Chevigny's "ride-around" view of police abuses, *Police Power* (1969); Stark's study based on newspaper clippings, *Police Riots* (1972); Goldstein's report for the Police Foundation, *Police Corruption* (1975); the well-known Knapp Commission report (1972); and finally Sherman's study of corruption in four large cities, LEAA report, *Controlling Police Corruption* (1978), and his book, *Police Corruption* (1979).

The basic approach of these studies is to examine (1) how police officers corrupt other police officers, (2) the source of temptations, and (3) whether the payoffs are regular (for example, the pad) or a one-time affair. The studies include advice to management on how to break up internal cliques and bring about more central control. However, there is very little discussion of the effect of primary group cliques on the formal structure.

Sherman focuses his concern on breaking the linkages between local politics and police corruption and proposes various strategies that police managers can use to control their staff (Table 2–1, next page).

Sherman's conclusions are (1978: 1)

1. Premonitory strategies (aimed at ongoing corruption) for corruption control can reduce the level of organization of police corruption.

2. Postmonitory strategies (aimed at past corruption) for corruption control do not seem to be as effective as premonitory strategies.

3. The same strategies for corruption control can be employed in a police department of any size, although the tactics may differ.

This scenario is found in some small and medium-sized cities throughout the United States. Basically this type of corruption cannot exist without the active cooperation of top police officials and major figures in the political hierarchy. As outlined by Dombrink (1991), every major city in the past decade experienced a corruption scandal—the new variable being narcotics. Still Sherman's model with a basis on management control of investigations and employee drug testing remains a viable strategy.

TABLE 2–1
MANAGERIAL STRATEGIES AND TACTICS FOR PREVENTING CORRUPTION

CITY AND TACTICS

STRATEGY	NEW YORK, N.Y.	OAKLAND, CALIF.	NEWBURGH, N.Y.	"CENTRAL CITY"[a]
1. High personnel turnover	Overt pressure on commanders	Quiet pressure on rank and file	Criminal prosecution (but not by management)	Overt pressure
2. Accountability	Punishing lax supervisors	Punishing lax supervisors	Not adopted	Not adopted
3. Tighter supervision	Decentralization: supervisors present at corruptive tasks	Centralization: rules, paperwork	Personal supervision by executive	Not implemented
4. Ending corrupting policies	End vice-arrest quotas; provide "buy" money; advance expense money	Not adopted	Not adopted	Increase funds for informer's fees
5. Changing the task environment	Reduce gambling enforcement; make bribery arrests	Increase gambling enforcement; make public appeals against "gifts"; make bribery arrests	Appeal to public to report corruption; repeal ordinance allowing gifts	Not adopted
6. Changing the political environment	Not adopted	Scare politicians into honesty	Initiate federal probe of political corruption	Not implemented
7. General management policy	Premonitory	Premonitory	Premonitory	Postmonitory

[a]"Central City" was promised anonymity as a condition of the study.
Source: Sherman (1978).

CORRUPTION, CLIQUES, MEAT EATERS, AND GRASS EATERS

One of the early research articles on police corruption that investigates primary group cliques in the police structure is that of Stoddard's "The Informal 'Code' of Police Deviance: A Group Approach to 'Blue-Coat Crime'" (1968: 202). Stoddard indicated that it was the cliques dominated by older officers that first corrupted the recruits. The Knapp Commission (1972: 3–4) showed widespread corruption:

> The overwhelming majority of those who do take payoffs are "Grass eaters," who accept gratuities and solicit five, ten, and twenty-dollar payments from contractors, tow truck operators, gamblers, and the like, but do not aggressively pursue corruption payments. "Meat eaters," probably only a small percentage of the force, spend a good deal of their working hours aggressively seeking out situations they can exploit for financial gain. including gambling, narcotics, and other serious offenses which can yield payments of thousands of dollars.

Leonard Savitz (1971: 697) has given management a very good reason why these negative police cliques develop, as he studied a cohort of Philadelphia police recruits over a three-year period:

> With a capricious, uncooperative, and unreliable citizenry, with a bureaucratic structure which does not always properly protect its own, there arises the possibility that latent structures develop which place the highest premium among fellow officers. Secrecy is defined as personal and conscious concealment of information not only from the public but also from supervisory and administrative levels with the organization.

---

case study
The Wincanton (Reading, Pa.) Protection System

The following account is taken from the task-force report on organized crime (National Advisory Commission, 1976) and is such a well-documented government report on how organized crime took over the criminal justice system that it has remained a classic. Despite the fact that this occurred over twenty years ago, this study is considered to be the classic on corruption and organized crime.

Two basic principles were involved in the Wincanton protection system—pay top personnel as much as necessary to keep them happy (and quiet) and pay something to as many others as possible to implicate them in the system and to keep them from talking. The range of payoffs thus went from a weekly salary for some public officials to a Christmas turkey for the patrolman on the beat. Records from the numbers bank listed payment totaling $2,400 each week to some local elected officials, State legislators, the police chief, a captain in charge of detectives, and persons mysteriously labeled "county" and "state." While the list of persons to be paid remained fairly constant, the amounts paid varied according to the gambling activities in operation at the time; payoff figures dropped sharply when the FBI put the dice game out of business. When the dice game was running, one official was receiving $750 per week, the chief $100, and a few captains, lieutenants, and detectives lesser amounts.

While the number of officials receiving regular "salary" payoffs was quite restricted (only 15 names were on the payroll found at the number bank), many other officials were paid off in different ways. (Some men were also silenced without charge—low-ranking policemen, for example, kept quiet after they learned that men who reported gambling or prostitution were ignored or transferred to the mid-

night shift; they didn't have to be paid.) Stern was a major (if undisclosed) contributor during political campaigns—sometimes giving money to all candidates, not caring who won, sometimes supporting a "regular" to defeat a possible reformer, sometimes paying a candidate not to oppose a preferred man. Since there were few legitimate sources of large contributions for Democratic candidates, Stern's money was frequently regarded as essential for victory, for the costs of buying radio and television and paying poll-watchers were high. When popular sentiment was running strongly in favor of reform, however, even Stern's contributions could not guarantee victory. Bob Walasek, later to be as corrupt as any Wincanton mayor, ran as a reform candidate in the Democratic primary and defeated Stern-financed incumbent Gene Donnelly. Never a man to bear grudges, Stern financed Walasek in the general election that year and put him on the "payroll" when he took office.

 POLICE TYPOLOGIES

Another approach to the study of internal groups has been the "typology of ideal types" study. The theory of ideal types, introduced into social science by Max Weber, says that models of reality can be created as an extreme form of that reality and used to clarify the relationships embodied in that reality. Wilson's (1968) styles of policing is the most widely used typology: legalistic, watchman, and service. The legalistic type would arrest a citizen any time any law was broken, with keeping the peace (watchman) and the delivery of human service to citizen (service) only emerging after the law was satisfied. "Has the legalistic style of policing ever existed in reality?" The usual answer is no, not as a style of a police agency or the style of an individual officer. However, some agencies prefer this type of policing, even though the other styles may also exist in a legalist style of police agency. The same is true of individual officers. What this and other typologies do enables the researcher and the student of police management and police culture to use the ideal typology as a tool to analyze police departments and police groups. We will see this tool in use when we look at styles of leadership and management.

Broderick (1987) created a typology that is widely used. He has three types. The enforcers "place a relatively high value on social order and keeping society safe and a relatively low value on individual rights and due process of law." (1987: 23) The idealists "place a relatively high value on individual rights and due process of law....They also believe that it is their responsibility to keep the peace, to protect citizens from criminals and otherwise preserve social order." (1987: 49) "Realists place a relatively low emphasis on both social order and individual rights....Realists seem less frustrated than...other officers." (1987: 77) These realists are the ultimate cynics and feel that not much can be done about crime and criminals. Optimists "place a relatively high value on individual rights. That is, like the Idealists, they see their jobs as being people-oriented rather than crime-oriented." (1987: 99) They are not crime-oriented, they like helping people, and they feel police work is rewarding.

This is a typical typology. The author then goes on to describe various police behavior of each type. Police managers need to deal with all kinds of police personalities. They would do well to look over some of these typologies to see if any relationship can be found between these social constructs and police behavior.

Hundreds of typologies for the study of police management and police culture have been produced. There are professional cops, street cops, by-the-book cops, bad cops, good cops, and many others. These studies look at whole departments, styles of leadership and management, and types of police officers. However, these studies rarely take even a brief look at how these models are also characteristic of groups of police officers in the agency.

Consider, for example, a chief with a service orientation who takes over a department that already has a legalistic style. He will send standard operating orders to the officers telling them they should spend time talking to citizens, delivering babies, teaching courses at the local schools, serving as guest speakers, and *also* apprehending criminals. The new chief will find tight and fast resistance because the prevailing style gives priority to enforcing the law and apprehending criminals.

If the chief does not understand the difference between his or her style of policing and the one prevailing in the department, he or she will fail. Police managers need to understand police styles on a daily basis if their orders are to be effective.

 ## MINORITY GROUP STRUCTURES

The research on minority law enforcement officers has generally been directed toward how blacks feel about being police officers and what group norms emerge. However, some work has been done on black police officers' clubs and social groups and their effect on police administration and management.

AFRICAN-AMERICAN OFFICERS

From December 1964 to October 1965, Nicholas Alex interviewed 41 black New York City police officers with a series of open-ended questions. The result was the first book on black police, *Black in Blue* (1969). Alex discovered that black police officers were often accepted as brother police officers but were often socially excluded from white officers' social activities (1969: 87): "It's wonderful in the station house....We are going to do police work together— wonderful. But off duty, that's different. It's funny. When you walk into a room of white cops getting together for a few drinks with their wives, there's a very cold feeling." He quotes another black police officer (1969: 97) as belonging to a black officer's social club: "Several years ago I belonged to a club. It was a social club of Negro cops and corrections men." However, that is all we find out about this club.

He also shows ethnic rivalry (1969: 111) in terms of blacks being exclud-ed from the detective division: "The Irish are the bosses. It's an Irish job and they want to keep it. They can't stop you on the promotion jobs, because you take a test and the marks are posted, so everyone knows. But they can stop you from getting into the Detectives, Youth Division, and Plainclothes." There are some data here, but this is basically a descriptive study with little analysis, except in terms of general racial discrimination.

A 1973 (Bannon and Wilt) article on black police officers based upon a disclosed number of interviews with Detroit black police of various ranks (fall 1970 to spring 1971) found that black cops were more often referred to sim-ply as good or bad cops by white police officers. Black police officers did not want to lower the standards to bring more blacks into the police agency since they felt this would lower their own status in the eyes of their fellow police officers. Here you see a closer identification with the prevailing police culture.

However, many of the same problems persisted. Blacks felt that opportu-nities for promotion had improved over the years. However, they were still dis-turbed that (p. 27) "assignment to preferred jobs often occurred on a friend-ship basis, rather than strictly on a qualification basis." The basis of group friendships and its analysis was not carried forward. The social exclusion of black police officers persisted. As one black Detroit police officer states (p. 28): "I have observed a certain amount of discrimination in that white officers tend to keep to themselves and exclude blacks from their groups not only socially but even in everyday relations at station houses." No group activities of blacks were documented.

From January 1974 until January 1976, Eugene Beard had 947 (90 per-cent) of the black officers on the Washington, D.C., police force complete a self-administered questionnaire under orders from the chief of police. The questionnaires were turned in to the officer's desk sergeant. Ten percent were from black female police officers. Nearly 84 percent of the respondents held the rank of private, and more than "65 percent reported that they trusted few or no white officers; black officers rarely socialized with white officers; more than 80 percent believed that blacks were discriminated against in hiring, job assignments, enforcement of rules and regulations and job performance ratings" (1977: 51). Beard also reported that 58 percent felt that "the lack of trust of black police personnel by white police was not a problem (p. 50)."

In a follow-up study to Alex's work, Leinen (1984) discussed racial discrimination in the New York City Police Department from the Civil Rights era to the beginning of the 1980s. Until the 1960s, black officers were assigned only to black neighborhoods and were neither promoted nor assigned to special units. Disciplinary actions against black officers were inequitable when compared to those against white patrol officers. In the last two decades many improvements have been made in these procedures. Based on a series of interviews with black patrol officers, detectives, and supervisors, Leinen found that institutional discrimination had largely disappeared. He felt this was due to the legal, social, and political events of the civil rights era, along with the efforts of black officer associations such as the **Guardians**. Leinen (1984: 255-56) reported that there were some white officers who continued to deny blacks and other nonwhite officers opportunity and mobility in the New York City Police Department. This problem, he maintained, was compounded by the senior positions held by these racist white officers. Although blacks and other minorities have made strides in the department, there was still the obstacle of the racist senior officer to contend with.

A study by McBride (1986) on the recruitment and training process for three medium-sized police departments in New York State found that blacks were generally accepted by their white colleagues based on the black officer's ability to do the job. Based on a series of face-to-face interviews, the study found some instances of discriminatory treatment toward black officers during employment selection and police training.

Black recruits indicated that they had encountered difficulties during field training because of both personality clashes and the treatment of black citizens by their field training officers. The same recruits indicated they had little difficulty in dealing with the areas to which they were assigned after field training, regardless of the racial makeup of the suspects and victims in the area. They felt that the isolated instances of cries of **"Uncle Tom"** came from citizens who had a bad attitude toward police in general.

The number of minority officers, blacks, hispanics, and asiatics on the force and in officer ranks has continued to grow over the years, as a result of affirmative action programs. Even as the research becomes more sophisticated, it is still evident that blacks and other minority officers are generally treated equally on the job by white police officers but continue to be generally isolated from white police officer social affairs.

Black and Hispanic police officers have been growing in number and percentage in the fifty largest city departments. The largest percentage of African-American and Latino Police Officers (Macguire and Pastore, 1995: 49–50) are:

Police Department	Percent 1983	Percent 1992
African-American		
Washington, D.C.	50.1	67.8
Atlanta, GA	45.8	54.6
Detroit, MI	30.7	53.3
New Orleans, LA	20.9	39.2
Memphis, TN	17.5	30.2
Latino		
El Paso, TX	56.9	61.1
Miami, FL	39.2	47.2
San Antonio, TX	32.9	36.3
Albuquerque, NM	32.7	34.2
Los Angeles, CA	13.6	22.3

Latinos and African-Americans are no longer minorities who are also police officers. They are police officers who happen to be African-American, Latino, Irish, French, German, Italian, and so on. In 1996, unlike 1956, these people are just "cops."

FEMALE OFFICERS

The first woman officer was appointed in the Los Angeles Police Department in 1911 (Sherman, 1973a: 383). As was pointed out by Owings in *Women Police* (1925), the female officer was normally used in three areas: vice, juvenile work, and the handling of female prisoners (police matron). Sherman (1973a) indicated that women, at that time, still constituted only 2 to 3 percent of the national police force and that surveys showed that women still held the traditional women police jobs in the male-dominated departments around the nation.

In 1968, Chief Winston Churchill of the Indianapolis Police Department assigned two women to car 47 to do regular patrol work. He thus earned the distinction of having the first women doing "regular" duty. As Sherman points out, "The crew of car 47 has earned open if grudging acceptance from most Indianapolis policemen." "Grudging acceptance" exemplifies the place of women in policing. Police management decides to take a chance to assign female police officers to regular duty. Over a number of years, these female officers earned the grudging acceptance of the male police officer.

Of the many stories that come from jurisdictions around the country, the following trends are well documented.

Catherine Milton (1972) found that women officers were used as secretaries and dispatchers but were infrequently accorded equality with men. By 1974 there were enough female police executives in Pennsylvania that Barbara Price could publish an article entitled, "A Study of Leadership Strength of Female

Police Executives." Susan Martin, a policewoman in Washington, D.C., interviewed 32 officers on feelings. She concluded (1979: 322) that

> policewomen as tokens in a male-dominated occupation face a number of dilemmas....They face performance pressures, isolation from co-workers, tests of loyalty and entrapment in stereotypic roles. Expected to outperform others, closely watched for any sign of weakness yet pressured at the same time to conform to typically feminine behavior and punished with such labels as "bitch" and "lesbian" for failure to act in stereotypic ways, policewomen indeed work under different structural conditions than male officers.

She also pointed out that there was a lack of unity among female police officers and that they fail to act as a political faction or as a group. Instead, they compete individually and lack internal political clout.

Let us examine some quotations from women police officers (Dreifus, 1980: 18, 20, 25).

> People are always asking me what I'm trying to prove...
> Winning acceptance took time. I did it by striking a balance between being tough and funny.
> A woman on patrol will never have the equivalent of a wife. No guy wants to be that tolerant.

In 1993, female police officers made up 9.4 percent of sworn police officers and 63.1 percent of civilian employees of police departments in the United States. (Macguire and Pastore, 1994: 55)

In 1971, women were only 1.4 percent of sworn police officers. (Martin, 1993: 328) In 1990, Martin found that women were 10.5 percent in cities over 50,000 and 11.3 percent in the suburbs. In 1986, nonwhite women were 40 percent of the female officers. Female officers in that year represented 3.3 percent of all supervisors in municipal agencies. (Martin, 1993: ;328) In 1993, the four women police chiefs in major cities were Elizabeth Watson, Austin, Texas; Elaine S. Hedtke, Tucson, Arizona; Leslie Martinez in Portsmouth, Virginia; and Mary F. Rabadeau in Elizabeth, New Jersey. (Schulz, 1995: 372)

The courts have backed women when they have been discriminated against in hiring and promotion. In Webb v. City of Chester, Ill., Webb testified that on the day she got her badge, a member of the Board of Fire and Police Commissioners told her, "I don't want you here, you are a woman and a woman has no business being a police officer." Even though she was at the top of her police academy class, two and one-half weeks after graduation, she was fired. The jury awarded her $20,250 for embarrassment and humiliation and $9,750 as compensation for lost wages, and the judgment held on appeal. This was done under Section 703(a) of Title VII of the Civil Rights Act of 1964, which states it is illegal to discriminate because of sex.

In Thomas v. City of Evanston in 1985, and Baurney v. Pawtucket in 1983, courts decided that a physical agility test discriminated against women. In 1979 in Vanguard Justice Society v. Hughes, and U.S. v. North Carolina in 1981, courts decided that certain weight requirements also discriminated against women. Hale and Menniti conclude from these and other cases that "where the success rate of a plaintiff class is less than 80 percent, a finding of a disparate impact is appropriate for the courts." (Hale and Menniti, 1993: 181–183) This means that if 80 percent of a certain class flunks, then the test or criteria is suspect.

Balkin in 1988 did an empirical study titled, "Why Policemen Don't Like Policewomen." He quoted one respondent, "If you are sleeping with someone you are a slut; if not you are a dyke." (Balkin, 1988: 92) The reasons why women police officers have such a hard time being accepted by the male police force are once again the three S's: secrecy, solidarity, and social isolation. Balkin (1988: 35) concludes, "This solidarity is in the service of ameliorating the men's sense of isolation from the public and the dangerousness of their work. Women in policing undermine this solidarity. They are not like them and are [therefore] opposed.

Leslie Kay Lord found (1986: 89) that "male officers still harbor grave reservations about women's suitability to be competent police officers." In a study of stress on the female officer, Wexler and Logan indicated that these types of attitudes put a great deal of stress on the female officer. As one officer in their study said: "The academy said they didn't want women. We stuck together and said we were going to make it. One training officer said, 'This is my personal opinion. I don't think you should be in this job. You should go home and have babies'" (Wexler and Logan, 1983:50). The study concluded: "After 6 years of women on patrol, the men in the department still did not seem to accept them as officers. They were ignored, harassed, watched, gossiped about and viewed as sexual objects. The hostility of the male co-workers has been so substantial that other stressors receded in comparison" (Wexler and Logan, 1983: 52).

However, another study showed that when the researcher controlled for age, the younger officers were more accepting of the female officer (Weisheit, 1987). Yet another study reported that women reported higher stress than men but that "improvement in status and income associated with entry into male-dominated employment may ameliorate stress consequences for policewomen in comparison to other employed women" (Pendergrass and Ostrove, 1984: 308).

A final issue that has had a negative impact on policewomen and their relationship to their fellow officers and the community is a charge that policewomen are cowardly (Homant, 1983). Some male officers also accuse the female officer of being emotionally unstable in the face of violence. However, a 1987 study refutes these stereotypes. Sean A. Grennan (1987: 83) in a study of the New York City police department found that there was no gender difference in the number of injuries sustained in patrol. "There is no basic difference between the ways a male or female officer, working in a patrol team, reacts to violent confrontation." He also concluded (1987: 84) that "women police officers, in most cases, are far more emotionally stable than their male counterparts and lack a need to project the **macho** image that seem to be inherent in the personality of most male officers. The female officer, with her less aggressive personality, is more likely to calm a potentially violent situation and avoid injury to all participants." He showed that in a male/female team, the male was more likely to discharge his firearm.

It is going to take time for the female officer to be accepted in the male-dominated occupation of law enforcement. However, the female officer will become more accepted as the older officer leaves the force, and the younger, more tolerant, officer who went through training with female officers, starts filling up the ranks. This problem of acceptance of women and blacks as subgroups within the law enforcement will disappear when both the public and the police themselves respond to the uniform rather than to the person wearing the uniform.

case study
Canal City Police Department

The Canal City Police Department is a traditional, hierarchical department in a small city on the East Coast. The middle-sized department reflects the social and political makeup of this municipality, which is dominated by one ethnic group. The informal relationships that have developed over the years have created a number of strong cliques based upon kinship and a variety of interests.

One ethnic group dominates the police hierarchy so much that other officers complain how these officers stick together. The perception of the other officers is that these officers do favors for each other, including preferential treatment for promotion, shift assignments, and attendance at special training programs outside the city. This is quite similar to the behavior of the Irish in Boston and Scandinavian and German groups in areas of the Midwest. Unlike the New York City Police Department, where a number of ethnic groups compete with each other, in Canal City there exist only the one ethnic group and the unorganized others. In Canal City, the "rabbi" who will help you up the promotion ladder will be from this ethnic group. In New York City, he most likely will be Irish, then Jewish, and least likely Italian or German.

Kinship permeates the ethnic cliques. Favors are performed by uncles, cousins, and godfathers of higher rank for those related in the lower ranks.

Naturally, in this traditional, autocratic department, the chief and his cronies form the most powerful clique; moreover the chief retains power and influence, not just through the normal means of command rank but also through a communication network operated by his clique. Officers who attempt to go against the chief are inevitably discovered by members of this clique that extends to the lower ranks. When a malcontent officer is identified, the information is conveyed to the chief, and the officer is disciplined.

A unique clause in the union contract allows command officers to participate fully in all union activities. Not surprisingly, the agenda of the Police Benevolent Association's meetings contain few criticisms of the chief or members of his clique. Thus control is exerted downward through the ever-watchful eyes of the chief's clique, even when he cannot be present.

One shift, shift C, has been a thorn in the side of this autocratic chief. Composed mainly of younger, college-educated officers, the officers in this shift have been known to pull pranks

Canal City Police Department (cont'd)

that make the chief angry. Once, while the chief was trying to transmit a radio message, members of the shift keyed their microphones in to the chief's frequency, causing considerable interruption. The culprits were invited to report to the chief's office. In the tradition of the fierce loyalty that police officers have for each other, no one reported and no one told the chief anything. Every man in the shift was ordered to one tour of foot patrol each month, and patrol partners were changed from day to day.

This was a punishment directly attacking the informal organization of the shift. Over the years, partners come together who like and trust each other. In Canal City, partners are often referred to as being "married" to each other.

Rotating the tours of duty broke up the partnerships and disrupted much of the informal organization of the shift. In sociological terms, this was probably the worst type of punishment the chief could devise in terms of the morale of his young officers.

Within shift C, the following cliques were identified:

> *The elite clique.* Three experienced and powerful men who are close to the chief and enjoy his protection. One is a patrolman, one is a lieutenant, and one is a captain. All have over 20 years of seniority.

> *The young ambitious.* These six with young families are aggressive officers in terms of making arrests and doing "real" police work. They privately voice their

opposition to the chief's dictatorial policies and fervently hope that he retires soon. Additionally, they feel that some members of the shift are lazy and corrupt and have little use for these officers.

Pistol clubbers. These three married officers belong to the department pistol club and take part in statewide competitions. The club provides a common meeting place away from the police station for socializing, sharing gossip and criminal information. The pistol club has the blessings of the chief.

Social drinkers. These five officers go drinking together sharing both police and private gossip. They all have at least seven years of experience and are known to socialize with their families.

The shift has sportsmen, golfers, and officers attending college. However, these are the main cliques. What makes this shift stand out from the rest is that cliques are formed mainly on the grounds of interests, not ethnic and kinship ties. Every officer knows that when you are dealing with one of these officers, you are also dealing with his clique and the relationship between his clique and your clique.

At times, the entire shift gets together at their favorite police bar for drinking and playing cards. On the evening shift, 4:00 P.M. to 12:00 A.M., there are frequent and rather rowdy get-togethers at local bars and in private homes. This has become known in

Wambaugh's terminology as "choir practice."

The officers are deeply imbedded in their various social and professional groups that define power relationships in the department. They also make a fairly large department with strong hierarchical relationships more humane and give the individual officer a sense of personal worth and security.

At present, traditional ethnic cliques dominate the department and support an authoritarian chief. If the young ambitious clique manages to form an alliance with a number of the stronger kinship groups, the chief may have problems and a new power relationship may be forged in the Canal City Police Department.

This is a real department, and participant observation research has been done in this department. However, considering the explosive nature of the analysis of the power relationships cited, the authors have decided not to reveal additional (geographical) details.

 ## CONCLUSION

This chapter has focused on the subculture and informal organizational structure as forces to be dealt with by police managers. We began by defining the concept of subculture and offered examples of how it appears in police work argot, isoteric knowledge, internal sanctions, unity, social isolation, perception of violence and psychological distance. The implications for police managers are obvious. Issues and problems that have basis in the notion of subculture have a tendency to become major.

Internal factions based upon the primary group organization will exist in every police department. It is up to the management to use these groups as positive reinforcement for the basic purpose of the organization. The deep ties of loyalty generated by primary groups operating through the informal social structure can make or break management in any police department. Most books on police management and administration ignore the effect of these groups on the operations of the basic organization and management style.

However, we can no longer afford to ignore the fundamental group dynamics that structure departmental activity on a daily basis. These groups, along with police subculture and unions (described in Chapter 14), operationalize management directives and determine the impact of management decisions on the operation of the organization, itself, and on the citizens. Primary groups shape and run most organizations in terms of the personal effect on individual officers. No policy can be implemented without taking these groups and their actions into account. The sophisticated police manager knows that there is a long way to go from the orders he issues from his desk to the implementation of those orders in the squad room and streets.

QUESTIONS FOR REVIEW

1. List the major characteristics of police departments as vocational subcultures; give special emphasis to the notions of social isolation and police unity.

2. Use the concept of police argot to explain some major tenets of police as a subculture.

3. How would you as a police administrator deal with the informal norms and sanctions while you were trying to introduce a different type of uniform?

4. Do police really have a daily perception of violence? How does this relate to the perceived need for psychological distance?

5. Explain the differences between the formal organization and informal organization.

6. Analyze the effect of police primary groups on the police organization.

7. What is the effect of peer group norms on police corruption? As a police administrator, how would you use these norms to deal with the problems of police corruption?

8. Describe, analyze, and apply the different styles of policing—watchman, legalistic, service—to a local police agency.

9. Based on the conclusions of the available research, compare and contrast how Latino, African-American, and women police officers fit into both the formal and informal police organization.

10. Do informal cliques help or hinder good police management? Why?

CLASS PROJECT

Compare and contrast the police as a vocational subculture to any other vocational subculture. Interview both a police officer and a member of the other vocation. In your interview, ascertain whether the interviewee feels that his or her occupation is characterized by such things as argot, internal sanctions, social isolation, unity, and the like.

KEY TERMS

argot	Guardians
blue minority	Hawthorne Study
coop	hook
Gemeinschaft	horse
Gessellschaft	informal organization

BIBLIOGRAPHY

AHERN, JAMES F., *Police in Trouble*. New York: Hawthorne Books, 1972.

ALEX, NICHOLAS, *Black in Blue*. New York: Appleton-Century-Crofts, 1969.

ARNOLD, DAVID O., *The Sociology of Subcultures*. Berkeley, Ca. Glendessary, 1970.

BALKIN, JOSEPH, "Why Policemen Don't Like Policewomen." *Journal of Police Science and Administration*. March, 1988. pp. 29–38. 16, no. 1.

BANTON, MICHAEL, *The Policeman in the Community*. New York: Basic Books, 1964.

BARKER, THOMAS, and DAVID L. CARTER, eds. *Police Deviance*. 2nd ed. Cincinnati, Oh.: Anderson Publishing, 1994.

BEARD, EUGENE, "The Black Police in Washington, D.C." *Journal of Police Science and Administration*, 5, no. 1 (March 1977), pp. 48–52.

BERGER, PETER L., and BRIGITTE BERGER, *Sociology: A Biographical Approach*. New York: Basic Books, 1972.

BLUMBERG, ABRAHAM, "The Police and the Social System: Reflections and Prospects." in Abraham Blumberg and Elaine Niederhoffer, *The Ambivalent Force*. Hinsdale, Ill.: Dryden Press, 1985, pp. 3–26.

BLUMBERG, ABRAHAM, and ELAINE NIEDERHOFFER, *The Ambivalent Force*. Hinsdale, Ill.: Dryden Press, 1985.

BRODERICK, J., *Police in a Time of Change*. 2nd ed. Prospect Heights, Ill.: Waveland, 1987.

CARTER, DAVID L., and DARREL W. STEPHENS, "Police Ethics, Integrity and Off-Duty Behavior: Policy Issues on Police Conduct." in Thomas Barker and David L. Carter, eds., *Police Deviance*. 2nd ed. Cincinnati, Oh.: Anderson Publishing, 1994. pp. 29–44.

CHEVIGNY, PAUL, *Police Power: Abuses in New York*. New York: Pantheon, 1969.

CHRISTOPHER COMMISSION, "Report of the Independent Commission of the Los Angeles Police Department" in Thomas Barker and David L. Carter, eds., *Police Deviance*. 2nd ed. Cincinnati, Oh.: Anderson Publishing, 1994. pp. 291–306.

CLARK, JOHN P., "Isolation of the Police: A Comparison of British and American Situations." *Journal of Police Science and Administration*. 56, no. 3. (September, 1965), pp. 307-331.

DIETL, BO, and KEN CROSS, *One Tough Cop*. New York: Pocket Books, 1988.

DREIFUS, CLAUDIA, "Portrait of a Policewoman," *Police Magazine*, 3, no. 2 (March 1980), pp. 18-26.

DRUCKER, PETER F., *Management: Tasks, Responsibilities, Practices*. New York: Harper & Row, 1974.

GARDINER, JOHN A., "Wincanton: the Politics of Corruption," in the President's Commission on Law Enforcement and Administration of Justice, *Task Force Report: Organized Crime*. Washington, D.C.: Government Printing Office, 1965.

GARNER J., and E. CLEMMER, *Danger to Police In Domestic Disturbances—A New Look*. Washington, D.C.: U. S. Department of Justice, 1986.

GERTH, H. H., and C. WRIGHT, MILLS, *From Max Weber: Essays in Sociology*. New York: Oxford University Press, 1946.

GOLDSTEIN, HERMAN, *Problem Oriented Policing*. New York: McGraw-Hill, 1990.

GOOLKASIAN, GAIL A., *Confronting Domestic Violence: A Guide for Criminal Justice Agencies*. Washington, D.C.: U. S. Department of Justice, 1986.

GRENNAN, SEAN, A., "Perspective on Women in Policing." in Roslyn Muraskin and Ted Alleman, eds., *It's A Crime: Women and Justice*. Upper Saddle River, N. J.: Prentice Hall, 1993. pp. 163-176.

_____. "Findings on the Role of Officer Gender in Violent Encounters with Citizens," *Journal of Police Science and Administration*, 15, no. 1 (March, 1987), pp. 78-85.

HALE, DONNA, and DANIEL J. MENNITI, "Discrimination and Harassment: Litigation by Women in Policing." in Roslyn Muraskin and Ted Alleman, ed., *It's A Crime: Women and Justice*. Upper Saddle River, N. J.: Prentice Hall, 1993. pp. 177-190.

HUGHES, HELEN MACGILL, *Social Organizations*. Boston: Hollbrook, 1971.

KELLING, GEORGE L., "Police and Communities: The Quiet Revolution." in Siegel, Larry J., ed., *American Justice: Research of the National Institute of Justice*. St. Paul, Minn.: West, 1991, pp. 121-128.

KIRKHAM, GEORGE L. , "From Professor to Policeman: A Fresh Perspective on the Police." *Journal of Police Science and Administration*. 2, no. 2 (June, 1974), pp. 127-137.

THE KNAPP COMMISSION, *Police Corruption in New York*. New York: Whitman Knapp, 1972.

LEINEN, S. , *Black Police, White Society*. New York: Basic Books, 1984.

LIGHT, DONALD, JR. , and SUZANNE KELLER, *Sociology*. New York: Alfred A. Knopf, 1975.

LORD, LESLIE KAY, "A Comparison of Male and Female Police Officers' Stereotypic Perception of Women and Women Police Officers." *Journal of Police Science and Administration*. 14, no. 2 (1986), pp. 83–97.

MACQUIRE, KATHLEEN, and TIMOTHY J. FLANAGAN, eds., *Sourcebook of Criminal Justice Statistics 1994*. Washington, D.C.: U. S. Department of Justice, Bureau of Justice Statistics, 1995.

MACQUIRE, KATHLEEN, and ANN L. PASTORE, eds., *Sourcebook of Criminal Justice Statistics 1995*. Washington, D.C.: U. S. Department of Justice, Bureau of Justice Statistics, 1996.

MARTIN, SUSAN E. , "*Police*women and Police *Women*: Occupational Role Dilemmas and Choices of Female Officers." *Journal of Police Science and Administration*. no. 3 (September, 1979), pp. 314–323.

MARTIN, SUSAN E. , "Female Officers on the Move." in Roger G. Dunham and Geoffrey P. Alpert, eds., *Critical Issues in Policing*, 2nd ed. Prospect Heights, Ill.: Waveland Press, 1993. pp. 327–347.

MARX, GARY T. , *Undercover: Police Surveillance In America*. Berkeley: University of California Press, 1988.

MCBRIDE, R. BRUCE, "Perceptions of Racial Discrimination Within Occupation Socialization Process As Held by Newly Appointed Police Officers in Selected New York State Police Department." Unpublished dissertation. Albany, N. Y.: SUNY at Albany, 1986.

MILTON, CATHERINE H. , *Women in Policing*. Washington, D.C.: Police Foundation, 1972.

MITTEAGER, JIM, "NYPD's Gay Cops." *The National Centurion*, 2, no. 1 (February, 1984). pp. 33–36, 71.

MOORE, MARK H. , and ROBERT C. TROJANOWICZ, "Policing and Fear of Crime." in Larry J. Siegel, ed., *American Justice: Research of the National Institute of Justice*. St. Paul, Minn.: West, 1991. pp. 129–136.

MORE, HARRY W. , *Special Topics in Policing*. Cincinnati, Oh.: Anderson Publishing, 1992.

NATIONAL COMMISSION ON LAW OBSERVANCE AND ENFORCEMENT, George P. Wickersham, chairman, *Wickersham Commission Report 14: Police*. Montclair, N.J.: Patterson Smith, 1931, reprinted 1968.

NIEDERHOFFER, ARTHUR, *Behind the Shield*. Garden City, N.Y.: Doubleday, 1969.

NIEDERHOFFER, ARTHUR, and BLUMBERG, ABRAHAM, *The Ambivalent Force*. Hinsdale, Ill.: Dryden Press, 1976.

NIGRO, FELIX A., and LLOYD G. NIGRO, *Modern Public Administration*, (3rd ed.). New York: Harper & Row, 1973.

OWINGS, CHLOE, *Women Police*. Montclair, N.J.: Patterson Smith, 1925, reprinted 1969.

PEAK, KENNETH, *Policing America*. Upper Saddle River, N. J.: Prentice Hall, 1993.

POLICE FOUNDATION, *On the Move: The Status of Women in Policing*. Washington, D.C.: Police Foundation, 1990.

PENDERGRASS, VIRGINIA E. , and NANCY M. OSTROVE, "A Survey of Stress in Women in Policing." *Journal of Police Science and Administration*. 12, no. 3 (1984), pp. 138-144.

RADANO, GENE, *Walking the Beat*. Cleveland, Oh.: World, 1968.

REICHER, LISA M., and ROY R. ROBERG, "Community Policing: A Critical Review of Underlying Assumptions." *Journal of Police Science and Administration*. 17, no. 2 (June, 1990), pp. 105-114.

REISER, MARTIN, "Some Organization Stresses on Policemen." *Journal of Police Science and Administration*, 2, no. 2 (June, 1974), pp. 138-144.

ROBERTSON, IAN, *Sociology*, 3rd ed. New York: Worth Publishers, Inc., 1987.

ROETHLISBERGER, F.J., and WILLIAM J. DICKSON, *Management and the Worker*. Cambridge, Mass.: Harvard University Press, 1939.

SAVITZ, LEONARD D. , *Socialization of the Police*. Final report to the Pennsylvania Criminal Justice Planning Board. Philadelphia: Temple University, 1971.

SHERMAN, LAWRENCE, "The Sociology and Social Reform of American Police 1950-1973." *Journal of Police Science and Administration*. 2, no. 3 (September, 1974), pp. 255-262.

SHERMAN, LEWIS J. , "A Psychological View of Women in Policing," *Journal of Police Science and Administration*, 1, no. 4 (December 1973a).

SHERNOCK, STAN, "An Empirical Examination of the Relationship Between Police Solidarity and Community Orientation." *Journal of Police Science and Administration*, 16, no. 3 (September, 1988), pp. 182-194.

SKOLNICK, JEROME H., *Justice Without Trial: Law Enforcement in a Democratic Society*. New York: Wiley, 1966.

SKOLNICK, JEROME H. , "A Sketch of the Policeman's Working Personality." in Abraham Blumberg and Elaine Niederhoffer *The Ambivalent Force*. Hinsdale, Ill.: Dryden Press, 1985. pp. 80-90.

SKOLNICK, JEROME H. , and THOMAS C. GRAY, *Police In America*. Boston: Little, Brown, 1975.

SMITH, RALPH LEE, *The Tarnished Badge*. New York: Thomas Y. Cromwell, 1965.

STANFORD, ROSE MARY, and BONNEY LEE MOWRY, "Domestic Disturbance Danger Rate." *Journal of Police Science and Administration*, 17, no. 4. (December, 1990), pp. 244-240.

STARK, RODNEY, *Police Riots*. Belmont, Ca.: Focus Books, 1972.

STODDARD, ELLWYN R. , "The Informal Code of Police Deviance: A Group Approach to Blue Coat Crime." *Journal of Police Science and Administration*. 59 (June, 1968), pp. 201-213.

STRATTON, JOHN G. , *Police Passages*. Sandusky, Oh.: Glennon Publishing Company, 1984.

TAUBER, RONALD K., "Danger and the Police: A Theoretical Analysis." *Issues in Criminology*. Summer, 1967. pp. 69-81.

THIBAULT, EDWARD, "The Blue Milieu: Police As A Vocational Subculture." in John W. Bizzack, ed., *Issues In Policing*. Lexington, Ky.: Autumn House Publishing, 1993.

THIBAULT, EDWARD A., and R. BRUCE MCBRIDE, "Institutionalizing the Community Police Model in Canalville: A Case Study." *Journal of Police Science and Administration*, 9, no. 4 (December, 1981), pp. 390-397.

THIBAULT, EDWARD, and NORMAN L. WEINER, "The Anomic Cop." *Humboldt Journal of Social Relations*, Fall, 1973. Reported in *Human Behavior*, 1974.

THIBAULT, EDWARD A., LAWRENCE M. LYNCH, and R. BRUCE MCBRIDE, *Proactive Police Management*. 2nd ed. Upper Saddle River, N. J.: Prentice Hall, 1990.

TYLER, EDWARD B., *Primitive Culture*, London: John Murray, 1871.

VAN MAANEN, JOHN, "The Asshole" in Peter K. Manning and John Van Maanen, eds., *Policing: A View From the Street*. Santa Monica, Ca.: Goodyear Publishing, 1978, pp. 221-238.

WALKER, SAMUEL, "Racial Minority and Female Employment in Policing: The Implications of 'Glacial' Change." *Crime and Delinquency*, 31 (October, 1985). pp. 355-572.

_____, *The Police In America*. New York: McGraw-Hill, Inc., 1992.

WAMBAUGH, JOSEPH, *The New Centurions*. Boston: Little Brown, 1970.

_____, *The Blue Knight*. Boston: Little Brown, 1972.

WEINER, NORMAN, *The Role of the Police in Urban Society: Conflicts and Consequences*. Indianapolis, In.: Bobbs-Merrill, 1976.

WESTLEY, WILLIAM A., *Violence and the Police*. Cambridge, Mass.: Massachusetts Institute of Technology, 1970.

WEXLER, JUDIE GAFFIN, and DEANA DORMAN LOGAN, "Sources for Stress Among Women Police Officers." *Journal of Police Science and Administration*. 11, no. 1 (1983), pp. 46-53.

WHEISHEIT, RALPH A., "Women in the State Police: Concerns of Male and Female Police Officers." *Journal of Police Science and Administration*. 15, no. 2 (1987), pp. 137-144.

WHITE, MERVIN F. , TERRY C. COX, and JACK BASEHART, "Theoretical Considerations of Officer Profanity and Obscenity In Formal Contacts With Citizens." in Thomas Barker and David L. Carter, eds., *Police Deviance*, 2nd ed. Cincinnati, Oh.: Anderson Publishing, 1994. pp. 223-246.

WILSON, JAMES Q., *Varieties of Police Behavior*. Cambridge, Mass.: Harvard University Press, 1968.

WILT, G. MARIE, and JAMES D. BANNON, "Cynicism or Realism: A Critique of Niederhoffer's Research Into Police Attitudes." *Journal of Police Science and Administration*. 4, no. 1 (March, 1976), pp. 38-45.

3

Purposes and Principles of Police Organizations

Traditionally, most police agencies tend to be highly reactive **line** organizations; that is, the police wait for citizens to call them and then they react to that phone call for service. Albert Reiss, Jr. (1971: xii), found a solid empirical base for this interpretation in his study of the Boston, Washington, D.C., and Chicago police departments: "Most of the mobilizations, [that is] 81 percent originated with citizens telephoning the police for service and the department dispatching a one- or two-man beat car to handle the incident." In the reactive department, officers on patrol generally spend their time in a parked vehicle reading the paper, having coffee, or doing personal errands while waiting for that radio dispatch that sends them roaring to the scene of an incident or crime requiring police intervention. Interspersed will be attempts to garner sufficient traffic and parking violations to keep the supervisors off the line officer's back. Very little, if any, time is spent on police patrol.

O.W. Wilson, former superintendent of the Chicago Police Department and author of *Police Administration* (1950), used the term "the **omnipresent** police officer" to characterize the police officer who was everywhere in his random patrol duties, deterring crime by his mere presence. However, a study of the effect of **random patrol** in Kansas City seems to indicate that the mere presence of uniformed police and marked vehicles may not be the deterrent that we once thought (Kelling and others, 1978).

The **Kansas City Experiment** divided that area's 15 precincts into three approaches to patrol: (1) respond to calls only, (2) provide normal random patrol, and (3) provide two to three times the normal level of random patrol. The conclusions were (Kelling and others, 1978: 164): "The experiment found that the three experimental patrol conditions appeared not to affect crime, service delivery and citizen feelings of security." If this is true, a major activity of line officers has been a waste of time. This kind of research also shows the need for the administrators of an agency to play a more active part in the managing of patrol officers. The nation needs to develop a new breed of realistic police managers who are able to evaluate critically and implement selected innovations in the area of law enforcement. Proper applications of those appropriate programs should lead to a more proactive police agency.

 LAW ENFORCEMENT AS BIG BUSINESS

There are over 40,000 law enforcement agencies in our country, employing some 560,000 officers and 220,000 civilians (U.S. Department of Justice, Crime in the United States, 1994). The Bureau of Justice Statistics law enforcement survey conducted in 1993 found that the total annual operation expenditures by local police departments for the fiscal year was $24.3 billion. The average cost per citizen for police protection is about $131 (Bureau of Justice Statistics, 1996: 7). This figure includes not only federal, municipal, state, and county departments but also specialized departments such as campus, transit authority, railroad, housing, and environmental conservation units. Exclusive of school boards, the public agencies that make the greatest demand on the tax dollars of most communities are the big three: police, fire, and public works. Often the police department leads the field in using up available tax dollars.

The rational citizen, looking at a $20 million business would expect the most administratively competent personnel to be selected to lead this major corporation, the local police agency. Not so. Most police organizations are headed by former line officers who have worked their way up through the hierarchical, civil-service organizational structure. While these individuals were generally excellent operating personnel, many lack the skills and knowledge necessary to manage a police organization. Moreover, few have had the opportunity to expand their knowledge of modern management techniques necessary to perform their new responsibilities satisfactorily. Unfortunately, too, some communities even have it in their municipal charters that the new police chief has to be chosen from existing members of the police force.

If these agencies are to be effective, the traditional concept of police management needs to be changed. However, a number of obstacles must be overcome before a reality-based management approach, using modern business methods, can be incorporated into police agencies.

▶ CIVIL SERVICE/PROMOTIONS

In many states, the system of civil service, particularly the examinations, does much to inhibit management success. Consider taking the civil service examination for captain and having to answer the following vehicle and traffic law questions: "How far must a vehicle be parked from the curb?" "How far from a stop sign?" "What is the stopping distance on wet pavement?" This is important information for operating personnel. Any officer taking a captain's examination should know this information. However, wouldn't it be more useful to test the candidate's ability and judgments concerning the administration and management of human and physical resources? Continuing to espouse a line-officer management philosophy in a test for upper-level management positions gives official sanction to a continuation of bad management practices.

In addition, administrators' choices must come from among the top three candidates completing these examinations. In business or industry, on the other hand, we would seek out the best candidate possessing the qualification from within or without the corporation. The lack of lateral entry, the parochialism, the influence of police associations and unions, support the concept that the *best* must come through the ranks. We are not suggesting that civil service exams be abolished; rather, we would like to see them upgraded and made more relevant to the positions. They should not be used as the sole criterion for promotion. There should be some evaluation of the candidates' past performances—an oral interview and perhaps even a battery of psychological and management tests.

It seems that many agencies, especially in western states, have developed alternative methods of promotion with a more progressive approach to the selection of candidates for the respective positions. Namely, the promotion to sergeant, while being based somewhat on a written examination, is strongly influenced by assessment with established criteria. A promotion from sergeant to lieutenant, while being the prerogative of the chief of police, is often based on an assessment evaluation that includes oral interviews, with the final decision being the chief's. In many instances, promotion to captain or a higher rank rests in the hands of the chief and whatever additional criteria he may use to help in his judgment.

While there is no ideal or fool-proof way of getting the best candidates, the above suggests that it is a progressive administrator who has the greatest opportunity of getting (or removing) the persons he may feel are the most qualified and/or compatible with his goals and the goals of the community. There is always the problem of favoritism or "political" interference in the system of promotion. However, the professionalism of modern police agencies, and the expectations of its leaders, make this interference more difficult.

THE USE OF CIVILIAN EMPLOYEES

According to the Uniform Crime Report, civilian or non-sworn law enforcement personnel comprise about 28 percent of the workforce for police departments in the United States, and 62 percent were women (1994: 289).

This closely corresponds to a Bureau of Justice Statistics survey which found that 31 percent were civilian employees (1996: 1).

Heininger and Urbanek (1983) surveyed a proportionate stratified random sample of 100 medium-sized and large American cities to determine what effect the use of civilian personnel had on police agencies. Many police managers have been concerned about the replacement of the uniformed police officer by civilians and the hoped-for budget savings. Because of the increasing use of civilians in specialist positions with fairly high salaries, there were few savings in the budget. Here are their conclusions (Heininger and Urbanek, 1983: 205):

> Specifically, the findings suggest that using civilians may not lead to cheaper police protection, that using civilians probably does not "displace" sworn officers, and that there is no apparent relationship between civilians and either the quality of police protection or the risk of danger which must be assumed by sworn officers. These conclusions are more interesting in the light of secondary findings which show that (1) "real" police salaries are down; (2) police departments are commanding a diminishing portion of the municipal budget "pie" while at the same time, (3) both municipal expenditures and personnel levels rose sharply.

Important considerations for the hiring of civilian police personnel is a thorough background check, along with a psychological assessment. Civilian personnel are now being used in sensitive positions in records, dispatching, computers, and increasingly in making judgment calls that will affect the department and sworn personnel. This should emphasize the need for more attention by management for the proper training necessary to equip these civilians to perform efficiently and effectively.

 TRADITIONAL MEASURES OF POLICE EFFECTIVENESS

Look at the annual report of almost any police department in the country. First, you will see a covering letter from the administrator to his sponsoring institution. This is followed by a brief description of the department, usually accompanied by a standard organization chart. Then comes the bulk of the report, page after page of tabulated statistics, for example, on crimes in the community, cases cleared by arrest, traffic and parking tickets issued, percentage of stolen property recovered, accident rates, and so on.

These tabulations are supposed to show the efficiency of the agency. However, these are indexes of efficiency *after the fact*. At the time of reading, some citizens may have just been killed, injured, robbed, or arrested. The increase or decrease in crime as released to the media through the Federal Bureau of Investigation's **Uniform Crime Reports** are taken as an indication as to the effectiveness of the police agency. Unfortunately, such reactive measures tend to promote poor management, leading to the issuance of more traffic tickets, the growth of an unofficial quota system, and "fudging" of crime statistics. For example, it may be that the officer who stops citizens in traffic and advises them concerning their poor driving habits may be more effective than the officer who simply issues tickets. It takes a realistic, superior manager to recognize the difference.

As noted in Chapter 1, the Metropolitan Police Act of 1829 created the first modern police force in London, England. Sir Charles Rowan, in the force's first duty manual, stated the primary purpose for having a law enforcement agency (Reith, 1956: 135-36): "It should be understood at the outset, that the principal object to be obtained is the Prevention of Crime." Officers were specifically evaluated and rewarded for the attainment of this goal. This proactive, preventive approach led to better police-community relations.

Citizens are never happy about being the victim of a crime even if the crime is solved and the goods returned. From 1829 to the present, this citizen attitude has not changed. In a study of victims of crimes in inner cities outside the South, Block (1970) confirms this point of view. He found that follow-up and even arrest of criminals who attacked victims had only a slight effect on the victims in terms of their support for police. Victimization, itself, brought about a significant decrease in support for police. His conclusion backs up the basic insight of the 1829 manual (Block, 1970: 12) that "the best way for the police to gain support is to strengthen their efforts in crime prevention." O.W. Wilson, *Police Administration* (1950), agreed with this statement on how the police carry out their primary purpose in serving the citizens: "The police do this by preserving the peace and protecting life and property against attacks by criminals and from injury by the careless and inadvertent offender." A proactive department is more concerned with protecting the citizens from harm than with tallying up some kind of score of arrests after the citizen has been victimized.

Another principle, one presented in the nineteenth century by Robert Peel, concerned the efficiency of police. Peel felt that the best test of this efficiency was the absence of crime in society. Citizens should feel that they and their property are safe. This is a positive standard. The traditional standards all take a negative attitude. We should retain Peel's progressive approach in evaluating officers and promoting good management.

▶ TRADITIONAL PURPOSES OF POLICE ORGANIZATIONS

The traditional purposes most commonly accepted are

1. Protection of life and property.
2. Preserving the peace.
3. Prevention of criminality.
4. Apprehension of criminals.

Although these are legitimate purposes for policing, they have a major defect—they have become reactive. The activities used to carry out these purposes include routine patrol to discourage wrongdoers, arrest of criminals, recovery of stolen property, monitoring of sporting events, and such additional items as controlling traffic and pedestrian movements. Little encouragement is given to act in a proactive manner.

In some agencies, officers who attempt to initiate proactive programs are derided for being "gung ho" or "college cops" (the latter if they have had some formal education). Their supervisors often consider these officers to be troublemakers or wavemakers, individuals to be sharply disciplined and watched carefully. It takes a police manager of rare courage and talent to promote proactive officers. It takes a reality-based modern manager to put the wavemakers in charge. When it is done, it may immediately create a morale and a management problem. However, once the waves calm down, the resulting police department will have become an active force in the local community.

 # REALITY-BASED, PROACTIVE PURPOSES OF POLICE ORGANIZATIONS

Modern society calls upon all police managers to provide satisfaction for the citizens of the community in fulfilling the traditional purposes of policing. However, police managers also need to go beyond the traditional purposes of policing to the following areas of responsibility: (1) performance, (2) preparedness, and (3) progressiveness.

PERFORMANCE

Specific role definitions of police performance and productivity measures need to be created in terms of the daily activity of both the line officer and police manager. Criteria need to be developed to evaluate effectively and reward positive, proactive police activity. For example, how do you measure performance in terms of patrol activity? How do you evaluate the effectiveness of response to human-service calls and calls that entail referrals to other government and community agencies? Feedback mechanisms must be developed to monitor performance of line officers and police managers and to evaluate their activities so as to reward appropriate delivery of police services to the community. The focus is on measures of individuals in official positions and measures of organizational effectiveness.

PREPAREDNESS

Preparedness speaks to the needs of short-range as well as long-range planning, and entails the relation of the police agency to other community and government organizations, for example, social welfare and health agencies. Police organizations have normally planned only in terms of police rather than the whole human-service group of agencies. Today all personnel should be trained to handle future problems. Preparedness entails the need for better communication among all agencies. Time and resources need to be developed so that this type of thinking permeates the entire police organization.

PROGRESSIVENESS

This is a basic management-for-change concept where leaders are flexible and tolerant of ambiguity and are willing to institute new ideas because they may work. Such leaders do not feel threatened by such changes. The opposite of this type is the hierarchically orientated administrator who seeks closure and places limitations on his staff's ideas.

 # MANAGEMENT PRINCIPLES

To accomplish these purposes, management guidelines are needed. The following six principles allow for both the traditional reactive force and the aggressive proactive approaches: (1) respond, (2) regulate, (3) restrain, (4) recover, (5) repress, and (6) reinforce.

RESPOND

Most police activities are reactions to calls for service (Reiss, 1971; Cumming and others, 1965; Bayley and Mendelsohn, 1969; Webster, 1970). Even in large cities, the calls are largely service oriented. For example, of the 1,027,000 calls received by the Detroit police in 1968, only 16 percent were related to crime (Bercal, 1970: 683). Contrary to the television dramas, calls for crimes in progress are few. Police must also deal with on-scene confrontations, hostage situations, battered children, family crises, and the mentally ill, all of which call for a reaction response by the officers concerned. Many of these situations are highly dangerous and call for split-second response by a highly trained professional police officer.

Traditionally, police respond after a crime has occurred and there is a victim. And, as has been noted, victims are more hostile to the police after having been the target of a crime, even if the criminal is apprehended.

There is also a strong controversy in the field over response time. Most department are told to aim at 2 minutes or less when responding to a call. This early response time is only significant in cases of crimes in progress or calls of an emergency nature. Response time becomes important in the securing of crime scenes and the immediate apprehension of criminals. It is irrelevant to the majority of service calls. Too much management and training time is spent on this issue of response time.

REGULATE

Consider a long line of cars wending its way through the city streets with a funeral hearse in the front and police vehicle escort. Consider, too, vehicles parked at field days, ice cream socials, and ball games that require the police for traffic and crowd control. Police are also used as bodyguards and chauffeurs for visiting dignitaries and even some mayors. These are traditionally noncriminal police activities, and regulations are necessary to prevent crises in our communities.

RESTRAIN

This represents one of the traditional purposes for police, the apprehension of criminals. It should also include restraint of mentally ill persons and the prevention of one citizen from annoying or doing damage to another. For example a woman mowing her lawn with a power lawn mower at midnight just to annoy a neighbor with whom she is feuding might have to be restrained by police.

RECOVER

A major effort by police is the recovery of stolen property and its return to the citizens. **Sting** operations, in which a police agency sets up a phony fencing business to entice criminals to sell them stolen goods, result in the arrest of the criminals and some of their fences (those who deal in stolen goods). Millions of dollars in stolen goods are given back to the citizens in the course of such operations. This is one area in which the police provide a very useful service to the community and do recover considerable property of value, reducing insurance and personal losses.

REPRESS

It has become accepted that there are two important elements necessary for a crime to take place. First, the individual must have the desire to commit the crime; second, the opportunity must present itself for the satisfaction of this desire. Police have traditionally attempted to prevent crime by reducing the opportunity of the individual to commit the crime. The random patrol concept is justified by many police managers as a means of reaching this end.

In recent years, drug control strategies include targeting "hot spots," such as street areas and crack houses. Green (1995: 737-754) for example, reviewed a drug control program in Oakland, California that relied on police coordination against certain areas to decrease the amount of drug sales. This could be termed a repressive technique, in that city resources were targeted against a crime problem. The basic philosophy here is that it is very hard to buy and sell with increased police presence, which included raids, checks for violations of city housing codes, and legal actions against slum landlords.

Although actions such as these result in crime displacement, the study found that drug problems were decreased at target sites and that there was less displacement of narcotics activity in other neighborhood areas.

REINFORCE

This activity is designed to reinforce good citizenship and respect for the law and to encourage citizens to aid and assist officers and the agency. Examples of this type of activity are talking to citizen's groups and instituting traffic and bicycle safety programs. Operation **Neighborhood Watch** of the National Sheriffs Association teaches business owners and citizens to burglarproof their premises and watch out for their neighbor's property when a neighbor is on vacation. School programs such as the School Liaison variety in elementary schools and the teaching of criminal justice topics by community relations officers in high schools are also used.

In responding to this traditional purpose, police agencies have tended to create special units and focus on response activities to the detriment of effective service to the public. Although these are legitimate purposes, these purposes are not broad enough to contain the range of legitimate police activity. Each officer should consider himself or herself a community relations specialist.

To carry out these principles, it is necessary to come to an understanding of what the organization, itself, is all about. Here, we are looking for a definition of *organization* that will fit the requirements of both management and operations. This definition has to be broad enough to encompass the many tasks concerned with the creation of operational policy as well as the duties of administration.

Although a clear understanding of basic relationships specified by modern organizational structures is necessary, we must never forget that the tasks are carried out by real people with human concerns, needs, and emotions. Thus, any concept of organization from the perspective of current practices and theory is basically people oriented. The reason is that if any police organization is to operate efficiently, people have to be motivated to carry out tasks on the job and put out that little extra effort that makes organizations work.

 ## THE CONCEPT OF ORGANIZATION

In a staff paper that has been widely utilized at both the college level and for police executive training sessions, the Northwestern University Traffic Institute (1964:6) has stressed two aspects of organization as part of the basic definition: the mechanical/structural approach and the humanist approach.

MECHANICAL

One group says in effect: "Organization is the thorough arrangement and subdivision of activities to secure economy of effort through specialization and coordination of work, thereby leading to unity of 'action.' The key parts of this definition are 'subdivision to *secure economy of effort*' and 'specialization and *coordination leading to unity*.' This definition emphasizes the mechanics, or the physical aspects of organization.

The mechanical approach uses bodies to fill boxes in an organization chart, for example, assembly-line tasks and many military jobs. Police have been hiring and promoting to fill slots, without the concern for the personal qualifications of the individual.

HUMANISTIC

The other group of definitions can be summarized as "divising and grouping the work that should be done into individual jobs, and defining the established relationships between individuals filling these jobs." This definition emphasizes the people who make up an organization and through whom all work is done.
The humanistic approach is that used in most professional organizations where a particular skill must be developed at a particular level with the exact knowledge needed to fill a position. In a law firm, for example, you may need a new associate partner in corporate law. You are going to interview individuals, looking for specific knowledge, skills, and professional relationships that have developed over the candidate's lifetime in the field of corporate law. In the same way, modern police organizations should not be limited by a mechanical promotion exam. They should look for talent and professional skills. Just because you are promoted to lieutenant does not make you an expert in personnel even though the personnel department may need a lieutenant to operate as the manager of the department.

 ## THE TRADITIONAL CONCEPT OF BUREAUCRACY FROM MAX WEBER

Basic to any modern organization is the concept of bureaucracy. Police organizations, for example, are bureaucracies. Although the term *bureaucracy* has acquired negative overtones, it is the basis for modern civil service and a rational approach to administrating and organization. The German sociologist Max Weber (1889–1920) provided the formulation that has become the basis for all modern bureaucracies, including police organization (Gerth and Mills, 1946: 196–244).

A modern bureaucracy depends on having a money economy to pay salaries. The society also must subscribe to the view that success and rewards should be based on merit and hard work rather than on the condition of birth. Moreover, there should be a belief in treating each person equally and providing true equality of opportunity.

The following are, in shortened form, the general rules that Max Weber felt should govern and define a modern bureaucracy (Gerth and Mills, 1946: 196–204):

1. Regular activities are distributed in a fixed way as official duties.
2. Authority to give commands is distributed in a stable way, and coercive means of sanction are defined by rules in a consistent manner.
3. Only persons who have generally regulated qualifications to serve are employed.
4. Fixed jurisdictions are ordered by administrative regulations.
5. An official hierarchical system of superiors and subordinates, monocratically organized, exists.
6. Management is based upon *written* documents, normally called "the files."
7. Specialized officer of management requires thorough, technical, and expert training and knowledge.
8. Generalized rules are:
   a. Stable
   b. Exhaustive
   c. Learnable
9. Knowledge of the rules represents special technical knowledge that officials possess (in modern society, special officials who are rule experts are accountants and lawyers).
10. Office holding is a vocation and a career.
11. Officials have more status than the governed: insult of officials is proscribed by law with appropriate sanctions.
12. Bureaucratic officials are appointed by a superior authority (civil examination), not elected.
13. Tenure in the job is for life.
14. Regular pecuniary compensation, meaning the employees receive a regular and fixed salary.
15. Officials have a career in the hierarchy.

This is the ideal by which many modern public organizations are measured. When first developed and applied, it made capitalism work by providing a structural context for capitalists. Bureaucracy provides stability in the delivery of governmental services even though the political machinery may be in a turmoil. Politicians can fight all they wish, but while a modern bureaucracy exists in public service, citizens will receive their police and fire protection, have their mail delivered, and have their sewers fixed. This organizational concept will become more important as we examine how to carry out specific police management tasks in the modern police organization.

 ## ACCREDITATION FOR LAW ENFORCEMENT AGENCIES

The International Association of Chiefs of Police, the National Organization of Black Law Enforcement Executives, National Sheriff's Association, and the Police Executive Research Forum formed the Commission on Accreditation for Law Enforcement Agencies (CALEA). The commission set up 84 management guidelines that each member agency would have to address. These guidelines, which became known in law enforcement circles as standards, were divided into the following: (1) responsibilities and relationships; (2) organization and administration; (3) personnel structure; (4) personnel process; (5) law enforcement operations; (6) operations support; (7) traffic operations; (8) prisoner and court-related activities; and (9) auxiliary and technical services such as communications, evidence, and property management. For example, one standard related to administration calls for written directives that require the formulation, annual updating, and distribution to all personnel of written goals and objectives for the agency and for each organizational component within the agency (Commission, 1984: 1). Another example would be directive 33.3.2, on training instruction: "A written directive governs the tenure of instructors in all agency-operated training programs" (Commission, 1984: 33).

This has become a controversial program where the commission uses these standards to evaluate a police agency. The evaluation itself comes at a considerable expense for the department and has to be budgeted for. To meet the standards, there may be additional expenses and the local elected officials may not wish to spend money on upgrading the police agency. Although the standards are an excellent idea and go into enough detail to be operationalized, not all the standards may apply to all departments, especially the smaller police agency. However, given the increasing concern with civil liberty for both individual officers and departments, the meeting of professional standards promulgated by respected professional associations may become more important throughout the 1990s. The question of standards is often raised in civil suits.

Thus, the purposes of accreditation, according to CALEA, are to

1. Increase a department's capabilities to control crime.
2. Enhance effectiveness and efficiency of services.
3. Improve cooperation with citizens and with other agencies in the criminal justice system.
4. Increase citizen and employee confidence in goals, objectives, policies, and practices.

The accreditation process follows the similar program followed by colleges, universities, and professional groups for regional and professional accreditation which consists of (1) application and review of materials, (2) agency self-study to meet all standards, (3) site visit by accreditation team to review self-study and interview officers and community representatives, (4) response by agency to team review, (5) final discussion on points of dispute, and (6) awarding or denial of accreditation. As Behan (1989) points out, the standards are not prescriptive— the agency personnel must decide how to deal with such issues as personnel selection, training, and arrest procedures. Adopting state and national practices however, is not a one-time deal. Within a period of five years, the agency must seek reaccreditation and go through a similar review process. Thus, the agency is responsible for maintaining both accreditation and its operating standards.

An endeavor of this nature involves much time and work especially in the review of agency practices during the self-assessment period. Some may ask, "Why bother?" Proponents point out that accreditation is an important management tool. It allows the department to formally measure its strengths and weaknesses according to national norms with the goal of self-improvement. Accreditation also carries prestige for department members and the community. It is also reasoned that liability costs can be controlled since all high-risk activities will have operating and training guidelines. Further, it provides an opportunity to modernize certain equipment (provided budget support is available) as well as procedures and practices.

Not everyone is convinced that accreditation is all that it purports to be. It is very expensive and time-consuming in terms of staff and department involvement. According to Oettmeier (1992), reports, policies, and directives have to be reviewed and rewritten. This can result in the paper-tiger syndrome: the process becomes more important than anything else. Further, the objectives of accreditation may not immediately result in the stated purposes for accreditation. In other words, an accredited department may not be that effective and efficient in controlling crime or increasing cooperation with other agencies. Successful agencies, moreover, may not need accreditation since they are being proactive in addressing problems. What is lacking in the accreditation movement, Oettmeier feels, is the attention to the quality and other questions such as employee satisfaction and creativity. More importantly, critics suggest that CALEA and other groups involved in accreditation should look at what changes can be employed in an agency in such areas as training and practices.

CALEA does not hold a monopoly on accreditation. Because of the costs and an argument that CALEA standards cannot apply to all the states and to small departments (10 sworn employees or less), certain states such as New York, Colorado and Washington have begun their own accreditation programs. In New York, the number of standards for the state's accreditation program have been reduced to 400 to comply with existing statutes, statewide practices, and collective bargaining agreements. According to McCarty (1993), New York state provides technical assistance to departments interested in developing policies related to standards.

In summary, accreditation, whether national or state, is a useful managerial process for departments to measure their operations according to a set of professional standards. It is probably a necessary tool for departments attempting to deal with poor personnel practices, negative community relations, corruption problems, and administrative ineptitude.

▶ CONCLUSION

Managing a police department effectively requires considerable organization. Although humanistic concepts and democratic principles are useful in enhancing morale and producing even-handed personnel policies, they have to be dealt with in the context of a traditional bureaucratic structure.

A police department is a big business with a budget of hundreds of thousands, and in some cases, millions of dollars. The traditions of a nineteenth-century civil service are part and parcel of the organizational style of most police agencies. Part of the reality of modern police administration is the traditional civil service/Weberian bureaucratic structure. To perform the police function, orders have to be written and orders have to be carried out. Over the years, it has been shown that a traditional hierarchical organization can be an effective medium for fulfilling the major purposes of the police function.

The reality-based, proactive approach adds another dimension to the traditional bureaucratic structure: forward planning. The central core of the proactive approach is the need for police management to have the necessary planning skills to anticipate events. This is in good part what is meant by the three P's:

1. Performance
2. Preparedness
3. Progressiveness

A reality-based, progressive department is flexible enough to adapt to changing events and a changing society. It is prepared with adequate resources to deal effectively with future events and crises. The performance of this department speaks for itself by any reasonable measure of police effectiveness.

Although it is necessary to use the principles of the traditional bureaucratic structure to administer the modern, proactive police department, these principles are applied in a flexible manner. One of the problems with reactive police departments is that they become so bound by rigid, bureaucratic procedures that they lose sight of the real purpose of policing: providing a service to the community. The flexibility instilled in the traditional police structure allows for the anticipation of events and the ability to deal with an ever-changing society. The ideal police structure is the synthesis of proactive, traditional, democratic, and authoritarian styles. This department may be viewed by the citizens as an effective force in achieving a stable community—a good place in which to live and raise children.

QUESTIONS FOR REVIEW

1. Agree or disagree with the traditional purposes of the police organization. Has the modern police organization fulfilled these purposes? Should it?

2. Distinguish between a proactive and reactive police agency. What major characteristics identify the more proactive police agency?

3. Describe the role of planning in terms of (a) performance, (b) preparedness, and (c) progressiveness.

4. Place the following six management principles in order of priority and justify: (a) Respond, (b) Regulate, (c) Restrain, (d) Recover, (e) Repress, and (f) Reinforce.

5. If you were going to create your own police organization, what type of management would you prefer—mechanical or humanistic—and explain why. If you have trouble subscribing completely to either view, specify what mix of humanistic and mechanical concepts of police organization would perhaps work best.

6. Apply Max Weber's concept of bureaucracy to a local police agency and contrast Weber's model to what actually is going on in the local bureaucracy.

KEY TERMS

accreditation
humanistic organization
Kansas City Experiment
line
mechanical organization
Neighborhood Watch
Officer Friendly
omnipresent
performance
preparedness

progressiveness
random patrol
recover
regulate
reinforce
respond
restrain
sting operation
Uniform Crime Reports

BIBLIOGRAPHY

BAYLEY, DAVID H., and HAROLD MENDELSOHN, *Minorities and the Police*, New York: Free Press, 1969.

BEHAN, CORNELIUS J., "The Accreditation Process," in James J. Fyfe, ed., *Police Practice in the 90s*. Washington: International City Management Association, 1989.

BERCAL, THOMAS E., "Calls for Police Assistance: Consumer Demands for Public Service," *American Behavioral Scientist*, 13, no. 5/6 (May/August 1970), pp. 681–91.

BLOCK, RICHARD L., "Support for Civil Liberties and Support for the Police," *American Behavioral Scientist*, 13, no. 5/6 (May/June 1970).

BUREAU OF JUSTICE STATISTICS, *Local Police Departments, 1993*. Washington: U. S. Department of Justice, 1996.

BUTTERFIELD, RONALD W., "Deming's 14 Points Applied to Service," *Training*, 28, no. 3 (March 1991), pp. 50–59.

CLAUSER, FREDERICK J., and GEORGE E. CARPENTER, "Law Enforcement Accreditation: Getting It Done." *Police Chief*, 55, no. 1 (January 1988), pp. 60–63.

COMMISSION ON ACCREDITATION FOR LAW ENFORCEMENT AGENCIES. *Standards for Law Enforcement Agencies*. Fairfax, Va.: The Commission, 1984.

CUMMING, ELAINE, IAN CUMMING, and LAURA EDELL, "Policeman as Philosopher, Guide and Friend." *Social Problems*, Vol. 12 (Winter 1965), pp. 276–86.

GERTH, H. H., and C. WRIGHT MILLS, *From Max Weber: Essays in Sociology*. New York: Oxford University Press, 1946.

GREEN, LORRAINE, "Cleaning Up Drug Hot Spots in Oakland, California: The Displacement and Diffusion Effects." *Justice Quarterly*, 12, no. 4 (December, 1995), pp. 737–754.

HALBERSTAM, DAVID, *The Reckoning*. New York: William Morrow, 1986.

HEININGER, BRUCE L., and JANINE URBANEK, "Civilianization of the American Police: 1970–1980," *Journal of Police Science and Administration*, 11, no. 2 (1983), pp. 200–205.

HOLPP, LAWRENCE, "Making Choices: Self-Directed Teams or Total Quality Management?" *Training*, 29, no. 5 (May 1992) pp. 69–76.

KELLING, GEORGE L., AND OTHERS, *Patrol Experiment: A Summary Report and a Technical Report*. Washington, D.C.: Police Foundation, 1978.

NATIONAL ADVISORY COMMISSION ON CRIMINAL JUSTICE STANDARDS AND GOALS. *Police*. Washington, D.C.: U.S. Government Printing Offices, 1973.

NEW YORK CITY POLICE DEPARTMENT. *Operation 25*. New York: The Department, 1955.

NORTHWESTERN UNIVERSITY TRAFFIC INSTITUTE. *Improving Police Effectiveness Through Organization*. Evanston, Ill.: Northwestern University, 1964.

O'CONNOR, MARTIN, "Brief Notes Regarding the ADA," Yapank, NY: Suffolk County Police Department, 1991

OETTMEIER, TIMOTHY N., "Can Accreditation Survive the 90s?" in John Bizzack, ed., *New Perspectives: Issues in Policing*. Lexington, KY: Autumn House, 1992.

REISS, ALBERT J., JR. *The Police and the Public*. New Haven, Conn.: Yale University Press, 1971.

REITH, CHARLES. *A New Study of Police History*. Edinburgh: Oliver & Boyd, 1956.

U.S. DEPARTMENT OF JUSTICE, *Uniform Crime Reports, Crime in the United States: 1994*. Washington, D.C.: U.S. Government Printing Office, 1994.

U.S. DEPARTMENT OF JUSTICE, *Uniform Crime Reports, Crime in the United States: 1986*. Washington, D.C.: U.S. Government Printing Office, 1986.

WEBSTER, JOHN A., "Police Task and Time Study," *The Journal of Criminal Law, Criminology and Police Service*, Vol. 61 (1970), pp. 94–100.

WHITAKER, GORDON, ET AL., *Basic Issues in Police Performance*. Washington, D.C.: U.S. Department of Justice, 1980.

WILSON, O.W., *Police Administration*. New York: McGraw-Hill, 1950.

WILSON, JAMES Q., *Thinking About Crime*. New York: Basic Books, 1975.

_____. Explaining Crime. New York: McGraw-Hill, 1975.

4

Operating Principles

In any organization there are three major areas of work:

1. Administration
2. Supervision
3. Operations

Administrative functions are performed by top management and the immediate subordinates of the top-management team. They create and set **policy** (a course of action), providing guidance for the organization. *Supervision* is normally performed by the immediate supervisors of line personnel. They help to set the tone of the organization and ensure that the policies created by top management are actually carried out by the line personnel. *Operations* are performed by line personnel who normally have direct contact with the public and carry out the daily police activities.

ADMINISTRATION

POSDCORB is a classic theoretical model that helps to describe the major functions of any organization and how these functions are carried out. The acronym

POSDCORB stands for Planning, Organizing, Staffing, Directing, Coordinating, Reporting, and Budgeting (Gulick and Urwick, 1937: 1–45).

PLANNING

This activity includes short-range and long-range planning specifying goals and objectives in cooperating with other public agencies. Cooperating with other public agencies is a primary requisite. More and more, urban police departments are seeing that they have to involve themselves with the long-range planning of urban renewal agencies, social service agencies, health agencies, and so on. Even smaller departments and those in rural areas are beginning to see how long-range planning can help them deal with the increasing complexity of the police role and rural crime on the urban fringe.

ORGANIZING

Organizing deals with the creation of the formal structure of the police organization, the work of the enterprise. The goal is to coordinate all the organizational units to perform in the most efficient manner so that the purposes of the organization are met.

The organization, itself, becomes the total responsibility of the manager and reflects the organizational ability of the top-management team. Modern business principles are combined with a knowledge of public administration and modern police activities. The key to success is to create an organizational structure where the right talent will be doing the right job at the highest efficiency with the correct level of personal and organizational morale.

STAFFING

This function of management covers such aspects of the organization as hiring, firing, and training as well as assigning personnel to specific tasks and roles. There is also a concern with establishing satisfactory working conditions, including safe and appropriate physical facilities. For example, patrol cars should operate so as not to endanger the life of an officer. Included also is the need to provide tools necessary to carry out the job and to provide them in functioning order.

In theory, staffing includes developing job descriptions. Each job should be clearly defined and filled by a qualified employee. Qualified means that the employee has the necessary skills, background, and training to accomplish the tasks that the job description calls for.

Job satisfaction should also be considered. Every attempt should be made to match each employee to a job where he or she is:

1. Satisfied
2. Qualified
3. Gratified

DIRECTING

In this category the manager needs to (1) act as the overall leader of the organization, and (2) direct the day-to-day activities of the enterprise. As leader of the police organization, the manager has to make decisions and issue orders. Using modern management principles, this is normally a team process where the leader receives information and advice from the top management team. The information that is obtained through this consultative process should lead to a firm decision.

A police manager using this approach should seek advice from local community leaders as well as from top-management staff and experts in law enforcement. Then once a decision is made, the team should be expected to carry out daily the specified directions and procedures.

COORDINATING

The two major activities in this category are (1) the need to coordinate police agencies with other private and public agencies in the community and (2) coordination of activities within the police department itself. Coordination is designed to bring about agreement on specific courses of action to specific problems.

Typical problems that involve the coordination functions include legal ramifications of policy decisions, and deciding who is going to be in charge in cases involving overlapping jurisdictions. For example, a visit from a foreign dignitary might entail coordination among civic organizations and local, state, or federal authorities; it could require long-range planning to prepare for problems or situations that might occur. Coordination is an often-overlooked but essential part of police management.

REPORTING

Reporting entails keeping the flow of information going up, down, and across the organization. It also includes reporting to the police organization's political superiors, mayors, county executives, and the like. The annual report to the public and legislature has become a major means of communicating organizational goals and accomplishments.

Communication is never just one way if it is to be effective. Communication flows in an organized manner through a three-dimensional matrix to all superiors and subordinates. Increasingly important for modern management is lateral flow to specialists and staff.

BUDGETING

Budgeting includes preparing an annual financial plan and operating within the confines of the plan. Budgeting is a form of fiscal planning and requires knowledge of the kinds of budget models available. Typical examples are (1) planned program budgeting system (PPBS), (2) line-item budgeting, and (3) zero-based budgeting. There is increasing pressure on police departments for fiscal account-ability and expertise in the realm of financial stability, analysis, and reporting.

Running any law enforcement agency is like running a corporation but expending many public, not private, dollars. Most private corporations have appropriate numbers of well-paid executive managers, financial experts, and qualified staff. But there is little of this expertise for such positions in the public corporation we call a police agency. There is little doubt that police administra-tors need more training in financial matters.

▶ SUPERVISION

The supervisor's position in the organization is a vital link between line employ-ees and management. A major problem is that line officers promoted to supervi-sory positions often do not make the transition to thinking as supervisors. The primary reasons for this are (1) promotion by civil service examinations that often do not test for police management skills, and (2) lack of timely in-service training and resocialization into the supervisory role. With these handicaps, it is hard for that newly appointed line officer-supervisor to perform well as a super-visor in charge of other officers.

As a supervisor, the newly promoted sergeant will have to modify actions that he or she may have condoned as a line officer. As one officer, newly pro-moted, said to one of the authors, "The hardest thing about this job is disciplining personal friends, fellow officers with whom I went to the academy." With the cor-rect resocialization into the management role, that line officer can make an excel-lent supervisor. This takes planning, time, and money. With the supervisor being a key member of the total management team, it is well worth it.

Supervisors are often appointed to open slots in the organizational chart without any reference to past training, needed training, or knowledge of the offi-cer being promoted.

In a small police department of less than 10 officers, the supervisor's role is closer to that of the line officer, with the supervisor often sharing many of the duties of the line officer. Because the role is less narrowly focused than in the case of a large department, the role of the supervisor of the small department deserves special consideration.

Current research in policing focuses mainly on big-city police departments. But training and education have to be concerned with the broad-based, general-ist, smaller law enforcement agency supervisors as well. The most common prob-lem for supervisors and chiefs in small agencies is that they may have established personal relationships that make it difficult to delegate or assign tasks in a fair and impartial manner. Invariably, any promotion from within often causes hard feel-ings because someone will always be mad at being passed over.

Police administrators and supervisors in small departments readily admit that they are forced to become generalists, simply because they may be the only person on duty during a specific shift. Thus, the chief may be performing the daily routine of the street officer, as well as dealing with administrative tasks. On the other hand, there are very tangible benefits in the absence of a complex chain of commands, especially in the areas of direct supervision and communication. Regardless of size, the role of the top administrator requires conceptual skills, the ability to develop long-range goals, and the ability to communicate with all areas of the community. If anything, by the very nature of their presence in the community, small departments indeed practice community policing from knowing virtually everyone in the community and providing a wide range of services.

 # THE RESPECT APPROACH TO SUPERVISION

POSDCORB has been a useful approach to organizing basic management functions. What is proposed here is a similar approach to the functions of the supervisor who usually has the rank of Sergeant or Lieutenant. The acronym RESPECT stands for

R	Reporting and communicating
E	Evaluation and inspection
S	Services and community relations
P	Planning and implementation
E	Ethics and morale
C	Control and resource utilization
T	Teaching and directing

Because the supervisor is the vital organizational link between the street officer and management, the duties and functions of the supervisor need to be systematically analyzed. The following functions can be applied by both the small department and the large urban police department. While the applications will differ, the principles remain the same.

REPORTING AND COMMUNICATING

A police organization, among other things, is a communication network. The supervisor receives reports and needs to review these reports for information, clarity, and accuracy. This is a vital responsibility since future actions involving citizens are based on these reports.

In the important area of internal communications, management needs to know what the officers are thinking and how they are acting. The line supervisor and the internal department supervisor are in a position to perform this vital communication function by reviewing reports and recording observations.

Orders need to be communicated to staff, and it is the supervisor who converts orders to operational activities. Communication is a vital two-way flow for every police organization.

Supervisors need a basic knowledge of communication skills and communication links if they are to perform effectively. The supervisor needs to distinguish between statements and feelings: techniques for achieving effective communication will be fully developed in Chapters 10 and 12.

Accurate, brief reports are necessary if a department is to operate effectively. Reports have to convey the maximum amount of information in the minimum of space. Time is valuable, and the reading of reports is an expensive way in which to spend time in any organization.

EVALUATION AND INSPECTION

The supervisor's basic responsibility is to evaluate the officers in terms of their appearance, use of equipment, habits, and performance. *Habits* refer to behavior, mannerisms, use of language, and professional attitude; *performance* refers to the knowledge of the job and the ability to do the job in terms of professional qualifications. Dress and demeanor are also part of this evaluation and inspection process.

Even such "unmeasurables" such as empathy and the ability to deal with people have to be a solid part of the evaluation and inspection process. The supervisor becomes the enforcer of professional standards while helping the officers conform to these standards through a solid management support system.

SERVICES AND COMMUNITY RELATIONS

Since the police department is a public service organization, one of the supervisor's first responsibilities is to maintain the quality of the delivery of services to the citizens. This is done by making community relations activities part of the evaluation of each officer. The supervisor helps the officer to understand that he or she represents law enforcement in the community. With support from supervisors, community policing is not just relegated to a public relations department in the police agency but becomes the responsibility of each officer.

The officer needs training in order to deal with emergencies and the myriad of other services that constitute police work. Although arrest and apprehension of criminals is the most visible part of the business of law enforcement, the human-service function is just as vital. Top management must thus constantly reward its supervisors for the effective delivery of human service. Thus, an effective law enforcement support team can create a department deeply concerned with helping each citizen of the community.

PLANNING AND IMPLEMENTATION

This refers to both long-range and short-range planning and implementation. Supervisors are normally involved with daily planning activities such as scheduling the roster and reviewing patrol and detective assignments. Management needs to involve these supervisors in longer-range planning, specifying the needs of the unit(s) for the next month, year, or even a decade.

Supervisors are close to information needed for planning. They generally know the conditions in the street. A major rule in management communication is that the closer you are to your data, the more accurate knowledge of the data you have. Supervisors, as the first line of management, are vitally needed if planning is to be implemented.

Much of what top management intends in long-range planning has failed because the supervisors closest to essential planning data were neglected. It is the supervisory managers who will be in charge of actually carrying out the detailed implementation of such long-range planning. Supervision and planning need to come together if implementation is going to be accomplished.

Supervisors have to understand the plans and intent of management and have some general agreement as to the implementation of policy. If a hostile attitude is taken by the supervisors, the line officer will not readily implement a policy. There are too many obvious and subtle ways to not implement policy. The line officer in the street has a great deal of discretion and can use this discretion to support or harass management. Policy can be implemented so slowly, for example, that the impact of the policy decision is diffused and wasted. Or it can be implemented so rapidly that there is no thought of the side effects of implementation. The voluntary cooperation of supervisory personnel is necessary in any implementation of policy. Policy can work in the field only with the active understanding and cooperation of supervisory personnel.

ETHICS AND MORALE

Professional organizations, including police organizations, have a code of **ethics** (standards of conduct and moral judgment). Implementation of the profession's code of ethics is dependent upon the individual supervisor and is strongly related to the morale of personnel. A management guided by ethical principles with a reputation for integrity is more apt to have an organization with high morale.

Morale is also determined by a management that has sympathetic knowledge of line personnel problems. As stated previously, an effective communication system will bring management the necessary knowledge of line operating conditions and problems. Problems arise due to lack of communication and inaction. Finally, management's own code of ethics needs to be operational, since each supervisor becomes an ethical role model for personnel in the organization.

CONTROL AND RESOURCE UTILIZATION

Effective management needs to control both personnel and materiel, providing guidance and instilling a sense of responsibility. With increasingly scarce resources available for public agencies, their efficient use will be a paramount measure of management success in the future.

Knowledge, and effective use, of personnel becomes dynamically important since 70 to 90 percent of most police budgets are devoted to personnel. Personnel hours are money. Reactive management wastes human resources by failing to plan aggressively. Having officers reading the newspaper in the patrol on duty is basically a waste of personnel resources. The management of the future will be held accountable for spending human resources wisely and efficiently. An aggressive, proactive, reality-based management will develop an efficient and accountable police force.

TEACHING AND DIRECTING

The supervisor is concerned with personnel reaching their highest potential. By constantly training personnel in the use of proper procedures for obtaining the objectives of the police organization, supervisors become teachers. The supervisor selects specific individuals for in-service training and evaluates the training in terms of the enhanced worth of personnel to the organization. As corporate management has learned, regular in-service training is needed to run an efficient organization. Training is needed to develop leadership as well as skills. Included in this function is the need to direct personnel, which is also a teaching skill.

The acronym RESPECT then symbolizes the need for management to show *respect* for the basic integrity of the individual and to treat each employee in a professional manner. In the absence of such an approach, the organization will be inefficient and autocratic and will reflect many morale problems. A positive climate conducive to cooperation is created when basic respect is shown by management for all personnel and personnel for management. It is always a two-way street—a two-way street that pays big dividends for the modern, reality-based police department.

OPERATIONS

Operations is defined as all the activities necessary to carry out the basic goals of the organization. Controlling crime and providing service are the major goals for law enforcement agencies. Good management carries out these goals without wasting resources on irrelevant activities. Operations include (1) line functions, (2) staff or administrative functions, and (3) auxiliary or service functions. This is the basic way the police organization is structured.

LINE FUNCTIONS

For close to a century full-service enforcement agencies have organized line functions into the following categories: (1) patrol, (2) traffic, (3) investigation (detectives), (4) vice, and (5) juvenile. Recently, some agencies have had to change, consolidate, and even eliminate some of these functions. This will be discussed in a later chapter.

Patrol

In modern communities, when there is felt to be a need for a new police organization, the first function that is thought of is that of patrol. This function provides a public manifestation of the police through uniformed personnel being visible in marked patrol vehicles.

This leads to home rule pride and the creation of many new, small police departments. A major concern for modern police management is the consolidation of police forces to eliminate overlapping police jurisdictions and provide more efficient delivery of services. Thus, the patrol function, although central and essential to law enforcement, also creates its own variety of problems that need to be resolved. As we shall see later, the random patrol controversy in the efficient use of patrol services has become a central management problem in an era of scarce resources.

The patrol function, as used in many departments, treats the patrol officer as a generalist—a professional who can handle anything happening in the streets of the jurisdiction. It also requires the patrol officer to hand over certain activities to police specialists after the immediate street action has been handled. Thus, when treating the patrol function in terms of management, we must always be aware of dealing with the generalist-specialist controversy and targeting specific solutions for this continuing problem area.

Traffic

This function deals with both the motoring public and pedestrians. Considerable time is spent on accident investigations and traffic enforcement. When an ever-increasing traffic problem takes too much of an officer's time from normal service and patrol functions, an independent traffic unit may become justified.

Investigation/Detective

This is a nonuniformed follow-up force. Basically, this specialized unit develops in a department when the patrol officer does not have time to do investigations and when a certain level of expertise and experience is needed to deal with crime cases. A vital function of this unit is the preparation of cases for prosecution after arrest.

Vice

This nonuniformed, investigative function focuses on specific crimes such as prostitution, gambling, and narcotics. Many of these crimes have been called **victimless crimes**, although this designation is considered quite controversial by many law enforcement managers. Vice units also handle crime that is considered organ-ized such as receiving and transporting stolen goods, extortion, and other continuing criminal conspiracies.

Juvenile

It is estimated that roughly 80 percent of street crimes are committed by youths between the ages of 8 and 18. The crime statistics are showing increasingly younger offenders, however.

Juvenile laws and due process for juveniles differ from adult penal and criminal process statutes. Officers assigned to this function require specialized training so they can work closely with juveniles, parents, and various juvenile authorities.

STAFF/ADMINISTRATIVE FUNCTIONS

The administrative staff directly assists top management. They have no command or patrol duties, but are responsible for the everyday activities that concern the management team.

Staff/Administrative Units

Personnel	Inspections Office
Training	Intelligence Office
Legal Advisors	Research and Planning Office
Public Relations	Budget Office
Community Relations	Crime Prevention

These administrative functions are necessary to support the line functions. The line functions are directly related to the output services of the agency. Auxiliary functions are important, but the management team normally does not need daily input from these units, and, in a normal staffing chart, they are delegated down the line from management.

AUXILIARY/SERVICE FUNCTIONS

Auxiliary functions are the support and maintenance jobs that need to be performed by any organization. Basically all patrol and investigation units will make use of these functions at some time or other. The following is a list of services that might be included in the police organization:

Auxiliary/Service Units

Records	License Section
Data Processing	Maintenance Section
Identification Bureau	Communications
Jail	Crime Laboratory
Transport Sections	Animal Complaints
Property Clerk's Office	

Over the years, police departments have inherited functions that would normally be serviced by other units of the government. Many of the licensing functions have been relegated to police agencies for historical reasons only. Some of these functions may not be properly placed in police agencies and should be placed in other governmental agencies. This management problem will be discussed in a later chapter.

▷ CONCLUSION

The functions discussed in this chapter are the normal functions that exist in any full-service police agency. Every student of management needs to be aware of how these functions are carried out. They also need to be aware of the kinds of criteria that can be applied to determine the success or failure of police agencies in carrying out these functions.

To do this type of examination, the student needs to look at how specific departments are organized and how these structures successfully implement or fail to implement these functions. Of course, in the specific application of these functions, judgments must also be made concerning the worth of the function to departmental goals and general law enforcement goals. In later chapters, this will be done with case histories. At this point, the student needs an understanding of these functions and how they interrelate before undertaking a more elaborate analysis and application. However, the practical application of principles is vital if management is going to be proactive and reality based.

QUESTIONS FOR REVIEW

1. Place the following in terms of importance: (a) administration, (b) supervision, and (c) operations. Justify your decision.

2. POSDCORB has been used by management since 1937. Why is it so useful? Relate the planning function to the other functions of POSDCORB.

3. Explain the difference between the administration of a small-town police department and a large-city police department.

4. Rank in order of importance the functions of the supervisor as listed in the RESPECT approach to supervision. Justify your decision.

5. How does the operational job of supervision differ from the overall tasks of management?

6. What are the essential elements of a supervisor's job? Why?

7. What management and personnel skills does a supervisor need? Why?

8. What are the major distinctions separating staff/administrative functions from auxiliary/service functions? Explain.

KEY TERMS

auxiliary/service functions
budgeting
control
coordinating
directing
ethics
line functions
operations

organizing
planning
policy
reporting
staff/administrative functions
staffing
habits v. performance

BIBLIOGRAPHY

BOPP, WILLIAM J., *Police Personnel Administration*. Boston: Holbrook Press, 1974.

ETZIONI, AMITAI, *Modern Organizations*. Upper Saddle River, N.J.: Prentice-Hall, 1964.

GULICK, LUTHER, and L. URWICK, eds., *Papers on the Science of Administration*. New York: Institute of Public Administration, Columbia University, 1937.

IANNONE, N.F., *Supervision of Police Personnel* (4th ed.) Upper Saddle River, N.J.: Prentice-Hall, 1980.

LYNCH, RONALD G., *The Police Manager* (2nd ed.). Boston: Holbrook Press, 1975.

NEWMAN, WILLIAM H., *Administrative Action* (2nd ed.). Upper Saddle River, N.J.: Prentice-Hall, 1963.

STAHL, O. GLENN, and RICHARD A. STAUFENBERGER, eds., *Police Personnel Administration*. Washington, D.C.: Police Foundation, 1974.

WHISENAND, PAUL M., *Police Supervision: Theory and Practice*. Upper Saddle River, N.J.: Prentice-Hall, 1976.

WILSON, O.W., and ROY CLINTON MCLAREN, *Police Administration* (4th ed.). New York: McGraw-Hill, 1977.

5

The Art and Style of Proactive Police Leadership

One of the critical management issues of today is leadership. Too often in these past years, the public media has discussed the so-called crisis in leadership or why leaders can and do not lead. At a recent leadership conference, we rhetorically asked, Who are the most prominent police leaders in the United States today? The class cited prominent police figures but they had a hard time naming police leaders that they would want as models for their own careers.

The irony here is that many of the police leaders that we cite in Chapter 1 were not held in high esteem by their subordinates during their tenure in office. Others, such as former Los Angeles chief of Police Darryl Gates, were respected by the troops but damned by the rest of the public for insensitivity and errors of judgment for the department's handling of the Rodney King incident.

Reflecting on leadership as described by Etzioni, Richard Hall (1996: 139–140) points out leadership is a special form of power closely related to the ability of the leader to elicit the followers' voluntary compliance in a broad range of matters. Leadership is distinguished from the concept of power in that a leader has influence over subjects, while power implies that subjects' preferences are held in abeyance.

Perusing our personal libraries we came up with over 30 different definitions of leadership. Simply summarized, **leadership is the ability to get things done under the right circumstances**. So much for definitions. The real challenge is for students to examine and understand the problems and theoretical parameters involved with the characteristics of leadership in American policing. We decided for this edition to mix some of the classical leadership theories required of all graduate students for comprehensive exams with those of some current theories being discussed in the business world.

 PROACTIVE LEADERSHIP

Proactive leaders anticipate day-to-day events. They do not wait for events to reach them; they plan for events. They form a team that is flexible enough to seek a wide variety of solutions to the everyday problems of police management. This entails a deep commitment to contingency planning so that the eventual crises that do reach their desks do not overwhelm them. Crises, for a proactive police management team, are something to be dealt with and learned from, not simply reacted to.

To exercise this proactive leadership, three essential areas of competence are needed:

1. Talent
2. Experience
3. Training/education

While a whole range of competencies is needed for the exercise of leadership, these three areas are significant enough to become prerequisites for other competencies.

TALENT

Authority in an organization can be exercised in two ways: through the person of the officeholder or through the office itself. Of course, the reality is that authority is exercised in a synthesis combining both ways. However, the emphasis can go either way.

Max Weber's concept of **charismatic authority** is one of the earliest and clearest conceptions of authority being exercised through the person rather than the office (Weber, 1961: 628). Weber describes the three major bases for legitimate authority:

1. *Rational grounds*—resting on a belief in the "legality" of patterns of normative rules and the right of those elevated to authority under such rules to issue commands (legal authority).

2. *Traditional grounds*—resting on an established belief in the sanctity of immemorial traditions and the legitimacy of the status of those exercising authority under them (traditional authority).

3. *Charismatic grounds*–resting on devotion to the specific and exceptional sanctity, heroism, or exemplary character of an individual person, and of the normative patterns, the order revealed or ordained by the person (charismatic authority).

In its purest form, charismatic authority creates the authority of the office in terms of the person holding the office. Modern figures who are supposed to have exercised a great deal of their authority through the charisma of their person include such figures as Mahatma Gandhi, John Kennedy, and Eleanor Roosevelt.

Many police chiefs and sheriffs often depend upon the strength of their personalities in exercising public office. However, such authority is short lived. According to Weber (1961: 1297), "In its pure form, charismatic authority has a character specifically foreign to everyday routine structures. The social relationships directly involved are strictly personal." To create stability in the organization, charismatic authority needs to be channeled into the mechanics of a routine bureaucracy, thus taking on all the trappings of legitimate authority based upon legal and rational grounds. Charismatic authority with its reliance on personal relationships creates inconsistent policies based upon personal whims, and often breaks down.

Over time, the charismatic figure institutes the normal legalistic aspects of a rational bureaucracy, namely (1) a set of written rules that persist over time and that are adhered to, (2) a clearly identified set of administrative officials with their authority specifically defined and limited, and (3) a hierarchical organization with publicly known operational lines of authority.

A chief who has a strong personality and good rapport with the public may be able to operate for a time, depending upon charismatic authority, by ignoring the rules of rational bureaucracy. Modern, organized society, however, is basically a bureaucratic society based upon rational **legal authority**. Some charismatic sheriffs who are inconsistent administrators are kept in power by political party officials because of their vote-getting power. However, the rational rules of the organization take over the day-to-day business of the police department and even the most powerful sheriffs have to recognize this, especially when they see their power curbed by police unions contracts and the courts. However, a certain amount of charismatic authority is valuable and useful in exercising the duties of police leadership.

A talented police leader is one who also has a high degree of intelligence. He or she must be able to understand theoretical concepts as they relate to the job and be able to create abstract plans and operationalize these plans. This involves a high degree of abstract manipulation of data and the ability to comprehend and make the most use of the computer age.

Talented police leaders must also have what has been called a certain native shrewdness, that is, they have to have a grasp of politics and be pragmatic problem solvers. They must also be goal oriented, that is, individuals who truly want to get the job done. Police leaders have to balance many demands on their time along with conflicting demands that bear upon their decisions. Special interest groups, politicians, fellow police leaders, and their own officers, including the diverse groups within the official police community, all create pressures upon their decisions. A leader must have a sense of fair play and balance to get the job done amid the conflicting pressures.

Our police leaders must also be excellent communicators. They need to be clear and forceful yet be able to listen and understand other points of view. Their ideas of leadership need to be marketed just as business and industry market ideas. Police leaders have many publics, including their own officers, various community groups, and the governmental and criminal justice leaders. Communication ability is crucial. Former New York City Police Commissioner William Bratton was a master at this by appearing at important police events and communicating with the print and electronic media on the progress the department was making in the "crime war." Unfortunately, his media fame and public stature came into conflict with Mayor Rudolf Guiliani's, and Bratton retired in 1996.

After reading these few paragraphs on talent, the reader might begin to wonder if every police leader has to be a comic book superhero. The answer is, not quite. Too often, we have been satisfied in police management with mediocre leadership. The demands of the 1990s on police management will no longer allow us this luxury. The police leader of the 1990s may not have to be a superhero, but he does have to be a supremely talented human being who can bring talent to bear on the exercise of office.

EXPERIENCE

There is experience and there is experience. A police leader does not need twenty years of experience, one year at a time, where nothing is learned about the exercise of leadership talents.

He does not need simply operational experience. He really does not need to know how to fix a patrol car, how to write a parking ticket, or even how to drive a motorcycle. Management skills are developed through the exercise of management and administrative experience. They may seem obvious, but many departments operate when choosing their leaders as if this statement did not exist. If there were advertisements in the local newspapers for police chiefs, in terms of the history of electing and appointing police leaders, most of them would read like this:

JOB VACANCY FOR POLICE CHIEF

NO EXPERIENCE IN MANAGEMENT NECESSARY

What is being emphasized here is that experience is necessary, but it has to be experience of a certain kind and quality. Technically trained, operational administrators need experience in how to make decisions based upon complex, often incomplete facts and the human situation.

Experience in the day-to-day activities of police work is valuable and contributes to being a good police administrator. The operational and technical skills needed for administrators need to be superseded by the necessary human relations and conceptual skills needed to manage a police department.

Some of this lack of experience can be made up with a good management training program. Police leaders can be trained in how to draw up and present a budget, in what is necessary in exercising leadership skills in relation to personnel and in what goes in to such items as contingency planning and communication networks. Thus what is necessary in the exercise of proactive police leadership is a careful blend of ability, experience, and finally, training/education. Let us now examine this last area of competence.

TRAINING/EDUCATION

Police leaders are promoted, appointed, and elected, in most cases, without any further training in management skills. In the mid-1970s, the International Association of Chiefs of Police (**IACP**) surveyed the heads of the 49 state police and highway patrol agencies, all of the chiefs and sheriffs who headed agencies of 100 or more sworn personnel, and a 20 percent national sample of those chiefs with fewer than 100 sworn personnel and concluded (National Advisory Commission, 1976: 31):

> A majority of the police chiefs surveyed indicated that some law enforcement and management training should be required for future police chief executives. Training tends to refine executive capabilities derived from innate leadership ability and meaningful work experience....For the two-thirds of the police chief executives who advanced from within their organization, training is especially important to prevent agencies from becoming ingrown.

In terms of selecting a police chief, "Ninety-seven percent of police chief executives and 96 percent of their superiors believe that law enforcement training is an important or very important factor." The superiors surveyed were those governmental persons who supervise police chief executives (mayor, city manager, legislative group).

IMPORTANCE OF MANAGEMENT SKILLS

Over the years, a number of private and public agencies have developed courses for police officers and manager. Police academies in the largest agencies routinely offer some management courses as does the Federal Bureau of Investigations and the International Association of Chiefs of Police. Although both organizations perform an important function in updating the police chief executive and future police executives in the current issues such as hostage negotiation and crises and stress management, there remains the lack of a systematic approach to basic training for all police managers.

Although the survey did not identify a specific curriculum content for police management academies, it did identify 14 significant police management skills (Table 5-1) and asked the surveyed police executives to rate the importance of each skill on a scale of 0 to 10, with 10 being the most important (National Advisory Commission, 1976: 25).

TABLE 5–1

IMPORTANCE OF MANAGEMENT SKILLS FOR POLICE CHIEF EXECUTIVES

SKILL AREA	RATING BY POLICE CHIEF EXECUTIVES*
1. Motivating personnel and maintaining high morale	8.7
2. Developing subordinates into an effective team	8.6
3. Relating to the community	8.4
4. Organizing agency personnel and functions	8.0
5. Administering internal discipline	7.9
6. Maintaining internal review and control	7.9
7. Communicating with all levels within the agency	7.9
8. Establishing and communicating objectives and priorities	7.8
9. Forecasting, planning, and implementing agency activities	7.8
10. Resolving employee relations problems	7.7
11. Budgeting and fiscal management	7.7
12. Utilizing advanced technology	7.2
13. Coordinating agency activity with other organizations	7.2
14. Securing and managing grant-funded projects	6.2

*0=Lowest score; 10=highest score.
Source: National Advisory Commission on Standards and Goals (1976).

The study of this list of skills would, indeed, make a fine curriculum for a modern police management academy. When we analyze this list, some skill patterns emerge: organization and administration skills, technical skills such as fiscal and knowledge of advanced technology and overwhelmingly, communication skills on all levels.

Major metropolitan areas normally maintain their own police academies and offer some management training programs. However, the medium and smaller departments do not have the economies of scale of the larger municipalities and thus have neither the budget nor the continuing demand for such large-scale training. There is a need for systematic leadership/management courses for newly promoted police executives. These should be readily available on a systematic, recurring, and regional basis. Upon promotion, new administrators should have the opportunity to attend a regionally based training academy.

In 1921, the Wickersham Commission stated (National Commission, 1967: 44): "Not infrequently the chief is wholly incompetent to discharge the onerous duties of his position. He may lack experience, executive ability, character, integrity or the confidence of his force or all of them put together."

In 1967, the task-force report, *The Police*, of the President's Commission on Law Enforcement and the Administration of Justice reported the following path to the police executive suite at that time (p. 44): "The time-honored, uninspired path of promotion sees an administrator fish-laddering his way through the ranks, without being prepared in anything more than a "by chance" manner for the new and difficult responsibilities of successive commands. The consequence is that many of today's police commanding officers are simply promoted policemen, not professional administrators carefully prepared for demanding roles in the complex enterprise that is the hallmark of contemporary police work."

In 1976, in the *Police Chief Executive*, the International Association of Chiefs of Police (IACP), a group that normally defends the quality of police executives, stated (National Advisory Commission, 1976: 2): "Some jurisdictions have neglected to develop people within the police agencies to assume the leadership role. Where this is true, the job of police chief executive may go to someone who is not prepared for the important position—who does not meet minimum standards and who has not demonstrated the essential leadership and administrative qualification." In fact, one of the standards recommended for the selection process by the IACP tells us by what is left unsaid, the state of affairs today (National Advisory Commission, 1976: 49): "Police chief executives should not be selected solely on the basis of seniority without a determination of merit. Selection solely on the basis of seniority is not professionally acceptable." The question then becomes: How does a department select for talent, experience, and education and training? The obvious answer is to set up rigorous criteria, in writing, enforce these criteria, and use as wide a pool of potential talent as possible.

Today in the 1990s, the criteria for police executive selection in progressive departments is like selecting a business executive. Community search committees are looking for personnel who have a combination of education, training, and field experience. In addition to the management skills presented in Table 5-1, police chief candidates must also be able to define what is the department's organizational vision of the future. As Garner (1993: 3–4) discusses, this vision includes communicating a clear mission statement which is derived from discussion among employees and community leaders.

▶ MANAGEMENT STYLES

Over the years, numerous management profiles have been taken from the areas of public and business administration and applied to police management. There is a great deal of overlap in this area with communication models since style of police leadership is directly linked to the communication process within the agency. When communication goes from the top to the bottom, with no feedback system, for example, the management style tends toward the hierarchical and autocratic. When communication is two-way, ongoing, and considered to be effective in deciding policy between equals in an organizational structure, the management style tends toward the democratic, and team, approach.

The following approaches will be examined in terms of their applicability to the art and style of proactive police leadership:

1. Total Quality Management (TQM).
2. Reengineering.
3. Herzberg's eternal triangle.
4. Katz's three skills approach.
5. Maslow's need hierarchy.
6. Herzberg's hygiene versus motivators factors.
7. McGregor's Theory X and Theory Y.
8. Theory Z.
9. Tannenbaum and Schmidt's leadership patterns.
10. Blake and Mouton's management grid.

Each approach will be given in summary form and then applied to police leadership.

TOTAL QUALITY MANAGEMENT

Total Quality Management or TQM has become the standard agenda item at police management conferences in the 1990s. Although apparently new to management theory discussions, the foundations for TQM were written and discussed before and after World War II by W. Edwards Deming, who served as the leading organizational consultant during the rebuilding of Japanese industry. According to Halberstam (1986: 380), Deming is held with same regard as General MacArthur by the Japanese with regard to his contributions to postwar economic development. In the United States, however, Deming's ideas were never seriously discussed by organizational theorists until serious inquiry was made into Japanese management practices in the 1980s. In fact, the authors of this book came upon Deming's theories as an aside during leisure readings on a comparison of auto industries of the United States and Japan.

By itself TQM is defined as a strategic, integrated management system for achieving customer satisfaction. TQM involves all managers and employees and uses human resources and managerial and quantitative methods to continually improve organizational processes. According to TQM proponents, it provides attentive leaders, trained workers, data and measurement, a guiding vision, and operating values for any organization.

For example, the Xerox Corporation, which adopted TQM in the early 1980s, makes the following statement in a recent company brochure:

Xerox is a quality company. Quality is the basic business principle for Xerox. Quality means providing our internal and external customers with innovative products and services that satisfy their requirements. Quality improvement is the job of every Xerox employee.

This statement becomes the cornerstone for employee training, assessment of customer satisfaction, creation of management teams, and the corporation's recognition and reward system. An important component in TQM is **benchmarking**, which is defined as "the continuous process of measuring our products, services, and practices against our toughest competitor, or those recognized as world leaders and to identify areas that need improvement" (Xerox, 1991).

The basic components of TQM are summarized according to the **14-point** philosophy presented by Deming. As discussed by Butterfield (1992, 50–59) on their application to the service industry, they are as follows:

1. A consistency of purpose toward improvement of product and service.

2. The adoption of the quality philosophy by management which must begins with the corporate leaders.

3. An emphasis on improving work processes rather than relying on mass inspections.

4. Awarding of contracts and business on the basis of quality rather than price tag.

5. Constant improvement on production and service.

6. Much attention to training.

7. Uncovering barriers to workmanship.

8. Driving out fear such as the fear of asking questions or expressing ideas.

9. Breaking down communication barriers between departments.

10. Eliminating slogans and targets for zero defects and new levels of productivity. Instead, management concentrates on showing people how to do their work more accurately and efficiently.

11. Eliminating work standards that dwell on numerical quotas. Instead, use leadership to look for differences in performance.

12. Remove barriers that rob hourly workers of their pride in workmanship. This is often created by communication barriers between management and employees related to job performance or ways to improve services.

13. Instituting a vigorous program of education and self-improvement for workers for new or improved skills.

14. Having everyone in the organization working towards the objective of quality.

It is important to stress that TQM does not mean any change in the traditional organizational structure postulated by Weber. There is still the hierarchy and management is still in control. Quality teams, with the approval of management, are brought together to define and solve problems related to their sphere of influence but they may have little impact on overall company strategy. Comparing TQM to directed teams, Holpp (1992, 72–73) shows that the main difference is that directed teams in theory are given all kinds of flexibility for production and problem solving.

At the time of this writing, TQM remains an important concept in organizational theory. It should be noted that in the 1950s Deming used royalties from his books to create the Deming prize for Japanese companies and their quality control initiatives. Ironically, in the United States today, there is a Deming prize and a Baldridge award, which are both awarded to companies that have outstanding quality control mechanisms.

As discussed in Chapter 1, an important component of TQM is leadership. For Deming, leadership is important insofar as managers must remove barriers to producing quality goods and services. Organizations committed to TQM are committed to quality. If some process does not work or produce the right result, then the components that lead to the output are analyzed by a work team to find solutions. A mid-sized police department could use TQM to facilitate the return of recovered stolen property to the rightful owners. A team would be formed to look at the problems inherent with the current system. The team might include an evidence technician, patrol supervisor, patrol officer, and a representative from the district attorney's office interested in evidence for criminal cases. The team would then ask some basic questions such as, Why do we have to keep certain items? Could some items be immediately returned? How long after a court disposition do we keep items? How are the items properly tagged and inventoried? What do we do with unclaimed items and how do we destroy contraband such as drugs? Each question would be broken down to various distinct components and the team would try to provide new thinking and processes to these questions. This is not a one shot deal. The team would look at how other organizations deal with the problem of overloaded evidence supply systems. New ideas would be tried and victims (the customers) would be asked by phone or by mail to evaluate the method used to return their property. The idea is to get the property back to their rightful owners as soon as legally possible and to keep the evidence rooms free of junk. The leadership role in this enterprise is for management to permit formation of the team and allow it to constructively attack the problem without cumbersome red tape or meddling supervision.

Obviously this quest for quality begins at the top and filters down to all layers of the organization. Quality controls and innovations are tied to promotions and rewards. For TQM proponents, there must be true commitment and not lip service; otherwise the program becomes another fad. According to Halberstam (1986: 313) Deming had little use for managers who had not graduated from the factory floor. At that time, the science of management was exerting itself in many organizations and many managers dealt with abstractions rather than practical experience.

REENGINEERING

As businesses were adopting TQM as a way to improve the quality of their goods and services, a concept called *reenginering* was being developed by certain companies as a way to review how tasks were being performed. The term was coined by MIT professor Michael Hammer in 1980 as he observed radical reorganizations undertaken by many major companies. In their book, *Reengineering the Corporation,* Hammer and co-author James Champy wrote that reengineering is the fundamental rethinking and basic redesign of business processes to achieve dramatic improvement in critical contemporary measures of performance such as cost, quality, service, and speed (1993: 4). In comparison to TQM, reengineering involves a radical review of the entire organizational structure, while TQM programs exist within the framework of existing organizational structure.

Hammer and Champy present the following questions when a company or organizational unit is considering reengineering:

1. Why do we do what we do?
2. Can we disregard all existing structure and procedures and invent new ways of accomplishing work?
3. Do we need dramatic improvement? Should we blow up the old and replace it with something new?
4. What is the range of activities that creates output which is of value to the customer (1993: 32–36)?

This concept came about because of competition, cost, and the drive for quality facing American companies from Asia and Europe. According to the authors, companies that have undertaken reengineering have ranged from those that were in deep trouble, such as auto manufacturing, to those that were having no discernible difficulties but were not satisfied with current performance. Walmart, Hallmark, Kodak, and others are cited as examples of successful companies that used reengineering as a method to keep an upper hand in their markets.

Companies that have undertaken reengineering are not tied to the idea of centralized control. The development of informational technology, which resulted in information being shared throughout the organization, contributes to this concept by tearing down distance. Units that are miles apart can now teleconference, e-mail, fax, video sell, digitize, internet, and so on.

For his work, *Time* hailed Hammer as one of the 25 most influential people in the United States in 1996 (1996: 73). Many observers, however, have used the term reengineering in connection to "downsizing," "flattening," or "rightsizing" the organization, which in basic terms means reducing the size of the organization, producing less, and creating more profits for shareholders and executives. In most cases reengineering means that the company will produce more with less departments and levels of control, which indeed results in reduced organizational structures.

In a more recent work, Hammer wrote that reengineering had not just modified ways of working, it had transformed many organizations into structures that could not be recognizable. He states, "...the radical character of reengineering, however important and exciting, is not its most significant aspect. The key word in the definition of reengineering is "process": a complete end-to-end set of activities that together create value for a customer" (1996: xii).

Reengineering operational concepts appear somewhat similar to TQM guidelines. Problem-solving teams are formed to develop new products or processes to achieve results. Managers have to be retrained to think as coaches rather than traditional supervisors. Workers and managers, who share joint responsibilities, are rewarded according to results, not activity. Returning to our TQM discussion on ways of returning property to their rightful owners, a review team undertaking a reengineering of the recovery of stolen property would ask certain questions relating the process to the entire property operation, such as, why do we have to keep the property in an evidence room? Do we have to have an evidence room? Why can't the district attorney keep the evidence, since they deal with the evidence at trial? Okay, let's say that we keep the evidence room but the property is videotaped and returned to the owner immediately.

In this process the role of the leader is critical. The leader must have a vision and persuade others that reengineering is important. For policing, the chief must be able to delegate responsibility to the review team to come up with ideas and make them occur. Depending on the size of the organization, the chief or assigned deputy must run interference for the review team and give active support to team members. He or she must keep those with vested interests at bay, and allow the team to have an open discussion. Once a new process is achieved and tested, the management team must make sure that it goes into operation (Hammer and Champy, 1993: 104–105).

The above discussion understates the complexity of reengineering planning and decisions undertaken by major corporations with multinational sites. So far we have seen few examples of reengineering case studies applied to the public sector, mainly because most public organizations are still the sole providers of services in a given geographic area, and work rules are tied to union contracts and civil service procedures. Reengineering for police organizations may become part of the lexicon for managers because many large departments are being decentralized through modern technology and community policing, which together place command, information, and responsibility on local units. Traditional departments are being challenged by community and political groups as expensive, not responsive and, at times, not necessary in view of the overlap of competing jurisdictions that occurs in many areas. There is also increasing competition for support and resources between certain public departments and private security organizations. Reengineering as a concept provides a method to review the organizational structure in order to improve police services.

HERZBERG'S ETERNAL TRIANGLE

Herzberg's eternal triangle consists of the following three elements:

1. Organizational theory (work flow)
2. Industrial engineering (jobs)
3. Behavioral science (attitudes)

According to Herzberg, the organizational theorist says that "If jobs are organized in a proper manner, the result will be the most efficient job structure and the most favorable job attitudes will flow as a matter of course." The industrial engineer, on the other hand, tries to create "the most appropriate incentive system and to design the specific working conditions in a way that facilitates the most efficient use of the human machine." Naturally, optimal organizational design is expected to produce positive work attitudes. The behavioral scientist "emphasizes some form of human relations education, in the hope of instilling healthy employee attitudes and an organizational climate that he or she considers to be felicitous to human values." Naturally, this approach is expected to lead to "efficient job and organizational structure."

What needs to be emphasized here is that, if the leadership style is to be effective, it must include all parts of the eternal triangle. Most police department managers are limited to the organizational theory approach to management. They feel that if there is a proper organizational chart and if the officers understand their job description and operate in terms of the boundaries of this job description while obeying the traditional authority structure, the organization will have high morale and will perform optimally. In many cases, this has degenerated into *management by memorandum* where additions to the rules and clarifications of the organizational structure are seen as sufficient incentive to motivate personnel to do an efficient job. However, this is not sufficient to provide high morale because of a lack of understanding on management's part as to what motivates people to want to perform in an optimal fashion. As we examine the differing approaches to management style, what does work, in terms of a synthesis of approaches, will become clearer.

KATZ'S THREE SKILLS APPROACH

Robert Katz attempts to answer the question (Katz, 1975: 23), "What observable skills does an effective administrator demonstrate?" He states (1975: 24):

It is assumed here that an administrator is one who (a) directs the activities of other persons and (b) undertakes the responsibility for achieving certain objectives through these efforts. Within this definition, successful administration appears to rest on three basic skills, which we will call *technical*, *human*, and *conceptual*.

According to Katz, **technical skill** "involves specialized knowledge, analytical ability within that speciality, and facility in the use of the tools and techniques of the specific discipline." This is the skill most easily trained for. It is more operational than managerial. More complex is **human skill**, which Katz describes as "the executive's ability to work effectively as a group member and to build cooperative effort within the team he leads." Human skill means that the police executive is sensitive to other people's feelings and is aware of his or her own feelings.

This human relations skill involves (1) tolerance of ambiguity and (2) empathy. Tolerance of ambiguity means that the manager is able to handle problems where insufficient information precludes making a totally informed decision. The effective manager must also have a keen sense of appreciation and understanding of widely different viewpoints and cultures and be able to approach problems and people with no preconceptions.

Empathy is the ability to put oneself in another's place. A good police manager is able to put himself or herself in the place of the patrol officers emotionally and intellectually and thus understand the effect of any issued orders on these officers. The manager must be able to look at a situation from the viewpoint of the minority groups in the community and from that of the superior officer. The effective manager must also be willing to act in terms of these perceptions.

Katz's approach to **conceptual skill** is in terms of an organizing and integrating function (1975: 27), "coordinating and integrating all the activities and interests of the organization toward a common objective." This is not meant to be simply an intellectual process, as Katz considers such skills to include "an ability to translate knowledge into action." Police managers with conceptual skills are able to see their relationship to the rest of the organization of the department and understand how their orders and policy will affect the various structural relationships within the department. For example, an order concerning the use of evidence needs to be examined in terms of how it affects detectives, court cases and evidence flow, the laboratory, the property room, and the work of the line officer. Besides these internal relations, good conceptual managers are also able to understand and operationalize in their daily behavior the relationship their policies have to the place of the police department in the local government, community, and when necessary, state and nation.

As Katz points out, these skills are divided for analytical reasons. However, in the day-to-day activities of the police manager, all these skills are brought into play with the emphasis changing depending upon the problems and the organizational context of the department. Katz also emphasizes that these skills can be taught to current and future executives just as any other skill can. Thus good administrators are not simply born but can be trained in the classroom and by practicing the skill in the field. His conclusion should be printed in capital letters and placed in the office of anyone who has a hand in choosing and/or training police executives (1976: 33):

> The administrator needs: (a) sufficient technical skill to accomplish the mechanics of the particular job for which he is responsible; (b) sufficient human skill in working with others to be an effective

group member and to be able to build cooperative effort within the team he leads; (c) sufficient conceptual skill to recognize the interrelationships of the various factors involved in his situation, which will lead him to take that action which is likely to achieve the maximum good for the total organization.

MASLOW'S NEED HIERARCHY

Maslow attempts to understand what motivates human beings. If police managers understand this, they should be able to motivate their personnel and understand their own needs and satisfactions, so that they can become more effective. According to Maslow, first there is a basic need to feel secure and have one's physical needs taken care of. Next is the need to have good social relations. The third need is that of feeling worthwhile in terms of one's work and place in the organization. Many police administrators call this need a need to be respected by one's fellow officers and superiors. Fourth, there is a need to feel that one has enough authority where one's opinions are listened to and that the individual is actually participating in making policy in the organization. Finally there is the ultimate need that some people will never have satisfied, what Maslow calls the need for self-actualization or self-fulfillment. This combines a feeling of wanting personal growth along with such factors as being a creative self-starter who will be able to grow to his or her potential as a human being in this job. This hierarchy of needs is often diagrammed as a triangle going from basic needs of security to self-actualization at the top (see Figure 5–1).

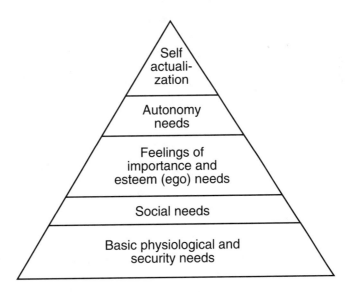

Figure 5-1
Maslow's Need Hierarchy.

I. Security Needs

   1. The feeling of security in my police management position

II. Social needs

   1. The opportunity in my police management position to give help to other people
   2. The opportunity to develop close friendships in my police management position

III. Importance, self-esteem

   1. The feeling of importance a person gets from being in my position
   2. The importance of my position inside the agency (that is, the regard received from others in my police agency)
   3. The importance of my position outside the agency (that is, the regard and esteem received from others who are not members of my police agency)

IV. Autonomy needs

   1. The authority connected with my police management position
   2. The opportunity for independent thought and action in my present police management position
   3. The opportunity in my police management position for participation in the meeting of agency goals
   4. The opportunity in my police management position for participation in the determination of methods and procedures

V. Self-actualization needs

   1. The opportunity for personal growth and development in my present management position
   2. The feeling of self-fulfillment a person gets from being in my police management position (that is, the feeling of being able to use one's own unique capabilities, realizing one's potentialities)
   3. The feeling of worthwhile accomplishment in my present police management position

To obtain a full range of answers concerning the police executive's feelings about his or her position in terms of fulfilling his or her needs, three rating questions are recommended: (1) How much of the characteristic was connected with your police management position? (2) How much of the characteristic do you think should be connected with your police management position? and (3) How important is this characteristic to you? It is obvious that if the manager is to operate successfully, this hierarchy of needs must be satisfied. Maslow warns us that executives vary in terms of how much of the need has to be fulfilled and which needs have priority; however, some attention in any organization has to be given to these needs if managers are going to feel that they are being rewarded for their efforts. Herzberg has tried to operationalize a similar scheme.

Herzberg's Hygiene/Motivators Approach to Job Satisfaction

Frederick Herzberg feels that the externally generated, traditional kick-in-the-pants approach, which he calls **KITA**, has not worked (1975: 13):

> KITA—the externally imposed attempt by management to "install a generator" in the employee—has been demonstrated to be a total failure….The absence of such "hygiene" factors as good supervisor-employee relations and liberal fringe benefits can make a worker unhappy, but their presence will not make him want to work harder. Essentially meaningless changes in the tasks that workers are assigned to do have not accomplished the desired objective either. The only way to motivate the employee is to give him challenging work in which he can assume responsibility.

Herzberg looked at what he called **hygiene factors** contributing to job dissatisfaction and found in a sample of 1,685 employees that these factors contributed 69 percent to job dissatisfaction and only 19 percent to job satisfaction, whereas what he calls **motivators** contributed 81 percent to job satisfaction and 31 percent to job dissatisfaction. Police managers who wish to be effective in motivating their employees and even themselves need to be aware of these dimensions of job satisfaction. Herzberg's chart (Figure 5–2), outlines his findings. As can be seen, Herzberg's positive motivators are similar to those of Maslow. However, Herzberg also gives specific recommendations concerning how, for example, a police manager might apply these motivators to members of his management team (1975: 19).

Herzberg's approach is to apply what he calls motivators to management personnel. He does this by relating certain principles to the motivators involved. By removing a certain amount of controls but still keeping the principle of accountability, he feels that personnel will retain a sense of responsibility and personal achievement. He emphasizes that by holding individuals increasingly accountable for their work, a sense of responsibility and personal recognition will be achieved. Along this same line, he recommends giving personnel an area of work for which they are responsible, which will result in a sense of achievement, responsibility, and recognition. Decentralizing authority and thus allowing more job freedom should also bring about an increase in these three areas. Internal recognition is obtained by sharing periodic reports with personnel as well as supervisors. Personnel are seen to achieve growth and learning through the handling of new and more difficult tasks. Finally, growth, achievement, and responsibility are increased by allowing personnel to become experts through the handling of specialized tasks.

The whole idea of motivating employees is an important concept begun by Herzberg that continues today under the heading of "empowerment." Empowerment is defined as allowing employees to actively participate in setting and achieving department or unit objectives. This results in a sense of ownership and pride in the tasks that are performed (Garner, 1993: 4). In the police case studies where empowerment as a concept was presented, the main motivators were those described by Herzberg that lead to extreme satisfaction. Police managers also must pay attention to hygiene factors because officers and staff may leave for better-paying organizations. As with any participative management scheme, the chief must be able to share and delegate power.

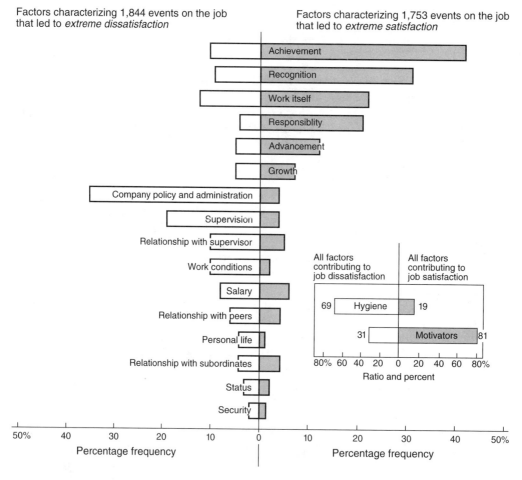

Figure 5-2

Herzberg's Factors Affecting Job Attitudes.

(Source: Reprinted by permission of the *Harvard Business Review*. An exhibit from "One More Time: How Do You Motivate Employees," by Frederick Herzberg (January/February 1968). Copyright©1968 by the President and Fellows of Harvard College; all rights reserved.)

CHAPTER FIVE — The Art and Style of Proactive Police Leadership

McGregor's Theory X and Theory Y

Douglas Murray McGregor's approach to management is similar to Herzberg's insofar as McGregor's advocates an industrial humanism that would provide a check against the autocracy created by stifling, autocratic hierarchical discipline (McGregor, 1978: 188-92). See Table 5-2.

Most police organizations currently operate according to Theory X. It will take a great deal of commitment for departments to develop the more modern approach of Theory Y.

TABLE 5-2
McGregor's Theory X and Theory Y

THEORY X (TRADITIONAL, HIERARCHICAL MANAGEMENT)	THEORY Y (HUMANISTIC, PARTICIPATORY MANAGEMENT)
1. Management is responsible for organizing the elements of productive enterprise—money, materials, equipment, people—in the interests of economic ends.	1. Management is responsible for organizing the elements of productive enterprise—money, materials, equipment, people—in the interests of economic ends.
2. With respect to people, this is a process of directing their efforts, motivating them, controlling their actions, and modifying their behavior to fit the needs of the organization.	2. People are not by nature passive or resistant to organizational needs. They have become so as a result of experience and organization.
3. Without this active intervention by management, people would be passive, even resistant to organizational needs. They must therefore be persuaded, rewarded, punished, controlled. Their activities must be directed. Management consists of getting things done through other people.	3. The motivation, the potential for development, the capacity for assuming responsibility, and the readiness to direct behavior toward organizational goals are all present in people. Management does not put them there. It is a responsibility of management to make it possible for people to recognize and develop these human characteristics for themselves.
4. The average person is by nature indolent—he works as little as possible. He lacks ambition, dislikes responsibility, and prefers to be led. He is inherently self-centered, indifferent to organizational needs. He is by nature resistant to change. He is gullible, not very bright, and the ready dupe of the charlatan and the demagogue.	4. The essential task of management is to arrange organizational conditions and methods of operation so that people can achieve their own goals best by directing their own efforts toward organizational objectives. This is a process of creating opportunities, releasing potential, removing obstacles, encouraging growth, providing guidance.
5. Management is by control.	5. Management is by objectives.

Source: McGregor, (1978).

THEORY Z AND POLICE MANAGEMENT

McGregor's management approach talked about a humanistic approach to management. However, we have a corporate culture that involves both **high touch**, that is, the humanistic approach for terms of personnel management skills, and the use of *high technology* for day-to-day business. John Naisbitt, author of *Megatrends*, in his book *Re-inventing the Corporation*, states that (Naisbitt and Aburdene, 1985: 36) "the old bureaucratic layers are giving way to the more natural arrangements of the new information society." This is also true of police managers, who have to learn new ways of processing information. However, as Naisbitt and Aburdene state (1985: 149): "Information is no substitute for thinking and thinking is no substitute for information."

It is not simply information or using a new technology. As Peter F. Drucker states: "The 'new technology' is entrepreneurial management." It is a management that knows how to use the new technology in a context of being able to motivate the workers to be efficient and loyal to the organization. (Drucker, 1986: 11) The latter is actually a reformulation of McGregor's humanistic approach but in the context of the new technology.

One approach to the use of both high touch and high technology is Theory Z, as characterized by the following: (Ouchi, 1981: 60-79).

1. There is a guarantee of lifetime career and employment in the agency.

2. One's career develops with different jobs throughout the agency rather than being limited to one specialization.

3. Decisions are developed relying on a high-technology total information system.

4. Management is characterized by the use of modern information and accounting systems, formal planning, management by objectives, and formal means of control of the system by management.

5. Decision making is initially consensual and democratic, where employees take a great deal of time agreeing to changes and talking about it. When a decision is made by top management, everyone is expected to go along with it and carry out the new decision.

The Japanese style of consensus building is foreign to American management philosophy as well as police management, which tends to be autocratic in dealing with individuals. However, some of the principles of the Type Z approach are already characteristic of many police organizations, including a lifelong career and both a formal and an emotional support system for the individual officer. Police management is used to giving orders from the top and the Japanese group culture may not work in America. On the other hand, American police managers dealing with the new information society may want to look at ways of building a consensus before major decisions are made in a police agency. Some of the mechanisms of decision making and placing of responsibility and authority lower down the chain of command might work for some departments. Access to new technology and information processing all the way down to the line officer may mean that the police management of the 1990s may have to look at new ways of making decisions and become more flexible in the granting of authority to first-line supervisors and line officers.

TANNENBAUM AND SCHMIDT'S LEADERSHIP PATTERNS

The question that Tannenbaum and Schmidt attempt to answer is: How should the manager lead his or her organization? As the authors point out (1975: 118): "The concept of leadership the article defines is reflected in a continuum of leadership behavior....Rather than offering a choice between two styles of leadership, democratic or authoritarian, it sanctions a range of behavior."This is an excellent approach for police managers to adopt since the different functions of the police agency demand different management styles. Emergency situations may demand a hierarchical, authoritarian response, whereas, the planning that goes into this response and the day-to-day workings of the department may demand a more democratic, participatory response.

In the original article (1958) the **continuum of management** decision-making style ran from "boss centered" to "subordinate centered." Recognizing the realities of the influence of labor unions and other pressure groups on management decisions, the authors changed this terminology to a continuum from manager power and influence to nonmanager power and influence. This more neutral terminology also served to encompass operational management, pressure groups, and such individuals as the line officer in the police department. The authors also allowed for a more realistic societal and organizational environment given modern demands on police managers.

This continuum from manager-oriented authority to group-centered authority has been graphically illustrated by Tannenbaum and Schmidt. (1975: 119). Table 5–3 (next page) has been adapted with minor modifications for the sake of clarity and applicability to police executive needs.

The authors stress the interdependency of the relationship between management and various groups effecting management decisions. For example (1975: 118), "the interplay between the manager's confidence in his subordinates and their readiness to assure responsibility and the level of group effectiveness."The police executive, no matter how autocratic, is not operating in a vacuum. His decisions influence others and they influence him.

Let us look at the various approaches that have been presented and see how they can operate on a practical level for police management. Since the 1920s business and public administration have exhibited a preference for the group-centered management style. Considering the various management styles that we have examined so far, however, we must remember that the modern police agency demands a mix of approaches because of the complex demands made upon management.

TABLE 5-3
TANNENBAUM AND SCHMIDT'S MANAGEMENT AUTHORITY CONTINUUM

MANAGEMENT-CENTERED POWER AND INFLUENCE						GROUP-CENTERED POWER AND INFLUENCE
TELLS	SELLS	TESTS		CONSULTS	JOINS	
Manager must be able to make decisions that group will accept	Manager must "sell" his decision before gaining acceptance	Manager presents decisions but must respond to questions from group	Manager presents tentative decisions subject to change after group inputs	Manager presents problem, gets inputs from groups and then decides	Manager defines limits within which the group makes decision	Manager and group jointly make decision within limits defined by organization- al constraints

Source: Reprinted by permission of the *Harvard Business Review.* An exhibit from "How to Choose a Leadership Pattern" by Robert Tannenbaum and Warren Schmidt (May/June 1973). Copyright ©1973 by the President and Fellows of Harvard College; all rights reserved.

There is a murder. The investigating officer arrives on the scene. The public, press, officials from other agencies, lab technicians, and others are on the scene. One person has to be in charge simply to protect the crime scene so that evidence docs not get destroyed. This situation demands a management-centered, hierarchical, authoritarian style.

The chief has to implement a new grievance procedure that has been demanded by the union contract. He consults with his management team and various operational officers concerning their feelings. Finally, he sits down with the Police Benevolent Association representatives and the members of his management team who are concerned with internal discipline and morale. They work out the details and decide to give the implementation procedures a three-month testing period and revise the program according to results and conditions. This is a group-centered management style; there has been time for group consultation and morale could be damaged without it.

BLAKE AND MOUTON'S MANAGERIAL GRID

Another approach that focuses on management style relates it to the two orientations of (1) a concern for people by management and (2) a major concern for production. In this case Blake and Mouton are concerned with large-scale organization development and executive development in relation to five theories of managerial behavior (Blake and others, 1975: 162). See Figure 5-3.

This is a program based on behavioral science concepts primarily drawn from the organizational development approach to management. The author's objective, through various training programs, is to bring the organization around

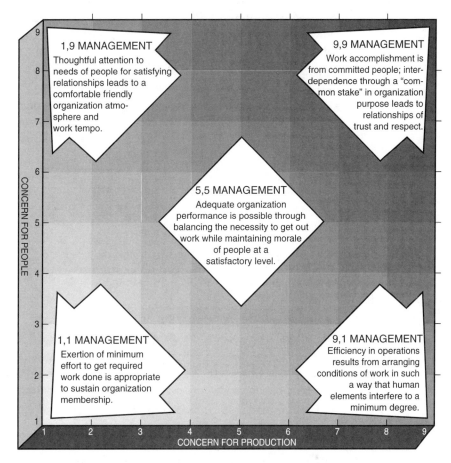

Figure 5-3

Blake and Mouton's Managerial Grid.

(Source: Reprinted by permission of the Harvard Business Review. An exhibit from "Breakthrough in Organization Development," by Robert R. Blake, Jane S. Mouton, Louis B. Barnes and Larry E. Greiner (Novermber/December 1964). Copyright ©1964 by the President and Fellows of Harvard College; all rights reserved.)

to the 9,9 part of the grid with a maximum concern for both people and production using a team concept. Some of the training approaches include (Blake and others, 1975: 163–64):

1. *Laboratory-seminar training.* 12 to 48 individuals are assigned to be members of problem-solving teams with face-to-face feedback. The focus is on managerial styles rather than personal behavior characteristics.

2. *Team development.* The focus is on the operating practices of the agency once the ground rules and relationships have been established.

3. *Intergroup development.* Group-to-group working relationships within the organ-ization are established on an operational level.

4. *Organizational goal setting.* The groups work on specific problems (e.g., union-management relations, promotional policies). "The goals prove to be 'practical' when managers who must implement them also establish responsibilities for implementation."

Finally, using a case method similar to the Harvard Business School approach, specific problems are worked out by the management-organizational development teams and the approach is stabilized as a permanent working relationship for the organization. The authors, working with Barnes and Greiner, implemented their approach in one industry and came to these conclusions concerning the type of organization that can successfully implement their approach (Blake and others, 1975: 181):

> Demanding but tolerant headquarters
>
> An enthusiastic and involved top manager and senior management group
>
> Educational strategy that effectively and continuously builds team problem solving and mutual support into work-related issues
>
> An organization whose work requires some interdependent effort and common values

Most police agencies have the potential to implement this approach for a good deal of the organizational procedure in the department. However, many have a long way to go to meet the conditions necessary to implement this organizational development strategy. Because this strategy can give members of the management team an insight into their individual working philosophies and how these philosophies affect their superiors, peers, and subordinates, this approach to managerial leadership will operate best where there is no pressure to make immediate decisions.

▷ CONCLUSION

The art and style of proactive leadership is based on talent, experience, and training and formal education. Proactive leaders are goals oriented and have the ability to communicate their vision and the agency mission to all members of the department and to the community. They have had a variety of learning and leadership experiences on their way to the top of the organization hierarchy. They do not look upon critical situations as problems but rather as leadership opportunities.

The greatest dilemma facing police managers once they have achieved higher-ranking positions is in the area of continuing training and education. The focus of police training courses today remains directed to line and supervisory personnel on operational skills and not towards executive development. Many large departments and state training agencies are just beginning to fill this void with management courses for chiefs and their deputies and higher education degrees in criminal justice management as a formal or informal norm for promotion. To this day, we begin our own management seminars with the question, "What is the latest book or article you have read regarding police management?" Unfortunately, the question draws much nervous laughter which forces us to conclude that greater attention must be directed to management training.

The chapter also introduced the leading organizational theories related to proactive police leadership. These range from the traditional concepts found in every management course (Maslow's need hierarchy, Theory X and Y) to newer concepts developed in the late 1980's (Theory Z, TQM, Reengineering). Each concept has an application to a wide variety of department and management problems in police organizations. Right now TQM is a popular topic at police conferences and seminars and it forms the basis for service delivery for departments that have adapted to community and problem-oriented policing. As with any concept, however, it is not a quick fix for departments with serious problems. It assumes that the organization already has a solid management and operations foundation. The best example we use at seminars is telling police managers not to adopt TQM if they don't have an existing departmental manual of rules or if they are not prepared to use TQM principles for the next ten years.

QUESTIONS FOR REVIEW

1. Make a chart comparing styles of leadership along a continuum from totally democratic leadership to totally authoritarian leadership.

2. Create your own theory of leadership and defend this theory in terms of maximizing employee morale.

3. Defend or attack Herzberg's eternal profile as it applies to a local police agency.

4. Is Maslow's need hierarchy relevant to police work? Why or why not?

5. Explain why McGregor's Theory X and Theory Y is so popular among textbook writers concerned with police leadership. Would this theory be

useful in a local police department? Why or why not? Why would it make sense or not in terms of a police department of 10 professionals or less?

6. Analyze and apply the managerial grid to a large metropolitan police department that has a corruption problem.

7. Review the theories concerning leadership and choose the one that you consider the best. Defend your choice as it would apply to a medium-sized police department that has both team policing units and traditional patrol units.

KEY TERMS

14 points
benchmarking
charismatic authority
conceptual skill
continuum of management
eternal triangle
hierarchy of needs
high touch
human skill
hygiene factors
IACP

KITA
leadership
legal authority
management skills
managerial grid
motivators
reengineering
technical skill
Theories X, Y, and Z
TQM

BIBLIOGRAPHY

BLAKE, ROBERT R., and JANE S. MOUTON, "Grid Organization Development," in *Classics of Public Administration*, pp. 268–75. Oak Park, Ill.: Moore, 1978.

_____, JANE S. MOUTON, LOUIS B. BARNES, and LARRY E. GREINER, "Breakthrough in Organization Development" *Harvard Business Review* (November/December, 1964); reprinted in *Business Classics: Fifteen Key Concepts for Managerial Success*, pp. 159–81. Cambridge, Mass.: Harvard University Press, 1975.

BUTTERFIELD, RONALD W., "Deming's 14 Points Applied to Service," *Training*, 28, no. 3 (March 1991), pp. 50–59.

DRUCKER, PETER F., *Innovation and Entrepreneurship*. New York: Harper & Row, 1986.

GARNER, RONNIE, "Leadership in the Nineties," in *FBI Law Enforcement Bulletin*, 62, no. 12 (December, 1993), p. 4.

HALBERSTAM, DAVID, *The Reckoning*. New York: William Morrow, 1986.

HALL, RICHARD H., *Organizations: Structures, Processes and Outcomes*. Upper Saddle River, N.J.: Prentice Hall, 1996.

HAMMER, MICHAEL, *Beyond Reengineering*. New York: Harper Business, 1996.

HAMMER, MICHAEL, and JAMES CHAMPY, *Reengineering the Corporation*. New York: Harper Business, 1993.

HERZBERG, FREDERICK, "One More Time: How Do You Motivate Employees" in *Business Classics: Fifteen Key Concepts for Managerial Success*, pp. 13-22. Cambridge, Mass.: Harvard University Press, 1975.

HOLPP, LAWRENCE, "Making Choices: Self-Directed Teams or Total Quality Management?" *Training*, 29, no. 5 (May 1992), pp. 69-76.

KATZ, DANIEL, and ROBERT L. KAHN, *The Social Psychology of Organizations*. New York: Wiley, 1966.

KATZ, ROBERT L., "Skills of an Effective Administrator," in *Business Classics: Fifteen Key Concepts for Managerial Success*, pp. 23-35. Cambridge, Mass.: Harvard University Press, 1975.

LIKERT, RENSIS, *New Patterns of Management*. New York: McGraw-Hill, 1961.

_____. *The Human Organization*. New York: McGraw-Hill, 1967.

_____. "Profile of Organizational Characteristics," in John P. Robinson, Robert Athanasiou, and Kendra B. Head, eds., *Measures of Occupational Attitudes and Occupational Characteristics*, pp. 276-80. Ann Arbor: Institute for Social Research, University of Michigan, 1969.

MCGREGOR, DOUGLAS MURRAY, "The Human Side of Enterprise," in *Classics of Public Administration*, pp. 187-93. Oak Park, Ill.: Moore, 1978.

NAISBITT, JOHN, and PATRICIA ABURDENE, *Re-inventing the Corporation*. New York: Warner Books, 1985.

NATIONAL ADVISORY COMMISSION ON CRIMINAL JUSTICE STANDARDS AND GOALS, *Police Chief Executive*. Washington, D.C.: U.S. Government Printing Office, 1976.

NATIONAL COMMISSION ON LAW OBSERVANCE AND ENFORCEMENT, George P. Wickersham, Chairman, *Wickersham Report 14*, Police. Montclair, N.J.: Patterson Smith, 1931, reprinted 1968.

OUCHI, WILLIAM G., *Theory Z*. New York: Avon Books, 1981.

PORTER, LYMAN W., *Job Attitudes in Management: Perceived Satisfaction and Importance of Needs*. Berkeley: Institute of Industrial Relations, University of California, 1964.

_____. "Need Fulfillment Questionnaire for Management," in John P. Robinson, Robert Athanasiou, and Kendra B. Head, eds., *Measures of Occupational Attitudes and Occupational Characteristics*, pp. 148-50. Ann Arbor: Institute for Social Research, University of Michigan, 1969.

PRESIDENT'S COMMISSION ON LAW ENFORCEMENT AND THE ADMINISTRATION OF JUSTICE, *The Police.* Washington, D.C.: U.S. Government Printing Office, 1967.

TANNENBAUM, R., and W. H. SCHMIDT, "How to Choose a Leadership Pattern," in *Business Classics: Fifteen Key Concepts for Managerial Success*, pp. 115–24. Cambridge, Mass.: Harvard University Press, 1975.

WEBER, MAX, "Power and Bureaucracy," in Kenneth Thompson and Jeremy Tunstall, eds., *Sociological Perspectives*. Middlesex, England: Penguin, 1961.

XEROX, "The Xerox Quest for Quality." Rochester, N.Y., 1991.

Police Information Management

 PROACTIVE POLICE MANAGEMENT CONTROL OF TECHNOLOGY

Welcome to the 21st century. Computers and advanced technology have revolutionized police management. However, the same tasks that confronted the 19th century police chief confronts the 21st century police manager.

This chapter begins with a review on communications theory. Communication with police administrators, middle management, and line officers must be clear and effective. Police administrators and officers also need to communicate effectively to the various police publics: citizens, pressure groups, media groups, and legislators. Records need to be stored, made accessible, and secured. This is also a communications and investigation function to include local, regional, national, and international record-keeping. Protocols need to be established concerning record access, categories that determine various types of information, and security.

The police manager has to assume leadership and be in charge. Police managers cannot allow the technology to drive policy decisions.

When police went from walking a beat to patrolling in cars, the technology drove policy. Police rode around in their patrol cars and were insulated from the public. It took a proactive use of community policing to move beyond the isolated officer in the patrol car. The 911 universal emergency phone number has once again resulted in technology controlling management policy. The enormous growth of service calls from 911 created a reaction-driven department overwhelmed by these service calls, from critical emergency calls through trivial calls. The proactive police manager institutes a split force, prioritizes the responses to the calls and takes control of this unique communication system (see Chapter 8 on patrol).

As all institutions become more information-driven, linking information access to policy making through computers becomes vital. This information has to be managed through proactive planning, packaging, and accessing. Computer mapping makes good use of crime data and 911 information, to pinpoint hot spots and help decide different levels of service in different neighborhoods at specific times during a day. Linking information from radio, 911, and computer communication to policy decisions concerning deployment and even personnel decisions is a smart use of information.

Laptop computers only became useful when there is a management system in place to take advantage of them. Secure information channels and organized reporting systems have to be in place before any computer is turned on. This means that the computer is only as good as the information put into the system and the intelligent use of the computer information system by human beings. If you put bad information into your computer system, a bad decision will come out of that system. The bottom line is that police managers need to make sure they are in charge of the system. If that is accomplished, the system becomes a valuable tool for every police manager, from a village police chief to the police commissioner of a major city.

 ## COMMUNICATIONS DEFINED

According to Richard A. McDonnel in his chapter on information management for *Local Government Police Management* (1977: 406), "Communication is essentially a social affair involving the sharing of information." He goes on to add: "The ultimate conclusion was that the most valuable tool that could be made available to the police officer, on whatever specific assignment, was *information*." This broad-based approach to communication encompasses the essentially two-way street of basic human interaction as well as the more narrow approach of technological communication. The emphasis is always on the sharing of information between two communicators. Communication should never be one way. The more sharing that is involved, the clearer the message.

In most police departments, communication has traditionally included such factors as dispatching, radio communication, and records. These essentials of good policing must be part of any well-ordered management plan for communication. However, police information management entails more than these technological aspects. Information management also includes, as McDonnel emphasized, communication as a social affair, involving the sharing of information between two or more human beings. The emphasis for proactive management is on the sharing aspect of communication.

In one-way communication, the chief gives orders to his or her subordinates. The subordinates then give orders to the line officers, and some action is expected to take place. Conversely, the social sharing of information is essentially a two-way process. When we talk to anyone, we expect **feedback**. This feedback could be as varied as a nod, a stance, an answer to a question, an agreement to orders, or recommendations to modify orders. The recognition and feedback that we continually receive keeps the communication process clear. Feedback enables the sender to know that the message was sent, received, and understood in some manner by the receiver.

Thomas C. Neil has summarized the typical model of communications that is in most general use (1980: 17):

> A typical model...contains the following parts: the *sender* of the original message; the *receiver* of this message; *encoding*, which is the translation of personal meaning into symbols; *decoding*, which is the reverse of encoding; and *channel*, which is the means by which stimuli are sent and received [author's emphasis].

The sender could be a police chief and the receiver could be a line officer. The encoding is normally in the form of an order in writing such as a standard operating procedure (SOP). Decoding takes place when the line officer reads the order and attempts to place it in behavioral terms. The channel in this procedure is the written order that is transmitted through a standard communication process.

The chief might, for example, be worried about the line officers wasting time talking to each other on duty. Let us also assume that the chief happens to be authoritarian. The following is a paraphrase of an actual order in an actual department.

Standard Operating Procedure, Order 538.71

> No sworn officer shall converse with another sworn officer while on duty for more than two minutes, unless the conversation shall consist of information concerning official duties.

The chief has encoded his concern into an order. The receiver, the line officer, decodes the message: "I'd better watch the time I spend socializing and having coffee with the other officers. I might have to justify that time in terms of some departmental business. That two-minute limit really doesn't make much sense given the nature of our patrol duties. So I'll ignore the two-minute part of the message, but I'll watch the time I spend socializing." The line officer also took a look at the **medium** of the message: an official order. The officer will take this message more seriously than if he had heard a rumor that the chief was worried about officers socializing too much.

The channel has also been called the "medium by which the message is sent." It can be the difference between a rumor and a written memorandum. Teletype messages are expected to be short, fact-filled pieces of information. The same incident described in a teletype message would have different details and content when provided by a newspaper story. An officer telling a fellow officer at a social affair concerning the same incident might fill out the story with details and colorful words that would never appear in an official report. The incident may be the same, but the messages are decidedly different. Media used to convey the messages—teletype, official report, newspaper story, casual conversation at a social affair—change the messages.

Although we do not agree with McDonnel that the medium is the message, since there is content to every message, we do agree that every police manager has to be aware of how different communication media can affect the interpretation of the content of messages. Thus police managers have to use both the formal and informal communication systems to send different kinds of messages. By using both media effectively, chiefs will find that they can communicate effectively and receive both informal and formal feedback to their messages. In the two-minute talking-limit example, it is hoped that this chief will receive feedback through informal channels that the memorandum is unrealistic. Then, if the chief has developed any good communication skills, he will modify the message to meet the needs of the line officer.

 ## ENCODING/DECODING: THE MEANING OF MEANING

Whenever we use language, we are taking an incident and encoding it into a prestructured formula. General semantics indicates that the symbol is not the thing and the map is not the terrain. **Symbols**, which include all words, stand for something else. When we pull down a map of the ocean, we do not get wet, because the map is a symbol for the wet ocean—the map is not the ocean itself. Therefore, the map, and words, are something less than an immediate apprehension of the ocean. In short, a map of the ocean is less than the experience we would have standing on a sandy or rocky beach, listening to ocean sounds, smelling the ocean smells, and gazing at the endless horizon. What does this mean when we try to communicate?

We all talk in **subscripts**. Subscript one might be what the sender means by a word. The various receivers might be receiving subscripts two and three, and so on. Let us try an illustration.

Officer Smith tells Officers Jones and Brown that he arrested a juvenile in a tough section of town on his duty shift, late at night. Officer Smith is thinking of a blond-haired, middle-class boy who had run away from home and found himself in a tough neighborhood. Smith's juvenile is JUVENILE$_1$. Officer Jones, who knows that neighborhood, might be thinking of a young tough who smokes marijuana, has black hair, and runs with a gang. Jones' juvenile is JUVENILE$_2$. Officer Brown might be thinking of a young girl he had picked up recently in that neighborhood for prostitution. She is a crack user. Brown's juvenile is JUVENILE$_3$. Unless there is some kind of feedback to Smith's message and a clarification from

Officer Smith, the symbol *JUVENILE* might lead to some real problems in this communication.

Very simple words, for example, *desk*, *car*, *juvenile*, can refer to a number of different actual things or types. Language is actually a form of shorthand. It is hard for every communicator and receiver to have experienced everything that they may want to discuss. The shorthand of language is used where general descriptions of the symbols are accepted until specifics are added. However, in the case of symbols, people normally add their own subscript, thereby shaping the reality of the spoken word into a picture that may or may not be meant by various communicators. It is necessary to add subscripts to the word symbol since the word symbol can never encompass all the empirical referents. The symbol is often used to describe a particular sensory experience, for example, that middle-class juvenile boy with blond hair that I picked up while on duty last night.

A perfect process would occur when the encoder and decoder know exactly what each symbol means and what the relationship of each symbol is to every other symbol. This happens in simple mechanical means of encoding the decoding such as Morse Code. You have a symbol chart and you simply relate dot-dash to the symbol chart and come out with letters. However, encoding and decoding language and orders entails a more complex process prone to error. Continual feedback to the encoder, explaining what the symbols means to the decoder, keeps messages clear.

▶ FEEDBACK

Two-way communication is always clearer than one-way communication. One-way, hierarchical communication lacks the essential feedback that tells the encoder that his or her message has been decoded in the manner he or she desired. With no feedback mechanism, the encoder/sender will not know if the decoder/receiver will receive the message in terms of (1) JUVENILE subscript one or (2) JUVENILE subscript two or (3) JUVENILE subscript three, four, and so on.

To have consistency in message communication, the decoder must have the same basic understanding of the encoding language that the transmitter has. The receiver must decode the message and fulfill the intentions of the person doing the transmitting. That is one reason why law enforcement officers often use codes and other shorthand devices. They know that the receiver, that is, another police officer, will understand the message since the decoding content of the message has already been agreed upon. Thus when an officer hears the code for an officer in trouble, he or she knows that this message (1) demands immediate action and (2) has top priority.

Feedback is what makes management aware of problems in the communication process. Orders sent down the line may get lost if there is no feedback. For example, there could be a fairly general order issued concerning checking certain businesses at night. Sergeants would then detail this duty to specific officers in the area during the times specified. However, the police administrator may have no idea that action is taking place unless there is feedback. The administrator needs to know at a minimum (1) if the message was clear and specific enough, (2) what kind of action took place as a result of the message (order), and (3) what modifications should be made in the message as a result of the actions taken or not taken?

WHO COMMUNICATES TO WHOM AND HOW

When we consider communication in context, we are looking at a situation. Is the situation an emergency, or is it routine? What are the ranks of the message sender and the message receiver? Will citizens be receiving the message? Who communicates with whom and how are the elements to be considered in communication. Let us look at some examples.

A judge tells a citizen that he is convicted of a crime and will be sent to prison. The context is the court setting. The result is a change of status of the individual from civilian to prisoner. The context is charged with authority, and there is a powerful difference in the status of the judge and the citizen who is about to be sentenced.

It is of vital importance that top police management understand the effects of their communication within the context of authority relations. We also have to consider what audience hears the message (for example, civilians or uniformed officers). The chief can take an officer aside and reprimand him or her for wearing a sloppy uniform. Or the chief can communicate this at lineup in front of fellow officers. Or the chief can give the officer the same message while the officer is engaged in an investigation in the presence of news reporters. It is the same message but different audiences. It also makes a difference whether it is the chief of the department or some fellow officer making the same statements. In this case, it is the same statement, different message. From these examples, we can understand that managers who wish to communicate clearly have to understand

1. The authority context of any message, giving the relative status of the sender and receiver of messages.
2. The audience receiving the message.
3. The effect of the message on both the person receiving the message and the audience that may be also hearing the message.

The style of delivering messages deserves consideration, too. Messages from police commanders and other management personnel in law enforcement tend to be brusque, unfeeling and in the form of orders. In a tense street confrontation with immediate potential violence, for example, this might be the correct approach. However, in many situations, this brusque approach will only tend to alienate line officers and citizens.

A commander could tell a line officer, "You are ordered to change your vacation time because the department needs more personnel at that time." Or the commander might say, "I know that you planned this vacation time and that it is important to your family. However, we have a special event and we really need the extra coverage. I would really appreciate it if you would change your vacation time or maybe you could trade with another officer who has that time off. Try to work something out. You know if we can't work something out, I'm simply going to have to draft an order. I would rather not do that. Could you see me in a couple of days concerning this matter. I really appreciate your help here. Thanks." What did we accomplish with the second version of the message? The commander told the officer that he knew and felt sorry about inconveniencing the officer's family. He also told the officer that no matter what, the department was going to need the extra officers. He also gave the officer some flexibility in fulfilling the departmental need. Yes, it would have been easier to have simply written the order. However, the second message would make for a department with much higher morale than a department that simply writes orders.

In the second message, the police commander was also telling the officer to use his support **network**. In every police department, over the years, everybody owes somebody for something. It could be simply a cup of coffee after a bad moment. It could be some help with a family affair or backup in a difficult situation. That is the nature of the police business: a supportive network of fellow officers is built up over the years.

What is important for an officer to learn—from the first day on the job—is that one of the officer's strongest psychological and emotional support resources is the existing network of fellow police officers. This means that when messages go out, even though they are hierarchical in form, they are actually going to a network. The network exchanges messages continually with everyone. Given all the messages a police officer receives and sends from his fellow officers in one 24-hour day, each officer would be surrounded by so many lines that it would be hard to see the officer in the midst of this concentration of messages. This networking approach to communications is often called **all-channel** communication. All-channel communication is a participatory management style with communication channels open between all parties.

Most departments, although deeply imbedded in the police network style of communication, have an official departmental style of formal communication called *chain* communication. Chain communication is the **chain-of-command** style where person 1 does not communicate with person 4 except through persons 2 and 3. This means if a line officer wants a message to reach the chief, he or she has to give that message to the sergeant, who gives it to the lieutenant, who gives it to the captain, who gives it to the chief or even the deputy chief. It also means that if the chief wants to communicate with that line officer, he has to go through the chain of command. The communication process is most rigid going from the bottom to the top. A top officer may bypass part of the chain of command.

However, while this formal process is going on, at least two interesting phenomena are occurring. First, the networking effect takes over, and all kinds of people in the uniformed department have either part of the message or various versions of the message. The informal communication network in policing is very strong.

Second are the friendships that have been formed that skip a rank. For example, sergeants do not normally become great friends with lieutenants; captains and sergeants are more likely to become friends as are lieutenants and line officers. This means that the message may, in fact, informally skip some of the chain of command while formally going up or down the chain of command. Except for routine communications that are noncontroversial, the chain of command is a cumbersome communication process. The chain of command becomes especially costly in two important areas: distortion of messages and the time it takes a message to reach the bottom and have the feedback reach the top.

Another style is **"Y" communication**, in which two superiors communicate to the same subordinate. The subsequent communications may go from subordinate to subordinate. An example of this is one secretary with two bosses. Pity the poor secretary when she receives priorities or contradicting messages from each boss. If this style is to work at all, there must be a key communicator at the junction of the "Y." Then two bosses give messages to the key communicator who sorts out priorities and eliminates contradictions and sends the messages to the subordinates. In general, "Y" communication systems fail because of the built-in conflicts.

 ## OBSTACLES TO COMMUNICATION

People fail to communicate with each other even when they truly want to reach out and communicate. A major problem is that we communicate through symbols. As mentioned earlier, what one officer means by *juvenile* may incorporate violent actions whereas another officer may consider a *smart kid* who talks back to be a juvenile delinquent. Police officers rely upon penal law definitions in part for the official purposes of arresting offenders.

Another problem is **inference**, as when we attach meanings to a message that the message giver never intended to be part of the communication. For example, Officer Brown says, "We need to roust that kid." Officer Smith says, "Yeah, I know. I'll go over to his house tonight, stand him up against the wall, threaten to arrest him, and see if he will agree to let me take a look at his room." Officer Brown says, "No, I didn't mean for you to do that. I think we could just stop by and question him concerning the crime. He has helped us in the past, and there is no reason why he wouldn't help us again." The key is "I didn't mean for you to do that." Officer Smith created a message by inference. He thought that the original message included content that was not actually in the message—by inference.

Officers make **assumptions** about messages that become part of the message but were not meant to be part of the message originally. Assumptions exist when you think that there are specific grounds for the content of a message and these grounds may or may not exist. Assumptions may be warranted or unwarranted. For example, Officer Brown may feel that a juvenile who has a record of violent crime and with whom he has dealt personally in violent situations may, in fact, be responsible for a violent crime. Now, if there is evidence that matches the youth's profile, Officer Brown may be correct. He has a warranted assumption concerning the potentiality of that particular youth's behavior. His assumption is based on reasonable evidence.

On the other hand, Officer Brown may have known that another youth comes from a bad family. He may have arrested that particular youth's brother for burglary and known that the youth's sister was a drug addict. Therefore, when there is a burglary in the vicinity and that youth is seen around the burglarized premises, Officer Brown may assume that the youth from the bad family is a likely suspect. Unknown to Officer Brown, this particular youth is an honor student at school and has just been awarded an athletic scholarship to a good college. Officer Brown's assumption is unwarranted because it is not based on good evidence. In fact, by saying that all members of the family are most likely bad, he has unfairly labeled every child in that family.

Bypassing, another obstacle to communication, occurs when two people talk to each other and miss each other with their meanings; that is, the same words can mean different things to different people. Bypassing is a common occurrence in the ordinary life of a line officer. For example, a sergeant asks a line officer to finish up a sick officer's reports. The line officer then stays overtime to finish the reports. The next day, the sergeant tells the line officer that he meant for him to finish the reports during normal duty hours. The line officer says, "I thought you meant, immediately!" Another obstacle to communication, **overgeneralization**, is basically a variation using unwarranted assumptions. A common example is when a police officer refers to someone as "a good guy." The general meaning of a "good guy" is someone who is helpful and will assist anyone recommended by the officer simply by dropping a name; for example, "Hello, Dr. Forest. This is Sgt. Francis over at Riverview Station. I spoke to Detective Williams and she said you're someone who could give me an assist on a case I'm working on."

The "good guy" is simply a generalization that is used for network referencing and assists in daily communication within and between complex organizations. However, in situations involving misconduct or corruption, a "good guy" is someone who may assist in a coverup or turn the other way "to see nothing." A "good guy" can also be one to bend the rules; for example, "Lou, be a good guy and don't report that dent I put in the fender of car 203 last night."

Proactive police managers need to have a basic awareness of these problems and prepare strategies that provide for better communications before miscommunications occur.

⏵ THE JOHARI WINDOW

This is a basic exercise in communication flow that monitors how information is passed from the police manager to others and back again according to interpersonal style. It is a basic two-by-two table based upon (1) information known and not known to yourself about yourself and (2) information known and not known to others about you (see Figure 6–1).

When you and others share information, this is called region I, the *arena*. Mutually held information becomes the most valuable approach to communication. If others know information and you do not know the information, you may suffer a *blind spot*, region II. It is a personal handicap for the manager since he or she cannot understand the behavior of others if he or she lacks essential information concerning why they behave the way they do. This was involved in the example of Officer Brown thinking that a youth from a bad family was a likely crime suspect. Brown lacked information that the youth was an honor student with a good career ahead of him. This was Officer Brown's Johari window blind spot.

When you have information that is unknown to others, it is called region III, the *façade*. The façade is a protective front where information is withheld from others to protect the self. The question is how much defensiveness should be tolerated before the withholding of information interferes with good management communication.

When information is unknown by self and others, it is considered an area of potential creativity, region IV, *unknown*. As management communication becomes more effective, the unknown becomes known and region IV diminishes in size.

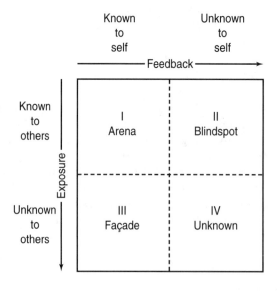

Figure 6-1
Johari Window.

The two basic processes for the creation of information are exposure of self in terms of giving information, including information about emotions and attitudes, and the feedback process, where others expose themselves and give information to self. The model calls for a climate of mutual exposure to achieve maximum communication and thus calls for an open, democratic management model. This would normally be in direct contradiction to the strict hierarchical chain of communication model.

The model calls for four types of communication in relation to the two processes of exposure and feedback. Type A is an impersonal style characterized by minimal exposure and feedback: the traditional police chief-dominated department. Type B minimizes exposure of self but attempts to maximize feedback. Management distrusts others but wishes emotional and general information from others. This normally results in a basic management model based on mutual distrust, often reverting back to type A.

Type C is an overuse of exposure to self and a minimal use of feedback from others, a giant ego ride. This is the "cult of personality" police chief with idiosyncratic policies. You generally know what the chief is thinking and the chief doesn't care what you think or feel. This style triggers feelings of hostility and resentment from the general officer population, especially the line officer population. The preferred style according to this model of communication is type D, open and frank communication; that is, a mutuality of maximum exposure and feedback. It is hoped that over time a context of trust and creativity will be created in the police department. Given the various demands of police departments, especially for emergency procedures, this is difficult to achieve. Type D communication will most often be found in a police department dedicated to a democratic management style. It is often tied in with some variation of team and community policing styles.

The basic exercise is for individuals to answer a number of questions concerning their exposure/feedback styles and then, using standard scores for the model, see where they stand in terms of the four regions. You then examine various strategies that would bring the maximum number of members of the police management team into the open communication model designated as the arena. According to the model, the larger the size of the arena in relation to the other three regions, the more effective will be the management communication model used by the police organization. The secret seems to be to bring employees, colleagues, and supervisors into a feedback/exposure position, which will maximize their communication with each other in the arena.

This type of model can be useful—up to a point. Everyone in the department is expected to spend some time communicating his or her emotions to everyone else in the department to gain maximum feedback, but there probably is not enough time to fulfill this requirement completely. Also, normal psychological health demands a certain amount of private space for individuals. Exposure and feedback in terms of producing some basic honesty in human relations can be useful for getting the job done, but spending too much time discussing emotional relationships can become counterproductive. After all, the department still has to arrest criminals and deal with myriad social problems.

As with other theoretical models drawn from the social sciences, business, and public administration, the Johari window communication model also needs to be tempered by the reality of managing real police departments with real problems. For too long, police organizations have been closed and rigid in their authoritarian management style. Conversely, however, reliance on feelings and democratic ideals will not work for police organizations either. The proactive approach is a tempered approach: consultative with enough exposure and feedback to do the job with sensitivity and efficiency. It is a forward-looking communication model where feedback becomes part of the planning process, and the planning process is a consultative process for all members of the police agency. This is an effective use of the Johari window as another analytical tool used to bring about consultative, effective communication.

 ## OPERATIONAL COMMUNICATIONS

This type of communication normally takes the form of writing. Written documents have one advantage in that they can be referred to with ease. They are also normally more precise than informal and verbal communication. They provide a certain consistency of standards along with rules and norms for the police organization.

Certain objectives need to be established and met if the organizational goals of the police agency are to be accomplished. These goals are achieved through the six objectives of written communication:

1. To make plans operational.
2. To carry on day-to-day operations.
3. To relay and interpret policies.
4. To provide details for activity completion.
5. To complete assignments satisfactorily.
6. To provide for evaluation and feedback.

TYPES OF ORDERS

Specific assignments are needed to give managers and line officers direction concerning how to carry out the vital activities of the police agency. Traditionally, these written activities have taken the following forms:

SOP	Standard operating procedure
TOP	Temporary operating procedure
GO	General orders
SO	Special orders
MEMO	Memorandums

There are the written **directives** necessary for the daily operations of any responsible police agency that may be gathered into a volume called the **duty manual**. These directives are expected to operate consistently over time. While duty manuals should be kept up to date, they generally change in only minor ways from year to year and from police administration to police administration.

SOPs: Standard Operating Procedures

These are the procedures that will affect the total department on an ongoing basis over time. They have a specific starting date but no ending date. They are changed by the creation of a new SOP that says the old SOP is no longer in effect. They are numbered and dated for filing purposes.

Basically all new SOPs should be incorporated into an annually revised duty manual. This way, all the officers in the department will have access to an organized set of rules. In the event that this does not occur, the duty manual becomes dated and new officers have to resort to file cabinets of SOPs to learn the basic rules of the department. Even experienced officers can become confused when the duty manual consists of hundreds of files.

SOPs include what is and is not acceptable communication under a wide variety of circumstances and authority relationships as they are met in the normal course of police business. The duty manual is simply an organized way of having all of the SOPs in one place.

TOPs: Temporary Operating Procedures

These have all the characteristics of SOPs with one exception: they have a termination date. That means that on the termination date, the TOP is no longer in effect. Of course, they are dated and numbered. Events that are handled by TOPs would be one-time events such as sporting events, parades, and visits from dignitaries.

GOs: General Orders

Like SOPs, these are numbered and dated and go to all personnel. The GO is created for informational purposes whereas the SOP and the TOP are operational orders. Legal changes such as those created by search and seizure cases would be GOs. New procedures for handling drunken persons according to new state directives would go out as GOs. Relations with mental health or probation agencies might go to all personnel in the form of GOs.

SOs: Special Orders

These are numbered and dated and refer only to personnel matters. They are very specific and refer to such items as transfers, job assignments, promotions, and disciplinary actions.

MEMOs: Memorandums

MEMOs are written to communicate information or orders of short duration. These are dated but not numbered. They are generally for very limited distribution. MEMOs are used when a verbal order is adequate but putting the order in writing will eliminate all possible misunderstandings. (They might apply in such mundane matters as having a patrol car fixed by the police mechanic.) MEMOs are especially useful in maintaining continuity of information to a staff that is operating on various shifts over a 24-hour period and seven-day week.

Basically these directives are of vital importance for the maintenance of communication in a department. All should be written with care. There should also be a time period when these various types of communications are either destroyed—all copies—or codified in some manner. Operational orders that last over time should be incorporated in the duty manual. Personnel matters become parts of permanent personnel files when they are of enough significance to affect an officer's performance appraisal. Occasionally, the department may wish to resort to microfilm or microfiche for the storage of some of these materials. However, at the end of a specified point, most of this paperwork should be destroyed. This will normally entail a change in some state laws concerning document retention.

THE EFFECTIVELY ORGANIZED DIRECTIVE

Reports can be effective or they can be jumbled and vague. Reports should be both precise and concise. Police departments tend to drown in a sea of ill-conceived, badly worded phrases that lead from nowhere to nowhere. If the department is to be effective, these general rules for writing directives should be followed:

1. The contents of the directive must be achievable and reasonable. To carry out the order, the recipient must have the means and the ability to act effectively.

2. The instructions concerning the directive should be sufficiently detailed to ensure the completion of the task. An example might be a directive concerning the disassembly of weapons. A directive that simply says that the officer must be able to assemble and disassemble his or her weapon does not contain enough information. Detailed information is needed concerning the variety of weapons at an officer's disposal. The directive might also include specific training procedures for officers needing additional information and skills to disassemble specific weapons.

3. Directives should use normal English language that would be understandable at the tenth-grade reading level. Although all police officers are high school graduates, they may not be able to read at a twelfth-

grade level. Many college texts at the freshman level are being written with a tenth-grade vocabulary. It is vital that technical terms be clarified in simple English.

4. Orders that need explanation should be given some justification concerning why the order has been issued. This enhances morale, compliance, understanding, and two-way communication.

5. Orders should be edited. First drafts should be examined for clarity by a close colleague of the originator. If possible, the directive should be edited by a member of the management team other than the author. After editing for clarification and use of language, you can then decide whether the order actually means what you meant.

6. The directive should be of sufficient importance to the management of the department to justify its being written. Given today's proliferation of paperwork, directives should not be written unless there is a proven need. In general, a directive should
   a. Be an order of some complexity.
   b. Extend over a fairly long period of time.
   c. Go to more than one officer.
   d. Affect a fairly large number of personnel.

   Basically, the more personnel affected by an order, the greater the justification for putting the order in the form of a written directive.

7. A feedback mechanism should be part of every order. Some directives may be followed up automatically, but this does not always happen. A police management team is only as good as the information at its disposal. Management needs to know if the directive (a) was carried out, (b) in what manner, and (c) with what effect.

 THE DUTY MANUAL

The codification of the written rules of the police agency is variously called the operations manual, the procedures manual, rules and regulations, and even standard operating procedures. The usual title is "duty manual."

The duty manual governs many aspects of an officer's private life as well as his or her behavior during a tour of active duty. Most duty manuals are very specific. For example, concerning a part-time job, a duty manual may specify that the officer needs the permission of the department. It may also specify the length of hair, the length of sideburns, and the width of mustaches. Officers are expected to be fit and ready for duty at all times. They are often expected to carry their badges and even their guns while off duty.

The duty manual of the London Metropolitan Police in 1829 specifies how the duty manual was expected to be used (Reith, 1956: 135):

The following General Instructions…are not to be understood as containing rules of conduct applicable to every variety of circumstance that may occur in the performance…of duty; something must necessarily be left to the intelligence and discretion of individuals; and according to the degree in which they show themselves possessed of these qualities and to their zeal, activity and judgment on all occasions will be their claims to future promotion and reward.

Duty manuals were rightly expected to contain some flexibility in terms of interpreting the general rules of the department. A professional police agency must leave a great deal to the intelligence and discretion of the individual police officers.

O.W. Wilson ably stated what is now considered the normal definition of the duty manual (1963: 33):

DUTY MANUAL: Describes procedures and defines the duties of officers assigned to specific posts or positions….Duty manuals and changes in them should be made effective by general order; the changes should be incorporated into the first revision of the duty manual.

The duty manual usually has a chart of the organization and some job descriptions. This is to fulfill the need for consistency and fairness in normal departmental regulations.

A typical duty manual might describe the general duties of a sergeant as follows:

A Sergeant of Police will be responsible for the enforcement of all laws and ordinances, Department Rules and Regulations, orders, procedures, discipline, punctuality and attendance, appearance, good order, and efficiency of members of the police agency within assigned jurisdictions.

Besides this general job description, a good duty manual would also outline some of the specifics of the job of sergeant:

1. Train, direct, supervise, and evaluate members in their assigned duties. Recommend remedial or disciplinary action for inefficient, incompetent, and unsuitable members.

2. Inform his or her relief of all necessary police matters.

3. Report to his or her commanding officer absentees and any deficiencies in personnel and equipment.

4. Ensure that recovered property is handled in accordance with department orders.

5. Without unnecessary delay, visit all officers of the force on duty in the territory subject to supervision. Advise them of all important

information or details relating to the efficient operation of the department functions and inquire as to the conditions of the member's post. Report all matters requiring police action to the desk officer.

6. Visit at least twice during each tour of duty the patrol officer(s) assigned to special posts, hospitals, or other details located within the territory subject to supervision.

Of course, many other duties, both general and specific, could be spelled out. However, this gives some idea of how the duty manual is organized and how specific it should be. The duty manual must provide enough detailed information so that the job can be accomplished with the maximum amount of efficiency, and yet not be so detailed as to abolish that necessary use of intelligence and discretion that makes for good police work.

The duty manual is a clear, concise, and logical way in which to order procedure in a police department. It also helps to order normal business by describing the duties of each rank of officer and the way in which the ranks relate to each other. It can and does succinctly incorporate procedures to be used for such emergencies as natural disasters. The general rule is that the operations mandated by the duty manual along with personnel procedures must be of a recurrent nature. This is something that the department will have to deal with on an ongoing basis.

Some duty manuals often become very specific. This happens when incidents that occur in one example are used to create a general rule. Often, these rules become unrealistic, and good management must always be on the lookout to make sure that the duty manual specifies rules and regulations that are efficient, humane, and above all, reasonable.

Examples of some very specific rules from an actual duty manual follow:

 No smoking on the job. No member of the department shall smoke on post or beat while in uniform or while conducting an investigation of any nature.

No entering places where intoxicants are sold. No member of the department, while on duty, shall enter any place in which intoxicating liquors are sold except in the immediate performance of his or her duties.

No inebriation off duty. No member of the department shall drink intoxicants at any time off duty to the extent he or she becomes unfit for duty.

Two-minute limit for talking on duty. Conversations of more than two (2) minutes between members of the force on patrol, unless concerned with their immediate performance of duty, are prohibited.

Rules and Regulations

Are trivial rules enforced so that autocratic and often unprofessional police leadership can exert control and harass professional police officers? The following is adapted from a newspaper account of an actual incident.

A man ran into the station house with a loaded shotgun. After the man was disarmed, the officers saw that he was cut with a knife and the man was taken to a hospital. Meanwhile, a television camera crew interviewed an officer who had handled the incident. The officer appeared on television: hatless! The commissioner gave the officer an official reprimand for appearing hatless on television. The officer said, "In the confusion, I inadvertently left my hat in the station house."

The commissioner decided not to take disciplinary action against the officer, but gave out a strongly-worded memorandum the next day concerning proper dress. The commissioner stated in his memorandum, "Any violations of the procedures and regulations concerning the wearing of proper and mandated articles of uniform will be dealt with severely. Disciplinary action, which could result in charges against a violator, will positively be taken. The most flagrant violation of the regulations concerning the wearing of uniform relates to not wearing the police cap."

This is a good example of the misuse of the duty manual. A normal regulation referring to the wearing of a uniform, neatly, has been used to harass police officers in the performance of their duty. Adverse publicity was generated and the chief looked like he was an incompetent and a petty tyrant.

Many regulations are either too specific or too general to be obeyed. Their purpose often derives from the chief's need to exert internal control over his officers. With modern civil service legislation, it is difficult to fire a police officer. Therefore, the chief may write down a number of rules simply to pinpoint an officer who is violating the rules. This is not a good way to handle internal police discipline, since many of the rules are unfair and cannot be enforced in a just manner.

If the rules of the duty manual are seen as being unreasonable and used to "set up" officers, the agency will have a growing morale problem. The duty manual *will not* be seen as an effective instrument for the implementation of policy. When the rules are clear and reasonable, the duty manual can legitimately be used for official reprimands and even the firing of an officer. In general, the rules contained in the duty manual should

1. Be kept short so that everyone can read and understand the total manual in a relatively short time span.

2. Be consistent.

3. Be reasonable.

4. Conform to principles of good management.

5. Be humane.

6. Be enforceable.

7. Be stated in an unambiguous manner.

8. Be related to the actual operations of police procedures.

9. Not deal with the trivial.

10. Be written in a good English format with a professional tone to the choice of words.

It is especially important (see principle 10) that any words that denote an autocratic, arbitrary manner should be deleted.

An effective and fair duty manual is an essential tool for the efficient operation of a police agency. If an officer is reprimanded or fired because of failure to comply with the rules and regulations of the duty manual, he or she must be able to see some essential honesty and fairness involved in this procedure. At that point, the duty manual becomes an effective management communication tool and legitimately produces general rules for the social control of the civil service police force by the police management team.

▶ PROACTIVE COMMUNICATION MODEL

A proactive communication model must include the following elements:

1. Planning

2. Organizing

3. Operationalizing

4. Evaluating

All these elements have to be related to an ongoing feedback system if this communication model is to operate effectively. These elements are naturally related on an ongoing basis to actual operational procedures and the objectives of the police organization.

The proactive communication grid in Figure 6–2 (next page) shows how these elements are interrelated. The double-headed arrows show that each element has to be related to every other element of communication and that all the elements need to be related to an effective feedback system. Figure 6–2 gives the breakdown of the individual parts of the basic elements of the proactive communication grid.

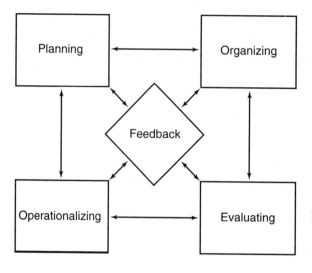

Figure 6–2
The Proactive Communication Grid.

Planning

1. Identification of need
2. Forecasting
3. Research and development
4. Conformity to goals and objectives
5. Use of staff in developing the planning process
6. Police personnel input
7. Outside consultation and coordination
8. Decision-making process

Organizing

1. Hiring of personnel
2. Training
3. Rules of procedure and directives created
4. Development of auxiliary services and infrastructure of support
5. Service, capitalization, and maintenance of physical plant and equipment
6. Implementation orders drawn up

Operationalizing

1. Supervision of implementation procedures
2. Continuing direction and control
3. Coordination of various parts and segments of the police agency
4. Coordination with outside agencies

Evaluating

1. Development of standards that lead to operationalized evaluations
2. Listing of criteria of success
3. Evaluation procedures developed and related to empirical standards of success
4. Creation of centralized data file
5. Creation of centralized staff of research analysts
6. Outline of inspectional procedures
7. Feedback with recommendations to planning

MICROCOMPUTER AND MAINFRAME APPLICATIONS TO INFORMATION MANAGEMENT

Before computerization, paper records got lost, created storage problems in terms of bulk, and were hard to handle. In order not to lose information, there was great redundancy in all police information systems. It took considerable time just to find things. Files would occasionally get misfiled or lost, with disastrous results. Accessibility and security were in constant conflict. How could police management provide instant access to all records for appropriate police personnel while keeping the access limited in terms of security considerations? There was no solution until the computer. Now information can be processed in a rapid manner while access is limited by use of security codes.

However, the computer is simply a tool, a machine, to process information. The computer does not create solutions, manage problems, or become a panacea for all solutions. Police managers manage and solve problems using the computer. Given this warning concerning the overreliance on computer technology, we also have the opposite end of the spectrum; that is, fear of computers. There are still police managers who cannot operate without hard copy; that is, a piece of paper, and who are fearful concerning the use of computers. These managers need to be retooled or retired. This may sound harsh, but the realities of the information age in terms of an efficient means of organizing so much information are overwhelming.

When mainframe computers first came into existence, data were generated with huge amounts of output overwhelming police managers and administrators. When one of the present authors first did a survey run of police attitudes on an old IBM 360, he ran hundreds of tables, creating a paper pile over 3 feet high. The second thing he did was throw away this 3-foot-high stack of tables. The police managers, with their mainframes, also threw out hundreds of feet of output. Why? What happened?

It was so easy to get the data and the data output that police managers asked for everything without thinking through what they wanted. Managers need to use computers as tools and ask only for the output they need to get their jobs done in the most efficient manner. The ability to *ask the right question* is the basic talent needed for police administration.

Police managers need to free up their time in terms of detail while having access to essential information. The major areas that lend themselves to the optimum use of data processing for the police manager are

1. *Payroll:* periodic payroll records, actual paying of personnel, and analysis of payroll records in relation to time sheets, court time, sick time, and so on, with enhanced fiscal planning ability.

2. *Budget:* fiscal control of the existing budget with up-to-date record of expenditures; fiscal impact of any emergency/overtime procedures; planning capability in terms of generating future budgets; the manipulation of fiscal data for mayors, city managers, legislators, police management, and so on.

3. *Purchasing:* uniforms, supplies, equipment, and so on—provides controls for purchasing, especially when correlated with maintenance and depletion schedules, for example. The cost of uniforms provided for personnel by contract in many departments can be a large expenditure where there is a need for good control. Also, there is a need for controls in terms of bulk versus retail purchases with the use of a cost/benefit subroutine.

4. *Vehicle maintenance:* includes patrol cars, boats, bicycles, and so on. There is a need for detailed records in order to get comparative cost per mile and such items as the optimum trade-in mileage.

5. *Annual report:* gathering of the necessary data to justify department operations to the legislature, administrative officials such as mayors and county executives, and the general public.

6. *Inventory:* adequate control of departmental assets along with replacement schedules and similar details.

7. *Personnel:* maintaining current personnel records, allowing convenience of updating with a subroutine that permits selective information to be readily available to the police manager.

8. *Training records:* maintaining a level of information relative to past, ongoing, and future training needs of the members of the department. This has become increasingly important in today's litigious society, where training is an issue in relation to liability.

9. *Scheduling of personnel:* one of the most difficult tasks is to schedule 24-hour, seven-day coverage for patrol officers patrolling a community. The police manager needs to consider a number of

variables, such as shift changes, vacation time, rest days, and training time. There is also a need to have enough personnel to cover
effectively the different numbers of calls for service at different
times. Computer programs have come a long way in making such
scheduling easier.

10. *Community relations:* maintaining records on the speaker's bureau,
tours of the department, press and media relations, and so on, including the use of desktop publishing for newsletters and news releases.

Productivity can be increased throughout the department by using data processing, at least in the following areas:

Crime reports	Found property
Evidence control	Warrant files
Modus operandi	Court appearances
Traffic tickets	Burglar alarms
Vacant house checks	Daily bulletin
Hazardous conditions	

The use of microcomputers, which allow data input into a mainframe system or the interconnection of the microcomputers with any adequate data storage, enhances the ability of administrators and officers to have instant and adequate input and output of essential information. Security codes and a sophisticated security system can protect files while giving access to personnel who are
authorized to have access.

COMPUTER-AIDED DISPATCH

Computer-aided dispatch **(CAD)** enhances calls for service from the public
and the dispatching of police cars and personnel. The CAD system verifies
addresses, determines the beat of incidents, and gives a case number and priority number to each call. Some systems even report "dangerous histories." The
computer automatically records all calls and can recommend to the dispatcher a choice of units to dispatch to the call. The time of dispatch is recorded as
well as time on the scene and time the unit is free. Thus CAD provides real-
time monitoring of vehicle status, a continuously updated incident file, and
allows supervisors to monitor the incident status and provides telephone,
radio, and digital activity statistics. The system can also generate crime statistics reports, flag deviations and trends, automatically generate required data
for resource allocation models, and provide on-line information for line supervisors, administrators, and officers. The system's features are summarized in
Table 6-1.

TABLE 6–1
CAD: POSSIBLE SYSTEM FEATURES

FUNCTION	CAD-RELATED FEATURES
Needs identification	Complaint clerk enters incident-related information into the computer CAD adds routine data (incident number, date, time, etc.) Computer checks data validity (address verification, etc.) Computer assigns a call priority Computer assigns a beat number Computer checks for previous incidents at this address or related data (e.g., hazardous information) Computer estimates length of time until a unit can respond to the call Backup operator handles lengthy calls
Status monitoring	CAD provides real-time monitoring of vehicle status (and vehicle location, if tied to AVM or Automatic Vehicle Monitoring) CAD maintains a continuously updated incident file (assigned, unassigned, cases cleared, etc.) Supervisor can monitor unit and incident status by calling up complaint clerk and dispatcher displays
Response/ adjustment	Operator has computerized files of frequently used telephone numbers (ambulance, tow, etc.) CAD routes incident information to appropriate dispatcher Computer provides a summary list of incidents in the system Computer recommends which unit(s) to select (based on estimated unit location) Computer automatically times calls and raises a "flag" if a call takes longer than a specified time Computer provides telephone, radio, and digital activity statistics Unit status can be updated automatically (with MDC Mobil Data Computer) or through an operator (using CAD or a separate system) Personnel can automatically sign in as "available" at shift change using remote terminals Data base queries can be handled automatically (via MDC) or through an operator (using CAD or a separate system) Dispatcher can have one, two, or more video monitors Computer maintains temporary situation files (e.g., traffic and street repairs) CAD supports coordination of multiple unit (and/or agency) assignments to one incident CAD provides a basis for officers' daily incident reports Computer handles routine log-off operations (e.g., adds time and date, and stores in closed incident file)
Resource management	Computer periodically generates crime statistics reports for state and federal use Computer reports can be generated off-line Computer provides statistics by any desired set of categories (type of crime, area, time of day, etc.) Computer generates management reports from CAD for departmental use (e.g., incident logs, officer activity logs) Computer can automatically flag deviations or trends One-time, special reports (e.g., particular crime activity patterns) can be generated Computer can automatically generate required data for resource allocation models On-line information is available via remote terminals for patrol personnel, sergeants, etc.

Source: Colton et al. (1983: 23-24).

CAD is widely used throughout the United States and is increasingly used for management planning by matching the allocation of police resources in relation to calls for service. Following are the goals of CAD as stated in a study of 26 cities (Colton and others, 1983: 30):

To monitor and better display data, including outstanding calls, ongoing incidents, and patrol unit status and activities.

To provide better information to personnel, including complaint clerks, dispatchers, and supervisors.

To help decide which patrol unit(s) to assign to a call for service based on estimated unit locations.

To reduce response time through reductions in call answering, call processing, unit assignment, and travel times.

To improve officer safety by more effectively monitoring unit status and responding more rapidly in case of emergency.

To facilitate access to remote data files, including outstanding warrants, stolen property, and state and national inquiry systems.

To improve the quality of data maintained from the dispatch process through address verification; automatic assignment of case numbers, dates, and times; elimination of duplicate assignment of case numbers, dates, and times; elimination of duplicate entries; and so on.

To better manage police resources through the use of better data and a better understanding of the command and control process.

To improve service to the public through quicker response time, better dispatch data, and improved management of police resources.

MOBIL DIGITAL COMMUNICATION

Mobile digital communications **(MDC)** provides a nonverbal means of transmitting dispatch and status messages between a law enforcement communication center and patrol units, as well as accessing data files by both the communication center and the patrol units. A mobile digital terminal is the basic element of the system, along with an encoder and decoder with message switching and display of messages controlled by a microcomputer. The goals of MDC are as follows (Colton, and others, 1983: 43):

To reduce voice congestion and expand the communications capability of existing radio channels using digital signals which have a higher transmission rate than voice signals.

To increase officer effectiveness through easier access to remote data files, which could potentially result in more "hits" (i.e., apprehensions and recoveries).

To increase dispatcher effectiveness by relieving the dispatcher of routine data inquiries, patrol status updates, message repetitions, and/or dispatches of some (noncritical) calls for service.

To increase officer safety through easier data base access, increased communications capability, and an "Emergency" button on MDT units.

To improve message security using digital signals which are more difficult to decipher than voice messages.

To improve accuracy and decrease message repetition using mobile digital terminals that can provide hard copies.

To allow selective routing of messages using terminals that can be addressed either collectively or individually, on an "as need to know" basis.

To allow unattended message reception using terminals that can record messages while an officer is out of a vehicle.

Various departments have operated using MDC on a widely varying level of sophistication. Table 6-2 shows the various ways of using the MDC system in police agencies.

TABLE 6–2
MDC: POSSIBLE SYSTEM FEATURES

LEVEL OF DIGITALIZATION	DESCRIPTION	COMMENTS
Status only		
One-way	Mobile unit can report status by pressing a single key on mobile unit console. Dispatcher's console maintains indication of last status transmission. All messages from base station are by voice.	Minimum hardware in mobile unit and minimum expense; useful in reducing channel congestion where there are many cars per channel, since status reports constitute a significant portion of traffic.
Two-way	As above, plus comparable capability for base station to transmit status or other "canned" messages (primarily acknowledgements) to mobile units by a single console key. Mobile unit displays messages as lights (no text) or numbers.	Advantages as above, plus saves significant amounts of dispatcher time used to acknowledge status messages. lack of an acknowledgment capability by either mobile or base unit is generally not acceptable.

TABLE 6-2 (CONT'D)

LEVEL OF DIGITALIZATION	DESCRIPTION	COMMENTS
Full text plus status	As in two-way status above, plus a full alphanumeric keyboard and display (luminous and/or printer) in mobile unit plus function keys for status and other "canned" messages.	Requires a telecommunications controller at the base station. Reduces dispatcher work load significantly and further reduces channel congestion over status-only capability.
Direct data base query capability	Mobile unit can make data base queries directly of local state, and national data bases without relay through dispatcher.	Requires additional hardware (modems to interface with remote data base lines) and additional switching software for minicomputer. Dispatcher control and/or monitoring can be provided.
Computer-aided dispatching	Computer performs computations to help dispatcher locate nearest available unit or units to assign to a given incident. Verifies jurisdictional boundaries, valid address, prior complaints, and possible dangerous condition.	Can be added to any system with a computer, requiring primarily additional software. Can be provided with any level of dispatcher control. May require larger computer and more peripherals.
Automated data collection and report generation	Computer logs all messages or selected types and automatically generates reports of traffic by message type, car, time of day, or other breakdowns. Officer reports can be entered through mobile terminals, and used as part of Field Officer Daily Report, although this can increase traffic significantly.	Requires additional software. Useful capability to monitor system performance and usage, trends in message traffic, etc. May require larger computer and more peripherals.

Source: Colton and others (1983: 39).

AUTOMATIC VEHICLE MONITORING

Automatic vehicle monitoring **(AVM)** provides the location and status of the vehicle, such as in pursuit, en route to scene, door open, and so on. It is more inclusive than an automatic vehicle location system (AVL), which simply provides a vehicle's location. Location is provided by four devices: (1) a navigation (hyperbolic) system which uses a radio location techniques called Loran C, a system used by ships at sea; (2) a trilateration system uses radio location from three or more fixed sites; (3) a signpost/proximity system, locating a vehicle through the use of fixed electronic signposts located throughout an area; and (4) a dead-reckoning system where computer-assisted instruments are used to track vehicles on a city map; for example, utilizing an advanced geocoding system.

The first AVM program, a signpost transmitter system, was installed in Monterey, California, in the early 1970s. Both the St. Louis and Dallas police departments have installed AVM systems. The stated objectives of the AVM systems are as follows (Colton and others, 1983: 52):

> To reduce response time through reductions in dispatch and travel times.
>
> To increase apprehension rates through reduced response time.
>
> To improve officer safety by continually monitoring the status and location of police vehicles.
>
> To improve dispatch efficiency and coordination by providing the dispatcher with precise data on unit status and location.
>
> To improve tactical command and control through on-line direction of such special tactical events as high-speed chases, bank robberies, emergency deployment, and support for covert operations.
>
> To improve patrol efficiency and effectiveness through the availability of *direct* information regarding the location and allocation of the patrol force, and through the *indirect* realization of patrol officers that they are being monitored.
>
> To improve supervision of the patrol force through better on-line supervision of officers in the field and through the use of the management information generated from the AVM system.
>
> To reduce voice-band congestion when linked with some type of mobile digital communications (MDC).

One reason for the controversial nature of the AVM becomes very obvious to both management and line officers: that is, there is greater control and supervision of the patrol force. It stands to reason that if supervisors know the condition of all patrol cars and where the cars are at all times, they also have a pretty good idea of where the patrol officers are and what the status of the patrol officer is. This has great potential for increasing police productivity in terms of service to the public.

911

The **911** system provides one phone number for calling all police agencies in a geographic area with one central dispatch system. The 911 system has achieved a high degree of acceptance from the police and the public.

Generally, when this system is not in existence, it is due to interference by local politics, rather than technical difficulties, which have been and can be overcome. A basic 911 system also provides a number of useful features: (1) automatic identification and display of the calling number and address of the person calling the 911 number; (2) jurisdiction selective routing (JSR), which allows routing of the 911 call to the appropriate jurisdiction; (3) supplementary dispatch/support data (SDSD) gives the police beat, firebox area, and ambulance zone of the location of the call; (4) internal selective routing (ISR) allows routing of calls to the appropriate operator in large law enforcement jurisdictions; and (5) automatic registered name identification (ARNI), which gives automatic display of the name of the person owning the origination phone for the call. Although the 911 system should be adopted by every jurisdiction, there are two major problems that need to be dealt with: (1) the problem of duplication of street names and (2) mobile phones that move through too many locations (Colton and others, 1983: 63).

The objectives of the basic and advanced 911 systems are as follows (Colton and others, 1983: 63):

Basic 911 System

To have an easy-to-remember number for emergency purposes.

To reduce emergency response times.

To increase apprehension rates and decrease the level of property damage.

To promote citizen involvement in public safety.

To improve coordination of emergency services.

Advanced 911 System

To overcome the disparity between jurisdictional boundaries and the telephone company's central office exchange boundaries using the automatic location identification (ALI) and jurisdictional selective routing (JSR) options.

To reduce the number of false alarms, bomb threats, and other malicious calls using the ARNI (automatic registered name identification) and ALI option.

To allow for call-back and address identification in case a distressed caller gives inadequate information using the ARNI and ALI options.

To minimize the number of complaint clerk transcription errors using the ALI and ARNI options.

To enhance an emergency operator's area familiarity, awareness of resource availability, and identification of redundant calls using the ALI, supplementary dispatch support data (SDSD), and internal selective routing (ISR) options.

A regional communication system **(RCS)** is a plan whereby a number of law enforcement agencies cooperate in the creation of a common communication network. RCS decreases operating costs, especially personnel and total equipment and installation costs. Jurisdictions are able to afford computer-assisted communication systems that would otherwise be out of reach of their budgets. This approach can also overcome channel congestion problems, coordinate police actions during emergencies, and provide a regional base for attracting outside funding. As with 911, many efforts at establishing a regional communication system have been blocked by petty politics. However, it is hoped that savings and cost and the increasing efficiency provided by the system will overcome these obstacles (Colton and others, 1983: 73).

There are a number of reasons for establishing an RCS, and the form of the actual RCS implemented will reflect the particular benefits expected by the jurisdictions involved. Possible objectives for RCS include (Colton, 1983):

> To decrease operating costs, especially personnel-related costs.
>
> To decrease equipment and implementation costs.
>
> To overcome radio channel congestion problems.
>
> To provide a means of coordinating police actions during certain emergencies.
>
> To establish a joint entity which would more easily attract federal and state subsidies.

A major reason for adopting an RCS is cost savings: through consolidation, a regional communication system may decrease operating costs (especially personnel-related costs), and total equipment and installation costs. Furthermore, by creating an RCS, cities may be able to afford technologies—such as CAD—that they may not be able to afford on their own.

To implement and fully utilize a computer-assisted *police command, control,* and *communication system* (PCCCS), it is recommended that the following steps take place (Colton and others, 1983: 79):

1. Needs assessment.
2. Careful identification of PCCC philosophy and approach (for example, management versus operational perspective).
3. Preparation of a needs statement based on the needs assessment and overall philosophy, generally in the form of a request for proposal (RFP).
4. Responses from vendors to the RFP and selection based not only on cost, but also on quality concerns.
5. Specific commitment of vendors to a measurable level of performance.

6. Careful orientation, training, and involvement of operations personnel.

7. Evaluation and revision to assure that the system continues to meet the ongoing needs of users.

Naturally, these steps cannot always be followed precisely, and flexibility and adaptability are essential. Furthermore, such an approach by itself will not guarantee success. However, it is our judgment based on our literature search, surveys, and site visits that using this kind of process as a checklist will make a major contribution toward successful PCCC system implementation. The structure of a fully integrated system is shown in Figure 6-3.

Ideally, all these systems would be in place and then, of course, they would be integrated with regional, statewide, national, and international networks. Any police agency in the United States should be able to access information on criminals from all resources.

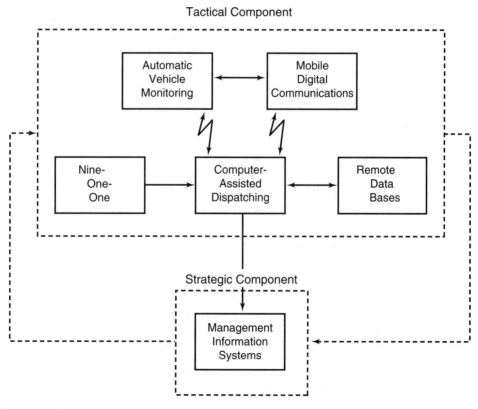

Figure 6-3
An Integrated PCCCS System.

National Crime Information Center

The National Crime Information Center (**NCIC**) maintains a computerized filing system, including such information as wanted persons, stolen property, criminal history, and information on identifiable persons in relation to investigations on reported crimes. The NCIC system is supported by the federal government and has a national advisory board made up of police administrators from all over the United States. This advisory board makes recommendations to the Director of the Federal Bureau of Investigation in terms of NCIC policy. Since its creation in 1967, the NCIC has accomplished the following goals (*NCIC Operating Manual*, 1985: Intro-1):

1. Enhancing the development of state, county, and metropolitan computerized criminal justice information systems, thereby making NCIC information more readily available to the officer on the street.

2. Establishing uniformity of coding standards for the exchange of criminal justice information.

3. Increasing the probability of criminal detection by providing law enforcement with the timely and accurate information necessary to combat today's highly mobile criminal.

4. Improving the overall crime solution rate.

With the number of mobile data terminals and agency users currently at 110,000, the system is currently involved in an upgrading program entitled NCIC 2000. The purposes of the enhancements will be to

1. Establish national distribution system for data sets stored by states instead of keeping a central data base.

2. Establish the National Fingerprint File which will allow for electronic transmittal and identification of fingerprints.

3. Establish the Alcohol, Tobacco, and Firearms Violent Felon File which will create files of people who are terrorist suspects or of interest to law enforcement officials.

Automated Regional Justice Information System

The Automated Regional Justice Information System (ARJIS) operates in California and is similar to other state data networks, such as the Criminal History and Information Recovery System (CHAIRS) network in New York State. ARJIS consists of nine components:

1. Arrests and juvenile contacts.
2. AWDI (automated worthless document index).

3. Citations (misdemeanor citations, traffic citations, traffic warnings, traffic accidents).
4. Crime analysis.
5. Crime cases.
6. Field interviews.
7. Master operations index.
8. Personnel.
9. Property (pawned/wanted property).

Each police agency has one or more terminals which allow on-line access for either inquiry or update activity. For example, the worthless document index deals with forgeries, while crime analysis allows searches by name, partial name, or nickname; date; pawned, stolen, lost, or found property; addresses, and so on. Crime cases allow for searches by **modus operandi** or method of procedure. It is obvious that when these systems are in place, a great deal of sophisticated information sifting can take place. In California, as in most states, the following information is also accessible from their standardized files, called the Criminal Justice Information System (CJIS), which contains six systems:

1. Stolen vehicle system (SVS)
2. Automated boat system (ABS)
3. Wanted persons system (WPS)
4. Criminal history system (CHS)
5. Automated firearms system (AFS)
6. Automated property system (APS)

The latest developments in computer technology have further increased the applications for law enforcement. The increase in the use of **microcomputers** as opposed to mainframe operations allows each department to manage records, personnel, and crime data from one or several machines. According to Julian (1989) the fourth generation (4 GL) of computers allows nonprogrammers to devise various applications. In fact, some of the best applications for local crime analysis and parking are now being developed by law enforcement officers who caught on to computing in recent years.

In the first and second editions of this book we wrote that computer time sharing for small departments was a necessity because of cost. Not so anymore. The cost for hardware and software is relatively inexpensive. However, going into the computer age of the 1990s is not without horror stories and hardships. Case studies written by command personnel in *Police Chief* and other law enforcement management publications attest to the importance of planning and field testing to avoid failure (defined as obtaining expensive equipment that no one in the department will use).

THE PAPERLESS POLICE DEPARTMENT

Related to the new changes in computer technology is the transformation that has occurred in report writing and recordkeeping. Every police activity or crime incident demands a report on some kind of form. The majority of police patrol reports written before 1975 were handwritten; typewriters were reserved for detectives who needed four carbon copies for depositions and court papers. Standardized forms were introduced at this time to assist in data processing for mainframe crime analysis and to reduce the narrative portion of the report. Writing reports and completing forms takes time. Booking processes for the average misdemeanor take about two hours. Police administrators continue to look for ways to reduce the paperwork associated with arrests and investigations.

Today, officers can write reports on small notebook computers located in the front seat of the patrol units; discs are handed in at the end of the shift for hard copy needs. Cursor keys and spell-check functions in these report programs are useful time-saving features. Personnel in the Dade County Metropolitan Police Department who cannot type can now use a pen-pad computer which changes handwriting on a pad to typewritten form. Recording is another popular strategy, the most advanced form being digital dictation. As reported by Blanchard (1989) Warwick, RI officers dictate reports by phone into the department's main computer. The system permits the officer to review and edit reports at the time of dictation. Reports can be transcribed at a later date. As opposed to hand-held tape recorders and tape systems, the officer and patrol commander can get into the report at any time without going through miles of tape or locating individual diskettes. Dictation into department computers is also achieved by cellular phones that have become a very popular tool for investigators.

Laptop computers with forms-based software and smart keys that conform to the police forms can make police more efficient. The paperwork done on arrest, for example, can be spell-checked and ready for downloading to the main computer for access by administrators, prosecutors, and defense lawyers. With proper encryption programs and security codes, information can be obtained from data systems throughout the world.

Electronic mail can be distributed to administrators and can bring experts on-line during an on-going investigation. Legal statutes, community and human service addresses, and personnel can be directly accessed during routine calls. Information and forms can be printed and handed to administrators and citizens as needed. Everything from warrant checks and stolen vehicles, to mug shots and detailed maps, is immediately accessible.

Recordkeeping is another problem that is being addressed through imaging technology. The Syracuse Police Department in New York reported that it was making 26 copies of every record or about 4 million copies a year (Proceedings, 1993: 136). To reduce the "paper monster," the department invested in computerized imaging which scans the record and then stores it on a 12-inch optical disk. One disk can store 35,000 pages. Although paper records have not entirely disappeared, the amount of time and number of employees devoted to copying and retrieval has been reduced.

NEW TECHNOLOGIES FOR POLICE MANAGERS

What is possible today? Each officer can have a Personal Locator Transmitter (PLT) which keeps track of the officer and offers hands-free communication. The Remote Control Information System (RCIS) is portable and has full-color video, two-way audio, officer location, and monitors and transmits vital signs. A smart card with storage capacity that turns itself off with tampering, will provide secure identification in the size of a credit card. People can be identified with computerized signatures provided by fingerprints, DNA, and voiceprint.

The Advanced Regional Justice Information System in California is being updated, from a textual mainframe system to a user-friendly, client-based, PC system that uses a mouse to get information for an investigation, or just information needed by a beat officer. Graphics such as computer mapping and photo line-ups will be available in the field, along with form-based software for field reports via the laptop.

Each officer will have access to an immense amount of data, including graphic and photographic interfaces for identification of suspects. Officers can interview a victim while calling up an identity kit program to focus on victim image, and then compare this to suspect profiles and modus operandi. Eastman Kodak has a writable CD that provides 20 file cabinets full of storage, combining image processing technology with case management functions for the detective on the street or in the courtroom. Voice recognition technology is now available for officers to talk their reports into the system.

The WorldWide Web provides incredible services but needs organizing. IACP has its own Web page, as do agencies such as the DEA, FBI, Federal Bureau of Prisons, National Institute of Justice, Supreme Court Decisions, ERIC gopher on juvenile delinquency, Bureau of Justice Statistics, RAND, National Criminal Justice Links, U.S. Department of Justice, and a Criminal Justice e-mail listserv. Online newsletters are available such as American Police Beat, Justice Information Distributions List, Journal of CJ, and Popular Culture.

The United Nations Criminal Justice Information Network (UNCJIN) provides a worldwide automated system used for communicating and exchanging criminal justice information including a gopher-based electronic discussion forum. The United Nations Online Justice Clearinghouse (UNOJUST) will provide access to criminal justice member holdings all over the world, including an e-mail service.

There are sites called Cops, Help Locate a Fugitive, Internet Crime Writing Network, and many, many others. For example, Justice Technology Information Network (JUSTNET) "provides information on new technologies, equipment and other products and services available to the law enforcement, corrections and criminal justice communities." JUSTNET provides news and information services, chat line, topic board, and data and publication services. For registered law enforcement and correction users there are data links to agencies that have used the products.

One of the major issues is security, including encryption protocols and privacy for address linkages and chat groups. What if you are tracking a serial killer and want to set up a law enforcement board, data link, and some kind of round-table discussion group? It would be important to **not** transmit this information to the criminal community. Personal encryption holds some solutions where only the person getting the message can decrypt the message.

Computer Assisted Dispatch (CAD) is being teamed up with record management systems (RMS) to look at CAD patterns and past patterns—crime locations, vehicle locations, officer response, etc.—to make policy. It acts as a paper for every single incident, with appropriate linkages to police investigation, court, and human service data banks, dispositions and feedback. There are over 200 RMS companies in the United States that are eager to provide these services to police management. Once the programs are in place, data only has to be entered once into the system and then it is on its way to data bank linkages and a Proactive Management Based Information System (PMBIS).

PROACTIVE MANAGEMENT BASED INFORMATION SYSTEM (PMBIS)

This is where you combine your CAD system and an RMS with linkages to other systems. The innovation here is the use of installed management-based software configured for your police department with this combined system.

The best review in the field concerning this high technology is found in an article in the *Police Chief*, "High Technology Solutions" (Pilant, 1996). Pilant gives us an example of this type of system. "Dispatch Automation…has a Records Information Management System (RIMS) that not only does computer-aided dispatching, records management and mapping but acts as an interface for state and NCIC information for mobile computers; CLUES (Comprehensive Law Enforcement Systems, Inc.,) which offers CAD/RMS and acts as a common data base so agencies can share information." (Pilant, 1996: 45–46).

Communication between cars and dispatch will also include conferencing, monitoring vehicle location, and in-vehicle information. The chief will know where the vehicle has been on a computer map (and be able to trace a route with time and date), when the door was opened and closed, how long the motor ran, what is gas mileage, and, with a few sensors, if the officer has been smoking in the car and possibly the brand of the cigar. This makes for close monitoring and data messaging by anyone who has access to the system. Open architecture allows the department to add on system modules from a variety of sources. The RMS capability, along with management software, makes this enormous amount of data usable for policy making.

These systems work best when management can fully utilize them. For example, Distributed Collaborative Planning (DCP) systems that link commands at multiple locations are useful for large departments, regional police problem-solving, and interagency collaboration. DCP provides real time software decision-making models, shared information retrieval, digital video teleconferences, and shared computer desktops including textual, verbal, digital, and pictorial information. Current and archival data can be shared for homicide investigations; for example, crowd control during riots with each unit providing and sharing information (Rome Laboratory Law Enforcement Technology Team, 1996).

Management needs to step in to control and organize this information so that it doesn't break down into information overload, static enhancement, and plain babble. The decision-making tree may help but some kind of prioritization needs to be in place along with an information flow system of command capability.

These systems are useful when police managers are in charge. Buy a system that is expandable open technology so you can add more systems and capability when you need it. You need a company that has been around long enough to establish a reputation. You need a system that works for your department rather than one that fits a Star Wars 21st century that makes no sense to you and your officers.

Buy the latest tested technology that works for your management team. In this world of technology, everything is getting better and prices will drop. Buy what will work today, and hopefully tomorrow, for your department. Make sure that there is a maximum of training available and reliable, affordable technical assistance from human beings that talk in English, not some obscure technical language.

 CONCLUSION

In this section we have reviewed available information systems and previewed the more sophisticated systems of the future. However, all these systems are limited by the programs that are used for sorting and labeling information and the human beings who use these systems. Police managers must understand the potential of these systems and be able to use them if they want to successfully manage modern police departments.

The central concern of police communication is mutual, unambiguous understanding among all communicators. Communication can and does shape the nature of the police organization. If it is all one way, from the top to the bottom, and with little or no feedback, the department will be organized in an autocratic manner. The autocratic style, although effective in terms of rapid response, actually fosters inefficiency. Management needs to know which orders are effective in operation and which are not, and this is determined through a solid feedback system. With such a system, ineffective orders can be eliminated or modified until they become effective.

For communication to be understood by all parties involved, orders should be written in a consistent and organized manner. Unambiguous communication is especially important in police work, where the professional officer has to respond time and again to citizens in crisis. The line officer has to be an effective communicator. But this can be achieved only when the officer is supported by an orderly process of departmental communication. With so much time spent on paperwork, as well as on giving and receiving of orders, all police organizations should develop an ongoing, proactive communication system.

QUESTIONS FOR REVIEW

1. Interview a police supervisor. Ask a series of questions concerning one-way and two-way communications. How does his or her answer compare with the recommendations of this chapter and why is there a similarity and/or a difference?

2. You are a patrol officer on the radio discussing a tense hostage situation with a commanding officer. Identify (a) the sender, (b) the receiver, (c) the encoding, (d) the decoding, and (e) the channel.

3. If you were a supervising officer of a patrol operation, describe the feedback system you would institute. Defend the efficiency of the system in terms of its information flow patterns.

4. One of the major problems in communications is misunderstanding and misinformation. Explain how you would deal with these two problems in terms of a small, rural police agency. Also identify how you would deal with these problems in terms of communications with other police agencies in nearby jurisdictions.

5. List the major obstacles to communications in the day-to-day work of a police agency and detail the major strategies you would use to overcome these obstacles.

6. If you were a police commander, in what part of the Johari window would you locate yourself and why? Choose another student in class and state where you would locate him or her in the Johari window grid and justify your judgment.

7. You have noticed that many of your patrol officers are wasting a great deal of time in stores. It is not just a question of gaining information and community support but an inefficient use of most of your officers' time. Specify the type of orders (SOP, TOP, GO, SO, MEMO) you would issue and justify your choice in the face of a grievance from one of your officers concerning your order.

8. Define *reasonable* in police management terms, and apply this definition to what you would consider a reasonable duty manual.

9. Apply the proactive communication approach to a local police department. How does this communication model work when placed in the field in the midst of the normal amount of practical difficulties?

10. Visit a local police department and compare its operations to the concept of a paperless police department.

KEY TERMS

assumptions	bypassing
AVM	CAD

decoding	microcomputer
directive	NCIC
duty manual	network
encoding	overgeneralization
feedback	RCS
GO	SO
inference	SOP
Johari window	subscripts
MDC	symbol
MDT	TOP
medium	911
MEMO	WorldWide Web

BIBLIOGRAPHY

BLANCHARD, WESLEY, "Digital Dictation a Boon for Warwick," in *Police Chief*, 57, no. 3, (March 1989) p. 53.

BOWKER, ARTHUR L., "Downloading Computer Information." *Law Enforcement Bulletin* (June, 1966), pp. 1–10.

COLTON, KENT W., MARGARET L. BRANDEAU, and JAMES M. TIEN, *A National Assessment of Police Command, Control, and Communication Systems*. Washington, D.C.: National Institute of Justice, 1983.

CURTI, KEITH, J., Laptop Computers. *Law Enforcement Bulletin* (February, 1996), pp. 1–9.

DOERING, R.D., *Vehicle Location Feasibility Study: Final Report*. Orlando, Fl.: Florida Technological University, 1974.

GABRIEL, CHARLES E., "Onondaga County Police Agencies Make Mobile Radio District Idea Work," *Law and Order* (February 1975), pp. 42–51.

JULIAN, JAY, "Fourth Generation Languages: The New Law Enforcement Combat Masterpiece." *Police C..., *56, no. 6, (June 1989) pp. 41–43.

KASHEY, DANIEL, R., "Mobile Digital Terminals: Police Communicators of the Future." *Law and Order* (February 1978), pp 26–38.

LARSON, G.C., *Evaluation of an AVM System Implemented City-Wide in St. Louis: A Summary Report*. Cambridge, Mass.: Public Systems Evaluation, Inc., 1978.

LIVELY, G. MARTIN, "Thinking Globally To Act Locally." *National Institute of Justice Journal* (February, 1966).

MCDONNEL, RICHARD A., "Information Management," in Bernard L. Garmie, ed., *Local Government Police Management*. Washington, D.C.: International City Management Association, 1977.

NEIL, THOMAS C., *Interpersonal Communications for Criminal Justice Personnel*. Boston: Allyn & Bacon, 1980.

OFFICE OF TELECOMMUNICATIONS POLICY, *Nine-One-One: The Emergency Telephone Number—A Handbook for Community Planning*. Washington, D.C.: U.S. Department of Commerce, 1973.

PILANT, LOIS, "High Technology" *Police Chief* (May, 1996), pp. 38-51.

Proceedings: Criminal Justice System and Technology Conference. Albany, New York: Department of Criminal Justice Services, 1993.

REITH, CHARLES, *A New Study of Police History*. Edinburgh: Oliver & Boyd, 1956.

RICH, THOMAS F., "The Use of Computerized Mapping in Crime Control and Prevention Programs." Washington, D.C.: National Institute of Justice, 1955.

ROME LABORATORY LAW ENFORCEMENT TECHNOLOGY TEAM, "The New Horizon: Transferring Defense Technology to Law Enforcement." *Law Enforcement Bulletin* (April, 1966), pp. 10-20.

SOHN, R.L., *Application of Computer-Aided Dispatch in Law Enforcement: An Introductory Planning Guide*. Pasadena, Calif.: Jet Propulsion Laboratory, 1975.

U.S. DEPARTMENT OF JUSTICE, NCIC Operating Manual. Washington, D.C.: U.S. Government Printing Office, 1985.

WEST, WILLIAM L., JR., "Automated Dispatching for Small Town Communications," *Communications* (February 1979), pp. 20-25.

WILSON, O.W., *Police Administration* (2nd ed.). New York: McGraw-Hill, 1963.

7

Basic Line Functions

Although patrol is the major line function, policing encompasses a variety of other functions designed to provide an entire range of law enforcement services to the community. These services involve four additional line functions, other than patrol, normally classified as

1. Traffic
2. Vice
3. Juvenile
4. Investigations

Other specialized line functions include hostage and negotiating teams, arson task forces, and special weapons and tactics (**SWAT**) squads.

In larger departments, these four functions as well as patrol are organized as separate entities and are assigned specific responsibilities; in smaller departments, each officer may provide the entire range of services. During one tour of duty, it would not be unusual for a village police officer to investigate a car accident, follow through on a continuing burglary investigation, and arrest a juvenile suspect. In larger departments, these tasks would be handled separately by the traffic division, the investigation unit, and the juvenile unit.

The number of divisions that exist in a department depends upon the size and history of both the community and the law enforcement agency. Specific problems may warrant the creation of new organizational units. A city with a large banking community may have a fraud unit, whereas a city with a large warehouse district might have a warehouse and loft squad. In the department of 140 sworn officers, the traffic division handled all matters related to traffic enforcement: accident investigations, issuing of parking tickets, processing drunk driving arrests, and even supervising the installation of traffic signs. In another department of similar size, these tasks were delegated as general patrol work.

In discussing this matter of police line functions, it must be stressed that although similar tasks need to be carried out and thus the general readings are useful, specific organizational structures will vary. The variables of agency size, community need, and history are of great importance when making realistic comparisons of police organizational structure.

 ## GENERALIST–SPECIALIST CONTROVERSY

A question that normally arises at this point is: Why not simply have the patrol officer handle every type of complaint and situation? This is the standard generalist-versus-specialist argument that police have been engaged in for decades. Realizing that all police officers have to be generalists, there are good arguments for specialization and organizing of departments into specific divisions.

The first major argument is that of control. Especially in larger departments with hundreds of personnel involved, organization into divisions becomes a mechanism with which to direct the overall activities of the agency. Thus personnel are allocated according to bureau or division to address specifics in a certain category of police problems.

Second, priorities have to be set and work has to get done in an organized manner. Given the wide range of tasks confronted by police agencies, the commander of a division and the chief in charge of all divisions can set up priorities. The delegation of duties by division or squad is traditionally taken to remedy the delivery of specific police services. For example, there may be an outcry in the community concerning juvenile crime. The resources of the juvenile division can be expanded and the commander in charge of that division can set priorities depending upon community demand.

Finally, there is the traditional argument—namely, that specialization leads to expertise and the police agency receives the benefit of efficient, knowledgeable experts by organizing according to divisions. Over time, the delegation of the same type of responsibilities to the same officers means that these officers are continually gathering current information concerning these specialized problems. It means that the department can allocate its in-service training resources to send a few specialists to high-powered training sessions in their fields of expertise. These expert professional law enforcement officers can then apply this specialized knowledge in their divisions. As a consequence, the department does not need to send every officer to every specialized training session to have their offices informed and up to date.

An example might help to clarify this issue. An officer assigned to the traffic division dealing with traffic and accident investigation will expect to be familiar with a wide variety of traffic topics. Subspecialties might be developed in traffic-flow planning, community education, accident investigation, vehicle and traffic law, and drunk driving. One officer might specialize in controlling high-speed chases by having made plans to reorder traffic flow and institute blockades. Another officer might develop expertise in disaster planning; for example, blizzards, hurricanes, and floods and their relationship to traffic flow and accidents.

Looking at the other side of the generalist-specialist controversy, "What occurs when specialization goes too far?" The answer is often that communication breaks down among divisions and individual commanders begin to build bureaucratic empires, wherein one bureau tries to outdo another in competition for perceived glory and resources.

This happens too often in the competition between the patrol and detective divisions. Patrol officers are tightly supervised and are expected to control the crime scene and report the crime to the detective division. Detectives are expected to give the reporting officers credit for their work and follow up the crime with analysis and investigation. Patrol officers are often jealous of the status and control over time that an officer in the detective division enjoys. They also feel that patrol officers may be the first on the scene but the last to receive credit and praise. Often, detectives do feel they are superior and neglect the patrol officers. Over time this can result in patrol officers rationalizing: "Why go out of our way for those guys [detectives]?" or "Let the detectives do it, it's not our job." Sloppy jobs are done on crime scenes and detectives end up *not* utilizing the talents of the patrol officers. Management has to be aware of these tendencies in all divisions and take constant steps to improve communication.

In discussing the duties and responsibilities of line functions, we shall also be looking at certain general principles that can lead to managerial improvements:

1. Assignments for all personnel should be based on the assumption that the job should present new challenges and lead to the acquisition and development of professional skills.

2. The best person should be selected for the job based upon ability, credentials, and track record.

3. Accept that there is a need for certain specialists but keep the number of such specialists and their areas of specialization within reason.

4. On a periodic basis, each agency should review the number of subgroups that exist in the formal organization and the need for their existence. This evaluation should take place in terms of each bureau's contribution to the police mission and whether its functions should be merged or returned to another bureau or division (for example, patrol).

In agencies where the patrol officer is a generalist, performance improvement is best reviewed by tasks rather than by bureautic function. This is done in other sections of the text.

▶ TRAFFIC

In the United States, traffic enforcement has always been a police function since it is related to the police role of protection of life and property. The proliferation of automobiles after World War I, followed by a concomitant rise in fatalities and injuries due to improper automobile usage, prompted many states to enact laws dealing with vehicle use that would be enforced by the police. Today, despite police regulation, traffic deaths and injuries continue to climb each year.

Against this background, the role of the police in this function is multivaried, involving

1. Elimination of accident causes and congestion.
2. Identification of potential traffic problems and hazards.
3. The regulation of parking on the street and at municipal facilities.
4. Investigation of property damage and personal-injury automobile accidents.
5. Directing public awareness toward the proper usage of motor vehicles and bicycles.
6. The arrest of offenders.

Of all the police functions, traffic enforcement is deemed by many officers to be the most frustrating. In the public's mind, traffic offenders are not criminals per se. Therefore, a person receiving a ticket for some violation does not think of himself or herself as a criminal, and resentment is directed toward the officer and the police in general. Moreover, enforcement of the various complex traffic laws produces an endless variety of excuses on the part of the offenders. One police magazine had a column devoted solely to the range of excuses that traffic officers hear before they decide to issue a ticket. Similarly, traffic summonses and parking tickets are the most common of the police processes to be the target of the "fix." The offender and the officials of the justice system feel that the violation was minor compared with the punishment of levying a money fine or the loss or suspension of a license.

However, the police will continue to be the prime enforcers of vehicle and traffic codes for the foreseeable future. Traffic-related problems will continue to be the most common attended to by all line police agencies. Many officers also feel that crimes are discovered and even solved through the process of day-to-day traffic enforcement and traffic stops. At this time, many departments in medium and large cities have specialized sections that deal exclusively with traffic problems. Considerable state police time is devoted exclusively to traffic enforcement on interstate highways and expressways.

EFFECTIVE MANAGEMENT IN TRAFFIC MATTERS

The amount of resources and personnel devoted to traffic enforcement will, of course, depend on the needs of the community. We do, however, offer the following guidelines.

1. Parking enforcement should be done by civilians or traffic wardens. There is little need for trained police officers to be solely involved with issuing parking tickets or directing traffic. These functions are, for the most part, mechanical and do not require a high level of expertise.

2. Patrol officers should be trained in all areas of traffic enforcement, including preliminary accident investigations, use of speed and alcohol detection devices, and knowledge of the vehicle and traffic laws. This aspect of police training is especially important due to the high number of traffic cases that make their way into civil and criminal courts that require review of the actions of the investigating officers and the policies of the department.

3. Certain officers, according to their interests, should be trained in specialized topics such as traffic planning, fatality investigation, and community awareness programs. A number of excellent programs, funded by state and federal highway safety grants, are available for such training. One such example is the course offered by the Traffic Institute sponsored by Northwestern University.

Traffic is primarily a patrol function, since officers on street and road units are in the best position to observe and address traffic violations and hazards. Officers use their investigation skills in work related to accident causation, statute violations, and victim/suspect identification. As has been previously noted, traffic enforcement frequently uncovers other criminal activity. Traffic enforcement frequently uncovers stolen cars, wanted persons, and contraband. Some danger is involved in this aspect of police work since the officer can never know whether the driver or passenger is armed.

▶ VICE

Vice is generally considered to be crimes against public morals. Examples of vice offenses are

1. Pornography
2. Prostitution
3. Gambling
4. Illegal drugs (controlled substances)
5. Illegal sale and manufacture of alcohol

These have historically been a province of the police because of public clamor for enforcement of laws created to eliminate these activities.

Often these offenses are considered victimless or nonpredatory crimes. The offender is normally offering a service or buying a service. If there were no customers for vice crimes, there would be no vice. In the area of drug addiction, however, there are secondary victims, as the drug addict attempts to "feed his habit" through street crimes. Also, there are cases of pimps placing young women on habit-forming drugs to enslave them in a life of prostitution. However, because these crimes are perceived as victimless by much of the public, vice laws are especially hard to enforce. In some communities, there is political pressure not to enforce certain of the vice laws. In other locales, what is a crime in one community may be legal a few feet across the county or state line. This is especially true in states that have legalized gambling.

Since the repeal of Prohibition, vice activities are traditionally perceived as being under the control of nationwide syndicates. Research in this area found that although there is syndicated crime, it is not as organized as was once believed (Rubinstein, 1973; Ianni, 1974; Blakley and others, 1978; Fowler and others, 1978; Steffensmeier, 1986; Rowan, 1986). For example, in one survey of gambling enforcement (Fowler and others, 1978: iii–iv), the following major conclusions were reached:

1. Legislators have given police a relatively unattractive job for which police can get little credit if they do a good job and considerable abuse if they fail.

2. The laws against public social gambling and commercial gambling probably are enforceable to the extent that other comparable laws are enforceable. Consistent with the relatively low priority of gambling, the resources devoted to gambling law enforcement are very modest. The results, with a few notable exceptions, are modest as well.

3. Citizens are very likely to view nonenforcement of gambling laws as an indication of police corruption.

4. Regional, multiservice criminal organizations were reported to directly control all or a substantial portion of illegal commercial gambling operations in about half the cities surveyed. Three cities were more likely than others to have had publicly disclosed gambling-related corruption in the past. In the balance of the cities, bookmaking and numbers operations were said to be run primarily by local, independent organizations that specialized in gambling. There had been no significant publicly disclosed gambling-related corruption in any of these cities in the past ten years.

5. The prosecutors of gambling cases generally do not recommend penalties for conviction, which any reasonable person would think would be a deterrent to further involvement in commercial gambling.

With the exception of drug traffic, these conclusions could be reached in the study of most vice statute enforcement programs.

The use of drugs by criminals is becoming increasingly widespread. According to federal report *Report to the Nation on Crime and Justice* (U.S. Department of Justice, 1983:39), more than 75 percent of all inmates had used illegal drugs, about double the rate for the U.S. population. One-third of all inmates drank heavily and two-thirds of these inmates drank heavily every day. Twenty-eight percent of the inmates used heroin, 41 percent used cocaine, and 40 percent used amphetamines and barbiturates. The Rand study of career criminals found that "felon drug abusers committed more burglaries, con-type crimes and drugs sales than burglars, con-men and drug dealers who did not use drugs." Forty percent of the inmates said that they were very drunk or under the influence of drugs when they committed their offense.

James Inciardi, in his book, *The War on Drugs*, concluded (1986: 131–32) that "drug related crime is out of control....Since less than 1 percent of the crimes committed result in arrest, it would appear that the efficient control of drug-related crime is well beyond the scope of contemporary policing." He interviewed 573 narcotic users in Miami and discovered that they had committed 215,000 crimes. Now, 82,000 crimes or 38 percent were drug sales, while an additional 22 percent were victimless crimes such as prostitution and gambling. However (Inciardi, 1986: 126–27), "the same 573 narcotic uses were also responsible for almost 6,000 robberies and assaults, and almost 6,700 burglaries, almost 900 stolen vehicles, more than 25,000 instances of shoplifting, and more than 46,000 other events of larceny and fraud." However, we must agree with Inciardi that narcotic addiction does not "cause" crime; rather (Inciardi, 1986: 130), "narcotics drive crime. When comparing the two groups, the narcotics users were involved with greater frequency, intensity, diversity and severity than the non-narcotic users."

This mini crime wave of 215,000 offenses resulted in 609 arrests; that is, 0.3 percent or one arrest for every 353 crimes. With an estimated half a million drug addicts in the United States, law enforcement management has a major problem on its hands. The drug crime problem is interjurisdictional, international, and often entails prominent members of the community. Interagency and interjurisdictional cooperation and the protection of the drug enforcement unit from politics are policies that make sense in this sensitive area. However, there are few strategies that have worked in controlling the overall problem of crime and drugs. Given the magnitude of the problem it won't go away. It will take up an increasing amount of any department's time as the drug abuse problem becomes more widespread and violent.

Prostitution at one time flourished in most American cities in red-light districts and brothels. Today the traditional brothel has been replaced by street walkers, massage parlors, dating services, and "weekend" hookers who may or may not be organized.

Regardless of the controversy on the organizational structure of syndicated crime, vice street offenses present the police agency with an immediate host of problems, especially if they occur in a specific area. Beyond the commission of the offense, a variety of secondary effects can occur: customers can be "rolled," other crimes may be committed, and the area may undergo an economic decline. Vice activity that operates without interference by the police, either in a concentrated or nonconcentrated area (citywide), is perceived by the public to mean that the police are being paid to look the other way.

The enforcement of vice laws is equally frustrating to police officers. The dictum that "the offender goes back on the street before the arresting officer completes the paperwork" is true! This is due to the relative ease with which offenders raise bail or pay the nonjail fines that are meted out by the courts. Police officers often agree with a common public attitude that vice offenses are less harmful when compared with violent crimes. This view can be reflected in organizational policy in terms of low priority for vice enforcement. Gambling enforcement is generally viewed by police officers as a source of frustration and is an unpopular assignment.

While there is a need for some personnel to have a long-term assignment to vice investigation to establish continuity, generally vice assignments should be of short duration. Continuity is needed to understand the scope of the problem and the nature of investigation methodology, to establish solid interjurisdictional working arrangements, and to train new officers. Short duration is needed for most vice assignments because faces soon become known, especially in undercover work, and officers lose much of their investigative value. Vice investigation is demoralizing, frustrating, and dangerous, and often without the kind of backup officers would like to have. It takes a special kind of individual to work undercover, and it creates definite morale and personnel problems for police management.

Units to investigate organized crime are usually found in federal law enforcement agencies and large city and state police departments because of the multijurisdictional and international nature of cases. Investigations are very expensive in terms of personnel and equipment requirements. Organized crime units investigate the following activities:

1. The distribution and manufacturing of narcotics.
2. Unlawful gambling enterprises.
3. Professional theft and fencing network.
4. The lending of money at high rates of interest to be collected by force or financial takeover.
5. Bribery, extortion, embezzlement, and fraud in unions and businesses.
6. Corruption of public officials.
7. Economic crimes involving financial offenses against business, investors, and consumers.

Since the prosecuting element is so important in ongoing organized-crime investigations, the most effective units are those that include representatives from the district attorney's offices.

The organized-crime unit needs state and federal and, at times, local representatives along with intelligence analysts and other experts. Areas of expertise include those that involve technical skills in the areas of photography, electronic surveillance, polished detective skills, and content expertise in the various areas of organized crime such as narcotics and fraud. There is a need to include special security controls, including location and protection for informants and witnesses. Since much of this type of investigation, along with a spillover into white-collar crime investigation, means having to follow a line of money to discover the criminals and convict them, an investigative account is essential to the work.

To be successful, there must be a major investment in skilled personnel and equipment accompanied by a great deal of multijurisdictional cooperation. With ongoing investigations, a "screened" representative from the local vice squad may prove useful. (*Screening* means that the individual has been carefully investigated in terms of the need for security for the total investigation.)

Added to this area of crime investigation is computer crime. Computer crimes include a number of offenses such as invading systems to scan information, change data, transfer funds and steal money, or place a "bomb" in a program that will "zap" data. These crimes also include the commission of crimes with the aid of the computer, such as financial fraud. Because of increased reliance on computers for daily transactions in all areas of life, individual consumers and computer systems are subject to criminal use and invasion and destruction. Examples of computer crime in the daily news are common. However, computer crime investigation units on the state and local level are a rarity.

Obviously, personnel involved in computer crime units must have advanced training in computer science and programming and Internet applications. Computer case investigation is very arduous and difficult to prosecute, mainly because most judges and juries have a difficult time understanding case evidence.

 ## YOUTH SERVICES AND JUVENILE AID UNITS

The police are the main component in the criminal justice system with whom juvenile offenders come into contact. And the police confrontation is highly significant in determining the number and types of cases that eventually proceed to juvenile court. Many jurisdictions agree with the *least coercive* recommendation of the task force in *Juvenile Justice and Delinquency Prevention* (National Advisory Commission, 1976: 186): "To respect family autonomy and minimize coercive State intervention, law enforcement officers dealing with juveniles should be authorized and encouraged to use the least coercive among reasonable alternatives, consistent with preserving public safety, order and individual liberty."

Thus, in most jurisdictions, almost all police-juvenile interactions and confrontations result in informal action or are settled with warnings of future severe action. The task-force recommendations on when counseling and releasing should take place rather than court action are a general guideline used by most jurisdictions (1976: 210):

1. *The nature of the alleged delinquent act.* In cases of minor delinquent acts such as disorderly conduct where there are no other serious negative factors, police should consider releasing the youth.

2. *Juveniles' previous behavioral history.* The presence or absence of a prior history of serious law violations should be given substantial weight in making a release decision.

3. *Circumstances possibly contributing to the alleged delinquent act.* Investigation may turn up important information about the youth's neighborhood or associates, which may be influencing negative behavior.

4. *Juvenile's willingness to reform.* The juvenile should demonstrate a cooperative attitude; assurance of good conduct is an important factor.

5. *Parental supervision.* Interest and attitude of the parents or guardians toward the juvenile and the alleged law violation as well as their ability to provide the necessary supervision and guidance.

The task force also recommends interviewing the parents at home. Judgments can be best made by the police officer concerning the youth's living conditions and the ability of the parents to supervise the youth in the youth's home environment.

In cases that are more serious or that involve repeat offenders or suspects who have attitude problems, the result may be official action followed by an appearance in family court. This also happens when the complainant presses for some official action. In large departments, this action might take place at the juvenile bureau that was part of the investigation division; in medium-sized departments, this action might take place in the juvenile unit that was part of the patrol division; in smaller departments, most likely a juvenile officer who reports directly to the chief would handle this matter.

BACKGROUND

Juvenile-aid divisions were formed in the early part of this century in response to urban crime and related social problems involving children, many of whom were newly arrived immigrants. The legal and social reforms that gave certain protections and services to children were based, in part, on two theories developed in the common law: that of **doli incapax**, a child under a certain age is incapable of wrongdoing, and that of **parens patriae**, the state must assume the role of the parents if the parents cannot live up to their responsibilities in the care of the child. In all states, children under a certain age, usually 16, are accorded the title of *juvenile* for criminal and civil matters.

Until the 1960s, the rules of criminal prosecution for children regarding their legal rights under due process were ill defined. In 1967, in a case titled *In re Gault*, the U.S. Supreme Court ruled that children must be afforded the same legal protections as adults. In many localities, the investigation and prosecution of juvenile cases is strictly defined by state statute and is reinforced by rules and procedures of juvenile court. In most states, a juvenile suspect cannot be questioned unless accompanied by a parent. The place where the interrogation occurs has to be in a nonpolice atmosphere, which is defined as being a room or office away from the mainstream of police activity. Juveniles cannot be confined in adult jail lockups but must be transported and held in special juvenile facilities.

The range of juvenile offenses, however, also incorporates offenses that would not be considered offenses if the act or activity were committed by an adult. We are referring here to **status offenses**. These include running away from home, truancy, not behaving according to parental rules in the home.

Many officials and the general public remained concerned about the rise of juvenile crime versus the revolving-door system of justice that appears to let juvenile suspects go free with no punishment. Charles E. Silberman, in his review of the criminal justice system (1980:355), found that most juveniles do not receive any type of sentence in juvenile court until they have been before a judge the fourth or fifth time. He concludes:

> If "nothing happens" until the fourth or fifth offense (or, in some instances, the ninth or tenth), young offenders are persuaded that they have an implicit contract with the juvenile court permitting them to break the law. Therefore, when something does happen—when a severe sanction is imposed at an earlier point—delinquents feel that their contract has been violated unilaterally and their sense of justice is outraged. "I was sent here on a bum rap," a youngster in a California training school told me, in tones of great moral indignation. What he meant, I discovered, was not that he was innocent of the robbery charge on which he had been convicted, but that "the judge sent me here on the third offense, instead of waiting until the fifth."

As a result, many states are lowering the age at which the juvenile is treated as an adult if he or she commits a felony, which means criminal court and adult arrest procedures and incarceration. Thus, rape, robbery, arson, and murder become adult offenses if they occur within a certain age bracket and under certain circumstances. The trend is to "get tough," a posture that will have a significant effect on how police behave with juvenile offenders.

ROLE OF JUVENILE AID

Having this general background in mind, the police juvenile aid operation or division performs a variety of activities. First, it must act as a protector of children's rights, seeing that the rules of criminal prosecution for criminal and status offenses are maintained. Then, it must see that the security of the community is maintained—the public has the right to be safe from youth crimes. Third, it must deal with children who are victims of parental abuse or neglect.

In summary, the juvenile aid division does the following:

1. *Investigation of juvenile cases.* This involves not only criminal cases where the suspects may be juveniles but also cases where juveniles are victims. Generally, cases involving adult crimes committed by juveniles are handled by regular investigative and patrol personnel. When an arrest has been made, or a suspect has been brought in for questioning, the juvenile aid personnel should be notified. Those cases involving status offenses or child victims should be handled by the juvenile aid personnel. In many situations, cases of this nature do not involve a typical police response but demand patience, knowledge of referral agencies, family crisis intervention skills, and counseling techniques. The officer may need to handle child abuse. Or there may be cases of simple neglect. In one case, an officer walked into a home and saw a child being bathed on one side of a tub while there were feces on the other side. It takes a strong stomach to handle these cases. Normally, social agencies are available to work with these parents, but in the long night hours immediate police action may be necessary.

2. *Screening of cases.* Cases forwarded to the juvenile aid division must be screened for a future course of action. The recommendations of the investigator or the patrol officer should be taken into consideration in view of their familiarity with the circumstances surrounding the case. It is at this stage that the juvenile aid officer may wish to divert the case from the normal progression found in the criminal justice system to either a formal or informal mode of treatment. Such options include referral to a community agency, police counseling, or **stationhouse probation**, where the offender reports to the juvenile aid division on a regular basis to account for his or her actions during the week. The case may be disposed of if the situation warrants restitution and it is made, or there are no grounds for future action.

3. *Preparation of cases for juvenile court.* The necessary paperwork and evidence must be gathered by the officer if the case is forwarded to the juvenile court. The experienced juvenile aid officer will know how to present the documentation needed for the court as well as be able to keep track of when the case will be called. The officer should follow the ultimate disposition of the case, and advise the initial arresting officer(s) of the results.

4. *Community liaison.* This is an important aspect of the juvenile aid function. The police should be viewed as the experts in all areas of crime in the community, especially that related to youth. This will be important for the planning and funding of special programs undertaken

by community groups for juveniles. At the same time, the police should maintain an active liaison with community groups that are involved with problems with juveniles such as the YMCA/YWCA, Catholic Charities, and the school district.

Another aspect of community liaison involves keeping abreast of community programs where children may be referred if there is a need for special treatment. Those might include those programs involving youth employment, professional counseling vocational training, and recreational activities.

JUVENILE RECORDKEEPING

Information regarding youth crime must be stored in an area that is maintained separate from adult files. In most cases, the case folder is confidential and not subject to any review except by youth-division personnel. At the same time, there is a need for information on youth crime, projected trends, and gang activity that must be available and disseminated to the department and, at times, to the community.

While all officers should have the training to deal in all aspects of juvenile crime, specialization in this area is needed due to the ever-changing rules and statutes on juvenile prosecution as well as the development of new skills and knowledge. In short, personnel assigned to juvenile duties should be trained for and considered experts on all matters of juvenile crime and procedure. They should be consulted by members of the department for their expertise and continually called on for juvenile interactions, especially by the patrol section.

PERSONNEL SELECTION FOR JUVENILE AID

In the past, the juvenile aid units were staffed by women officers and older "father figure" officers. This was unfair to both the older officers and females since it stereotyped their professional roles. Personnel in juvenile departments should be highly trained individuals who are picked or volunteer because they have some talent in working with the juvenile offender. The task force report, *Juvenile Justice and Delinquency Prevention*, was very clear about this (National Advisory Commission, 1976: 256):

> Police juvenile officers should be assigned by chief executives on the basis of departmental written and oral examination rather than being appointed by a civil service or merit commission. Juvenile officers should, if possible, be selected from among the department's experienced line officers. Selection boards established to interview candidates for the position of police juvenile officer should include police department command officers and selected individuals from the juvenile justice system and public youth agencies.

In addition, it is recommended that qualified officers be able to pursue a career as police juvenile specialists and have the same opportunities for advancement and promotion as are available to the other officers in the department.

ORGANIZATION OF JUVENILE AID OPERATIONS

As discussed before, depending upon the department, a specialized juvenile unit should be organized. In the smaller departments, at least one officer should have the specialized knowledge needed to deal with juvenile offenders.

A juvenile specialist provides the department with an expert in the juvenile court procedures and juvenile offenses that are normally handled differently from adult offenses. This officer can also develop ongoing useful relationships with whatever youth-service agencies exist in the area. Interestingly, he or she can provide useful information in the solving of cases for the detective division. Many a case has been solved through information that juvenile offenders have mentioned casually to the juvenile police specialist.

Some departments have initiated a family service bureau. Most problems with juvenile offenders start and end in the home. Police officers have found time and time again that the troubled youth of the community come from disrupted families. To deal with this situation, some departments have combined juvenile services and domestic crisis intervention so that a total approach to potential offenders can be developed. Also with the family-service-bureau approach it may be more likely that the agency can provide proper referral service for the whole family. For example, the father might be an alcoholic, the mother might be out working, and there is no adult babysitter in the home. The older boy becomes a juvenile delinquent while the younger children wander the streets, say, a couple with drug problems and the younger sister, still in junior high school, is pregnant. This family needs help, but it might not be provided if only one family member at a time is seen by police officers. Bureaus dealing with such families have proved successful in Dade County, Florida, and Dayton, Ohio.

The task force on *Juvenile Justice and Delinquency Prevention* summarizes the basic organizational structure of the juvenile unit as follows (National Advisory Committee, 1976: 245): "This unit should be functionally centralized to the most effective command level; and should be assigned responsibility for conducting as many juvenile investigations as possible, assisting field offices in juvenile cases and maintaining liaison with other agencies and organizations interested in juvenile matters." The basic recommendation is a separate unit in medium-sized and larger-sized departments. This unit would have its own command structure and should be commanded by an officer of sufficiently high rank to deal effectively with the command structure of patrol and detectives while interacting with the heads of major youth-service agencies such as probation, juvenile court or a state division for youth. In most departments, this would normally mean the rank of lieutenant or captain. It would also show other officers in the force that one could rise in rank in juvenile work and that the chief respected the juvenile unit.

Officers in this juvenile unit could also specialize. One officer might learn the juvenile law and keep abreast of late-breaking legal developments. Another might specialize as a liaison officer with various juvenile agencies in the community. And another might develop relationships with local merchants to help solve and prevent juvenile crime directed toward business and commercial establishments (shoplifting, burglary).

However the unit is organized, it can be of great value to the total department. The department will have its own team of experts on juvenile offenders to be used as referrals, for their knowledge and for training.

Related to traditional juvenile aid responsibilities are gang monitoring and suppression. Juvenile gangs are defined as groups comprised of youths between the ages of 11 and 18 who commit crimes over a long period of time. These groups have a succession of leadership, are clearly identifiable by various types of dress, and are held together by race, ethnicity, or common geographical area.

Dealing with youth gangs involves monitoring members, training parents and groups dealing with juveniles on gang trends, intercepting and investigating criminal activities, and counseling members when they decide to leave the gang. The activities of gang intervention personnel also become pivotal when city or area resources are directed to gang suppression, whereby leading members are arrested and prosecuted.

MODEL YOUTH PROGRAMS

The following descriptions are taken from a variety of police youth programs found in a variety of police agencies throughout the United States. Not every agency may wish to promote every item in this program. This model can, however, serve as a source of ideas when youth programs are developed for specific agencies. Let us examine some general guidelines for these programs:

1. All programs should be open to all youths regardless of gender or background. Although delinquent youths may be the target population, it would be unfortunate to have all program participants labeled "bad." Thus, the police are said to run this program for "bad kids and hoods." This outcome will most likely further rather than prevent delinquency. So once again, open the programs to all community youths.

2. The program should not be expensive to join. Unless they steal or burglarize, most delinquent youths cannot afford expensive equipment. Thus, most programs have to be subsidized or not need expensive equipment. Once again, the programs must be open to all the youths in the community.

3. The objectives of these programs are to prevent delinquency and to enhance the image of police officers among youth of the community. A secondary objective is to develop information and informants concerning juvenile activity. Thus, many programs that may seem, on

the surface, unrelated to police activities, such as baseball games or canoe trips, become valuable as part of the work of a police juvenile specialist.

Following is a discussion of a variety of programs that have been tried—some with more success than others. All programs will have to be adapted to local conditions.

Mobil neighborhood watch

Patterned after traditional neighborhood watch programs, participants use their own vehicles and are equipped with mobile phones to call in for police assistance with juvenile gang activity. Other activities may include graffiti removal, clean-up programs, and youth athletic programs.

Neutral zone

Activities are provided in a designated area during high crime hours or weekends for area youth. In Mountlake Terrace, Washington, the police department and volunteers run such a program in the local high school and provide meals, athletic opportunities, tutoring, and a food and clothing bank. According to the Crime Prevention Coalition (1996) a key concern is safety for the participants; thus, gang affiliation clothing is prohibited and pat-down searches are required for entry into the area.

Parent networks

This is a venture whereby parents are urged to get to know their children's friends and to share ideas and concerns about behavior and activities. Juvenile units provide brochures and speakers to talk about networking and responsible hosting of parties and sleepovers.

Explorer Posts

Many departments have established police explorer posts to work with youths who have indicated an interest in law enforcement. The Boy Scout model of exploring involves the formation of a post, sponsored by a host agency, that will involve youths between the ages of 14 and 21 in a vocational or educational field. Some larger police departments, such as Suffolk County, New York Police, are able to sponsor as many as seven different explorer posts throughout their jurisdiction.

The explorer concept is designed to allow youths to gain firsthand information on law enforcement operations and career possibilities. Explorers are assigned various station-house tasks in addition to formal classroom learning. Many agencies even allow their explorers to ride along with regular officers on patrol. Explorer post members can also be of great assistance at parades, field days, and other large public gatherings requiring personnel for traffic and crowd control. Many departments issue their explorers a distinctive uniform for this purpose.

While the explorer concept offers unending possibilities for police-youth interaction, some drawbacks must be pointed out. Agencies that invest their total youth resources on exploring soon learn that not all youths are attracted to this type of program, especially those who would be termed "delinquent." On the other hand, some youths are attracted to police explorer or other volunteer groups since they provide the youth with the opportunity to act out authoritarian tendencies or to capture the excitement of police work. Members of explorer posts can be subject to ridicule and abuse in the school setting, since they are looked upon by peers as police informants. Therefore, the continuance of such a program by the police agency can, at times, be a trying experience. The role of the police advisor will vary from personnel and recruitment manager, to counselor, and to general troubleshooter.

School Liaison Programs

In many communities, the presence of police patrol cars in the school parking lot signifies that there is trouble of one form or another, since school officials generally call for the police only as a last resort. In reality, the police presence at school has become commonplace in many cities and communities due to rise in teacher and student assaults, drug use, and property crime occurring during regular school hours. In many cities, police units patrol the school grounds and buildings as a normal assignment.

As a result, many schools and police agencies have initiated formal and informal relationships in dealing with school crime. Sitting down and discussing mutual concerns can be viewed as an important first step for many communities whose citizens may perceive the school and immediate grounds as "out of bounds" for regular police operations. An important part of this relationship is an agreement as to how and when police officers will be summoned for school-related situations, including arrests on campus or during school hours, the types of incidents that result in immediate dispatch of officers, the interception of non-student trespassers on school property, and crowd control at school events.

As one solution, the school-liaison-officer program, a police officer is assigned to a school on a continuous basis. The officer's presence in the school is not so much for law enforcement or intelligence purposes, rather, it is a learning and community resource for school administrators, teachers, and students. Here the officer might teach a course on crime problems or police operations, assist teachers in the preparation of course materials related to law enforcement and criminal justice, or meet informally with students to discuss issues that are of concern to them.

Drug Abuse Resistance Education (DARE)

This program is presented by specially trained officers to reduce drug, alcohol and tobacco use by children. Instead of using scare tactics, the program teaches life skills such as making choices and dealing with peer pressure. Program topics include drug information, assertiveness, stress, personal safety, and the consequences of behavior. The 17-week elementary school curriculum for fifth and sixth graders is taught in classrooms during the regular school day. Begun in Los Angeles, many states have adopted this program for implementation in all schools. Posters, T-shirts. DARE patrol vehicles and other visual aids are augmented through private contributions.

Athletic Programs

In the early part of this century, many urban police departments formed athletic programs to offer underprivileged youths a chance to participate in organized sports programs. Today, these programs, Police Athletic Leagues, still exist but in name only. Private charities eventually took over the entire responsibility for the programs. The police connection exists only for fund-raising purposes.

Sports and athletic programs provide a good environment and opportunity for police-youth interaction. In most communities, officer volunteers provide the staffing support. Frequently, the department or the police union may sponsor a team in an organized athletic program such as Little League or Youth Hockey, with police officers acting as coaches or trainers.

Outdoor Adventure Programs

These programs are variations of the Outward Bound model offering youths a series of wilderness challenges. Programs of this nature cannot always be operated in a traditional shift time span and may run into political and union opposition as the following case study illustrates.

In the absence of opposition, many programs operate successfully for many years. It is hard to feel hostile toward the police officer who guided you on an overnight camping trip as many a potential delinquent and many an officer have found out to their mutual satisfaction.

POLICE YOUTH PROGRAM POTPOURRI

Ride-along programs. Youths ride along with officers in their patrol cars and observe police in action.

Drug-testing programs. Police agencies identify any suspicious materials found in the home.

Speakers' bureaus. Officers are available on a continuing basis to speak to various youth groups. Speakers can be generalists or specialists.

Columns in youth-oriented publications. Question-and-answer columns for youths on police matters are written for teenage publications; format can also be used as a weekly radio program on a youth-oriented music station.

Stranger danger program. Officers work closely with elementary schoolchildren to warn them of the dangers of going with strangers and to identify various entrapment techniques.

One summer, the Oakdale Police Department embarked on an ambitious program for youths in their community: a 10-day canoe trip to the nearby Allegheny Mountains. Youths who had been in trouble with the police during the year were selected as participants. The objective was to give these youngsters a chance to spend time in the outdoors, learn camping skills, and meet the police in a nonconfrontational atmosphere.

One of the two officers assigned to the group was a state-certified guide. Various civilian volunteers also accompanied the group. The officers were paid their normal salaries.

The trip was successful, and plans were made for another trip in the following year. Opposition to this concept arose from certain members of the city council, however, who argued that police officers should be paid to patrol city streets, not to conduct camping expeditions. As the controversy mounted, the officers argued that they could only accompany the group if they were paid overtime along with their normal salary, which since they were away from home for 10 days amounted to some 200 hours per officer.

Opposition to the program was stifled when community leaders and the newspaper came out in total support for the program.

In the final compromise, it was decided that only youths who lived in the municipality and one police officer would be allowed to go. The trip, moreover, was reduced from 10 days to 7 days.

Station house probation. This is a community restitution program whereby juveniles are sentenced to work at the police station.

Police probation counseling center. In this center, jointly administered by probation and police agencies, police officers bring youths in trouble and juvenile offenders for counseling and referral to youth service agencies.

 # INVESTIGATIONS

Investigations is the police activity concerned with (1) the apprehension of criminals by the gathering of evidence leading to their arrest and (2) the collection and presentation of evidence and testimony for the purpose of obtaining convictions. Investigations is normally divided into two major areas of activity: (1) the preliminary investigation normally carried out by officers in the uniform patrol division and (2) the follow-up investigation normally carried out by officers formally trained in investigative techniques, often part of a detective bureau.

In larger departments, a division or bureau is responsible for follow-up investigations; special investigations are assigned by the chief of police. Additionally, this function also covers the recovery of stolen property, the gathering of criminal intelligence, and the preparation of cases for trial. Organizationally, this division may be titled *Detective, Central Investigation*, or *Criminal Investigation*. For our purposes, we will use the simple title of *Investigations*.

The role of the investigator is probably the most glamorous one in the police department. This modern Sherlock Holmes is portrayed in movies, television, and novels as a meticulous and tireless gatherer of evidence that miraculously leads to the arrest and conviction of criminals. As shown on the television series *N.Y.P.D. Blue*, this super police officer is a bit unorthodox, normally at odds with his superiors, and normally willing to bend the rules, especially if this involves a deliberate violation of departmental directives. Embedded in a web of unsavory informers the heroic investigator maintains integrity in his unrelenting pursuit of crime and the master criminal.

The public, and to some extent the patrol officer, maintains this glorified notion of what an investigator is all about. Reality, as usual, is a mixture of fact and fiction. In some cases, detective work is all that the media says it is, but in most investigative jobs it is a series of monotonous tasks that may or may not lead to a break in case. Long, hard hours are put in interviewing neighbors after a major crime has taken place. One of the best examples of the everyday work of the detective is found in the portrait of Al Seedman, chief of the New York City detectives (Seedman and Hellman, 1974: 4);

> Throughout his career Seedman often obtained his solution by using his intelligence on the mundane, seemingly unrelated information that a record-oriented society can provide if only one knew how to find it.

For example, police in a small town found a male skeleton and asked Seedman for advice on how to find out who it was. Seedman asked if there were signs of dental work and the answer was no, even though the teeth were in poor repair. Normally, dental work is the easiest way of identifying a body, even though the investigator has to interview dentist after dentist until the correct records are found.)

Seedman then reasoned that if the person had had money, his teeth would have been repaired; also, the teeth would have been repaired if the man had worked in a union job or was on welfare. The skeleton didn't match any missing person report. Seedman told the local police to wait until the end of the year and then (1974: 5)

> go to the IRS and get a printout of all single males making less than $10,000 a year, but more than the welfare ceiling, who paid tax in the first three quarters but not on the fourth. Chances are the name of their skeleton will be on the printout.

This is the way many investigations are solved—step by laborious step. Unlike the outcomes on television and in the movies, clearance on crimes investigated against property is less than 20 percent. This means that over 80 percent of these types of crimes investigated are never solved.

PRELIMINARY INVESTIGATIONS

Cases would not be solved and offenders would not be arrested unless patrol officers were willing and able to use some preliminary investigation skills. The patrol officer's tasks in crime incidents normally entail both investigative and noninvestigative action. O.W. Wilson (1963: 282) gives us an excellent listing of these duties, under the heading PRELIMINARY:

P	Proceed to the scene with safety and dispatch.
R	Render assistance to the injured.
E	Effect arrest of perpetrator.
L	Locate and identify witnesses.
I	Interview complainant and witnesses.
M	Maintain scene and protect evidence.
I	Interrogate suspects.
N	Note all conditions, events, and remarks.
A	Arrange for collection of evidence.
R	Report incident fully and accurately.
Y	Yield responsibility to detectives.

One of the most important duties of the police officer responding to a crime call is to secure the crime scene. Cases are often lost because reporters, higher administrative officials, and various other personnel are allowed to indiscriminately contaminate a scene by handling evidence or walking through the area. There have even been cases of patrol officers taking weapons from a crime scene and turning them in two or three days later.

To win a case, there must be continuity of the evidence from the scene of the crime, to the vaults of the police laboratory or property room, to the hands of the prosecuting district attorney. Documentation must be made of any person who handled any piece of evidence and the circumstances under which these pieces of evidence were handled. Otherwise, alert defense lawyers can point to the discrepancies and win cases on technicalities.

It is a cardinal rule in most agencies that there should be only one person in charge at any crime scene. Once the scene is secured by the first officer(s) at the scene, those assigned to evidence collection should be in charge. In some instances this may be the responding officer who is also a trained evidence technician, or it may necessitate summoning others with the necessary expertise and equipment. In any event, no one else—victims, witnesses, higher police officials, other police officers not assigned to the case, reporters, TV crews—should be permitted access to the crime scene area until a thorough examination has been completed and all photographs taken and evidence collected.

Evidence should be photographed in place, marked properly by the person discovering it, placed in a sealed or appropriate container to prevent contamination, and prepared for transportation in a manner designed to maintain continuity.

The use of patrol officers for preliminary investigations, as O.W. Wilson points out, helps to relieve the detective force of many time-consuming tasks. This practice enables the detectives to concentrate their specialized skills on the tasks for which they have been trained as a more efficient use of skilled personnel. This use of the patrol officer is also important for the morale of the total agency.

Since the vast majority of positions in a police agency are for uniformed officers, the average officer will never have an opportunity to become an investigator. Expanding the uniformed officer's role, however, helps (1) make the officer more aware of his or her basic responsibilities in protecting the scene (2) promote the feeling of belonging to a team rather than being only a **reporter** called to contain the scene until the "specialists" arrive, and (3) the officer and the department to evaluate future assignments in the investigative areas.

Management should publicly acknowledge the positive contributions of the uniformed police officer as well as his or her detective counterpart in the successful conclusion of cases. When an officer can see that a positive contribution has been made and that he or she will receive recognition for that contribution, the officer will become a more positive and effective employee.

However, patrol officers have limited training in investigative skills and have little time to give to any investigation if the municipality is to have effective police coverage. As a result, the time-consuming process of follow-up investigation is often assigned to specialists.

FOLLOW-UP INVESTIGATIONS

This is actually a continuation of the preliminary investigation through the arrest stage and, it is hoped, conviction. The follow-up investigation can be divided into three phases: early, intermediate, and final. Each phase requires a variety of tasks. Harry Caldwell has spelled out these tasks clearly and concisely (1972: 62–63):

Early Phase

1. A thorough review of all reports relative to the offense.
2. A reinterview of all persons with information relating to the offense.
3. An attempt to relate the physical evidence to the crime.
4. A continuing search for persons with information relating to the crime.
5. A refinement of the pickup broadcasts on suspects and the distribution of pickups to the appropriate law enforcement agencies.

Intermediate Phase

1. Application of the modus operandi files to the particular offense in an attempt to identify the perpetrator.

2. Identification of the perpetrator by fingerprints, physical evidence, or eyewitnesses.

3. The filing of appropriate criminal charges against the perpetrator.

4. The arrest of the perpetrator and recovery of additional evidence associated with the crime.

5. The recovery of property stolen in the offense.

Final Phase

1. The preparation of reports upon which the prosecution of the case is based.

2. The provision of sufficient relevant testimony to prove all necessary elements of the offense.

3. The presentation, in court, of testimony relating to the follow-up investigation.

As long as we have our present court system, these tasks will have to be fulfilled. In the future, however, the intermediate phase will become increasingly complex as computers are used as a tool by investigative units. At the present, it is possible to do a computer search by alias, modus operandi, and thousands of other set sorts. Currently, systems are being interlocked so that a search can take in a local area, county, state, and in some instances, the nation. However, no matter how good the tools, cases will ultimately be solved by a well-trained investigator with an instinct for human folly.

TRADITIONAL STRUCTURE

Historically, the investigations divisions of large urban police departments have been removed from the mainstream of police operations in the station houses. In general, a person enters a detective or investigative squad room by invitation only.

In the early days of policing in the United States, it was the prime task of the police investigator to cultivate informers. This was relatively easy at the time as both the criminals and the police most often grew up in the same neighborhoods. Related to the cultivation of informers was another task—the regulation of vice activity. The combination of these two tasks, with few records being made of payoffs for information and the considerable amounts of unrecorded money surrounding vice activity, led to the problem in police corruption, a problem that has persisted to the present.

However, as any competent detective will continue to tell you, his informers are his stock in trade and he could not stay in business without them. In one crucial area, drug investigation, it has been well documented that these investigators could not operate without informants. As Skolnick states (1975: 120), "Without a network of informers—usually civilians, sometimes police—narcotic police cannot operate." Another study of the role of informant in narcotics enforcement (Williams and Redlinger, 1979: 24) agrees with Skolnick and concludes, "the use of flipped and paid informants gives narcotic agents their best opportunity to enforce drug laws which are, by and large, unenforceable." Interestingly enough, this study of six narcotic units throughout the United States considered other informants—John Q. Citizen types or other police—to be less useful than the paid or flipped informant. The **flipped informant** is an arrestee who agrees to inform for considerations such as nonprosecution, plea reduction, and so on.

In police departments that have a traditional organizational structure, the detective or investigative division still retains an elite position. According to Niederhoffer (1969: 82), many patrol officers aspire to be detectives or investigators not only for new challenges but to be able to wear street clothes and enjoy the relative freedom from constant supervision. Given the present conservative structure of most police departments, this holds true today.

In many cases, appointment to investigator does not entail an increase in rank or pay. What does occur is a raise in status as defined by the police subculture. A major way to gain status in the uninformed culture of the police agency is to get out of uniform. This signifies that the officer is reaching a more professional, executive status where he or she is able to take command of important departmental matters.

THE RAND STUDY

The value of the traditional investigative division in terms of crime solving and contributions to the overall role of the police agency was questioned in a study conducted by the Rand Corporation in 1976 (Greenwood and others, 1976). In reviewing the operations of 23 police departments, the researchers found that generally

1. Clearance rates by investigation divisions are unreliable. Most crimes are cleared (an arrest made) during the initial investigation by patrol officers.

2. Many reported felonies receive no more than superficial attention. In reality, minor property crimes are not even investigated.

3. Too much physical evidence is collected. Most items of evidentiary nature cannot be processed in the crime laboratory.

4. For many cases there is a serious gap between the prosecutor and the investigator. Key evidentiary facts that could help the prosecutor obtain a conviction are not documented by the investigator.

5. Too much time is spent locating witnesses and reviewing reports on cases that will never be solved. There is also considerable time that cannot be accounted for in the daily tour of duty, which leads to suspicion that too much time is spent on personal errands.

The conclusions raised by this study point out that perhaps investigators, in the traditional sense, may not really be all that effective in solving crimes. Is this to say that all investigation units should be disbanded? Not really, but the Rand study shows the need for reappraising the tasks performed by investigative divisions.

MANAGING CRIMINAL INVESTIGATIONS

The Rand study spurred the federal government, in particular the LEAA, to review and recommend changes in the investigations function in American policing. Through funding for initial research, a prescriptive package entitled *Managing Criminal Investigations* (**MCI**) was prepared in 1978 for local law enforcement agencies under the auspices of the University Research Corporation of Washington, D.C. The objective of the MCI program was to improve upon police investigative performance by increasing the number of arrests and convictions. After a number of workshops were held around the country, the key elements of the MCI plan were field tested in Birmingham, Alabama; Montgomery County, Maryland; Rochester, New York; Santa Monica, California; and St. Paul, Minnesota. These elements are as follows: (1) enhancement of patrol officers in investigations, (2) case screening, (3) management of continuing investigation, and, (4) improvement of police-prosecutor relations.

1. *Enhancing the Investigative Role of Police Officers.* As stated before, in many departments, the patrol officer is merely a reporter of crimes that come to the attention of the police; the important follow-up work is conducted by investigators. In many cases, when the investigation division is called to the crime scene, the same questions are asked over and over again to witnesses and victims. For minor felony property crimes, there is often a time lag of hours and perhaps days before the investigator actually arrives at the scene to ask questions, process the crime scene for fingerprints and photographs, and do neighborhood canvassing.

   As a result, many departments have expanded the tasks of patrol officers to include investigative work. In Fremont, California, patrol officers have a prime responsibility for investigating crimes. The Investigations section will follow up a case only if there are unusual circumstances such as travel to another city, a sudden flood of calls for patrol services, or the need for specialized knowledge. On a routine basis, personnel assigned to investigations and patrol are routinely briefed on all matters of criminal information. In Rochester, New York, teams of detectives and patrol officers have been created to handle all investigative matters in high-crime areas. Program evaluation showed high clearance rates for robberies and burglaries in those areas covered by these teams. Departments that wish to enhance the role of patrol personnel in investigatory work must (1) draw up guidelines on the types of crime or situations that patrol personnel officers will investigate; (2) implement procedures that will result in the call up of detectives and forensic personnel, if needed; and (3) institute a program of training in investigations.

2. *Case Screening.* How does one decide to continue further investigation of an incident? Typically, there is no set answer. By rule of thumb, a seasoned officer working a case can predict whether the incident has any chance of being solved based on the variety and amount of information gathered within a given period of time. One might ask, what types of information, what variety, and how much time? Experience might be the only answer. In an effort to quantify this process, researchers at Stanford University developed a screening instrument to predict the chance for future success of any given criminal investigation. The **Stanford Instrument** as presented here has been adapted and modified by many police departments in the United States (see Table 7–1.)

TABLE 7–1
STANFORD RESEARCH INSTITUTE ROBBERY INVESTIGATION DECISION MODEL[a]

INFORMATION ELEMENT	WEIGHTING FACTOR
Suspect named	10[b]
Suspect known	10[b]
Suspect previously seen	10[b]
Evidence technician	10
Places suspect frequented named	10[b]
Offender's movement description	
On foot	0.0
Vehicle (not auto)	0.8
Auto	1.5
Auto color given	1.5
Auto description given	2.3
Auto license given	3.8
Physical evidence	
Each item	1.3
Weapon used	1.8
Vehicle registration	
Query information available	1.1
Vehicle stolen	2.3
Useful information returned	3.4
Vehicle registered to suspect	4.6

Another variable of importance is the offender-victim race. If this variable were included, the weights listed next would be assigned. Since this variable is dependent upon the population makeup for Oakland, it is included as a footnote primarily for Oakland and for general interest. Its value in increasing the probability of correct classification is nil.

TABLE 7-1 (CONT'D)

INFORMATION ELEMENT	WEIGHTING FACTOR
Offender-Victim race	
Black offender, white victim	0.0
White offender, black victim	0.3
All other combinations or unknown	0.7
White offender, white victim	1.1
Black offender, black victim	1.5

[a]Directions: Circle the weighting factors that appear in the incident report. If the sum of the factors is 10 or above, follow up the case; otherwise, suspend it.

[b]The values calculated actually exceed the threshold of 10. The values provided here are conceptually simpler and make no difference in the classification of groups.

Source: Greenberg and Wasserman. (1979: 36).

An important aspect of case screening, and overall investigative processes, is the advisement of witnesses and crime victims on case progress. Too often, the victim who made a complaint to the police is kept in the dark as to what efforts were made to solve the case. With case screening, the person making the complaint is advised when the case is suspended based on lack of leads, or variables, related to the case.

3. *Managing Criminal Investigation* This important step of the investigative process involves assigning the case to a single investigator or a group of investigators to solve the crime. As Greenberg and Wasserman discuss (1979: 47), the follow-up portion of the investigative process "has been traditionally characterized by the absence of a management system for assigning, coordinating, directing and monitoring the continuing investigative effort." What usually happens is that crimes that need follow-up attention are assigned at random by whoever is on duty and according to the time at which the incident occurred. And since many investigators keep their leads in a personal file, the information acquired is available to no one else (Cawley and others, 1977). Citing earlier discussion on issues related to investigation management, Greenberg and Wasserman (1979: 47) conclude that "the lack of managerial control over the continuing investigation process undoubtedly leads to many shortcomings, such as inequitable case loads, improper assignment of cases, incorrect priority decisions, lateness of investigator responses, and the lack of investigative continuity."

To solve this problem, the basis of the MCI program, or any investigations management program for that matter, must rest with administrative controls. An administrator must be able to deploy resources, organize work loads, and determine economical and effective assignment polices for the investigative unit. The applications of such an administrative plan include:

Centralized filing of all investigative folders. This ends a tradition of officers keeping their own case folders in their desks and allows all investigative personnel and supervisors to review the folders and obtain information when necessary.

Allocation of review dates by a supervisor. Here, a date is assigned for all paperwork on the case to be brought up to date.

Use of investigative checklists of SOPS. The officer investigator can present the steps he or she took in the investigation in checklist form, with further explanation, if needed, recorded in the narrative summary.

Investigator's Checklist

Victim interviewed in person
Victim interviewed by phone
Victim interviewed at home (if not, explain)
Witnesses interviewed in person
Witnesses interviewed by phone
Residential/commercial neighbors interviewed in person
Residential/commercial neighbors interviewed by phone
Officer on scene interviewed in person
Crime scene visited
Crime scene searched
Area of crime canvassed
Fingerprint search conducted
Photos taken at scene
Other forensic support provided
Physical evidence search that produced leads
Modus operandi files searched
Photos of known criminals viewed by victim
Major offenders' files accessed
Local hospital record search (if appropriate)
Prison records on recent releases checked
Parole file checked
Local police departments checked
Checked recent aliases
Informant's file checked
Unit members checked for information sources

Administrative attention must also focus on assigning cases, according to the resources of the department or the nature of the case at hand. In the much-publicized murder of a violinist with the

New York City Philharmonic, a team of more than 50 detectives was assembled to work the case. Representing various areas of expertise, the detectives' tasks included checking all immediate leads in various cities all over the United States. As the leads diminished, the detectives were reassigned to their former cases. Throughout the process, one person was assigned the investigation and to coordinate the activities of the other investigators. For a relatively minor crime, such as a house burglary, one investigator will be assigned the case. Where a common modus operandi appears for a number of burglaries, a team may be assembled to work the case.

4. *Improving Police/Prosecutor Relations.* The police investigator and the person who will ultimately prosecute the case, the district attorney or the public prosecutor, often act in isolation with regard to the tasks that each performs. Seasoned investigators often look upon prosecutors as people who do not understand the reality of the case, which results in plea bargaining (referred to as "Let's make a Deal") or an inept presentation of the case in the courtroom. The prosecutor, on the other hand, often has to deal with a staggering case load (as does the investigator). Except in sensational cases, the prosecutor does not have the opportunity or the time to analyze every aspect of a criminal investigation. Moreover, the first thing that the prosecutor may observe when presented with the investigation case folder is poor grammar, spelling errors, and the lack of concise information needed to plug legal and criminal procedural gaps related to the case. While investigators are appalled when their hard work results in a dismissal or a reduced charge, prosecutors often wonder why the police even made the arrest. Neither side goes to the other and asks. "What is wrong here?"

What the Rand study, the MCI program, and various textbooks on criminal investigations recommend is that prosecutors and investigators start communicating on a more frequent basis before the disposition of the case. This communication can be formal or informal. Participants in the MCI program and other police agencies have initiated weekly meetings, with representatives of both sides talking about issues or procedures related to criminal investigation and prosecution. The MCI program advocates delegating one officer as liaison between the police and the prosecutor's office. The liaison officer's duties include mediating investigator and prosecutor grievances, providing advice on legal procedures and changes, and communicating day-to-day problems that arise between agencies. In Washington, D.C., the office of the general counsel plays an important role as liaison between the police and prosecutor. This office reviews all cases that may be disposed of by plea bargaining or trial.

Monitoring the System

Various measures of effectiveness that have been proposed include arrests, clearances, and convictions. Hastings gives us a convenient checklist (1977: 230):

1. Number of offenses citywide or in each district.
2. Differences in offenses between present and past reporting periods.
3. Number (and percentage) of cases closed after (a) preliminary investigation and (b) follow-up investigation.
4. Number of cases closed without follow-up investigation and comparison of resulting clearance rates for these cases and those receiving further investigation.
5. Number of convictions versus arrests.
6. Number of cases cleared by individual investigators versus number of cases assigned.

Numerous other measures can be identified. They should be based on the requirements that system users place on the monitoring system. Common requirements of the police chief, for example, may be personnel performance evaluation, resource allocation, case status, procedural effectiveness, and investigative outcome analysis. The monitoring system is the best method by which the police administrator can receive data on which these assessments can be based.

It might prove useful comparing the New York City list of desirable characteristics to the one created by former chief Thomas Hastings of the Rochester, New York, Police Department (Hastings, 1977: 228):

1. *Decisiveness:* readiness to make decisions or to render judgments.
2. *Judgment:* ability to reach logical conclusions on the basis of the evidence at hand.
3. *Planning and organization:* effectiveness in planning and organizing own activities and those of a group.
4. *Problem analysis:* effectiveness in seeking out pertinent data and determining the source of the problem.
5. *Impact:* ability to create a good first impression to command attention and respect, to show confidence, and to achieve personal recognition.
6. *Initiative:* actively influencing events rather than passively accepting; self-starting.

Does MCI Work?

Proponents of MCI report modest success with the program in terms of resources saved, investigative efficiency, and investigative effectiveness.

Although police departments in Birmingham, Alabama, and Santa Monica, California, reduced the number of personnel assigned to investigative divisions through case-screening processes, the other participant agencies did not reassign personnel. There were many inconsistent variables with regard to investigative efficiency in all participating departments. In some of the agencies, average monthly case loads were reduced in some sites but not in others. The time spent in follow-up investigations again decreased in some sites but not in others. However, there was a report of reduced case load for investigative personnel for all cities involved. As for investigative effectiveness, the researchers (Greenberg and Wasserman, 1979: 7) concluded

> Investigative effectiveness appears to be, for the most part, unresponsive to the implementation of MCI. Local evaluations in each site have demonstrated no significant change in arrest, clearance or conviction rates.

Although success with field test agencies who participated in MCI appears to have been limited, one should not disregard MCI completely. What is significant is that certain aspects of the program, adopted by over 200 police agencies, were found to be successful; for example, case screening and supervision of continuing investigations. The police administrator, therefore, must weigh each component of MCI and decide, based on local conditions, whether greater efficiency and effectiveness in investigations would result.

There will always be a need for effective police investigations. The experience of the 1970s indicates that the most effective investigative force is one that works closely with both the patrol division and the district attorney's office. Thus, effective management for investigations is really a case of creating an organization and atmosphere where there can be effective investigative teamwork.

 ## TARGETING LAW ENFORCEMENT RESOURCES ON THE CAREER CRIMINAL

There has been increasing concern among both law enforcement officials and prosecutorial officials on the small number of street criminals who are responsible for a disproportionate amount of crime (Chaiken and Chaiken, 1982; Wolfgang, Figlio, and Sellin, 1972; Tracy, Wolfgang, and Figlio, 1985). **Career criminals** are the highest-rate offenders who actively pursue a life of crime as a career. If police departments can focus their energies and target these career criminals proactively, something may be done to reduce crime, especially street crimes that concern the ordinary citizen.

The U.S. Justice Department has funded a number of projects around the country, for example, in Baltimore; New York City; Kansas City; Washington, D.C.; Albuquerque; San Diego; and West Covina, California. These projects include (1) using warrant service to screen, locate, and apprehend career criminals; (2) using prearrest surveillance techniques; and (3) targeting postarrest career criminal cases. The most successful approach was postarrest case enhancement followed by targeted warrant service. The least successful and most costly approach was the prearrest program. Although the most proactive method, this approach has two fundamental flaws:

1. The net for potential criminals who "might" be arrested is spread too wide and uses too many personnel.

2. In the United States you are considered innocent until proven guilty, and this approach may entail harassment and violation of civil liberties.

Table 7-2 is an outline of the various approaches.

TABLE 7–2
LAW ENFORCEMENT CAREER CRIMINAL PROGRAMS/OBJECTIVES AND ACTIVITIES

Type 1: **Post-arrest-Case Enhancement**

Objective:	Successful prosecution, conviction, and incarceration
Activities:	Assign case to experienced investigator.
	Develop suspect screening criteria.
	Develop and maintain a repeat offender list.
	Verify criminal records.
	Conduct extensive case follow-up.
	Assist prosecutor in case preparation.
	Provide victim/witness assistance.

Type 2: **Warrant Service**

Objective:	Immediate service of warrants
Activities:	Develop suspect screening criteria.
	Screen outstanding warrants for career criminals.
	Gather background information.
	Conduct surveillance.
	Locate and apprehend suspect.

Type 3: **Pre-arrest Suspect Targeting**

Objective:	Interruption of criminal activities
Activities:	Develop suspect screening criteria.
	Target repeat offenders.
	Recruit and cultivate informants.
	Verify criminal activities of target.
	Conduct surveillance of targets.
	Conduct property/drug buy/sell scams.
	Infiltrate criminal networks.
	Assist prosecutor in developing case.

Source: Gay and Bowers (1985: 6).

The general goals of the Baltimore, Maryland, program are listed in Table 7-3.

TABLE 7–3
REPEAT OFFENDER PROGRAM GOALS AND OBJECTIVES: BALTIMORE COUNTY, MD.

Goal: To identify repeat offenders quickly and to remove them from the community through long-term incarceration.

Policy: The department recognizes the need for removing from the community adults and juveniles who repeatedly commit criminal acts. It is, therefore, the department's intention to work closely with the state's attorney's office and the Juvenile Services Administration to identify and detain repeat offenders.

Objectives:

1. Identify repeat offenders at the time a warrant is issued, an arrest is made, or as early as possible within the criminal justice system.
2. Document and maintain a list of repeat offenders and establish a central location for directing departmental inquiries.
3. Prevent the repeat offender from returning to the street while awaiting trial/adjudicative hearing.
4. Enhance the investigation of all repeat offender cases for presentation to the prosecutor.
5. Work with the state's attorney's office and Juvenile Services Administration in the preparation and presentation of cases for timely prosecution.
6. Certify the repeat offender's criminal/juvenile history before the sentence hearing.
7. Seek maximum penalty allowed by law.
8. Establish a liaison with the Division of Parole and Probation and the Juvenile Services Administration to facilitate the exchange of repeat offender information.

Source: Gay and Bowes (1985: 26).

Many of the departments involved in the career criminal programs developed signed work agreements with informants. This document provided superior officers with a clear picture of what their officers were doing with informants. In addition, these units were concerned with following issues concerning informants: who controls the informant, performance standards, compensation, information verification, and confidentiality. Table 7–4 is a sample work agreement with an informant.

TABLE 7–4
SAMPLE INFORMANT WORK AGREEMENT

1. *Informant* agrees that he will plead guilty to a felony burglary violation of the state code.
2. *Informant* will set up and participate in the purchase of stolen property from a known source identified to the district attorney.
3. It is understood that if the transaction for stolen property, including arrests, do not take place, the whole of this agreement is null and void and neither party shall have any obligation to the other under this agreement.
4. It is understood that if the transaction described above does not take place for reasons beyond the *informant's* control, this agreement shall remain in full force and effect.
5. The district attorney agrees that the *informant* shall not receive a state prison commitment or be incarcerated in jail but shall be placed on probation as a result of his plea for a term not to exceed three (3) years. Should *informant* thereafter violate any term of probation, however, he may be sentenced by the court to the full punishment prescribed by law. It is also agreed that *informant* may receive courtesy probation supervision out of the State of California.
6. The district attorney agrees that any statements made by *informant* to district attorney or investigating officers or made in connection with testimony pursuant to this agreement shall not be used against him, as he shall be accorded use immunity to any such statements.

In the face of declining resources, departments need to concentrate their efforts on the optimum cost/benefit choice. This could be an efficient way to target the highly active criminal. If the career criminal is responsible for such a huge amount of crime, it would make sense to put this career criminal out of business. However, giving the increasingly evident relationship between drugs and crime, departments are going to have to look at more than one target. Both the drug and career criminal seem to be important sources of criminal activity and both need to be targeted.

▷ CONCLUSION

Line functions are complementary to the patrol function and form the core of the time spent on activities in the department. However, a major distinction needs to be made between the traffic function covered in this chapter and the other line functions: vice, youth services: and investigations. Officers assigned to the traffic functions must receive specialized accident-investigation training. Well-developed human relations skills are important for these officers who provide direct service to the public. For many small departments and for some state police forces, a good deal of the uniformed forces' time is spent on traffic. Traffic management should combine the knowledge and skills of a good traffic-flow engineer with computer skills that can be used to pinpoint crucial accident areas.

Vice, youth services, and investigations often involve considerable plain-clothes work along with a somewhat different set of skills compared with those used by the uniformed traffic officer. The youth service bureau operates in two major areas: prevention and ongoing investigations. The prevention programs are important to the department both in terms of public relations and in having youth and police on good terms with each other. As most officers who deal with youth have discovered, youths are some of the best informants available. They are everywhere in the community, and they are often willing to volunteer information to police officers they trust. The bulk of the nation's street crime is still committed by youths between the ages of 17 and 25. Thus it is mandatory that every police department, no matter how large or small, have police officers who specialize in youth work.

Vice and organized crime units are areas of police work that demand special knowledge and skills. It is well known that the only real way to control this type of crime is to be able to deal with the organizers near the top of the crime hierarchy. This means that the department will be involved in lengthy investigations, often with no immediate payoffs. Vice and organized crime is multijurisdictional and international in scope. This means that a department needs experienced officers and the commitment of specialized resources.

Investigations have come a long way since the days of Sherlock Holmes and Dr. Watson. They are no longer the purview of one person; today they have to be managed in terms of a reasonable return on the commitment of professional personnel. This is the major contribution of the MCI system for managing criminal investigations, a cost-effective method of justifying when to commit and not commit personnel to investigations. The system is also useful in providing a communication framework beginning with the patrol officer who might initiate an investigation and ending with the prosecution of the arrested felon in the district attorney's office.

A theme throughout this chapter is the generalist-specialist controversy. The answer to this controversy is related to the line function, the community that the department is policing, and the size of the department. The entire focus of community policing is to provide a wide array of services. In cities, a specific geographical area becomes defined as the community, and line officers are charged to deal with community expectations and needs. A suburban department of ten sworn offices really needs officers who can perform a wide variety of tasks from traffic through drug and vice investigations. For the smaller departments, the answer might be having a generalist-specialist community service officer. This means that each officer is expected to do a variety of generalist functions while certain individual officers also have specialties. One officer may be good at giving speeches, another a forensic expert, while another has a special knowledge of the youth community. The way you organize will depend on your department. What is important is that a major focus of police management skills should be devoted to the effective administration of the basic line functions.

QUESTIONS FOR REVIEW

1. How are the main line functions classified? Explain how organizational size affects the organization of these functions.

2. What is the controversy surrounding the generalist versus the specialist with regard to delivering basic line functions to the community?

3. What are the main objectives of traffic enforcement? Why is this considered to be frustrating to many officers?

4. How might management improve traffic enforcement?

5. Why is vice enforcement truly a managerial dilemma?

6. Why should vice enforcement be taken over mainly by state and federal agencies?

7. Explain the historical development of juvenile-aid divisions.

8. List the main objectives of juvenile-aid divisions.

9. How do the following programs aid in the juvenile-aid function: explorer post, school liaison, outdoor adventure, stranger danger?

10. What is the main role of police investigators?

11. What has been the historical basis of detective divisions? How does this affect the investigative function today?

12. Explain the significance of the Rand study and traditional investigations.

13. List and briefly discuss the main components of the MCI program.

CLASS PROJECT

You have been appointed Chief of Police, Wilkenson, Wyoming. Until last year, Wilkenson was a travelers' stop for the railroad and Interstate 89. Then oil was discovered. Within one year, the town grew from 5,000 to 25,000 in population.

Policing before the oil rush was done by the county sheriff's department assisted by the highway patrol. With the rapid population increase, there is now a need for a municipal police department. The town council has told you to create a police force regardless of cost.

Your first task is to create an organization showing the function. Your instructor will show you how to prepare a basic chart. Include in your chart all those functions that will need to be staffed in the next three years. Write a brief rationale for each position you have created in your organization.

KEY TERMS

career criminal

cases screening

DARE

doli incapax

flipped informant

In re Gault

MCI

Neutral zone

parens patriae

PRELIMINARY

ride along

reporter

Stanford Instrument

Station house probation

status offenses

stranger danger

SWAT

BIBLIOGRAPHY

BLAKELY, G. ROBERT, RONALD GOLDSTOCK, and CHARLES H. ROGOVIN, *Rackets Bureaus: Investigations and Prosecution of Organized Crime.* Washington, D.C.: U.S. Government Printing office, 1978.

BLOCH, P.B., and D.R. WEIDMAN, *Managing Criminal Investigations.* Washington, D.C.: U.S. Government Printing Office, 1975.

CALDWELL, HARRY, *Basic Law Enforcement. Pacific Palisades*, Calif.: Goodyear, 1972.

CAWLEY, D. F., H. J. MIRON, W. J. ARAUMO, R. WASSERMAN, T. A. MANNELLO, and Y. HUFFMAN, *Managing Criminal Investigations Manual*. Washington, D.C.: University Research Corporation, 1977.

CHAIKEN, JAN M., and MARCIA R. CHAIKEN, *Varieties of Criminal Behavior*. Santa Monica, Calif.: Rand Corporation, 1982.

CLARK, WARREN, *Traffic Management and Collision Investigation*. Upper Saddle River, N.J.: Prentice-Hall, 1982.

CRIME PREVENTION COALITION, *1996 October: Safer Communities Brighter Futures*. Washington, D.C.: National Crime Prevention Council, 1996.

FOWLER, FLOYD J., THOMAS W. MANGIONE, and FREDERICK PRATTER, *Gambling Law Enforcement in Major American Cities*. Washington, D.C.: U.S. Government Printing Office, September 1978.

GARMIRE, BERNARD L., ed., *Local Government Police Management*. Washington, D.C.: International City Management Association, 1977.

GAY, WILLIAM G., and ROBERT A. BOWERS, *Targeting Law Enforcement Resources: The Career Criminal Focus*. Washington, D.C.: National Institute of Justice, 1985.

GREENBERG, ELLEN, and ROBERT WASSERMAN, *Managing Criminal Investigations*. Washington, D.C: National Institute of Law Enforcement and Criminal Justice, 1979

GREENWOOD, PETER, and others, *The Criminal Investigation*. Santa Monica, Calif.: Rand Corporation, 1976.

HASTINGS, THOMAS F., "Criminal Investigation," in Bernard Garmire, ed., *Local Government Police Management*. Washington, D.C.: International City Management Association, 1977.

IANNI, FRANCIS A. J., *Black Mafia: Ethnic Succession in Organized Crime*. New York: Simon & Schuster, 1974.

INCIARDI, JAMES A., *The War on Drugs*. Palo Alto, Calif.: Mayfield, 1986.

NATIONAL ADVISORY COMMISSION ON CRIMINAL JUSTICE STANDARDS AND GOALS. *Juvenile Justice and Delinquency Prevention*. Washington, D.C.: U.S. Government Printing Office, 1976.

NIEDERHOFFER, ARTHUR, *Behind the Shield: The Police in Urban Society*. Garden City, N.Y.: Doubleday, 1969.

ROWAN, ROY, "The 50 Biggest Mafia Bosses," *Fortune*, 114, no. 11, (November 1986), pp. 24–38.

RUBINSTEIN, JONATHAN, *City Police*. New York: Farrar, Strauss and Giroux, 1973.

SEEDMAN, ALBERT A., and PETER HELLMAN, Chief. New York: Avon Books, 1974.

SILBERMAN, CHARLES E., *Criminal Violence, Criminal Justice*. New York: Vintage Books, 1980.

SKOLNICK, JEROME H., *Justice Without Trial*. New York: Wiley, 1975.

STEFFENSMEIER, DARRELL, J., *The Fence: In the Shadow of Two Worlds*. Totowa, N.J.: Rowman & Littlefield, 1986.

TRACY, PAUL E., MARVIN E. WOLFGANG, and ROBERT M. FIGLIO, *Delinquency in Two Birth Cohorts*. Washington, D.C.: U.S. Department of Justice, 1985.

U.S. DEPARTMENT OF JUSTICE: BUREAU OF JUSTICE STATISTICS. *Report to the Nation on Crime and Justice*. Washington, D.C.: U.S. Government Printing Office, 1983.

WILLIAMS, JAY R., and LAWRENCE J. REDLINGER, "The Role of the Informant in Narcotics Enforcement," Paper presented at the Academy of Criminal Justice Sciences, Cincinnati, Ohio, March 1979.

WILSON, O.W., *Police Administration* (2nd ed), New York: McGraw-Hill, 1963.

WOLFGANG, MARVIN E., ROBERT M. FIGLIO, and THORSTEIN SELLIN, *Delinquency in a Birth Cohort*. Chicago, Ill.: University of Chicago Press, 1972.

8

Patrol Operations and Community Policing

The increased use of technology and research has changed the face of patrol operations. Today's police supervisors can keep in constant communication with patrol cars and officers. Reports can be dictated into a computer and police can have access to nationwide information while working the streets. The advent of the 911 system has drastically changed citizen's access to law enforcement services. A 911-driven department is a totally reactive department that has no time for special programs and citizen interaction approaches, such as community policing.

The nation's police forces have moved beyond random patrol. This began with the conclusions from two Kansas City, Missouri studies that showed the ineffectiveness of random patrol and rapid response. "The study concluded that preventive patrol did not necessarily prevent crime or reassure citizens. Similar experiments with similar results were subsequently conducted in St. Louis, Missouri and Minneapolis, Minnesota." The study on rapid response concluded, "that police response time was unrelated to the probability of making an arrest or locating a witness and that neither dispatch nor travel time was associated with citizen satisfactions." (National Institute of Justice, 1994: 12).

A majority of a police officer's time is still spent on patrol and responding to calls for services. Police managers are increasingly looking for alternative ways of providing services. A major question in police management is how to control certain calls so that they don't overwhelm scarce police resources. The Police

Executive Research Forum developed a Differential Police Response System in which trained dispatchers coded all police calls as critical or noncritical. Noncritical calls were stacked with citizens asked to file reports and critical calls were answered immediately. Many police departments have adopted these procedures along with other systems of prioritizing police calls.

Police management wants to have various approaches beyond police response to 911. Some approaches are community policing, neighborhood policing, fear reduction policing, problem-solving and task force approaches, and hot spot targeting. In order to have these alternative approaches available, patrol forces have been split into a 911 response force for critical calls and a force that is reserved for these other approaches. A major issue is to have enough tax dollars to afford these split forces.

In this chapter, we will discuss new programs that have emerged as a result of study and discussion of this issue. We also will review the current managerial issues related to patrol, and offer suggestions for improvement.

 THE TRADITIONAL MODEL

Until this decade, administrative attitudes and practices toward police patrol had changed little since the London Metropolitan Police duty manual, written in 1829. The first police constables assigned to patrol had to walk designated beats within a given time span. Although the automobile replaced many foot patrols in the twentieth century, patrol beats were assigned on the basis of the needs of the community, geographical limitations, and available personnel.

Police patrol continues to consist of the following activities: calls for assistance, patrol-officer-initiated activity, preventive patrol, and administrative activities. The jurisdiction of the department is divided into various zones, and one vehicle is assigned to each zone each shift. Certain highly populated zones, such as shopping malls, business districts, and apartment complexes may be assigned a foot-patrol officer.

In the public's mind, and perhaps reinforced by television, the patrol officer and his or her partner cruise an area, answer a few calls, and occasionally spot a suspicious person or vehicle leading to a spectacular arrest. The practice of cruising is **preventive patrol**. The rationale behind this is that the deployment of various foot and patrol units can prevent and deter criminal activity. While many officers would like to roam an area in the manner just described, actual, preventive patrol depends upon numerous variables such as the number of crimes in a reported area, potential or consistent trouble spots, heavy traffic patterns at certain times, and the whimsey of the officer and his or her supervisor. In large departments, assigned sectors are strictly maintained or jealously guarded by officers and supervisors. Patrol units are not allowed to go beyond their designated sectors except when dispatched or in "hot" pursuit. Preventive patrol time is also spent goofing off, going on personal errands, having coffee, or meeting other patrol units to share gossip.

In smaller departments, the same runs true. The great difference is that the patrol unit(s) on duty are supposed to stay within the jurisdiction and not venture outside village or town limits.

Preventive patrol is interrupted by calls for assistance that may be of a criminal or a service nature. Upon receiving a call, the patrol unit is supposed to suspend preventive patrol and respond to a location. Calls for both criminal and noncriminal matters account for 25 to 40 percent of all patrol time, which, of course, depends upon the size of the sector, economic conditions (for example, inner-city versus suburban middle-class neighborhood), and number of units available for the entire jurisdiction during that shift.

Incorporated with preventive patrol are officer-initiated activities. These include questioning suspicious persons, stopping vehicles, operating radar, or conducting informal community service activities (for example, talking to businesspersons or schoolchildren or making unassigned business checks). Officer-initiated activities account for only 14 percent of patrol time, although this figure may be higher during early morning tours of duty when there are few calls.

The rest of patrol time is designated as administrative. Tasks of this nature include prisoner transport, writing reports, appearance in court, and vehicle maintenance. Administrative tasks consume large blocks of time during all shifts, especially during normal working hours of 9:00 AM to 5:00 PM since most administrative work occurs during this time period.

THE KANSAS CITY STUDIES

While many departments continue with traditional patrol in the manner just described, a few major urban departments began experimenting with new patrol tactics by the beginning of 1970. One most cited today is the so-called Kansas City Study conducted by the Kansas City, Missouri Police Department and the Police Foundation. The general hypotheses of preventive patrol were tested by dividing the southern portion of the city into 15 police beats. These 15 beats were then divided into five groups, each group having three matched beats. For these matched groups, there was one in which patrol was greatly increased; a second beat in which patrol was eliminated altogether except for calls for service; and a control beat, in which patrol continued at the same pace as before the experiment. As Wilson (1975: 109) reports:

> After a year, no substantial differences among the three areas were observed in criminal activity, amount of reported crime, rate of victimization as revealed in the followup survey, level of citizen fear, or degree of citizen satisfaction with the police.

In addition, citizen satisfaction was found to have increased in the second and the control beats, whereas it decreased somewhat in the beat where patrol was greatly increased. Today, many researchers and police administrators continue to discuss these conclusions. To be candid, there have been many criticisms of this experiment due to faulty experimental design and methodology. Nevertheless, this experiment opened the door for further discussion on the benefits of preventive patrol and the hypothesis that random patrol may be a waste of time.

Further issues were raised by a second experiment conducted in Kansas City in 1977 to study the relationship between response time and crime. The orthodox notion of police patrol maintains that crime will decrease if the police are quick to arrive upon the scene. The study found that since citizens generally take too long to report crime, response time has nothing to do with the number of arrests and crime. Moreover, for nonemergency calls, there were few citizen complaints of the police taking their time to respond to calls as long as the dispatchers advised the complainant what to expect in terms of estimated time of arrival for the patrol.

 RETHINKING THE TRADITIONAL MODEL

Although developed in the 1970s, Table 8–1 conceptualizes some of the problems that need to be dealt with by police administrators who are attempting to make improvements in patrol operations. The general goal for improvement is to (1) reduce administration, preventive patrol, and calls for assistance and (2) add to time spent on directed patrol and crime analysis related to directed patrol. Since 85 percent of all police interactions with citizens come from calls for assistance (Reiss, 1971), this category will remain the same or will expand by a few minutes. The major modification will be that all calls for assistance do not have to have a police car within 2 minutes. The phone operators, who will be trained for this task and have guidance sheets created by department administrative staff, will judge priorities of the call. Each call will have a priority code assigned to it, and the call will go out to the patrol cars coded in terms of high, medium, and low priority.

TABLE 8–1

Patrol Activity	Time Used (Percent per Shift Hour)	General Plan for Improvement
Administration	23	Reduce the amount of time such tasks detract from patrol
Calls for assistance	23	Manage calls better, especially those of noncriminal nature; create priority system of call returns
Preventive patrol	40	Incorporate specific objectives during this time period; reduce to less than 10 minutes of shift hour
Directed patrol	14	Based on time reduction of other tasks, more time will be available for this activity

Source: W. G. Gay et al. (1977b: 3).

PREVENTIVE PATROL

Although preventive patrol takes 40 percent of an officer's time, it is the crux upon which modern police practice rests. The reasons why patrol units are mobile and do not stay in a garage and respond as needed in fire-department fashion are the following:

Detecting crime

Apprehending criminal offenders

Recovering stolen property

Maintaining a sense of public security and confidence in the police for the community

Satisfying public demands for noncriminal services

These objectives raise many questions. For example, preventive patrol may have really nothing to do with detecting crime and apprehending criminal offenders. In reality, most arrests that occur "in progress" within a few minutes after the commission of a crime stem from the police having been at the right place at the right time.

The same may be true on the issue of deterrence. While many administrators assume that the police presence suggests a higher probability for the apprehension of offenders, there is little evidence to suggest that traditional patrol practice leads to this objective. The basis for this objective rests with the assumption that the criminals are always on the lookout for police patrols and view these patrols as a serious hindrance to the commission of a crime. Unfortunately, many crimes are spontaneous enterprises that lack long-term planning. In other cases, criminal activity occurs under the eyes of the police in certain areas that are high-crime districts. For example, drug sales on the street in large metropolitan areas may go on uninterrupted even as the police cruiser passes by.

Arrest data are often used to back up this assumption by way of crime clearance rates. Patrol is then deemed effective or ineffective on the basis of apprehensions in a certain area. However, even the freshman criminal-justice student knows that crime rates are affected by a number of factors that have nothing to do with the police presence (for example, family situation, economics, immigration). In short, we do not have satisfactory means for evaluating the effect of patrol tactics.

While recovery of stolen property is cited as an objective of patrol, the fact of the matter is that stolen property is usually recovered by investigators following up on a case rather than by the uniformed patrol presence. The only exception to this might be stolen automobiles. But even with a stolen auto, the recovery most often occurs due to the careless driving habits of the offender. It is rare for an officer to recover a stolen vehicle as a result of spotting the license plates or vehicle description. Many experienced officers know of vehicles that were parked for weeks in shopping malls, airports, or apartment complexes before being discovered as stolen due to an abandoned-vehicle complaint filed by the owner of the property or a security guard.

If anything, patrol may be the best public relations exercise utilized by the police in the United States. In essence, the citizen sees the patrol vehicle cruise by and may therefore perceive that the police are "out there" doing their jobs. Research, however, has shown that other factors have to be taken into consideration before one can conclude that the public is satisfied with the police. Such factors are overall crime rates, officer treatment of the public, the level of police corruption, and other community issues.

If anything, traditional police patrol does indeed provide a number of non-criminal services to the community that are dependent upon community norms. Historically, all police agencies respond to domestic disputes, lost-person reports, traffic accidents, loud-party complaints, and so on. In many areas, the community dictates what services the police provide above and beyond the traditional non-criminal tasks (for example, escorting funeral processions, directing traffic near churches on Sunday, providing oxygen to persons having difficulty breathing, transporting blood from a blood bank to a hospital). Yet, as Schell and his associates (1973) point out, these services may contribute nothing to public satisfaction with the police simply because the amount of these activities cannot be measured in terms of citizen satisfaction. Still, as one administrator remarked, "I agree with you, but you should hear the complaints that come in once it is found that we are not providing funeral escorts, blood runs, or other such goodies!"

CALLS FOR SERVICE

A common assumption made by the American public is that when you make a phone call for the police, the police will immediately respond—no matter how serious the incident may be. Many observers of patrol believe that there may be a need to dispel the tradition that all calls merit immediate response. In fact, perhaps 40 percent of all calls could be handled by communications personnel. This would save a great deal of time from dispatch to completion of a written report.

Many departments are starting to use various methodologies to handle complaints other than sending a patrol unit to the scene. Some departments are experimenting with mailed-out forms to collect information on traffic accidents of minor nature and petty larcenies. Other agencies advise the complainant to come down to the station at his or her convenience to complete any reports. Additionally, many agencies are developing community referral systems to refer complaints to other public or private agencies that might be of greater assistance to handle certain problems.

One immediate benefit seen by utilizing these methods involves improving officer morale. It is no secret that many officers dislike wasting time on so-called junk calls in which there are no suspects and the complainant really wants the police investigation report for insurance purposes. Nevertheless, when compared with procedures of policing, these are radical changes, especially for citizens who may feel that they are being given the runaround. Any new method for reducing patrol responses requires a period of public education by way of media campaigns, civic meetings, and coffee hours. It will also require the dispatcher or a supervisor of the officer on the street to explain these types of procedures to citizens or callers.

Another controversial method for reducing the time spent on nonessential calls for assistance by patrol units is called *stacking*. Stacking simply involves classifying calls in terms of priority, thereby increasing the amount of time that can be allocated for uninterrupted patrol for certain units. Table 8-2 illustrates the stacking system utilized for the Kansas City, Missouri, Police Department.

TABLE 8-2
KANSAS CITY, MISSOURI, CALL PRIORITIZATION GUIDELINES

TYPE OF CALL	TYPE OF RESPONSE[a]	TYPE OF CALL	TYPE OF RESPONSE[a]
Homicide		Alarm	
Homicide	Immediate	Holdup	Immediate
Suicide/attempt	Immediate	Burglar	Immediate
Dead Body	Immediate	Self-initiated duties	
Sex offenses		Traffic violation	Immediate
Rape/attempt	Immediate	Assignments	N/A
Molestation	Walk/phone in	Building check	Delay
Indecent act	Walk/phone in	Car check	N/A
Robbery		Foot patrol	N/A
Robbery/attempt	Immediate	Warrant/subpoena	Delay
Strongarm/attempt	Delay	Car chase	N/A
Assaults		Listing	Delay
Shooting	Immediate	Pedestrian check	N/A
Cutting	Immediate	Residence check	Delay
Other assault	Walk/phone in	Suspicious	
Burglary		Person	Immediate
Residence	Delay	Prowler	Immediate
Nonresidence	Delay	Car prowler	Immediate
Larceny		Occupant, parked car	Immediate
Larceny/attempt	Walk/phone in	Ambulance	
Holding person for	Immediate	Investigate need	Immediate
Purse snatch/attempt	Walk/phone in	Ambulance en route	Immediate
Auto theft		Fire or disaster	
Stolen/attempt	Walk/phone in	Fire	Immediate
Attempt to locate	Walk/phone in	Explosion	Immediate
Recovered stolen	Delay	Intoxicated person	
Miscellaneous report		Person down, injured	Immediate
Animal bite	Delay	Intoxicated	Delay
Loss	Walk/phone in	Disturbance	
Recovered property	Delay	Disturbance	Immediate
Destruction of property	Walk/phone in	Investigate trouble	Immediate
		Mental	Immediate
Open door or window	Immediate	Noise (specify)	Delay or refer to city prosecutor's office
Fraud	Walk/phone in		

TABLE 8-2 (CONT'D)

TYPE OF CALL	TYPE OF RESPONSE[a]	TYPE OF CALL	TYPE OF RESPONSE[a]
Traffic		Miscellaneous	
Handle traffic	Delay	Check abandoned	Delay
Check traffic lights	Immediate or notify	car	
and barricade	Public Works	Wires down	Immediate
Obstruction in	Immediate or notify	Explosive device	Immediate
street	Public Works	Gambling game	Delay
Illegally parked	Delay	Target shooters	Immediate
Traffic accident		Animal	Delay
Accident, property	Walk/phone in	Lost/senile	Immediate
damage	or delay	Assist motorist	Delay
Investigate, injury	Immediate	Open fire hydrant	Delay
Fatality	Immediate	Fireworks	Delay
Juveniles			
Lost juvenile	Immediate		
Disperse group	Delay		
Holding	Immediate		

[a]All calls marked "Delay" will be answered immediately if the incident is in progress, suspects are in the area or are known, and there is danger to human life or of property destruction. N/A means not applicable.

Source: Gay and others (1977b: 75).

Another method to reduce time on minor calls for service involves the use of nonsworn personnel or parapolice officers such as community-service officers. In many departments, these nonsworn personnel are assigned to a variety of duties including desk duty, writing parking tickets, directing traffic, conducting crime prevention campaigns, and other similar assignments.

ADMINISTRATIVE TASKS

In this technology age, many police departments are experimenting with new devices and procedures to cut down on the amount of time uniformed and plain-clothes officers spend on administrative tasks. With regard to police procedures ranging from arrests to prisoner transports, many departments are asking the question, "How can we improve the amount of time an officer can spend on crucial tasks?" In many cases, these require revisions of laws; for example, those mandating that the arresting officer must appear at arraignment with a defendant in court the next day. In other instances, the duty manual is subject to review and update to cut out unnecessary tasks.

While these issues are often resolved by in-house review, a basic problem that continues to plague all police officers is that of paperwork. On average, police agencies use over 50 different forms ranging from arrest to motor-vehicle-accident reports. In fact, the average arrest requires that more than 10 different forms be completed. While many of these forms can be eliminated or combined, there still remains the problem of writing reports.

Some agencies are adopting programs and procedures taken for granted in private business by having patrol officers tape record reports for future transcription or use lap-top computers. Some agencies have gone so far as to have the officer call in the report by telephone immediately after the investigation. At any rate, once these skills are mastered, it is found that administrative time is reduced.

DIRECTED PATROL

When administrative tasks, calls for service, and preventive patrol are reanalyzed, the final objective will be the allocation of greater time for directed patrol. For our purposes, **directed patrol** can be defined as the allocation of patrol services in a planned and rational manner. Many departments have various applications of directed patrol that will be discussed. In addition, directed patrol is dependent upon two other variables: crime analysis and shift design.

Crime Analysis

Too frequently, patrol deployment is made without referral to when and where the crimes are occurring. As Reiner (1977b) points out, many police personnel prefer to operate by tradition or rule-of-thumb methods rather than rely on crime analysis. A minority of police departments in the United States, however, delve into crime analysis with the assistance of federal grants. At present, crime analysis in the United States ranges from sophisticated computer programming to pin mapping.

One project sponsored by the former Law Enforcement Assistance Administration to encourage the use of crime analysis is the Integrated Criminal Apprehension Program, commonly known as ICAP. The birth of ICAP via LEAA was due to the rapid development of computer technology in the last decade followed by the federal government's insistence that crime programs be supported and evaluated by analysis. Over 30 police agencies today participate in the ICAP program. What then is crime analysis? According to ICAP (Reiner, 1977b):

> The crime analysis function is defined as a set of systematic, analytical processes directed at providing timely and pertinent information relative to crime patterns and trend correlation, to assist operational and administrative personnel in planning and deployment of resources for prevention and suppression of criminal activities aiding the investigation process, and increasing apprehension and clearance of cases.

After pertinent data are obtained from field reports, arrest sheets, or dispatch logs, the information is collated, analyzed, and then communicated to line supervisors and field personnel. With this information, the patrol supervisor is then able to make rational decisions for deployment of staff or to devise specialized patrol techniques.

Redesign of Patrol Shifts

Crime analysis can be very useful in analyzing work loads by shift or season. At present, most police departments allocate an equal amount of officers to each shift, usually three shifts in a 24-hour period. Despite this allocation, all departments realize that criminal activity increases between the hours of 4 p.m. and 2 a.m., which can present some problems with regard to police operations since officers are unable to perform directed patrol when they are having to rush from call to call. In recognition of this dilemma, many departments have redeployed their patrol personnel based on need rather than on equalization. For example, many agencies have designed to following programs:

9–40: In this program, the officer works 9 hours a day, 4 days a "workweek," 40 hours a week, for a total of 36 hours; the other 4 hours are taken up with physical fitness, in-service training, and roll call.

4–10: In this very common program, the workweek consists of 10 hours a day, 4 days per week.

In addition to these and other proposed designs, deployment extends beyond the traditional equal shift allocation in that the shifts are redesigned to provide increased coverage between the hours of 7 p.m. and 1 a.m. (Gay and others, 1977: 19-52; Ward, 1977). Agencies on a five-day 40-hour workweek would be able to do the same thing, provided that there were permanent shifts with more personnel being assigned to high-crime hours. The main problem with shift redesign in traditional agencies stems from union or personnel opposition, since most officers prefer the day shifts with as many weekends off as possible. Proponents of 9–40 and 4–10 point out that accommodations can be made with weekends off by way of a rotation basis.

Specialized Patrol

In some departments, directed patrol comes under the heading of specialized patrol, where specific units are assigned to a special area (for example, burglary squad, sneaker squad for inner-city street crime). Tactics that are commonly employed by these units include:

1. *Decoys.* In decoy squads, an officer is disguised as a "victim" who is assisted by several backup officers. This tactic is used for such crimes as muggings, purse snatchings, and assaults.

2. *Stakeouts.* In stakeouts, officers—either physically or by use of electronic equipment—are assigned to a likely target area. Crimes in progress are frequently interrupted.

3. *Suspect surveillance.* In suspect surveillance, police personnel watch and follow individuals who are suspected of committing offenses with frequency (for example, burglary, robbery, drugs, organized crime).

4. *General area surveillance.* As with stakeouts, general area surveillance is used against either persons who conduct criminal activities or in a wide area with a variety of targets. Some jurisdictions even go so far as to station television cameras on certain high-crime street corners.

The assignment of a specialized patrol unit to a problem is based on the analysis of crime data. Specialized patrol is an example of a proactive system that operates according to a rational plan of crime detection rather than randomly stumbling about waiting for something to happen.

Some of the advantages of this specialized patrol approach are:

1. Specific units are assigned to a specific problem so that management knows exactly who is responsible for solving that crime problem.
2. The unit normally exhibits a high degree of teamwork with high morale.
3. There is improved skill development in the specialized area over a period of time with officers being called upon by all members of the department in their area of expertise.
4. There is usually a great deal of positive public interest generated by media attention.

There are problems with specialized units that affect the whole department. There is always the problem of communication (e.g., deciding who is responsible for what problems, like having a burglary unit that may not respond to other street crimes). Officers in regular squads resent the "hot shot" specialists who attain glory and prestige while regular patrol has to take care of more mundane matters. This is especially acute in departments where factions operate in a negative fashion. Departmental morale can be destroyed by resentment over specialized units.

The use of aggressive enforcement tactics also produces negative public attention. People get upset when stakeout squads use heavy-caliber weapons to kill robbers. Citizens also complain about area surveillance, particularly the use of video cameras in high crime areas. While there is a generally positive outlook toward professional law enforcement services, serious questions are raised on the use of heavy-handed tactics and technology.

FOOT PATROL

Some police managers feel that automobile patrolling has led to a police alienation from neighborhoods and loss of a feeling of security that was generated by foot patrol. Foot patrol can have a positive benefit in high-density neighborhoods. When Newark, New Jersey and Flint, Michigan reinstituted foot patrol, they came up with these findings (Kelling, 1987):

1. When foot patrol is added in neighborhoods, levels of fear decrease significantly.
2. When foot patrol is withdrawn from neighborhoods, levels of fear increase significantly.

3. Citizen satisfaction with police increases when foot patrol is added in neighborhoods.

4. Police who patrol on foot have a greater appreciation for the values of the neighborhood residents than do police who patrol the same area in automobiles.

5. Police who patrol on foot have greater job satisfaction, less fear, and higher morale than do officers who patrol in automobiles.

Personal-contact patrol also brought about fear reduction in Houston. The police started "to drive through the neighborhoods, knock on doors and chat with pedestrians, thus creating a visible presence" (Sherman, 1987). The major object of these programs is not crime reduction, although this has happened in some cases. Foot patrol and personal-contact patrol do increase a feeling of security by citizens and lower the fear of crime.

BICYCLE PATROL

Police officers around the world have used bicycles for patrol purposes since the nineteenth century. With the advent of modern mountain bikes, police bike patrols have been established. The Seattle Police Department and other West Coast departments in the United States use bikes for patrol operations all year. The idea has become popular with university and college police departments. Other applications are found in airport parking lots, resort and recreation areas, and locations that impede motorized patrol units. In these locations, bike patrol personnel can respond quicker than vehicles to emergencies.

As with any other function, bike patrols require a great deal of planning with regard to equipment, training, personnel needs, and supervision. Equipment includes mountain bicycles, seasonal uniforms, helmets, and foul-weather gear. Equipment or contract services have to be purchased for parts and repairs. Personnel selected for this assignment have to be physically fit. Training programs, such as the one used by the University Police Department at the State University of New York at Albany, include such topics as bike nomenclature, proper riding and equipment, emergency response, tactical pursuit, and safety in such areas as woods, stairways, and shopping malls.

The bicycle patrols used by public safety agencies today provide the following benefits:

1. Increased interaction between officers and the community.

2. Access to remote or vehicle-denied locations.

3. An indirect wellness program for office participants.

Bicycle patrols should not be viewed as a specialized function but rather as a part of normal assignment.

Bicycle Maneuvers

The Power Slide

With the power slide, officers direct their bikes to slide to a particular location. When using the power slide, officers approach a subject at a high rate of speed. On reaching the suspect, they plant either their left or right foot on the ground with the knees slightly bent to make the bike lean away from the suspect. The officers then apply the rear brake with enough pressure to lock up the rear tire, causing the bike to spin around. Power slides can be performed to the right or left side depending on which is the officer's stronger side.

The Panic Stop

To stop the bike at any given moment, officers use the panic stop. In this case, they apply the rear brake to lock up the rear tire and move their center of gravity (torso) to the rear of the seat, causing a controllable skid and stop.

The Rolling Dismount

The rolling dismount is a technique used by officers to get off their bicycle quickly. Officers slow the bicycle down to a controllable speed with one foot on the pedal, while engaging the kickstand with the other foot. The rolling dismount is performed in a quick, fluid motion, ending with the bike in the standby/ready position.

Source: FBI Law Enforcement Bulletin, September 1993.

TEAM POLICING

In the 1960s the concept of team policing received considerable attention by criminal justice educators, planners, and practitioners. It was seen as a possible solution to the major problems faced by many American police departments: (1) poor police-community relations, (2) duplication of effort, (3) the rise of crime, and (4) the increasing costs of police budgets. **Team policing** involves decentralizing the existing police organizational structure and reorganizing services into specific subunits. These subunits are usually based on geographic, ethnic, and other socioeconomic boundaries found in particular communities. In each subunit, the team is charged with the allocation of patrol, investigation, and other police services and programs, according to the needs of the community.

HISTORY OF TEAM POLICING

The concept of team policing originated in Aberdeen, Scotland in the late 1940s as an experiment to counteract low morale and boredom experienced by single officers patrolling quiet areas. A change was made from the one-unit, one-beat method of patrol to teams of five or ten patrolling an area divided according to the concentration of crime and calls for service (Sherman, 1976, xiii). In 1966, due to a personal shortage, the Coventry constabulary in England began a form of team policing called **unit beat policing**, whereby constables were formed into teams and the team was assigned to a specific area. Information from the team was fed to a central collator who exchanged the information to other teams. Although the Aberdeen patrol method was abandoned in 1963, other British constabularies and a few American police forces have adopted similar plans.

In the United States the urban and campus unrest of the 1960s brought forth renewed interest in police patrol tactics and police community relations. It was generally concluded that a gap had developed between the police and the public. This was due to the decline of the neighborhood foot-patrol officer and the abandonment of many precinct stations in favor of centralization. The 1967 Presidential Commission on Law Enforcement and the Administration of Justice recommended that agencies introduce team policing as a means to lessen this gap. Team policing was also expected to increase community involvement with crime prevention and detection.

POSITIVE ASPECTS OF TEAM POLICING

The positive aspects of team policing are

1. The police services rendered by the team become more personal to the community, and in return, the relations between the police and the community are improved.

2. Team policing provides a flexible structure for its members in that innovation is made possible and professionalism is increased by the development of shared knowledge and peer review.

3. Patrol and investigatory functions are merged into one task, thus eliminating the social barriers of communication and status conflict between uniformed and plainclothes personnel.

4. A reduction is attained in the chain of command in that decision making is made by supervisors and operating personnel.

5. Each member of the team is given a chance to utilize discretion and enhance personal skills. As a result, greater work satisfaction is expected.

TEAM POLICING AND TACTICAL PATROL

Team policing is often confused with **tactical patrol** techniques. Tactical patrol deals with selective law enforcement for a specific problem in the area. Examples of this type of enforcement are robberies, murders, muggings, and purse snatching occurring in a routine manner, in a specific geographical area. With team policing, emphasis is placed upon territorial exclusivity, maintaining stable and close ties with the citizens of the neighborhood, participation in planning and management and an orientation toward results in presenting the police mission (Edgar and others, 1976: v).

TEAM POLICING ORGANIZATIONAL MODELS

Between 1970 and 1974, a number of municipalities introduced team policing into their areas, with and without assistance from federal and private funding sources. The teams fell into four categories (Gay and others, 1977):

1. **Basic patrol teams** involve the reorganization of the department into teams responsible for basic preventive patrol, radio dispatch service, and traffic duties. In this format, team policing is used as the basic organizational mode for the efficient delivery of patrol services. Officers on these teams, however, do not have community-relations or investigative responsibilities. Cities that used this organizational model were Richmond, Virginia; North Charleston, South Carolina; St. Petersburg, Florida; Syracuse, New York; and San Bruno, California.

2. **Patrol investigative teams** combine the features of the basic patrol team with the assignment of follow-up investigative responsibilities to the team. One of the best known models of this approach occurred in Rochester, New York. There, patrol officers were responsible for conducing complete preliminary investigations and certain investigative follow-ups. The patrol investigative teams are assigned to specific areas.

3. **Patrol community service teams** combine the duties of the basic patrol teams and community relations. In the team area, the officers were encouraged to provide assistance to people of the community, making job referrals for the unemployed, making medical referrals for the ill, and performing similar liaison services between the people and the social agency's network (Fink and Sealy, 1974: 155). In San Diego, individual officers were encouraged to become involved with community services in the area in addition to the community service offices working from a central community relations office.

4. **Full-service teams** are the most controversial in the discussion of team policing. In full service, specific portions or the entire organizational structure of the department is broken down into a team format. Patrol, investigations and community relations are the responsibility of the team. Full-service team policing is divided into two categories: multispecialist and generalist.

   In the **multispecialist** form, the team is composed of patrol and specialist officers (detectives and community relations offices) who are under the direction of a team leader. The specialist officers continue to do the same tasks but receive greater assistance from the team officers. The multispecialist approach was or is in current use in the Arbor Hill neighborhood in Albany, New York; Charlotte, North Carolina; Cincinnati, Ohio; Detroit, Michigan; Los Angeles and Palo Alto, California; and St. Petersburg, Florida.

In the **generalist** approach, the team members are expected to perform both basic patrol and specialist duties. This format was used in the South End section of Albany, New York; Dayton, Ohio; Holyoke, Massachusetts; and Menlo Park, California. In full-service team policing formats, there were a number of unique developments.

Full-service teams, such as in Albany, Mount Holyoke, and Palo Alto, adopted blazer-and-slacks uniforms to get away form the traditional military image portrayed by the police. These teams set up police stations in storefront sites in the heart of the team jurisdictions. For other cities, such as Los Angeles, and Cincinnati, there was no change in uniforms or in police station location. Using existing resources, the big change was a closer working relationship between patrol officers and specialists and greater leeway for the conduct of investigations. Community relations became a responsibility for each member of the team as well as for the community relations personnel.

In all the team-policing categories, there was one common variable. The team had complete jurisdiction of the area. Patrol units from the other divisions could enter the team area only for backup purposes or in pursuit of a suspect. On the other hand, steps were taken to ensure that the team members did not have to respond to calls outside their jurisdiction. For all the teams, formal and informal means of interaction were encouraged to discuss problems and share criminal information. Some of the teams had weekly meetings and in-service training for this purpose.

For the full-service teams, community relations was an important function that was conducted in a variety of ways, ranging from scheduling meetings with community leaders to organizing sports programs. As with the patrol/community service teams, making referrals to the social agency network or initiating action on behalf of citizens was also important. As one Arbor Hill officer in Albany, New York commented, "Before, if someone had their water turned off, it was not a police problem. With the Arbor Hill unit, we feel it is a police problem, and we try to do something about it."

IN MEMORIAM: TEAM POLICING

Evaluation of these programs brought mixed reviews. The Rochester, New York investigative-team program was deemed successful for improving clearance rates and reducing crime. The community investigative-team programs in New York City and Albuquerque, New Mexico, were assessed as failures generally due to overall departmental problems. In the New York City experience, the teams failed to change the role of the patrol officer or increase his or her job satisfaction. In

Albuquerque, New Mexico, it was found that the teams were unable to provide a higher level of community-service delivery.

San Diego, California, however, had greater success with their program. Here the officers adapted to their new role, delivered community services, and improved their attitudes toward the community.

For the full-service team, those in Albany, New York (Arbor hill); Cincinnati, Ohio; and Los Angeles, California were extensively evaluated and the results were somewhat mixed (Gay and others, 1977b: 41):

> While indicators of workload management, investigative effectiveness and police attitudes towards the community have improved, there has been no change in officer job satisfaction and community attitudes.

 ## PROBLEM-ORIENTED POLICING

In 1979, Herman Goldstein proposed what he described as a problem-oriented approach to law enforcement (Goldstein, 1979). In the late 1970s and throughout the 1980s, police managers, faced with more and more personnel with college degrees, attempted a number of approaches at improving job satisfactions—task forces, quality circles, and management by objectives. Problem-oriented policing is another one of these approaches that utilizes the educated police force in a more proactive manner. According to the authors, traditional police patrol is a reactive system where police departments deliver services by "reacting to individual events reported by citizens' gathering information from victims, witnesses and offenders; involving the criminal justice process and using aggregate crime statistics to evaluate performance" (Spelman and Eck, 1987: 3). In Newport News, Virginia, police were trained in a four-stage approach:

1. *Scanning.* Identify major problems; for example, burglaries in an apartment complex, downtown area thefts from autos, and prostitution-related robberies.

2. *Analysis.* Collect and analyze information from a variety of public and private resources, not just from police data.

3. *Response.* Work with other agencies and public to tailor actions suitable to the problem.

4. *Assessment.* Evaluate the effectiveness of the actions to see if the problem was alleviated or solved.

As a result of this approach, downtown robberies were reduced by 39 percent, burglaries in that apartment complex were reduced by 35 percent, and thefts from parked vehicles outside a manufacturing plant dropped by 53 percent.

Table 8-3 shows the Problem Analysis Model, which worked well for the Newport News, Virginia police agency problem-oriented policing.

TABLE 8–3
PROBLEM ANALYSIS MODEL

ACTORS	INCIDENTS	RESPONSES

Victims
  Lifestyle
  Security measures taken
  Victimization history
	Sequence of events
	  Events preceding act
	  Event itself
	  Events following criminal act
		Community
		  Neighborhood affected by
		    problem
		  City as a whole
		  People outside the city

Offenders
  Identity and physical
    description
  Life-style, education,
    employment history
  Criminal history
	Physical contact
	  Time
	  Location
	  Access control and
	    surveillance
		Institutional
		  Criminal justice agencies
		  Other public agencies
		  Mass media
		  Business sector

Third parties
  Personal data
  Connection to
    victimization
	Social context
	  Likelihood and probable
	    actions of witnesses
	  Apparent attitude of residents
	    toward neighborhood	

Source: Spelman and Eck (1987:6). *This is a true proactive approach!* Rather than waiting around for a citizen to get hurt, a team of police officers identified current problems that were unique to their community and then created a plan to alleviate these problems.

To find out what were important problems for the citizens, a number of city-wide and neighborhood surveys were conducted. Citywide problems included domestic homicides, gas station driveoffs, assaults on police officers, runaway youths, drunk driving, and disturbances at convenience stores. Specific neighborhood problems included drug dealing, robberies, vacant buildings, burglaries, larcenies, thefts from autos, and rowdy youths. In one apartment complex, the police successfully organized a building association, and had the city intervene in the maintenance of the complex, which resulted in better living conditions and a 35 percent drop in the burglary rate.

The problem-oriented process is summarized in the flow chart from the New York Bureau for Municipal Police (see Figure 8–1). What is important is that the community is involved in solving problems whether they be drug deals, stolen bicycles, or loud-noise complaints. The basic tenets of Goldstein's article were later incorporated into full discussion in his book *Problem Oriented Policing* (1990). The concept is used interchangeably with community-oriented policing **(COP)**, but there are some basic theoretical differences between the two. What problem-oriented policing **(POP)** does is provide us with a planning model to deal with specific issues in the wider view of community policing.

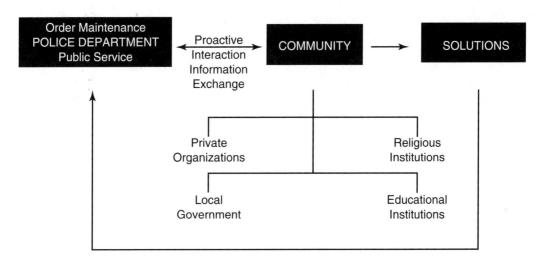

Figure 8-1

The Problem-Oriented Policing System Flowchart.

Source: Bureau for Municipal Police, Albany, N.Y., 1990.

 COMMUNITY-ORIENTED POLICING

In 1982, George L. Kelling and James Q. Wilson published an article titled "Broken Windows," which captured the attention of police administrators. They described how Philip Zimbardo, a noted sociologist at Stanford University, placed an abandoned car in a tough Bronx neighborhood and another abandoned vehicle in a wealthy area in Palo Alto, California. The vehicle in the Bronx was immediately vandalized and became a stripped hulk within a week. The car in Palo Alto remained untouched until Professor Zimbardo intentionally broke its window. The vehicle was also stripped of usable parts by vandals. Kelling and Wilson used this field experiment to present the idea that run-down neighborhoods attracted crime and fear. They recommended that foot patrol be established in neighborhoods to increase the perception of safety for citizens.

They recommended **foot patrol** in tough neighborhoods. The idea was not to simply reduce crime but to have a police presence to make people feel safer. Technology had allowed the police to abandon the streets of the city. Police officers with their fancy computers and communication systems riding around in police cars were simply not communicating with citizens. Foot patrol that had a goal beyond the simple reduction of crime, that is, giving citizens a feeling of safety, was tried around the United States beginning with Newark, N.J. in 1981. Other sites followed: Oakland in 1984, a second Newark program in 1985, Houston in 1987, and Boston in 1986. Although the crime rate did not usually go down, the general conclusion was that the citizens, "felt safer and less worried about personal property victimization" (Grenne, 1989:361). This evaluated over a number of years into fear-reduction programs and finally into community policing—all of which have their original roots in the team policing of the 1970s.

One of the major differences between the reactive patrolling of the 911 police force and community-oriented policing is that community-oriented policing can become proactive. By working closely with citizens, police can anticipate and prevent crime. Community policing, when done right, is one of the most proactive programs that a professional police department can adopt.

▶ TRADITIONAL AND COMMUNITY-ORIENTED POLICING COMPARED

One of the questions asked time and time again is, what makes community-oriented policing so different from traditional policing? In the past when an officer walked a beat visiting neighbors and business on a daily basis, we had a form of community policing. Now that police are barricaded inside their police vehicles, only reacting to citizen calls after a crime has taken place, we have the opposite of community policing.

Giving out traffic tickets is also reactive since it takes place after the fact. Police don't station themselves outside of bars where citizens are known to get drunk and then drive. Instead, police wait for those drunk drivers to drive many miles, possible injuring or killing somebody, before they give out their tickets—much, much too late. Working with the community outside such bars to stop drunken persons from driving would be both community-oriented policing and proactive policing.

The comparison of traditional policing with community-oriented policing in Table 8–4 was published by the National Institute of Justice (Sparrow, 1988: 8–9).

TABLE 8–4
TRADITIONAL VS. COMMUNITY POLICING: QUESTIONS AND ANSWERS

| | ANSWERS | |
QUESTION	TRADITIONAL	COMMUNITY POLICING
Who are the police?	A government agency principally responsible for law enforcement.	Police are the public and the public are the police: the police officers are those who are paid to give full-time attention to the duties of every citizen.
What is the relationship of the police force to other public service departments?	Priorities often conflict	The police are one department among many responsible for improving the quality of life.
What is the role of the police?	Focusing on solving crimes.	A broader problem-solving approach.
How is police efficiency measured?	By detection and arrest rates.	By the absence of crime and disorder.

TABLE 8-4 (CONT'D)

| | ANSWERS | |
QUESTION	TRADITIONAL	COMMUNITY POLICING
What are the highest priorities?	Crimes that are high value (e.g., bank robberies) and those involving violence.	Whatever problems disturb the community most.
What, specifically, do police deal with?	Incidents.	Citizens' problems and concerns.
What determines the effectiveness of police?	Response times.	Public cooperation.
What view do police take of service calls?	Deal with them only if there is no real police work to do.	Vital function and great opportunity.
What is police professionalism?	Swift effective response to serious crime.	Keeping close to the community.
What kind of intelligence is most important?	Crime intelligence (study of particular crimes or series of crimes).	Criminal intelligence (information about the activities of individuals or groups).
What is the essential nature of police accountability?	Highly centralized; governed by rules, regulations, and policy directives; accountable to the law.	Emphasis on local accountability to community needs
What is the role of headquarters?	To provide the necessary rules and policy directives.	To preach organizational values.
What is the role of the press liaison department?	To keep the "heat" off operational offices so they can get on with the job.	To coordinate an essential channel of communication with the community.
How do the police regard prosecutions?	As an important goal.	As one tool among many.

To summarize Table 8-4, community police consider themselves part of the public they serve. They work proactively by taking steps to eliminate crime and disorder. Community policing focuses on the citizens' problems and concerns.

 IMPLEMENTATION OF COMMUNITY-ORIENTED POLICING

According to *Implementing Community Policing: The Administrative Problem* by Kelling and Bratton (1993:4), the current police reformers who are carrying out community policing are using middle managers such as the leadership of line operating units and staff units (for example, planning and training).

Thus, the solution to the administrative problem in police departments was the establishment of a powerful mid-management group that: 1) extended the reach of chiefs throughout police departments and 2) became the locus of the practice and skill base of the occupation. As such, mid-managers became the leading edge in the establishment of centralized control over police departments' internal environment and organizational operations.

In order to establish useful and sustained change in any police department, police managers must overcome the overwhelming resistance of the established police culture. This is especially true in the case of community policing which attempts to reach outside the police department to involve civilians in police matters. The research on police culture, from Westley's (1970) dissertation on the Gary, Indiana police department in 1950 to Thibault's article, "The Blue Milieu," indicates that police have been socially isolated from the public (minority groups in particular), hostile to the public, threatened by any type of change, and very secretive (Thibault, 1992).

The only way a police chief can implement community policing is to have middle management convince the patrol officer that community policing:

1. Doesn't threaten his or her sense of identity as a police officer.
2. Doesn't lower the professional status or authority of a police officer.
3. Rewards police officers in terms of postings and promotions for implementing community policing.
4. Will remain a permanent part of departmental police procedures.

The old timers will say, "I remember that team policing crap. We worked with the community and formed what they would call today quality teams. Well the then chief felt that his power was threatened: BOOM! That was the end of team policing. Only middle management has the staying power to convince these officers, who have heard it all, that community policing is a permanent part of law enforcement.

In Dallas, the lieutenants (middle management) opposed community policing. As Kelling and Bratton report (1993:5), …before a single operational element of the strategy was in place {the police chief} was fired…and the planning unit…was renounced and liquidated." That was the end of community policing for Dallas.

In Cincinnati in the 1970s decentralized team policing was instituted by the chief and his managers without involving middle management. They jazzed it up with the behavioral jargon of management by objectives, further alienating the middle managers. The result was predictable (Kelling and Bratton, 1992:6):"By the end of 1975,…while some forms of team policing still existed, little of substance remained."

Kansas City, one of the most progressive police departments in the nation, used outside money to create problem-centered-policing task forces.

Middle managers were involved, for example, testing preventive patrol as a strategy and working on juvenile problems around the schools. The projects were successfully implemented; however, when the money ran out, the police went back to business as usual. This happened to team policing and directed-patrol strategies throughout the United States. In almost all cases, the departments went back to business as usual when the outside money ran out (Kelling and Bratton, 1992).

The city of Los Angeles faces major challenges in implementing community policing in the wake of the riots that followed the beating of Rodney King. In a city with so few police officers relative to the size of the population, the police barely have time to be reactive. There is little outside money. A limited amount of community policing—working through middle managers in selected neighborhoods—may be implemented, but at a high cost to patrol and 911 response.

SEATTLE: SUCCESSFUL IMPLEMENTATION OF COMMUNITY POLICING

In Seattle, a citizens group, the South Seattle Crime Prevention Council worked closely with the police department to target certain activities that the community wished the police to deal with:

> *Narcotic Activity Reports.* 1,219 citizen complaints of drug activity were actively followed up in the streets by teams of detectives.
>
> *Criminal Trespass Program.* More than 100 businesses signed up to give permission to police to enter their properties, which were posted No Trespassing, in order to cite or arrest individuals loitering in order to do drug transactions. Citations for cooperation were given to 1,044 citizens.
>
> *Pay Telephone program.* Pay phones were programmed for outgoing calls only so drug dealers could not receive incoming calls.
>
> *Owner Notification of Drug Trafficking.* Property owners were given notice that their tenants faced legal action for dealing drugs on their property.

Over time, other areas of the city were involved. A downtown business organization asked for strict enforcement of liquor laws and for foot and bicycle patrol where young people congregated. A crime-prevention division in the city police department, staffed by civilians, created a Block Watch program with organizers assigned to permanent stations in neighborhoods. Other city agencies such as the Seattle Housing Authority were involved.

Seattle's Public Action Plan

The voters approved an increase in resources including an addition of 147 sworn and civilian positions added to the department. Crime-prevention councils and police-department advisory councils were created to advise police in precincts through the city.

Community-policing teams of five officers and a sergeant were created. Members of the teams were considered full-time community police officers and did not answer 911 service calls. That Seattle was willing to devote part of its force exclusively to community policing marked a significant shift in departmental policy.

The Parks Department worked with police-officer volunteers to work with youth in an evening recreational program. The schools and the Department of Social Services were planning to work with police to actively intervene with youth in gangs and youth at high risk to join gangs.

Lessons Learned from Seattle's Community Policing

1. There is a need for police training in human relations skills.
2. The targets for community policing efforts have to be some problem that the community wants dealt with.
3. The impact is positive on both the police and the citizens.
4. Police get the benefit of civilian support in neighborhoods and businesses and support for the police budget.
5. The citizens get to know the police as human beings and as professionals.
6. The citizens see police in a positive light because the police are helping to solve the problems in their neighborhoods. (Fleissner and others, 1992).

COMMUNITY POLICING IN CHICAGO

In April 1993, Chicago's Alternate Policing Strategy (CAPS) was implemented in five districts. The burden of answering 911 calls was shifted to rapid response teams. Recruits, officers, and supervisors went through several training sessions. Advisory committees at the district level were formed, made up of police and citizens to support local problem-solving efforts. District advisory committees, with strong leadership that focused on specific short term issues were more successful than committees that focused on broad social issues. Beat meetings were divisive because citizens focused on community organizing and action while beat officers focused on police action. Locally-oriented volunteer groups with a crime prevention and local development agenda were the most successful groups.

There was a decrease in perceived crime problems and perceived physical decay. This included gang violence, drug dealing, building abandonment, and littered streets/sidewalks. Three districts experienced a decline in robbery and auto theft. Police supervisors involved in the CAPS program were more optimistic than supervisors not involved in the CAPS program. Chicago is currently implementing the CAPS program throughout the city. By reaching out to citizens, community policing produced a positive response to police efforts by the citizens of Chicago (National Institute of Justice, "Community Policing in Chicago: Year Two," 1995).

COMMUNITY POLICING IN HOUSTON

The goal was to involve the beat patrol officer with the community, with an emphasis on problem-solving. Officers were expected to keep citizens abreast of the police officer's activities. The description expressed an interest in power sharing with citizens but gave no examples of institutional implementation compared to what happened in Seattle and Chicago. The beats were redesigned to correspond to neighborhoods and beat officers were permanently assigned to specific neighborhoods. These beat officers were encouraged to become involved in the affairs of the community.

Some investigation was decentralized. Supervision and management were encouraged to support beat officers in solving neighborhood problems. The absence of criminal offenses, traffic accidents, and repeat calls for service became the criteria for evaluating the beat officer's performance. They said they managed calls for service by taking incident reports over the telephone, holding lower-priority calls and meeting with groups. Is this community policing? The answer is, it is a start but needs implementation with specific mechanisms. Just saying that beat patrol officers will talk to citizens doesn't create a community-policing model (Brown: 1989).

THE NEIGHBORHOOD SERVICE TEAM IN GARLAND, TEXAS

The team consisted of personnel from the police and fire departments, the planning department, and housing and neighborhood services. Field-level personnel interacted with citizens to identify problems and were empowered to initiate work without authorization from a supervisor. Training emphasizing teamwork with other departments included all levels of police supervision and line officers.

A community survey of one district was undertaken to identify community problems. Full-time NST officers did not have to respond to 911 calls. A short form with a "before" and "after" community survey was used to track the problem solving.

Neighbors wanted to clean up a neighborhood but lacked money for garbage tipping fees. The NST officer had the sanitation department provide trucks and a dumpster and the neighbors cleaned up the lots and streets. In another neighborhood, the housing department condemned and closed crack houses, and additional street lighting was provided.

To eliminate drug activity in an apartment complex near an elementary school, the NST surveyed the residents, adopted a zero-tolerance enforcement approach, enforced criminal trespass, evicted drug offenders, and code enforcement officials assisted management in making improvements. There was a 25 percent reduction in serious crime in the targeted area (Barber, 1996).

COMMUNITY POLICING IN BALTIMORE

This consisted of two approaches: a foot patrol, and an ombudsman officer. The ombudsman officer, like Houston's beat patrol officer, goes around and talks to citizens about their crime and community decay problems, and works with citizens to solve these problems.

There was a sharp increase in police visibility and a positive evaluation of police effectiveness by citizens in both the ombudsman police officer and foot patrol areas. Foot patrol resulted in a reduction in awareness of assault, robbery, larceny from person, larceny from automobiles, and vandalism. Ombudsman policing resulted in a reduction in the awareness of assault. There was also some reduction in some crimes but the author does not relate it to these problems (Pate, 1989).

▶ RECOMMENDATIONS CONCERNING THE IMPLEMENTATION OF COMMUNITY POLICING

How can a police manager decide if community policing is really taking place? The following four policies have to be in place:

1. *The agenda for police activities must be set by citizens*, not by the police administrators. This means there must be formal ways of finding out what the citizens want, such as surveys and the formal involvement of citizen associations.

2. *Middle management must be trained and directly involved* in the implementation of community policing, from the inception to final performance. This includes captains, lieutenants, and sergeants.

3. *There must be a split force.* Community policing has to be protected from 911 service calls so there is time to interact with citizen associations and to plan mutual problem solving with these citizens.

4. *Community policing must be a permanent policy of the department*, not dependent on grant money, which comes and goes. The policies and philosophy of community policing must be part of standard operating procedures. There must be a permanent reward structure for the implementation of community policing by line officers and supervisors.

Individual citizen involvement is not enough if community policing is to be truly implemented. As Skogan points out, there is a need to sustain community involvement. "One of the conclusions of the Chicago evaluation is that it is difficult to sustain autonomous citizen action, even with the support of the police. Organizations develop agendas that keep their energies focused, even when key leaders tire or turn to other affairs. They provide a locus for identification and commitment and they provide important social benefits to participants." (Skogan, 1996: 32)

Community policing cannot be implemented overnight. It takes time, training, a restructuring of departmental resources, and daily work with community groups. It can be done successfully as the Seattle experience has demonstrated. Middle management must become involved if the social isolation of the established police culture and the cynicism of the public is to be overcome. The line officer and middle managers have to be able to see the benefits of community policing or it will not work. We recommend that any agency that truly wants to implement community policing ask sworn police-officer representatives from middle management from a successful program to talk and work with their middle managers.

Without some additional resources in terms of new civilian and sworn-officer positions, it is very difficult for a reactive police department to implement community-oriented policing. But if you start small, say in one or two neighborhoods, and the people and politicians see that it is actually working, new positions and resources may become available. In the fight for additional resources in these tight-budget times, the best allies of the police are involved citizens who have seen community police programs work. It is not easy, but the benefits to both the police and community are worth the effort.

▶ HOT SPOTS

All of the various proactive patrol strategies, as well as community policing, only work when a police department has a split force. Patrol forces are split into a number of forces. The parts of the patrol force that are held back from servicing the reactive 911 calls are used for other purposes.

Larry Sherman found something very special while analyzing domestic violence calls to the police. He found that "Chronically violent couples can be identified and predicted. [And] Chronic locations of domestic calls can be predicted." (Sherman, 1992: 214) He found that "Over half (53%) of all domestic calls in Minneapolis occurred at buildings with four or more calls in 1986...." (1992: 227) A few years after this research, Sherman cites a case in the same city where 13 patrol cars responded to seven domestic calls in 48 hours for the same apartment. In Milwaukee he found that two-thirds of domestic calls "involved couples with two or more incidents in a 33-month period." (1992: 214)

This analysis can be applied to street crimes. In "Repeat Calls for Service: Policing Hot Spots" Sherman noted, "Three percent of the 115,000 addresses and intersections in Minneapolis were the subject of 50 percent of the 321,174 calls to police." (1989: 150) He noted under what he calls "dial-a-cop," his name for the 911 reactive system of policing, "The chronic locations are not given extra attention to try to reduce their heavy demands on police."

With a good data analysis management system tied into the 911 system, a proactive plan for policing hot spots can be created. There are a number of issues:

1. *Specific names are needed for specific locations.* For example, a bar can be known as Teddy's Twilight Bar at 110 Main Street. It can be known as (a) Twilight, (b) Teddy's, (c) 110 Main Street, (d) Twilight Bar, and so on. You might need a computer program to sort this out so that management knows that all calls came from one location.

2. *A criteria for the definition of a chronic location must be created.* Some examples would be: Top 50, 100, 250 called in terms of calls per year, minimum of 100 calls, 50 calls, etc. The size of the population would determine the criteria.

3. *The calls have to be categorized.* False alarm calls and lockouts would have policy implications in some jurisdictions while domestic violence and burglary would be important in other jurisdictions. Calls to discount stores, 24-hour convenience stores, various public and private apartments, medium- and low-priced hotels and bars are normal hot spots.

4. *An action plan would have to be formulated and implemented* to reduce the calls while dealing with the crime and problems generating the calls.

5. *An evaluation would be implemented* combining statistics related to a lowering of the number of calls per location and a questionnaire given to people at the hot spots. The evaluation would also take into account the displacement of crimes which would create new hot spots.

In Jersey City, New Jersey drug hot spots "made up only 4.4 percent of the street sections and intersections in the city but they accounted for 86 percent of narcotic sales arrests and 84 percent of emergency service...." The police met with area business owners and residents and used intensive crackdowns in cooperation with other government agencies. They maintained the gains made by close surveillance, foot patrols, and other forms of police presence. Major improvements were made in a few of the hot spots with little displacement to surrounding blocks.

Can focusing on hot spots work? Yes, if there is good analysis with a good police team involved in the planning and implementation efforts. It is better to focus on a few hot spots with an experienced team rather than spread the police resources too thin. It will also work with the help of other public and private agencies including liquor licensing authorities, the telephone company, department of health, and public housing agencies.

▶ CONCLUSION

Patrol is the most visible function in police operations. The concept of preventive patrol has come under great scrutiny based on the cost of vehicles and personnel and the seeming noneffect it has on crime incidents. Various studies and experimental programs have concluded that patrol should be directed to certain areas based on criminal activity and that all citizen calls do not merit a two-minute response time. The strategy is to cut down on patrol costs and create the optimum use of a professional police officer's time. However, political policy for many communities dictates the need for a police presence to reduce fear despite these fiscal and operational considerations.

The need for increased police presence and for new ways to address fundamental crime problems form the basis for community and problem-oriented policing. In this chapter, we have showed the theoretical differences between these two concepts as they are often used interchangeably. Some presenters on community policing often refer to community policing as the philosophy and problem-oriented policing as an analytical tool to deal with the causes of crime.

Community policing continues to attract much attention at professional conferences and seminars—perhaps even more so now that Federal and state grants are available for community policing projects and extra police personnel. The concept, however, cannot be perceived as a panacea for a community's crime problem and it involves a long-term political and fiscal commitment. Recall that team police programs were shelved once federal or state grant support ended. The key players for any change involve line and mid-management personnel in the department, which can be a difficult process in view of our discussion on police subculture.

QUESTIONS FOR REVIEW

1. What is meant by traditional police patrol? Of what activities does traditional police patrol normally consist?

2. What is the significance of the Kansas City studies?

3. What variables could lead one to conclude that traditional police patrol is a waste of time?

4. How are many agencies rethinking traditional police patrol in terms of administrative tasks and nonessential calls?

5. Why is crime analysis an important component of directed patrol?

6. What has been the "track record" of cities that have experimented with directed patrol? Team Policing? POP and COP?

7. How does directed patrol differ from specialized patrol? What are some examples of specialized patrol?

8. Why may proactive patrol be an important police methodology in the future?

9. Discuss the positive and negative attributes of community policing.

10. Explain the differences among tactical patrol, basic patrol, patrol investigation, patrol/community service teams, and full-service teams.

11. Present the various components needed for community policing implementation.

12. Outline the major management styles and leadership styles that would (a) be useful for implementing community policing and (b) be detrimental to the implementation of community policing and explain why.

KEY TERMS

basic patrol teams	neighborhood service team
caps	ombudsman police officer
community policing	patrol community service teams
crime analysis	patrol investigative teams
COP	police agent
CSO	POP
decoy squad	proactive patrol
directed patrol	preventive patrol
foot patrol	split force
full-service teams	stakeouts
generalist	surveillance
hot spots	tactical patrol
Kansas City Study	team policing
multispecialist	unit beat policing

BIBLIOGRAPHY

BARBER, ROBERT R., "Neighborhood Service Team," *Law Enforcement Bulletin* (January, 1996), pp. 17–22.

BLOCH, PETER B., and DAVID SPECHT, *Neighborhood Team Policing*, Washington, D.C.: U.S. Government Printing Office, 1973.

BLUMBERG, ABRAHAM, and NIEDERHOFFER, ELAINE, *The Ambivalent Force*. Hinsdale, Illinois: Dryden Press, 1985.

BROWN, LEE, "Community Policing: A Practical Guide For Police Officials," Washington, D.C.: National Institute of Justice, 1989.

BUREAU FOR MUNICIPAL POLICE, State of New York, "Seminar on Community Policing," New York, John Jay College, April 9, 1990.

CHAIKEN, J. M., *Patrol Allocation Methodology for Police Departments*. Santa Monica, Calif.: Rand Corporation, 1975.

DART, R., V. LUBANS, and R. SHOWALTER, *Plan to Increase Police Productivity: A Report on the Reorganization of the East Hartford Police Department*. Bethesda, Md.: Social Development Corporation, 1974.

ECK, JOHN E., and WILLIAM SPELMAN, "Problem-Oriented Policing in Newport News" in Roger G. Dunham and Geoffrey P. Alpert, eds., *Critical Issues in Policing*. Prospect Heights, Ill.: Waveland Press, 1993.

EDGAR, JAMES M., MARVIN MARCUS, ROBERT J. WHEATON, and ROBERT C. HILCOX, *Team Policing: A Selected Bibliography*. Washington, D.C.: U.S. Government Printing Office, 1976.

ELLIOTT, J. F., *New Police: A Description of a Possible Form of What the Municipal Police Will Evolve Into, Why They Must Change, and How Evolution May Be Accomplished*. Springfield, Ill.: Charles C. Thomas. 1973a.

_____. *Interception Patrol: An Examination of the Theory of Random Patrol as a Municipal Police Tactic*. Springfield, Ill.: Charles C. Thomas, 1973b.

_____, and THOMAS J. SARDINO. *Crime Control Team: An Experiment in Municipal Police Department Management and Operations*. Springfield, Ill.: Charles C. Thomas, 1971.

FINK, JOSEPH, and LLOYD G. SEALY, *The Community and the Police: Conflict or Cooperation?* New York: Wiley, 1974.

FLEISSNER, DAN, NICHOLAS FEDAN, DAVE KLINGER, and EZRA STOTLAND, *Community Policing in Seattle: A Model Partnership Between Citizens and Police*. Washington, D.C.: U.S. Department of Justice, 1992.

GARNER J., and E. CLEMMER, *Danger to Police in Domestic Disturbances—A New Look*. Washington, D.C.: U.S. Department of Justice, 1986.

GAY, WILLIAM G., H. TALMADGE DAY, and JANE P. WOODWARD, *Phase I Summary Report: Neighborhood Team Policing*. Washington, D.C.: U.S. Government Printing Office, 1977.

GAY, W.G., T.H. SCHELL, and S. SCHACK. *Improving Patrol Productivity*, Vol. I: Routine Patrol. Washington, D.C.: U.S. Government Printing Office, 1977b.

GOLDSTEIN, HERMAN. "Improving Policing: A Problem-Oriented Approach," *Crime and Delinquency*, 25 (1979), pp. 236–58.

_____, *Problem-Oriented Policing*. New York: McGraw-Hill, 1990.

GREENE, JACK R., "Police and Community Relations: Where Have We Been and Where are We Going?" in *Critical Issues In Policing*. Prospect Heights, Ill.: Waveland Press, Inc., 1989, pp. 349–368.

KELLING, GEORGE, *Foot Patrol*. Washington, D.C.: National Institute of Justice, 1987.

KELLING, GEORGE L., "Police and Communities: The Quiet Revolution," in Siegel, Larry J., ed., *American Justice; Research of the National Institute of Justice.* St. Paul, Minnesota: West, 1991, pp. 121–128.

KELLING, GEORGE L. and WILLIAM J. BRATTON, *Implementing Community Policing: The Administrative Problem.* Washington, D.C.: U.S. Department of Justice, 1993.

_____, and others, *Patrol Experiment: A Summary Report and a Technical Report.* Washington, D.C.: Police Foundation, 1074.

LARSON, RICHARD C., and MICHAEL F. CAHN, *Synthesizing and Extending the Results of Police Patrol studies.* Washington, D.C.: National Institute of Justice, 1985.

LEVINE, MARGARET J., and J. THOMAS MCEWEN, *Patrol Deployment.* Washington, D.C.: National Institute of Justice, 1985.

MOORE, MARK, H., and ROBERT C. TROJANOWICZ, "Policing and Fear of Crime," in Siegel, Larry J., ed. *American Justice; Research of the National Institute of Justice.* St. Paul, Minnesota: West, 1991, pp. 129–136.

NATIONAL ADVISORY COMMISSION ON CRIMINAL JUSTICE STANDARDS AND GOALS. *Police.* Washington, D.C.: U.S. Government Printing Office, 1973.

NATIONAL COMMISSION OF THE CAUSES AND PREVENTION OF VIOLENCE. *Rights in Conflict* (Walker Report). New York: New American Library, 1968.

_____. *To Establish Justice to Insure Domestic Tranquility*, Final Report. Washington, D.C.: U.S. Government Printing Office, December 1969a.

_____. *Staff Reports*, Vols. 1–15. Washington, D.C.: U.S. Government Printing Office, 1969b.

NATIONAL INSTITUTE OF JUSTICE, "Policing Drug Hot Spots," Washington, D.C.: U. S. Department of Justice, 1996.

_____, "Community Policing in Chicago: Year Two," Washington, D.C.: National Institute of Justice, 1995.

_____, *25 Years of Criminal Justice Research.* Washington, D.C.: National Institute of Justice, 1995.

PATE, ANTONY MICHAEL, "Community-Oriented Policing in Baltimore," in Dennis Jay Kenny, ed., *Police & Policing: Contemporary Issues.* New York: Praeger, 1989.

POLICE FOUNDATION, *On the Move: The Status of Women in Policing.* Washington, D.C.: Police Foundation, 1990.

PRESIDENT'S COMMISSION ON LAW ENFORCEMENT AND THE ADMINISTRATION OF JUSTICE. *The Police.* Washington, D.C.: U.S. Government Printing Office, 1967.

REICHER, LISA M., and ROY R. ROBERT, "Community Policing: A Critical Review of Underlying Assumptions," *Journal of Police Science and Administration.* June, 1990, 17. no. 2. pp. 105–114.

REINER, HOBART G., *Crime Analysis in Support of Patrol.* Washington, D.C.: National Institute of Law Enforcement and Criminal Justice, 1977a.

REISS, ALBERT J., JR., *The Police and the Public*. New Haven, Conn.: Yale University Press, 1971.

SCHACK, S., and W.G. GAY, *Improving Patrol Productivity*, Vol 2: *Specialized Patrol*. Washington, D.C.: University City Science Center, 1977.

SCHELL, T.H., and OTHERS *Traditional Preventive Patrol—Summary Report—National Evaluation Program—Phase I Report*. Washington, D.C.: University City Science Center, 1973.

SHERMAN, LAWRENCE, *Team Policing: Seven Case Studies*. Washington, D.C.: University Science Center, 1976.

———. *Neighborhood Safety*. Washington, D.C.: National Institute of Justice, 1987.

———, SHERMAN, LAWRENCE W., *Policing Domestic Violence*. New York: The Free Press.

SHERMAN, LAWRENCE, *Policing Domestic Violence*. New York: The Free Press, 1992.

———, "Repeat Calls for Service: Policing Hot Spots," in Dennis Jay Kenney, ed., *Police and Policing*. New York: Praeger, 1989.

SKOGAN, WESLEY G., "The Community Role in Community Policing," in *National Institute of Justice Journal* (August, 1996), pp. 31–32.

SPARROW, MALCOLM K., *Implementing Community Policing*. Washington: National Institute of Justice, 1988.

SPELMAN, WILLIAM, and JOHN E. ECK, *Problem-Oriented Policing*. Washington, D.C.: National Institute of Justice, 1987.

———, and JOHN E. ECK, "Newport News Test Problem-Oriented Policing." *National Institute of Justice Reports* (January/February 1987), pp. 2–8.

STRATTON, JOHN G., *Police Passages*. Sandusky, Ohio: Glennon Publishing Company, 1984.

THIBAULT, EDWARD, "The Blue Milieu: Police as a Vocational Subculture," in John W. Bizzack, *New Perspectives: Issues in Policing*. Lexington, Kentucky Autumn House Publishing, 1992.

THIBAULT, EDWARD A., and NORMAN L. WEINER. "The Anomic Cop," *Humboldt Journal of Social Relations* (Fall 1973), pp. 36–41.

THIBAULT, EDWARD, and NORMAN L. WEINER, "The Anomic Cop," *Humboldt Journal of Social Relations* (Fall 1973), reported in Human Behavior, 1974.

———, and R. BRUCE MCBRIDE, "Institutionalizing the Community Police Model in Canalville: A Case Study." *Journal of Police Science and Administration*, 9, no. 4 (December 1981), pp. 390–97.

TROJANOWICZ, ROBERT, and BONNIE BUSQUEROUX, *Community Policing*. Cincinnati, Ohio: Anderson Publishing Co. 1990.

VAN MANNEN, JOHN, "The Asshole," in Manning, Peter K., and John Van Maanen, eds. *Policing: A View From The Street*. Santa Monica, California: Goodyear Publishing, 1978, pp. 221–238.

WALKER, SAMUEL, *The Police In America*. New York: McGraw-Hill, Inc., 1992

WARD, STEVEN M., "Juvenile Programs." In Bernard Garmire, ed., *Local Government Police Management*. Washington, D.C.: International City Management Association, 1977.

WARREN, J. W., MARTIN L. FORST, and MANUEL M. ESTREALLA, "Directed Patrol: An Experiment That Worked." *Police Chief* (July 1979), pp. 49–78.

WESTLEY, WILLIAM A., *Violence and the Police*. Cambridge, Massachusetts: Massachusetts Institute of Technology, 1970.

WILSON, JAMES Q., *Explaining Crime*. New York: McGraw-Hill, 1975a.

_____. *Thinking About Crime*. New York Basic Books, 1975b.

_____, and GEORGE L. KELLING, "Broken Windows," in Roger G. Dunham and Geoffrey P. Alpert, eds., *Critical Issues In Policing*. Prospect Heights, Ill.: Waveland Press, Inc., 1989, pp. 369–381.

9

Administrative/Staff Functions

The term *administrative/staff functions* is utilized at the beginning of this chapter because many departments use either *administrative function* or *staff function* to describe the same set of services. We will use the term *staff functions* for the purpose of simplicity and clarity.

The police administrator must seek advice and counsel from persons who have various areas of expertise. The office of chief of police, while directing the overall police organization, cannot manage the daily operations of all units or functions as they do their daily tasks. Those areas of the police organization that assist in performing the advisory role are commonly termed administrative or staff services. In American policing, many of the following functions or divisions are usually included under this title: personnel and training, planning and research, legal advisor, public relations, inspections and internal affairs, and budget and community relations.

In reality, staff personnel actually command directly or indirectly, in that "advice" often constitutes a decision that is binding upon the chief administrator. For example, in personnel selection, the personnel supervisor presents a list of candidates who have successfully completed all requirements—civil service, state or county, and departmental—for the position of police officer. Much time and energy on the part of the personnel staff has gone into the preparation of this final list. With all these variables in mind, it would be difficult for the chief administrator to oppose these candidates. A tacit agreement or realization exists in organizational thinking, in which the chief acknowledges that the personnel supervisor is an expert in his or her field, having mastered all affirmative action and civil service regulations affecting this group of police recruits. The chief will review the list of candidates with the personnel supervisor.

The personnel supervisor will have to answer any questions if problems arise in the future; for example, a lawsuit based on departmental discrimination or an action grant being delayed because the department did not conform to civil service guidelines.

 ## LINE/STAFF CONFLICT AND COOPERATION

In the police subculture, persons assigned to staff services are often looked upon with disdain simply because they are considered to be "desk jockeys" engaged in "Monday morning quarterbacking" far removed from the everyday realities of police work being done on the street. The cause for this conflict is that, as Nigro and Nigro (1977: 165) pointed out, "The line frequently resents the controls exercised by staff officials." The reason for this is that the staff officers, no matter how tactful they are, "exercise a veto over the line...." Resentment can build up as the experts on the staff use their best judgment concerning line officers' activities. This judgment should and will entail denying line officers' requests. Although this conflict normally occurs between the line and staff officers, regardless of rank, the situation may be intensified when staff functions are operated and supervised by civilians.

Modern management principles applied to police functions normally result in a general recommendation for the hiring of civilians for many staff functions. The major reason given is that civilians may be less costly to hire than sworn personnel for some functions, and they can also be hired with prior training/education for specialized staff functions. The role of the manager is to be aware of the potential conflict between staff and line personnel and create a system that can accommodate these potential problems. One recommendation is to make sure that the civilian personnel on staff have enough authority in the department to carry out their functions. At the same time, there should be a process for line officers and staff personnel to appeal to upper management for conflict resolution.

This authority has to be clearly defined. Authority in the department goes from top management to middle management and then to the line officers and sergeants operating in the field. The staff officer and staff civilian personnel have authority concerning their internal functions and units. However, their authority does not extend to issuing orders to managers or line officers. Lines of authority need to be clear in any department if the department is to operate efficiently with a minimum of conflict. In this case, staff may recommend to management and line officers, but staff is not in the line of authority in operating the department.

On the other hand, as Nigro and Nigro relate (1977: 166), staff officers and civilians frequently look down on line officers. Such terms as *medieval, slow to change* and *ignorant* are frequently heard in discussions on this topic. It is easy to see how this attitude develops, for in reality, the staff personnel do have a major influence in the long-range and short-range policymaking for the police organization regardless of what the line officers feel. A good example of this type of this situation is shown in the following case study.

In this incident, management has obviously missed the mark in the positive utilization of staff officer Clement. It has missed the mark, also, in the effective utilization of staff information and recommendations by line officers. However, these problems can be dealt with in a positive manner.

---

case study
Ron Clement

Although Ron Clement deeply enjoyed police work, he felt that something was lacking in his life, and so he decided to go to college. He left police work as a patrol officer and applied his veterans' benefits toward a bachelor's degree. Ironically, he majored in criminal justice planning. Four years later, he walked through the front door of his old police station, only this time as a criminal justice planner.

Ron's responsibilities included preparing a daily summary of crime trends and analyzing different pieces of information that were gleaned from police reports. These daily summaries were copied and presented to patrol officers at the beginning of their shifts. He also assisted the chief of police and his deputies in overall departmental planning and soon became a part of the regular Monday morning administrative conferences.

"I didn't realize that there would be jealousy or animosity toward me. I mean, it was not too long ago that I was a patrol officer. But I suddenly realized that I had lost my connection with the street cops when I began to see my summaries in the roll-call-room wastepaper basket. I actually had to do a sales job with the cops, showing them how the crime summaries would be useful to their patrol work. The younger guys cooperated, but some of the veterans still shrugged off.

"It really hurt me when I overheard a conversation in the patrol locker room about me. One guy said, 'Clement has become a real jerk. He works inside and now he thinks he knows everything there is to know about running patrol. Why is it when a good cop, a brother patrol officer, goes inside, he becomes an arrogant jerk?'"

Realizing that this type of conflict is generally dysfunctional for the police organization and its personnel, we do have some recommendations for counteracting this state of affairs. These include

1. *Getting out of the office.* A common complaint is that staff personnel always stay in their offices or the station houses, thereby having little idea about what is going on outside. It is healthy for staff personnel, sworn and civilian, to ride along on patrol or be temporarily assigned to a line function, so as to keep in touch with the concerns of the line personnel.

2. *Rotating assignments.* Sworn personnel should occasionally be assigned to staff functions. Sworn police officers should be doing police work in the field. On the other hand, assigning line personnel to staff units from time to time can enlarge the former's perspective on the overall nature of police administration, so that they can better utilize staff work when they go back out on the streets. It also allows police administrators to review those individuals who have useful technical expertise or who are aspiring to become police administrators. Basically, this can be an excellent training ground for future executives.

3. *Implementing staff/line intervention.* In addition to ride-along or staff assignments, further interaction should be encouraged through meetings and seminars. For example, staff research on the right type of vehicle to be used for patrol should include patrol offices since they will eventually be affected by the decision. This is an often overlooked area of expertise. There are many personnel in agencies who, by virtue of their time on the job and experience, can contribute to the body of knowledge being gathered by staff as input to management decisions.

Although a great variety of staff functions exists, certain staff functions are either used in most police departments or are considered more vital to effective administration than others. In a text on police management that is also concerned with certain aspects of police operations as they affect the management of the department, only a limited number of specific operational functions and units can be examined.

▶ COMMUNITY RELATIONS

Many police agencies have established public relations or **community relations** units as a formal means of recapturing or establishing rapport with certain segments of the community. Program objectives of such units are aimed at target populations who either are prone to have violent confrontations with the police or have questions about police activities. The concept of community relations grew from the tensions of the 1960s, when many police and public officials realized that there was a gap in communication between the enforcers of the law and those they policed.

However, community relations are not just the responsibility of an organization unit in a police department; they must also become the personal responsibility of each and every professional police officer. Each officer presents the image of policing and his or her police department to the citizens. How each officer deals with the citizens in his or her daily work reflects on the department as a whole. Thus you cannot have officers who shrug their shoulders and respond to a request by a citizen, "Oh, that's the responsibility of a public relations unit. The officers out on patrol do not have anything to do with that community relations stuff." Instead, the officer should consider himself or herself a mini community relations unit.

This communications gap has derived from a number of factors. At an earlier time, police patrol officers generally had an intimate knowledge of the neighborhoods they patrolled. Even in immigrant neighborhoods, foot-patrol officers were accessible and generally visible as they made their rounds through the area. The decline of police-citizen contact occurred for a number of reasons. By the end of World War II, police patrol work was done by car, placing glass and steel barriers between officers and their publics. Neighborhood precinct houses, which were community centers of information and problem solving, eventually were closed down and centralized into a few station houses or a centralized police station, thereby becoming more inaccessible for the general public. Furthermore, traditional urban boundaries, shaped by ethnicity and geography, were broken down by politics and urban renewal. In many cities, these "old" neighborhoods were eventually populated by black, Hispanic, and other new immigrants, generally poor and unemployed, who sometimes look upon the police as an army of occupation.

This situation is not found only in the inner city. In many suburban areas, whose municipal boundaries are geographically far-flung, citizens may have difficulty identifying the community police since there are often too few officers to serve the population effectively. Or policing may also be carried out by a number of competing agencies that together may have conflict in providing the entire range of police services.

In discussing some popular programs and services that are offered by community affairs units, it will become apparent that each officer should in actuality be a community affairs specialist. In the final sense, the daily actions of the community police are the only one true variable that increases or decreases tensions within the community. Community relations, whether done by one division or by a single officer, provides a conduit for individuals and community groups to talk to the police. It also provides the department with a mechanism to undo or address perceived or real wrongs committed by officers in the course of their duties.

Public relations units are often responsible for providing the media with information concerning the department and official police activity. Officers who have been involved in a newsworthy story often do not recognize the incident when it is later written up in the newspaper. Newspaper stories are written to sell newspapers. If the department wants accurate reporting, it must have personnel who deal with the media and are familiar with journalism. These individuals have to establish a rapport with the media so that the latter are treated with respect and are given accurate information concerning police activity. Press police officers need to establish good relationships with professionals in journalism in order to correct any misinformation that may have been published. The word here is *credibility*. If the department is to have a positive relationship with the press, it must have a credible relationship. This kind of relationship takes time to develop and maintain, but it is vital to the image of the police department in any community.

PERSONNEL FOR COMMUNITY RELATIONS

Ideally, we see the specialized community relations assignment as short term and assigned to all officers. Realistically, this is not possible since the very nature of community relations assignment requires the officer to develop good relationships over a period of time. Moreover, there are those departments that may have a few officers that most police managers would prefer "kept under wraps" since their actions and attitudes would do nothing to improve police-community relations. Community relations should not be a "dropping ground" for officers who, for some reason or another, are not able to perform street duties or have been placed inside for disciplinary reasons.

FUNCTIONS OF THE COMMUNITY RELATIONS UNIT

The community relations unit functions in two major areas: crime prevention and public relations. However, it must again be stressed that the successful, effective department is one that is closely identified with the community and one in which the officers do not leave community involvement to a unit of the department. Actually, even though it is not tradition, a better name for this unit would be the community involvement unit, thus showing the close ties of the professional officer to the community. Following are some of the major functions of the community relations unit.

Public Speakers Bureaus

These normally involve the use of officers or administrators being available to make presentations on various aspects of police operations to community and school groups. As a rule, engagements should be planned days in advance and should employ the use of modern audiovisual techniques. The officer in charge of the community relations unit should review any topic that is to be presented with the department speaker so that there is a consistent departmental policy running through all presentations. The community relations department head should actively seek out those officers in the department who have an interesting topic to present and who have some public speaking talent, experience, or training. A list of these officers and their topics should be on hand when any community group requests a speaker. In the area of race relations, special care should be taken to assign only those individuals who are knowledgeable and able to keep their heads in the midst of often heated and sometimes rather "sharp" discussions.

Tours and Demonstrations

These programs provide an excellent opportunity to educate the public by reviewing specific police techniques and operations in a realistic setting. Tours should be scheduled in advance, and care and consideration should be given to the nature of the audience so that the operations can be shown and explained in the proper perspective. Care should be exercised so that the tour group does not interfere with police operations going on at the time. Demonstrations in and outside the police station on police methods that have proven to spark community interest include radar use, dusting for fingerprints, use of police dogs, alcohol and drug detection, and computer capabilities.

Department Homepages

The Internet has allowed citizens access to the so-called information highway which allows users to communicate, browse, and obtain information from millions of sites around the world. Proactive departments have created websites which allow users to obtain general information about the departments, crime prevention tips, and up-to-date information on crime incidents.

FAX Information Programs

This program allows the department to transmit general information or information related to crime incidents, by facsimile technology to a group of consumers. Consumers, as defined for this program, include businesses, neighborhoods, or even other government units in a county or area.

Ride Along on Patrol

Scheduled in advance by the community relations unit, a ride-along program provides members of the public with a chance to see their community from inside a police car. Departments with such programs have formulated strict procedures on the issues of liability and safety. Basically, we recommend that these programs take place only with officers who *volunteer*, without coercion, official or otherwise, to have ride-alongs in their patrol cars during their regular shifts.

Another problem concerns the selection of these ride-along citizens. In the case of criminal justice students, it is usually clear that these are people with a career orientation seeking knowledge. This may also be true of the ordinary citizen. The patrol officer has to do his or her job, and those who engage in the ride-along program should have some special training in how to handle citizens when tense situations develop. Rules and regulations governing these programs should be clear and in writing. Officers should be able to explain to the citizen the role of patrol in the total functioning of the department. Civilians need to be instructed in terms of what not to do. At a minimum, the following needs to be stated:

1. Civilians should never be armed though they may have a gun permit.
2. In case of a violent incident, civilians should not leave the patrol car and should leave any confrontation to the professionally trained police officer.
3. Civilians are not allowed to bring tape recorders and cameras.
4. Civilians should be aware that this is a working police officer who had duty to perform and that they should not, in any way, interfere with the carrying out of that duty.

Some officers do not work well with civilian observers. An officer with personal problems does not need civilians in the patrol car to add to the stress of the job. Thus, officers engaged in the program for these and a variety of other reasons need to be screened. If the department management wishes a ride-along program as a public relations tool, controls must be placed on it in order for it to be a positive force in the community and the department.

College Intern Program

Many colleges offering criminal justice degree programs have established student intern programs in which the student is allowed to study the activities of a criminal justice agency for a certain period of time. Mutually agreed-to guidelines should be drawn up between the institution and the police agency regarding the number of hours and activities that the student will be assigned (Gordon and McBride, 1995). One officer should be assigned to be a mentor for the student. While the student is able to combine theory and practice in a criminal-justice-agency setting, agency personnel act in the capacity of field teachers by showing the student how police operations are carried out. In many cases, former interns are later appointed as police officers since the intern period has given the agency and the student the opportunity to decide if policing is a proper career.

Crime Prevention Programs

Many larger departments have separate units that deal with the issue of crime prevention. As noted elsewhere, one major role of the police lies in the prevention of crime. To further this objective, many departments instituted crime prevention programs in the 1970s as a means to reduce crime. The target populations for these programs were community and special interest groups interested in how they could help in the fight against crime and at the same time, reduce the likelihood that they would be crime victims. Specific programs included in crime prevention were the following:

Operation Identification. In this program, the police department allows citizens to borrow an engraver and etch an identification number on certain valuable items. The item of property and its identification number are then recorded in a police log. This process is useful if the item engraved is stolen and later recovered.

Neighborhood Watch. This program, devised by the National Sheriffs Association, incorporates the ancient notion of frankpledge. Each person on a street block is responsible for watching out for suspicious persons and incidents, especially those related to burglaries. The role of the community relations unit for this program is to foster the need for collective security in the neighborhood and instruct citizens under what circumstances to call for the police. Residents are issued decals that are posted in windows and doors indicating that the residence participates in the program, thereby attempting to foster some sort of deterrence.

McGruff: Take a Bite Out of Crime. This national media campaign has had a positive impact on law enforcement. Its four major objectives are (O'Keefe and others, 1984: 5) "(1) to change unwarranted feelings about crime and the criminal justice system, particularly those feelings of frustration and hopelessness; (2) to generate an individual sense of responsibility among citizens; (3) to encourage citizens, working within their communities and with local law enforcement, to take collective crime prevention actions; and (4) to enhance existing crime prevention programs at local, state and national levels. [The] campaign uses a cartoon dog character 'McGruff,' arrayed in a trenchcoat and admonishing citizens to follow the example of 'real people' prototypes who through various means helped to 'take a bite out of crime.'" Twenty-two percent of a nationwide sample responded yes when asked if the campaign affected their behavior; of those who answered affirmatively, 34 percent got new locks for their homes and used them, 21 percent were keeping watch on their neighbors and reporting suspicious activity, and 24 percent said that they were "thinking about doing something in the future that was suggested by the ads that we have been talking about" (O'Keefe and others 1984: Table 4).

Many crime prevention programs have been half-hearted attempts to improve police community relations. Often a program is conceived and massive publicity in the media is generated, but after a few months the program dies. The main problem is that most crime prevention programs are never evaluated in terms of one question, "Does the program have any impact on crime?" After instituting the program, the police agency must encourage continuing citizen participation in the program. The truth is that most equipment for Neighborhood Watch, Operation ID, and other similar ventures eventually does nothing but collect dust in police property areas. Thus, each program needs to be evaluated in terms of its permanent value to the citizens and the department.

THE COMMUNITY RELATIONS OFFICER

The community relations officer (CRO) acts as a liaison between the department and media services and public interest groups. In many departments, this specialist might be assigned to a community relations unit or, in some cases, report directly to the police administrator. In smaller departments, the chief of police very often will act as his or her own public relations officer.

In addition to acting as a liaison with the media, specifically the role of the public relations officer is to

1. Prepare releases on police-related news. Such news would include a daily police log, the status of investigations, crime trends, and other information deemed necessary for public knowledge.
2. Coordinate the scheduling of press conferences.
3. Prepare or coordinate special audiovisual materials or pamphlets, such as slide shows, handouts, or videotape presentations that portray department operations.
4. Coordinate the creation of home pages or fax information programs.

In this role the CRO must have access to all divisions and personnel in the department. Importantly, his or her viewpoint must relate to the policies of the police administrator and the department.

As has been mentioned, the press officer needs some journalistic training and the ability to have a credible relationship with the press. One problem often encountered is the reporter with a "police blotter" mentality; that is, when the reporter, looking for copy for the next day's paper, simply wants to know what dramatic event happened that evening. The press officer should be trained to handle this kind of mentality and, maybe, guide it to a more positive attitude for the good of both the media and the department.

The press officer should also be trained to speak effectively before the cameras. He or she needs to dress the part of a professional police officer and be articulate. With the new technology of the news (instant replay, portable TV cameras, and mobile units), an incident could happen and an on-the-scene report could be before the television viewers either instantly or within hours. A well-trained, responsible press officer who can handle tough questions in tense situations is needed for the job. This person should be recognized as a high-priority factor in any police budget and should have higher status and rank than he or she does in most departments. We have to get beyond taking press officers from the ranks and placing them before the camera with no special training. This position is vital for the creation of a positive image for the professional police department.

One last note on the press officer's training and rank. The press officer must command enough rank so that he or she has the respect of fellow officers and enough authority to be seen to speak for the department. These officers should have enough time on the road and in rank so that they can be respected for their past police experience and knowledge of the department. Finally, they should have solid training in criminalistics and crime-scene control so that they can educate the public and the press, yet protect the confidentiality of an investigation. They must be able to relate to investigators and know what can be said and what should not be said. They are also, on that television set, the department, and these officers' demeanor, training, and knowledge should spell out that they are professionals. Since the press officer represents the department to the public, the officer's behavior and language must be at all times professional.

 ## THE LEGAL ADVISOR

The daily actions of any police officer are subject to legal review according to the parameters set forth by the courts; so too are the operations of the police organization. Traditionally on criminal matters, police may consult with the local district attorney for advice and assistance in the coordination of criminal procedures and investigations. While this criminal aspect remains important, the police organization and its personnel have only recently been the targets of civil suits from persons or organizations. At one time, the police, as agents of the state, could not be subject to civil suit. Citizens can now sue public officials through various civil rights acts, particularly in those areas of false arrest, employment discrimination, and brutality. The rise of civil suits for money damages necessitates the use of attorneys who specialize in these matters. The role of the police **legal advisor**, then, would be to oversee the disposition of civil cases against the department. In addition, his or her duties would include keeping the organization updated on changes in criminal and civil laws and procedures as well as advising the chief and staff administrators on methods to decrease the likelihood of successful civil suits against the department. The legal advisor would also be a good resource for the continual problem of search and seizure matters.

The role of the police legal advisor in the future appears most likely to increase with stature in that a civil suit, whether successful or unsuccessful, incorporates procedures that are expensive in terms of legal costs. In many situations, the department or its counsel settles out of court for a lesser sum demanded by the plaintiff simply because of these costs. Successful suits, however, have an effect on the financial and policy operations of the department.

Civil suits against individual police officers are becoming an increasingly important factor when deciding certain departmental policy and individual police behavior (President's Commission, 1967: 30–35; Broadway, 1974, Silver, 1992). Police benevolent associations are becoming concerned with the threats of such civil action and have become involved, through their counsel, in a number of such suits.

Police departments in small municipalities and counties rely on private attorneys or corporation counsels for legal assistance. However, a part-time counsel on retainer with the local department, however small, would be of more benefit, since such legal help would be experienced and knowledgeable concerning the special problems of police departments.

Another useful function for counsel hired by police departments is that of the screening of arrest charges. Because of the use of plea bargaining in reducing charges, police officers may tend to overcharge or undercharge in making an arrest. A good police department counsel or, in larger departments, legal staff would make for better arrest charges and create better cooperation with a district attorney staff. The prosecutors would know that there was a screened legal basis for the charges that are handed to the district attorney's office. Fewer errors and fewer citizens awaiting trial for charges that are going to be reduced or dropped also makes for good management, along with positive community relations. In the long run, there should be more and cleaner convictions for crimes committed.

Police attorneys may also find patterns of errors that officers are making. Over time, through internal training sessions and memorandums to management and staff, such errors can be eliminated. Over the long run, again, we should have a better conviction rate.

In terms of good management, of course, the problems become more complicated as we look at the police arrest-and-charging function in the context of policy concerning the total court system. In the decision to charge (Jacoby, 1977: 7), "the prosecutor must make his decision based on the belief that:

> the individual is guilty;
>
> the prosecution of the case will result in a conviction equal to the effort expended;
>
> the influence of public opinion will be in the prosecutor's favor;
>
> the resulting sentence will match the crime; and
>
> the jurors are not loathe to convict."

Jacoby also spells out the choices available to the prosecutor:

> "to charge
>
> not to charge
>
> defer prosecution
>
> divert; or
>
> return the case to the source of information for further investigation."

Police legal advisors can be the interface between the police department and the courts. They can deal with the courts and bring policies and opinions back into the department so that arrests are consistent with the prosecutor's policies. They can also explain to the prosecutor's office how difficult it may be for officers in the street to carry out these policies. In the long run, this individual or office can bring about consistent policies in a police/court system while chief administrators for police and prosecutor's offices change. Thus they are a help in transition periods as well as in the day-to-day work of the department, the courts, and the arresting discretion of the individual police officer in the street.

▶ PROFESSIONAL STANDARDS

Police corruption in the United States has been a persistent problem for administrators and the community. Just what actually constitutes corruption is a local topic of debate, but for our purposes, we will define **corruption** as any instance where a sworn officer abuses his or her authority to obtain personal gain.

In recent years, the term corruption has been used interchangeably with police deviance, which is used to describe the following activities:

1. Corruption and misconduct during normal work activities and while off-duty.
2. Abuse of authority tht includes physical, psychological and legal transgressions against suspects, prisoners, and witnesses. (Barker and Carter, 1994)

From colonial times, officials who enforced the law always had a great deal of latitude in committing crimes during the course of their duties. The histories of many major police departments are replete with accounts of brutality, nonfeasance, bribe receiving, and abetting the activities of gangsters. Although there were periods of reform, corruption generally returned after the ruckus died down (Smith, 1965).

After World War II, many citizens, state and local governments, and interest groups addressed the issue of police corruption in their communities. Spurred by the media, many major police departments in the United States between 1950 and 1974 (and many smaller agencies as well) experienced corruption scandals (Sherman, 1974). This raised issues that still remain unsolved: Who polices the police? and How do we stamp out corruption or deal with misconduct?

One rather spectacular failure involved the advent of civilian review boards that caused what many police administrators of the time (1960s) felt was trial by newspaper, thereby destroying police morale (Richardson, 1974). This was also felt by most police benevolent associations of the time, especially the PBA in New York City. In New York City the action involved line officers in a political campaign to abolish the civilian review board which resulted in a resounding victory for the line officers' associations. This is one of the first times that an individual police officers' organization felt that it had the support of the citizenry to bring about policy changes.

One solution to the dilemma of corruption was the formation of a special unit, termed the **internal affairs** unit, that would keep watch on the activities of departmental personnel and investigate alleged acts of corruption or misconduct. The title **professional standards** has replaced the *internal affairs* title in most police agencies. This reflects new thinking on the part of college-educated police administrators and officers. It represents more than just a label change. It reflects how professional police administrators view their ethical and moral responsibility to the public and their wish to be self-governing, using their own professional standards. The professional-standards unit is expected to enforce a model code of professional standards that would apply to all members of the department. As Fogelson points out (1977: 179), after the Los Angeles Police Department started an Internal Inspections Division for this purpose, virtually every major city adopted a similar model. Today, every police department, large or small, has either a division or a person who handles the internal affairs functions, which in addition to corruption, include investigating offenses defined by police duty manuals as "misconduct."

Those departments that have professional internal-affairs operations are often hampered in their effectiveness by opposition from the rank and file, which is then formally expressed in the union contract. Union rules may include the following for the investigation of police officers:

1. A ban against the use of polygraphs or alcohol-detection devices.
2. Defined hours when an interrogation may occur between a suspected officer and investigators.
3. Advance notice advising an officer that he or she is subject to an investigation. Such notice may include the name and address of the complainant and the alleged act.
4. Complex procedures that make it virtually impossible to dismiss or discipline an officer.
5. The right of an officer to pick certain members of the review panel that will hear his or her case.

While such tactics may appear to be self-defeating for addressing the issue of police misconduct and corruption, it must be pointed out that these "safeguards" emerged to combat certain investigatory techniques including interrogation during the early morning hours, not being informed of the nature of the complaint before being questioned by internal affairs, the use of decoys and entrapment tactics, and disciplinary action being taken against officers without due process. A review of an agency's union contract on this issue often reveals either real or perceived abuses of the internal affairs function on the part of the rank and file.

ANTICORRUPTION PROGRAMS

The existence of the internal-affairs functions is only one facet of a departmental stance toward corruption. In their manual on developing an anticorruption program, Ward and McCormack (1979) make recommendations that have practical value for the 1990s.

1. *Establish a working definition of what constitutes corruption.*
   While all agencies would agree that accepting a bribe to fix a narcotics arrest would be a corrupt act, accepting a free lunch might be okay for one department, but corrupt for another. Community norms must be taken into account. What do politicians and merchants con-

sider a corrupt act? Finally, an important question to be raised is: Can the department and its personnel live with the final decision?

2. *Determine the nature of corruption.* This simply involves asking the question: Does police corruption exist in the department? If so, what kind and to what extent? This will not be determined overnight, but must take into account meetings with administrative personnel, public officials, and review of intelligence data.

3. *Obtain commitments from authorities.* A chief of police who wishes to tackle a corruption problem in his department must have the backing of the political establishment of the community and the assistance of other components of the criminal justice system, especially the local prosecutor.

4. *Develop an anticorruption policy.* This includes broad policy statements that deal with specific and prevalent forms of corrupt behavior (for example, gifts, food, kickbacks from tow-truck companies). These policy statements should be communicated to all members of the department personally, if possible, and commanders and other field supervisors should be notified that they will be eventually responsible for seeing to it that these policies are obeyed.

Once these steps are taken, the final task is implementing the policy into an actual working part of standard operating procedures. The steps involving implementation include:

1. Having policies reviewed and discussed by various committees composed of rank and file and administrative officers.

2. Having the police legal advisor review the plan.

3. Designing an evaluation mechanism to determine the effectiveness of the program.

The result of this planning should be a written policy preferably in handbook form on the rules of conduct for members of the police agency. These comprise the basic policies that will govern the daily activities of the police. They will also notify the public of the agency expectations in their interactions with one another.

These directives have to be very specific; for example, "Acceptance of any gratuity will be subject to disciplinary action. This includes services, restaurant and fast food meals, and presents of all kinds including bottles of alcoholic beverages given during holidays. Minimum punishment is suspension without pay for two days."

Although we have extensive materials on training in another part of the text, it is valuable to review the training function in terms of anticorruption programs. Recruit training should emphasize departmental policies, procedures, and ethical standards and be followed up with practical role-playing exercises based on common incidents related to corruption problems on the street. In-service training should also be provided, perhaps in the form of roll-call training to keep these policies constantly in front of all personnel in the agency. We recognize that it is difficult to change attitudes and practices of veteran police officers; however, it is the responsibility of management to correct these problems.

The key to deterring corruption rests with each supervisor's interpretation and enforcement of consistent policies from management. A close liaison and understanding of departmental policy is a must for successful operation.

MANAGING THE PROFESSIONAL STANDARDS/INTERNAL AFFAIRS UNIT

Internal affairs is that section of the police agency that handles citizen complains or initiates investigations of officers committing crimes or misusing their authority. In larger departments, internal affairs is a separate division that receives complaints and conducts investigations. In smaller departments, the chief of police or a delegate may comprise the entire internal affairs unit. It is important to note that internal affairs is not the only section that handles complaints against police. Petty transgressions are handled on an informal basis by midline supervisors or the peer group. Serious complains, or those initiated by a citizen directly to the police department, usually become the province of internal affairs.

Internal affairs is viewed with suspicion from two fronts. For citizens, suspicions are often raised as to whether making complains will make any difference since they believe that the police will "whitewash" the incident. For police officers, internal affairs poses a threat in that it abrogates the entire notion of fraternity found in the police subculture—the inconceivable idea that fellow officers will prosecute another resulting in fines, suspension, forced retirement, or jail.

Outside input deals with most of these misgivings. In many cities, citizens have been added to committees to review police misconduct. A nice balance is shown when police management has a major input into what citizens would be added to these committees, thus protecting internal morale while having an outside check on police misconduct.

In various cities throughout the nation, outside agencies have become involved in citizen complaints concerning police misconduct. Complaints are received by what is considered an agency outside the department in the following cities: (1) Buffalo, New York—the Buffalo Police Commissioner's Investigation Unit receives the complaint; (2) Honolulu, Hawaii—can receive complaints at the Office of the Ombudsman of the State of Hawaii, the Office of Complaints and Information, or the Prosecutor's Office; (3) Kansas City, Missouri—has the Office of Citizens' Complaints; (4) Toledo, Ohio—receives complaints at its Human Relations Center; (5) Indianapolis, Indiana—the Human Rights Commission investigates complaints, and the police department is required to follow its recommendations; and (6) Washington, D.C.—the

Complaint Review Board reviews investigations conducted by the police and makes recommendations with the city commissioner as the final authority (Broadway, 1974: 518–30).

Essentially, all complaints should be reviewed and investigated, no matter how minor or serious. It is the responsibility of the police agency to publicize the procedure for filing a complaint against a member of the police force. To prevent false reporting, it should also be publicized that a false complaint may result in prosecution. To prevent charges of "whitewashing," the internal affairs unit should notify the complainant of the results of the investigation and the disciplinary actions taken on the alleged offender. For complaints found to be "unsubstantiated" or when a no-action-taken result occurs, the complainant should still be notified and told the reasons why. If he or she is not satisfied, the complainant should be directed to the district attorney, the U.S. Justice Department, especially in instances of alleged civil rights violations.

DISCIPLINARY ACTIONS

A number of disciplinary actions can be taken against a police officer who has been found to have committed crimes or to have abused his or her authority. If the officer is accused of having committed a crime, the district attorney's office would naturally prosecute. However, while that prosecution takes place, possibly over a period of months or years, the officer may be kept on the force (presumed innocent until convicted) or may be suspended with or without pay. If the officer is not convicted and has been suspended without pay, he or she is normally reinstated and given back pay. In some cases the officer may have to bring civil suit to obtain that back pay.

Disciplinary actions can be brought against an officer for a violation against department rules which legally may not be defined as a criminal offense. Examples of such violations include failure to wear proper uniform or use proper equipment, having long hair or dirty shoes, failure to make proper entries in log books, and being late for duty. More serious departmental offenses which would still not be considered criminal offenses might include discourtesy to a citizen during the performance of a duty, an accident with a patrol vehicle, or drinking on duty.

In these cases, there are a range of sanctions that can normally be employed:

1. Field counseling or verbal reprimand
2. Written reprimand/formal counseling
3. Loss of vacation days or fine
4. Suspension with or without pay
5. Reduction in rank or change of assignment
6. Dismissal
7. Criminal prosecution

In cases involving minor deviation from department rules, supervisors usually resort to verbal reprimands. However, when the deviation becomes consistent behavior, such as being late for work, more formal means of discipline are employed.

The philosophy of discipline that we advocate is termed *progressive discipline*. The elements of progressive discipline are:

1. *Documentation.* It is the duty of the supervisor to document infractions and bring them to the attention of the officer. In the case of continued tardiness, some kind of official action must take place the first time the officer is late.

2. *Sanctions.* The sanction to be imposed, again ranging from verbal reprimand to a more serious punishment, must be related to the seriousness of the offense. For example, termination from the job is not a proper sanction for an officer who is late for duty for the first time. Termination, however, may be appropriate if the officer has been documented late on 30 occasions over a two-month period.

3. *Administration.* The sanctions must be equally administered to all portions of the department. It is not correct practice if discipline is meted out to one shift or sector but not to another. There must be consistency—which is difficult because of the range of situations and personalities that get involved in supervision.

Department Rules and Collective Bargaining Agreements

Departmental rules or collective bargaining agreements related to disciplinary actions must be strictly followed. In collective bargaining agreements, disciplinary procedures follow a grievance-like procedure in terms of a written notice to the offender and in some cases, stepwise review by a state labor relations board.

For example, for the officer who is tardy, the supervisor may wish to have a formal counseling session. A counseling session should be done in private and on a one-on-one basis between the officer and the supervisor. A written memorandum should follow outlining the basis for the problem, the reason the problem occurred, and the actions that will be taken to correct the problem. The written memorandum should be signed by both the officer and the supervisor.

Department review boards and state arbitrators become very concerned if the procedure is not followed in disciplinary matters no matter how slight the occurrence may seem. For instance, in one case a labor-relations arbitrator dismissed the department's request for loss of six days' pay for an officer who was consistently tardy because supervisors had not formally counseled the officer in ten previous but similar situations over the year. The rule in disciplinary matters is that if the allegation is not in writing and in the officer's personnel file, then it never officially happened!

In cases involving a serious complaint or a criminal allegation, more formal measures are employed. As Weston and Fraley (1980: 153) discuss, the rights of a police officer suspected of wrongdoing involve the following:

1. Notice of the nature of the investigation and the name of complainant, if known.
2. Time and place of interrogation and/or hearing.
3. Right to legal counsel at interrogations and/or hearing.
4. The recording of interrogation and hearings.
5. Written notification of determination and disposition of the complaint, with reasons for such dispositions presented.

Immediate suspension with or without pay before the commencement of a criminal proceeding or departmental review process occurs only if the officer is deemed to be a threat to the public and co-workers, or has committed a crime. Consider the following examples based on rulings by state arbitrators and police department review boards:

- Suspension without pay was an appropriate measure when an officer was caught shoplifting in uniform during an unauthorized meal break.
- Request for termination for an officer arrested off-duty in early morning hours wearing only sneakers was inappropriate since the employee was not officially on duty.
- The basis for termination was having consensual sex with a woman in a patrol vehicle while on duty. Before entering into a final-step hearing, the officer agreed to resign in lieu of six months back pay. The attorney for the department agreed to this plea based on the poor investigation that went into the incident, which could have resulted in a not guilty verdict and reinstatement of this officer.
- Although criminal charges were dismissed based on lack of probable cause, termination of a police lieutenant was upheld based on the defendant's service record and complaints involving sexual harassment, and the seriousness of the disciplinary complaint—striking a female officer.

If there are three recommendations that can be provided police management in terms of dealing with equity and protecting departmental morale, they would be

1. Consistency
2. Consistency
3. Consistency

This means that written procedures are followed and punishment fits the conduct.

EXCESSIVE FORCE

The use of excessive force by police officers is a major problem, and it seems that a small minority of officers receive the most complaints. For example, of the 3,440 complaints against police officers in Boston in the 1980s, 61.5 percent were lodged against 11 percent of the officers (Barker and Carter, 1994: 267).

The Report of the Independent Commission of the Los Angeles Police Department (Christopher: 1994, 291–306) on why the beating of Rodney King took place showed major problems. The Commission found that there was a group of police officers who repeatedly used excessive force and were known to police supervisors, and that no action was taken. From January 1987 to March 1991, of the 6,000 officers who were involved in the use-of-force reports, 4,000 had one report. There were 63 who had 20 or more reports. They accounted for 20 percent of all reports.

They found that performance evaluations of officers who used excessive force were generally positive. In an analysis of taped messages from patrol cars, they found officers admitting to beatings. The tapes were not audited by any supervisor. The Commission also found that the complaint system was skewed against the complainant, and that Internal Affairs only investigated a few complaints. It was also documented that the department treated excessive force offenses more leniently than other misconduct.

Police departments experiencing problems including excessive force and other police deviance cases need to institute new policies. Some combination of the following policies needs to be implemented relative to the specific problems, size, and nature of the police department.

Intervention Policies

1. Identification of officers who consistently use excessive force or other police deviance, with active intervention through a combination of counseling, sanctions, or removal from the police force if necessary. The use of excessive force and obscenities should be reflected in the performance evaluation reports.

2. Analysis and random monitoring of tapes of patrol car messages, with special emphasis on officers who are part of a targeted excessive force group, and/or use a consistent pattern of obscenities and racist remarks.

3. Special investigation and intervention by a team of departmental investigators, lawyers, and counselors. This office needs resources and support by the chief of police.

4. Written procedures for all investigations of police deviance, including rules for witnesses and other rules of evidence to be published to all

police officers and the public. These complaints need to be resolved with resources and policies such as the use of mediators and the availability of a legal staff. This will protect the rights of both police officers and the public.

5. Specific departmental rules outlining the limits of force by police officers, published to both police officers and the public. This should include both legal guidelines and the departmental rules.

6. Ongoing analysis of excessive use of force should be part of the schedule of analysis and written reports by a departmental research staff, or if the department lacks expertise and staff time, outside consultants.

7. Swift prosecution of any illegal acts by police officers and any false accusations by citizens.

8. Establishment of ongoing training for dealing with stress and anger control. Officers should have access to counseling for these and other problems.

9. Inform citizens and officers of the outcome of any complaint, in writing, with documentation, in a timely manner.

10. Some kind of appeal panel that would hear unsatisfied complaints by both the officers and citizens to an authority outside the department needs to be established. It could include a civil service board, ombudsman, judicial panel, binding arbitration, and of course, the use of courts and torts.

The secret of success is to deal with excessive force or any problem in a swift and fair manner without any cover-up. This means that all written rules and procedures should be in clear English, short, and to the point. They should be made available for everyone. The rules then need to be followed in a fair and consistent manner for both the police officers and any complaining civilian. Once a reputation for fairness is established, both officer morale and citizen respect will increase.

▷ CONCLUSION

Central administrative functions structure the day-to-day activities of the police agency. These functions are part of management prerogatives and are central to the major administrative authority in the department. When management talks about the internal staff of the agency, it is referring to the support personnel that administer to the needs of the line operations.

There is a natural antipathy between line officers and the administrative staff. The administrative staff structures and carries out the basic policies of the department and delivers these policies to the management. Supervisory staff is expected to exercise authority over the line officers in carrying out these tasks. Full communication between line and staff is essential if the cooperation that is needed to have a well-run department is to be achieved.

Three major staff functions are community relations, legal advice, and internal affairs. Community relations can be as simple as an individual officer in the small department or as much as a separate unit in the larger department. Traditionally, community relation officers have given speeches and have participated in Officer Friendly programs and the like. However, proactive management approach advocates a more active role for the police officers in the community. This means that all officers are trained in community relations and are expected to make community relations a part of their duties as police officers, taking part, for example, in such activities as teaching a minicourse in criminal justice in the local high school and organizing sport teams for teenagers.

The legal advisor, something of an innovation over the last ten years, is usually a full-time attorney employed by the department who can provide up-to-date training in changes in the law and screen cases so that the department has a better conviction record. It is a cost-efficient position.

Professional standards/internal affairs is one of the most difficult units to organize. To be effective it must be even handed and represent both the rights of the citizens who are being policed and the officers who are doing the policing. It must be proactive in the sense of having an ongoing anticorruption program. This means that the rules and regulations concerning discipline and corruption are in place and operational before there is any hint of problems. Too many times these internal rules and regulations are written and organized in reaction to specific instances of discipline problems and corruption. These reactive rules are often inconsistent since they relate to specific instances rather than to general behavior. Consistency and fairness have to be the major goal of any internal affairs unit.

These administrative functions, although closely tied to management, are essential to the operation of the total department. They affect all the personnel and, in the instances of community relations and internal affairs, can have a major impact on the department's image in the community. If the department is to be considered a professional police agency by the citizens of the community, these administrative functions have to be managed with a great deal of skill, knowledge, and consistency.

QUESTIONS FOR REVIEW

1. In your community, what recourse is available to a person who wants a solution to a problem related to police misconduct or corruption? To what agencies may he or she submit a problem?

2. What are the causes of line and staff tension in police organizations? How can these problems be addressed?

3. It would appear that every police officer is a public relations person. Why, then, is it necessary to have specific personnel assigned to this task?

4. Explain the strengths and weaknesses of the following community relations programs: ride along on patrol, tours and demonstrations, college intern programs, and crime prevention programs.

5. In general, what are the duties of a community relations officer?

6. List the main points of the anticorruption program presented in the chapter.

7. Why has police corruption and misconduct been a persistent problem in the United States?

KEY TERMS

community relations	line/staff conflict
corruption/misconduct	McGruff
college intern	Neighborhood Watch
home page	professional standards
internal affairs	ride along
legal advisor	

BIBLIOGRAPHY

BARKER, THOMAS, and DAVID L. CARTER, *Police Deviance* (3rd ed.), Cincinnati, Oh.: Anderson Publishing, 1994.

BROADWAY, FRED, "Police Misconduct: Positive Alternatives," *Journal of Police Science and Administration*, 2, no. 2 (1974), pp. 224–32.

CHRISTOPHER, WILLIAM, "Report of the Independent Commission of the Los Angeles Police Department" in Thomas Barker and David L. Carter, *Police Deviance* (3rd ed.), Cincinnati, Oh.: Anderson Publishing, 1994.

FOGELSON, ROBERT M., *Big City Police*. Cambridge, Mass.: Harvard University Press, 1977.

GORDON, GARY, and BRUCE MCBRIDE, *Criminal Justice Internships: Theory Into Practice*, (3rd ed.) Cincinnati: Anderson. 1995.

JACOBY, JOAN E., *The Prosecutor's Charging Decision*. Washington, D.C.: U.S. Government Printing Office, 1977.

KRAJACK, KEVIN, "Internal Affairs." *Police Magazine* (1979), pp. 9–16.

NIGRO, FELIX A., and LLOYD G. NIGRO, *Modern Public Administration* (4th ed.), New York: Harper & Row, 1977.

O'KEEFE, GARRETT, and others, *"Taking a Bite Out of Crime": The Impact of a Mass Media Crime Prevention Campaign*. Washington, D.C.: National Institute of Justice, 1984.

PRESIDENT'S COMMISSION ON LAW ENFORCEMENT AND THE ADMINISTRATION OF JUSTICE, *The Police*. Washington, D.C.: U.S. Government Printing Office, 1967.

RICHARDSON, J.F., *Urban Police in the United States*. Port Washington, N.Y.: Kennikat, 1974.

SHERMAN, LAWRENCE, W., ed., *Police Corruption: A Sociological Perspective*. Garden City, N.Y.: Doubleday/Anchor, 1974.

SILVER, ISIDORE, *Police Civil Liability*. New York: Matthew Bender, 1992.

SMITH, RALPH LEE, *The Tarnished Badge*. New York: Thomas Y. Crowell, 1965.

WARD, RICHARD H., and ROBERT McCORMACK, *An Anti-corruption Manual for Administrators in Law Enforcement*. New York: John Jay College, 1979.

WESTON, PAUL B., and PHILIP K. FRALEY, *Police Personnel Management*. Upper Saddle River, N.J.: Prentice Hall, 1980.

10

Auxiliary Functions

Police organizations, no matter what the size, need personnel to direct and supply resources to those units or individuals that provide police services to the community. Portions of the organization that fulfill this function are titled *auxiliary services*. Auxiliary services provide the "behind-the-scenes" impact on the police organization. They could also be titled *supporting services* since these services are necessary, normally, to support the daily business of the police agency.

The discussion in this chapter concerns the major auxiliary functions that appear in most departments. Depending upon local conditions, other supporting services may be necessary; however, we are interested in the supporting services used by most police agencies. These auxiliary functions include (1) communications, encompassing case records, criminal records, and identification officers; (2) data processing, including records, personnel, and administrative functions; (3) crime laboratory, including photographic, chemistry, and physical evidence laboratories; (4) property control; (5) vehicle and building maintenance; (6) licensing; (7) holding facility (jail); and (8) emergency mobilization services.

▷ COMMUNICATIONS

Some agencies assign communications to the patrol division since a great deal of time in communications is related to the patrol function. However, communications serves the whole department. Traffic officers, detectives, laboratory specialists, and experts from other special units all have the need for access to communications. In a modern department, a centralized communications and record unit is considered the most efficient way to organize this major auxiliary section.

The efficiency and effectiveness of daily police operations depend on the nature of the communications unit maintained by the department. This unit must be able to provide the following capabilities:

1. Telephone reception for emergency, nonemergency, and inquiry calls,.

2. Base-to-field communications and return by wireless radio.

3. Retrieval of police information related to wanted persons, lost property, vehicle ownership, and motorist information (commonly referred to as the DATA function).

4. Interface with or scanning of area and statewide police agencies.

5. Interface with or scanning of area fire and ambulance services.

The degree to which these services are provided depends not only on the size and jurisdiction of the police agency, but also the degree of economic investment that the municipality wishes to make for computer communications equipment. At present, the advances made in communications and computer technology provide the opportunity for every police department in the United States to offer these services to personnel and the community as shown in the following case study.

case study
Communications

On April 12, 1996, Mrs. Stephen Jones telephoned the Riverside Police Department stating that her husband was threatening to kill her and that she had locked herself in a bedroom. Her call was recorded on a telephone tape unit. Units 303 and 410 were dispatched to the residence. While en route, the communicator replayed the conversation to the officers on channel 1 of their multichannel mobile radio. The officers responding to the scene therefore had a general picture of the situation as related by Mrs. Jones. At the conclusion of the playback, Unit 303 "punched" the husband's name into the mobil data terminal and found that a man of the same name and address had been arrested by the department four years ago for assault with a deadly weapon. Upon arrival at the scene, one officer noted that a black MG sportscar was parked in the driveway.

Using the mobile data terminal, the officer "looked up" the license plate and found that it belonged to a subject by the name of Stephen Jones who had three outstanding warrants for burglary and assault. A detective unit also arrived at the scene. Using a cellular telephone, the detective called the residence and asked for Mr. Jones. Using his powers of persuasion, the detective asked Mr. Jones to come outside to talk to him about the outstanding parking tickets issued to his valuable sportscar.

This incident illustrates some of the capabilities of modern communication systems. The nearest cars from the jurisdiction were dispatched since this was a regional communication system. Also the system had a tape-recording capability, which had not existed a few years previously. In addition, the dispatched officers had instant access to all records—local, state, and national. In terms of providing the maximum amount of information in a very short time, the system had lived up to expectations.

CONSOLIDATION

In an effort to solve communications inferiority, some police agencies have pooled their resources and have formed a **mobile radio district (MRD)**, making a centralized communications center the main reception center for telephone calls for police assistance. Member agencies in the MRD are dispatched according to their jurisdiction. If an officer is in trouble, or if a serious emergency occurs requiring the presence of many patrol units from the member agencies, the communications center will be able to act as the focal point for activity coordination. Computers for local and national police information are maintained and operated at the center, and member agencies are provided with a terminal to be used in their own station houses. Mobile, portable, and base-station radio equipment is procured and maintained under the coordination of the MRD. To solve problems or address issues that arise on procedures or situations where problems developed, the MRD has a representative committee of member agencies that meets frequently to "iron out" these problems.

Consolidated communications centers using the MRD model have been established all over the United States in heavily populated metropolitan areas. One problem that arises in MRD formation is the influence that the political faction or agency that controls the communications center may have on all police operations for that area. This is a common problem when an agency, such as the state police, the sheriff's department, or a town police department has concurrent jurisdiction with city, village, or town agencies. The question that always comes up is: Who will receive the "glory" calls? This is usually solved by de facto arrangements and formal guidelines ensuring that city units will respond to calls in their jurisdiction and that other units only respond in emergencies or at the request of the agency. The solution of this problem has been crucial in the formation of consolidated police communications networks.

COMMUNICATIONS PERSONNEL

The police subculture may view those personnel who work inside the station house as second-class citizens since they are not out on the streets doing "real police work." As a result, officers assigned to communications are looked upon with some measure of disdain. In some agencies, the communications assignment is viewed as being for those who have physical ailments or have "screwed up" in some way; yet there is nothing second class about police communications.

These attitudes are in the process of change due to the importance of the communications function and the amount of technological expertise needed. It is not uncommon for police communications supervisors in large agencies to have formal degrees in electronics, computers, and communications and to be able to write grants and computer programs for elaborate police information-communications systems. Because personnel with this type of background are difficult to recruit for general police work, many agencies have relied on civilians with relevant work and educational backgrounds to manage their communications systems.

Some departments have begun to use civilians as communicators. In addition to classroom training, the civilian communicator should be assigned to observe patrol observations so as to get a feel for the geography and personalities of the sworn officers with whom he or she will be working. In the same vein, rookie police officers should be assigned to the communications sector for the same reasons. Supervision of a shift or section in the communications section should be supervised by an experienced sworn officer, who, in addition to normal administrative tasks, will act as commander for emergency situations.

In small police departments, the communications function will be handled by one person, who in addition to police responsibilities, will also have to act as desk clerk and fire dispatcher. Again, there is no clear-cut formula for the number of persons assigned to this function. It depends upon the size of the agency and jurisdiction as well as on the amount of police activity that the agency has to handle.

PERSONAL ATTRIBUTES

Police communicators should be familiar with all aspects of police operations and agency procedures. A good communicator, in practice, will have the ability to screen calls and solve those situations on the phone that do not require the police presence at the scene. As most police communications personnel relate, working on the police telephones and radios is a stressful job. It requires a number of personal qualities—tact, politeness, coolness, rational decision making—and the ability to perform seven different tasks at once. For the police subculture, the chief client of the communicator is the officer on the street, as he or she is responsible for the safety and informational updating of each and every one of the officers. Experienced communicators know when an officer is in trouble simply by a nuance or failure to call back while doing a task (for example, a vehicle and traffic stop) in a reasonable length of time. Officers assigned to street duty realize this. One of the first inquiries made at the beginning of the shift is, "Who's on the radio?"

Today in police training, communications procedures is a standard part of the basic police curriculum. Academies with a good physical plant may have a classroom as a mock communications area where recruits respond to mock telephone calls and requests for information, dispatch patrols, and calm an irate citizen—all at the same time! Civilian personnel also must be trained according to the same procedures and methods as regular police officers. For example, Connecticut requires that all dispatchers receive a one-week training program in police communications. In addition to mock calls, dispatchers learn basic first aid, crisis management, and communications theory (Burke, 1995: 14).

▶ RECORDS

As in all bureaucracies and complex organizations, efficient recording and flow of paperwork are essential to the successful operation of the police agency. The records division is often considered part of the communication division or at least it works closely with the communication division.

Although often downgraded in terms of funding and personnel, the records division is an important tool for management. To allocate resources, personnel, and budgeted funds, an accessible information system is needed. *Accessible* means that the information has to be available in more than raw form. Thus, the chief task of **records** involves classification, filing, and indexing of police paperwork by numerical, alphabetical, and numerous other classification systems, so that this information is accessible for later convenient retrieval. Information is also needed for informing the public and other private and public agencies such as defense attorneys, prosecutors, and insurance companies:

For police operations, records may be divided into the follow subcategories:

Category	*Tasks/Operations*
Persons	Arrestees, complainants, victims, missing persons, wanted persons, (for questioning or by warrant) fingerprints
Motor vehicles	Accidents, inquiries, fatalities, moving violations, and parking tickets
Administration	Personnel, payroll, scheduling, budget, purchases, inventories, and fleet and building maintenance
Crime statistics	Arrests and crime reports by legal statute, area, age, race, and so on
Property	Lost, found, stolen
Other	Jail, operations, court dispositions, bail monies, and referral services

These six subcategories may or may not be centralized depending upon the management philosophy or operational history of the department. Each line, staff, or auxiliary division might maintain its own records system in addition to a centralized system. Investigative divisions, for example, often maintain a file of suspicious persons or incidents via modus operandi. Be it a centralized or a decentralized records system, the overall records function is a mainstay of police operations—providing data for investigative leads, allocating resources for certain types of cases, or preparing state or national crime reports.

One of the main goals of the records section is to present a total reporting picture which is critical for management decision making in such areas as work-load, types of incidents, and an assessment of hazards. The types of crimes encountered or reported are important for uniform crime reporting purposes. Disposition information is also critical as indicated by the following disposition descriptors:

1. Arrest made—(Refer to original offense report)
2. Assistance rendered
3. Canceled by radio
4. Citation issued
5. Civil matter
6. False alarm
7. Follow-up: (supplemental report made)
8. No police action possible/necessary
9. Peace restored without incident
10. Referred to agency other than PD
11. Referred to other PD division

ENTER THE COMPUTER AGE

Police organizations began to use computers in the early 1960s. Not only was the computer, by this time, an important tool for informational transmission and storage, but also it was beginning to be used for managerial decision making. As shown in other chapters, computers have been experimented with in determining patrol allocation and operations in many American cities. Plentiful funding for computer acquisition was available throughout the 1960s and early 1970s, which made it possible for many police departments in large metropolitan areas to establish computerized data and communication systems.

At present, computer utilization has been expanded for the records function. The following positive attributes of computer utilization for data retrieval are (Bureau of Justice Statistics, 1993):

1. Lower routine operating costs of data processing.
2. Faster availability of information.
3. Allows an audit of the system.
4. New information generated that has never before been recorded.
5. Greater consistency of reporting data.

6. Reduced data distortion as the data move from line operations to staff.

7. Development of a giant data inventory to be used for testing the environment.

8. Greater freedom from mundane, routine recordkeeping.

STORAGE OF RECORDS

Historians bemoan the loss or damage of nineteen- and twentieth-century records of many American police departments, especially by fire or paper decomposition. This continues to be a special problem since paper processing requires the use of acids that break down the paper. Also, it is not uncommon to see stacks of police files stored in cardboard boxes gathering dust and moisture in the dark recesses of the station house. This situation has been caused by the lack of storage space for the tons of paperwork created annually and an unprofessional approach to storage and record retention.

Except for those records that, by law, need to be kept in the original, all storage should be microprocessed. This means that all records are reduced by the various processes available to modern library systems: microfilm, microfiche, or electronic retention in computer-generated files. There also needs to be a specific retention period for all records. There are problems with this cost-efficient approach to record retention and retrieval: (1) the laws need to be changed, (2) the expense of processing of records into microform has to be reduced, and (3) the cost of a retrieval system including readers and machines to produce hard copy from microcopy has to come down. The costs of such a system are declining as more and more research libraries create systems using microprocessing of research materials. The U.S. government has encouraged and sponsored numerous research projects to bring down the cost of processing and using micromaterials.

Imaging technology, which copies records onto a computer disk, shows great promise in reducing the amount of paper that police departments store.

SECURITY, SEALING, PURGING, AND PUBLIC ACCESS TO RECORDS

Police departments generally desire that police records be kept confidential to maintain the effectiveness of law enforcement operations. This is especially important since a large percentage of police information involves the criminal history of suspects and arrestees. It is therefore imperative that the police agency ensures the confidentiality and integrity of criminal history information through administrative, computer, and physical security requirements. Based on department of justice regulations with regard to security of federally funded information systems, the following guidelines apply to all police agencies:

1. Access to criminal history information, namely, records, computer files, or the operating environments where police information is stored should be restricted to authorized personnel.

2. Police personnel that have access to criminal history information are responsible for protecting this information from unauthorized access, disclosure, or dissemination.

3. The supervisor(s) assigned to oversee the records function is (are) ultimately responsible for all records.

4. Through written directives, SOPs, and updated procedures, each member of the police organization should be familiar with the substance and intent of record security regulations (New York State Department of Criminal Justice, 1990).

While police organizations are intent on protecting the confidentiality of their records, there has been a nationwide trend for allowing citizens to have access to police information, especially when that information is related to the individual. In the 1970s, a number of acts were passed by Congress as reforms to the abuses of federal and state domestic spying and increased classification of government operations. The **Freedom of Information Act** of 1974 allowed citizens to request public records and to attend meetings of a nonconfidential nature. The Privacy Act, passed in the same year, gave individuals access to personal records and restricted the collection, maintenance, and distribution of personal information in both private and public agencies. In general, an individual requesting a federal document must go through a formalized process to obtain a copy of the record.

Federal and state regulations give every person who is the subject of a criminal-history record the right to

- Request to be shown a copy of the record at a reasonably convenient location and time.
- Review the record (with assistance of a reader/translator, if needed).
- Receive a copy of the record for purpose of challenge.
- Request that a record be corrected upon a showing of inaccuracy or incompleteness.
- Obtain administrative review of record-correction denial.
- Request, for purposes of correction, a list of noncriminal-justice recipients of inaccurate information. (Criminal-justice recipients to be notified directly by criminal justice agency.)

The regulations do not provide a right to review:

- Any information other than "criminal history information."
- Any information contained in intelligence or investigatory files.

State and/or local criminal justice agencies are required to establish procedures for

- Review of criminal-history information by the record subject.
- Challenge by the record subject of information which is believed to be inaccurate or incomplete.
- Review of source documents by the criminal justice agency to determine accuracy/completeness of challenged information.
- Administrative appeal by the record subject of an agency's refusal to correct a record.
- Correcting information which has been disseminated that is shown to be incorrect.

Citizens may or may not be allowed access to their own criminal files, depending upon the state. In the case of the FBI record, upon payment of a fee, or proof of indigency, a citizen may receive a copy of his or her record. However, the FBI will only accept corrections to the record from the agency that sent the FBI the original data.

For police operations, this right to privacy may come into conflict with the need for accurate data on criminal suspects. Yet much police data contains information of little value or outdated relevancy. For example, many people are arrested whose cases result in dismissal or acquittal. In other cases, for police information systems that keep a record of wanted or arrested persons by street address, it is often the case that the information is "old." The suggestion that a suspect may still be living on the premises indeed affects the officer's perceptions as he or she responds to a call to the location in question. Both hand-recorded and computerized police information systems, therefore, should have policies that allow the removal of outdated or incorrect information. Two methods that apply to this procedure are termed (1) **purging**, as when the record is either destroyed or returned to the individual (this often occurs for the arrest records and fingerprint cards of individuals who have been acquitted or found not guilty), and (2) **sealing**, as when general access to the information is strictly limited except for certain instances or individuals. Sealing is generally done for juvenile offenders in that only youth officers or officials of the juvenile court can officially have access to the information.

Purging and sealing are used for outdated or declassified information, or when legal changes are made; for example, decriminalization of alcohol or drug offenses.

 PROPERTY SECTION

The property clerk, who may be a sworn officer or a civilian, is the person in charge of this section. Property is divided into (1) inventory control of physical property, (2) evidence control for court cases, and (3) found property such as bicycles that have been abandoned in the street. Some police agencies that provide uniforms also have the property clerk serve as quartermaster, issuing and taking care of uniforms.

INVENTORY CONTROL

Inventory control of physical property can have a major impact on the budget in that this property is being used 24 hours a day, as opposed to the more normal 8-hour or 12-hour day. Thus, planning—including maintenance and replacement control on a regular basis—becomes significant to day-to-day operations. Several individuals use the equipment in a 7-day, 24-hour-a-day week; thus to control inventory, the property clerk has to be on top of what is happening to the physical property. Examples of physical property are desks, chairs, file cabinets, the buildings themselves, heating and cooling units, and so on. Desktop computers may cost over a thousand dollars each and have to be maintained and replaced on a regular basis with the department able to recoup residual values by the sale of such items as secondhand equipment. All this takes strict auditing as well as inventory control. Businesslike procedures created by a full-time property clerk are necessary if the department is to justify this part of the budget to legislative authorities. Estimates must be made of the life use of each item in a police setting with periodic physical inspections to confirm this life use.

In some cases, inventory purchases may be out of the jurisdiction of the property section because of a state or county purchase plan. However, the same principles apply. Also, any civilian agency has to be made aware of the special problems of the servicing of a 24-hour police department.

Evidence control will be treated more fully when we examine the basic management of the police laboratory. However, two major principles are seen to apply here: continuity and security. A record must be kept of anyone handling any police evidence, and detailed records must be maintained concerning what happens to a piece of evidence whenever it leaves the property room. The second principle of security is paramount in any police agency. However, in the use of civilian personnel, special background check should be made, and in-and-out security measures need to be strictly observed. One of the major problems relates to keeping drugs in the property room. Small amounts of certain drugs are worth so much money in the street that the temptation of civilians and officers to make a quick dollar is always there. Professional security measures using current technology should solve most of these problems.

CONTINUITY OF EVIDENCE

Continuity of evidence means that there is a clearly documented record of where a piece of evidence has been, along with a record of who handled the evidence and why, from the time the evidence is picked up at the crime scene until it appears in a court case. Any break in the continuity of evidence is an opportunity for a sharp defense lawyer to break a case. The property clerk maintains the security of evidence as it is delivered from the crime scene and documents continuity in the following way:

1. Evidence is collected by evidence technicians at the crime scene and is sealed in plastic bags or appropriate containers to prevent contamination. It is also marked for future identification giving date and circumstance of obtaining evidence on the package or article. On this container or article will be a form that everyone who handles the evidence will sign, date, and give a reason for handling evidence. Continuity is the principle followed here.

2. Evidence goes to the lab if necessary or to the property clerk. Any detective or police officer who handles any evidence during investigation signs in and out for any piece of evidence. All evidence is to be returned to the property clerk for safeguarding when not needed.

3. At the end of the investigation, evidence normally is transferred to the district attorney's office where continuity of evidence must be maintained in case of appeal. The evidence is considered to be the prosecutor's responsibility until he or she returns it to the property clerk.

4. In addition, there must be security and oversight measures by which high risk evidence (narcotics, money, jewels, and firearms) are inventoried on a routine basis and only certain personnel have clearance to enter the evidence area. There also must be a process by which old evidence is either returned to owners, auctioned, or destroyed. It is no secret that many property rooms are full of items gathering dust.

FOUND PROPERTY

Found property is something of a nuisance for the department to handle but can be a real service to the citizen who might be able to recover that $450 bicycle that was missing one day. At periodic intervals, after the property has been kept for a reasonable period of time, a public auction is held to sell what property remains with the money going into the general coffers.

VEHICLE MAINTENANCE

Next to personnel, police vehicle acquisition, operation, and maintenance represent a major portion of budgetary expenditures whether the department has a fleet numbering 3 or 300 vehicles. A fully-equipped police vehicle (lights, siren, radio, security devices) may well average over $26,000 per unit. And with today's gasoline prices, many police departments are seeking ways to reduce vehicle operating costs by redefining patrol objectives, increasing foot patrols, redesigning patrol sectors, or experimenting with smaller more fuel-efficient vehicles. Departments are also using bicycle patrols in certain areas.

Police vehicles are on the road a good part of the 24-hour day. They may normally clock between 80,000 and 200,000 miles before they are retired, depending upon increased maintenance costs and downtime records. A car used by police is normally an adapted stock vehicle. Adaptation normally includes special lights, communication insertions, heavy-duty shocks, alternators, and roll bars. Thus we have vehicles that are purchased in large quantities, often with a state or municipal contract, but have added features that result in added costs and lower gas mileage.

With these variables in mind, patrol vehicle selection is an important decision. The chief criterion depends upon the environment. Rural and suburban departments generally need vehicles that have space for equipment and passengers since the patrol car serves as an office. Municipal departments that operate comparatively close to the police station can be best served by fuel-efficient vehicles. Terrain and weather are also important considerations for the selection of four-wheel-drive vehicles that can operate in the snow, on hillsides, or in beach areas.

One problem affecting many departments is that exact specifications need to be drawn for specific job requirements. However, if the police vehicle cannot accelerate or corner better than the normal stock vehicle, then especially on highway patrol jobs, the police job simply cannot be done.

Each department should have a preventive maintenance program to detect problems before actual breakdowns occur. With the exception of patrol operations on interstate highways and rural areas, most patrol cars operate on "idle" or stop-and-start situations and then suddenly must increase speed from 0 to 60 miles per hour in emergency situations. Considering the potholed streets, bumpy parking lots, and fields, they must travel, it is no wonder that most patrol vehicles are functionally dead by 100,000 miles or less. Moreover, because of the lack of spare vehicles, many departments actually keep their cars running 24 hours a day with "time off" only for maintenance or shift changes.

Preventive and actual maintenance for vehicles is handled by police or municipally operated central garages or, in smaller communities, by private contractors. In any case, each administrator will have to decide which method is desirable based on cost effectiveness and availability of service and facilities offered by the municipal government. Mechanics who work on the police vehicles and maintenance records should be considered important resources for data on vehicle effectiveness, operating costs, and systems that are prone to break down (for example, electrical system, cooling, tires).

Preventive maintenance is further important because of the variety of drivers for each vehicle, the heavy use, and the use of the vehicles in life-and-death situations. Management needs to be aware of the driving habits of its personnel, including the need for review classes on driving habits and continual testing. Part of this process is the creation of an accident review board where the personnel involved in accidents is strictly analyzed. The result of such a review may mean disciplinary action against sworn personnel and vehicle maintenance staff. It can also mean that management will have to review when a vehicle should no longer be in use. Some models of cars last longer than others and safety can only be maintained through the use of continual review. Many departments prefer to purchase half their fleet every year, whereas smaller departments may wait for two or perhaps three years to update. Many factors enter into this decision, including the rotation of vehicles into other units of the agency requiring less demanding vehicle usage.

The most important aspect of this discussion lies with the individual officer assigned to the vehicle. Not only is he or she responsible for operating the vehicle in a safe manner but also reporting all minor and major defects that come to his or her attention. Preventive maintenance includes checking oil levels, tire pressure, and emergency equipment before each shift. Cleanliness of interiors is important for public appearance and morale. Some officers would agree that their patrol units look like the devil due to exterior dirt, ashtrays filled to the brim with cigarette butts and waste paper, and candy wrappers and dirt strewn about the interior.

As energy conservation becomes more widespread, police will be using lighter vehicles and have more use of motorcycles in inner-city work. European police forces have been doing this for many years with a great deal of success. However, with more reliance on lighter vehicles according the recent experience, and with civilian dependence on the lighter vehicle, there should be more bodily injury accidents of patrol officers. Maintenance may have to be considered on a more frequent schedule as well as fleet turnover if the lighter vehicles continue to be used in the manner of the present-day larger-car motor fleet.

PERSONAL PATROL CAR

The use of the personal patrol car has been a controversial topic. Ruegg, in his evaluation of the **personal patrol car programs (PCP)**, offers three reasons for their use (1975: 290):

> Some departments see a PCP as possibly offering a low-cost solution to the need for greater police presence. Others see it as a relative inexpensive means of supplementing officer pay. Still other departments believe a PCP to be an economically efficient alternative for meeting police vehicle requirements apart from any special benefits from the program.

He concluded that the use of the police car as a personal vehicle for the police officer "costs substantially more" than does a centrally located and maintained fleet, for the following reasons (Ruegg, 1975: 296):

> (1) large capital costs are required to implement the program, (2) empirical evidence casts doubt on achieving a large reduction in per-mile running costs with personal cars, and (3) additional mileage incurred in off-duty driving will tend to raise total running costs, other things being equal.

There are other problems for management with the personal patrol car. Although changing shifts in the field may be something of a time saver and save some gas in going to a central office, management loses control over the officer and direct communication. Supervisory problems are created in that traditionally an officer would be subject to inspection of his or her person and equipment at a station roll call. Lack of regular inspections can lead to potential abuses of personal hygiene or equipment violations. Also the lines of communication become more critical, and careful checks must be maintained to avoid miscommunicating the routine daily orders and directives.

In a few cases, there may be some justification for this approach, as when (1) the canine corps needs special vehicles, (2) undercover cars are needed for surveillance, and (3) rural areas of large distances are involved. In the case of rural areas, regional garages may help to modify the distance problems.

One last problem of personal-use police cars is that police officers while off duty may involve civilian friends and their families in police business where there is potential violence. This means increased insurance concerning potential harm of these civilians. It also could mean an increase in damage suits by civilians against the police agency. When the officer is off duty and wearing old clothes (for example, cleaning out a basement and then going to a hardware store), he or she does not evoke a professional image in a personal patrol car. Although the increased presence of police cars has been seen as a benefit, there is a question whether this is a positive or negative benefit.

The Escondido Police Department in California instituted a policy of providing each newly hired police officer with a personal patrol vehicle. The officer takes this vehicle home with him or her but can only use the vehicle to drive to and from work. The officer cannot use the police vehicle for personal business and must reside within a few miles of police headquarters. According to Chief Jimno, this policy has resulted in a longer vehicle life, improved vehicle appearance, and reduced maintenance (Lynch, 1988a). The Escondido Police Department is convinced that this is an efficient cost/benefit approach. At least, in Escondido with its policy of restricted private use, the presence of the police vehicle in the community is seen as a positive effect.

 PHYSICAL PLANT MAINTENANCE

Police stations in many cities in the United States are outdated facilities that retain most of the attributes of nineteenth-century architecture. In some cities, the police station was built like a medieval castle to protect the police from mob attacks. In smaller cities, towns, and villages, police facilities are tucked away in some remote recesses of the municipal building or fire station, generally as an afterthought to the original plans. Overall, it appears that all police stations, whether old or modern, share a common problem of maintenance and upkeep since they are 24-hour operations.

As the police station is a place where men and women must work and citizens must visit, we feel that it should be properly maintained and provide a sense of pride for the community. Sometimes officers loathe having tour groups come through their station houses because of deplorable conditions.

With many departments contemplating new police stations, a number of architectural designs exist that can be adapted to fit the community environment. For police building planning, however, we do offer the following suggestions:

1. *Security.* Most police stations in the United States are easy targets for terrorist attacks. Although we do not advocate that police station architecture return to medieval design, public access to the various areas of operations should be strictly controlled. While a main desk should be available for the public for information and complaints, the rest of the police operations should be sealed off by remote-controlled or keyed doors. Further security should be incorporated for communications centers, power plants, and lockup areas. Distinctive identification cards should be worn by personnel and visitors, and those persons not displaying such a card should be immediately stopped and questioned as a matter of course by any in-house personnel. Security considerations must also be extended to parking facilities and grounds within the proximity of the police station. Ironically, many property crimes occur adjacent to police facilities, especially to patrol and privately owned vehicles.

2. *Personnel facilities.* The police station should have separate locker rooms and shower and bathroom facilities for male and female personnel. A trend is occurring in some departments where a country club atmosphere prevails in terms of a television room being located within the confines of the police locker room. Although additions of this nature are paid through volunteer contributions or funds from the police union, a negative image can result in that certain segments of the public may feel that such equipment was paid by public monies. If any "fringes" are to be included in the police personnel facilities, we would advocate adding a wellness equipment.

3. *Location to public.* The community police station should be accessible to the general public; this means building in a populated, central area of the community with ample parking facilities and measures to accommodate handicapped persons. In many suburban areas, state and other municipal police departments have been experimenting with ministations or substations in areas of high public or business traffic, such as in shopping malls, on a full- or part-time basis, to provide this aspect of accessibility. Some college campuses are placing stations in the student unions.

4. *Backup power system.* We know of many cases of chaos that occurred once electricity was disrupted by weather or unexpected

emergencies. Each police administrator should ask the question, "Can my station function if regular electric power is withdrawn?" The solution to this dilemma, of course, lies with backup power generators or battery systems.

An example of the applications of the foregoing criteria is evidenced in the Carlsbad Police Department. According to Captain Suttle, the philosophy behind the construction of the Carlsbad Police Department building was based on needs for (Lynch, 1988b) (1) the building to be good looking and accessible to the public, (2) security without looking like "a fortress," and (3) a functional and comfortable place for police department employees.

The two-story stone building has a reception area facing an atrium. Off the atrium is a communication center protected by high impact glass. Sound and lighting levels are attractive and controlled in all areas. Off the lobby is a community-relations area, where people can meet in an inviting setting. Offices have mobile walls.

Interestingly enough, the parking places are more than egalitarian; the "brass" park farthest from the building and other employees park closest to the building. The building is self-contained, with a backup generator, and emergency sleeping, cooking, and eating facilities. The function and structure of the building increases employee morale and maintains security while providing an accessible and attractive setting for the public.

TEMPORARY DETECTION FACILITY

Certain states allow municipal and police agencies to maintain a **temporary detention facility**—often called a *lockup*—for prisoners awaiting arraignment, release on bail, or transport. It is here, however, where many serious problems occur. Jail suicide is a common occurrence in temporary detention areas since it is here when the offender finally realizes the various effects that arrest has on his or her personal life. In other cases, prisoners begin to plot an escape while they wait for the next stage of processing. In still other instances, prisoners have died due to complications arising from being intoxicated, drugged, or beaten by police or other suspects during and after the course of arrest.

It is important that detention facilities in the police station be tightly supervised, that rigorous procedures be maintained for searching inmates, and that careful inventory of property and contraband be maintained. We suggest that whenever possible, audiovisual tape recording units be maintained to monitor prisoners in the booking area. This protects the agency from civil suits arising from charges of brutality, theft of prisoner property, and negligence.

It cannot be stressed too highly that, for the purposes of police management, this is a temporary holding facility (jail) and is not meant to be a permanent correctional setting. This is basically a lockup pending court appearance for those awaiting bail or those unable to make bail. For stays of more than a few days, prisoners should be transferred to a permanent correctional facility.

There are also the normal problems of state and federal regulations concerning the separation of adults from juveniles and females from males, plus the security problem of smuggling in and using drugs. This is a crisis period for many detainees, and there is a strong potential toward self-destruction. Thus, there is a need for constant and professional security to be maintained in the cell area. In the case of separation of adults and juveniles, this may not always be possible in smaller facilities. When it comes to these standard issues of corrections, including that of contact visits, there is a need, at that point, to transfer prisoners to a more permanent location where correctional professionals are in charge.

 ## LICENSE SECTION

There is some feeling among professional law enforcement managers that licensing should be placed in the hands of civilians and possibly another government agency. However, there is also some disagreement because of the historical context of the licensing function. Licensing traditionally grew around three police problems:

1. *Vice control:* licensing of taverns, taxies, and bingo games.
2. *Crowd control:* parade permits, sports events, and rallies.
3. *Organized crime:* with an overlap on vice, such things as the licensing of jukeboxes.

Although it may not be necessary for the police department to have direct control over the licensing functions of municipal government, some control and good communication is needed. Police agencies need to be informed concerning activities taking place in the community so that they may take the necessary steps to provide the services needed to control the situation.

THE CRIME LABORATORY

Every department needs to have access to a laboratory. There are three main ways of identifying criminals.

1. Eyewitness testimony, which is generally unreliable.
2. Confessions, whose use has been severely curtailed by the courts.
3. Circumstantial evidence.

Thus criminal justice officials have been relying more and more on circumstantial evidence in helping to convict criminals. Circumstantial evidence is developed by good laboratory techniques both at the regional laboratory level and with good preliminary work in the field by evidence technicians.

Crime laboratories are found in large municipal and state police agencies in the United States. The main operations of the crime laboratory involve the following:

1. Chemical analysis or evaluation of inorganic materials.
2. Biological analysis or examination of physiological fluids and organic materials, such as blood, human tissue, and hair.
3. Firearms examinations and tool marks.
4. Document examination for items involving forgeries, primarily checks and handwriting and typewriting comparisons.
5. Processing crime-scene photos.
6. Latent fingerprint identification.
7. Photographic examples for court presentation.
8. Micro- and macrophotography.

Smaller agencies that are generally limited in equipment and personnel by budgetary restraints cannot afford to have specialists that are needed for good laboratory work. Also, they cannot afford to have their top command personnel tied up in laboratory work. Major forensic work, for these agencies, is then sent to a state regional laboratory or to the Federal Bureau of Investigation. To provide for the rapid deployment and acquisition of physical evidence at crime scenes, many departments assign officers as evidence technicians—trained to gather evidence, take photographs, dust and lift latent fingerprints, and make measurements of crime and accident scenes. This makes more sense than dispatching a criminalist from the laboratory or, when he or she is off duty, from his or her residence. The necessary equipment for processing crime scenes is kept in the patrol car and is available at all times.

First, however, we ought to define the difference between the terms *criminalistics* and *forensic science*. **Forensic science** applies scientific or medical knowledge to legal matters. **Criminalistics** is one form of forensic science concerned with the examination of blood, hair, glass, bullets, and other evidence found at crime scenes. Other forensic sciences include forensic toxicology (poisons and toxic substances), forensic pathology (examination of persons who have died under questionable circumstances), forensic anthropology (skeletal remains), forensic odontology (teeth), forensic psychiatry, and document identification. Most crime laboratories found in policing confine themselves to areas listed under criminalistics and include documents (Serrill, 1978: 22).

Basically the crime laboratory needs to serve either a large jurisdiction or multiple jurisdictions to justify the costs of the needed specialists. In most cases there is a need for civilian experts rather than uniformed officers who may be assigned but possess little or no technical skill.

Crime laboratories need full-time directors who work closely with detectives, evidence technicians, the courts, and the training unit. Typical functional subdivisions of a normal laboratory would be (Sullivan and O'Brien, 1980: 277)

1. Arson
2. Chemistry
3. Documents
4. Firearms
5. Hairs and fibers
6. Serology
7. Criminalistics
8. Field Teams

These authors show the evidence flowing in the manner shown in Figure 10-1. The laboratory supervisor would be in charge of quality control, distribution of cases, and coordination of laboratory services. The civilian manager in charge of this evidence flow, the director of the crime laboratory, should report directly to top command personnel when the laboratory is located in one police department. The crime laboratory should be equipped with sufficient technology and qualified personnel to do both dry and wet chemistry and micro- and macroexaminations with crime-scene reproduction capabilities. Most laboratories located in police agencies consist of photography laboratories along with physical-evidence examination capability and field narcotic testing. Any operations more complicated, that will stand up to courtroom cross-examination, entail a major capital and personnel investment.

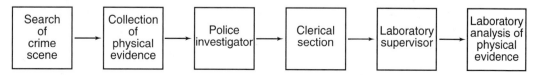

Figure 10-1
Flow of Evidence in a Police Investigation.

Eighty percent of the more than 300 forensic laboratories in the United States are located in police agencies. Most crime laboratories represent less than 0.05 percent of a police budget. A nationwide survey has indicated that 60 to 80 percent of a crime laboratory's caseload consists of fingerprinting and drugs, with the next most frequent use being firearms, blood and bloodstains, and semen (Peterson, 1987: 3). The study also found that "cases where scientific evidence is analyzed are cleared at significantly higher rates." The study also found that drug and alcohol cases, which represent more than 50 percent of a laboratory's caseload, were displacing other cases, such as burglary and robbery. Police managers need to be aware of these trends and look closely at the relationship between funding and caseload of the laboratories. One recommendation of the study that will become increasingly important in the future is: "Increased funding should be used primarily to broaden and intensify the caseloads of crime labs beyond predominant analysis of drug and alcohol analysis" (Peterson, 1987: 5).

The trend should be toward the use of independent regional laboratories funded by a fee system, even though most forensic laboratories are still located in police agencies. The necessary distribution of cost factors would help to increase this trend. Services and expert testimony would be readily available to local agencies with this limited decentralization of regional facilities. It is expected that if this trend continues, most police agencies will be developing and expanding the use of evidence technicians rather than maintaining local laboratory facilities.

Perhaps the most innovative and controversial innovation in forensic science is DNA testing. Deoxyribonucleic acid (DNA) is a molecule that is found in all life forms and defines their genetically inherited characteristics. According to Bashinski and Peterson (1991: 512), the genetic code found in a specimen is unique for every individual. Thus, the genetic code found in a specimen of blood, semen, or hair can be directed to one individual.

The successful prosecution of a criminal for physical and sexual assaults receives much media attention. For example, in Buffalo, New York, the "University Heights rapist" eluded police capture for over two years despite his repeated attacks. He was eventually prosecuted after his identity was learned and his blood was matched with the semen found at crime scenes through DNA testing. The advantages of DNA testing include the use of small samples, the possibility of testing one lab sample against another lab sample, and the computerization of results. The main drawback of DNA testing is its expense for equipment and the experience and training required for serologists to achieve technical expertise. DNA testing is only done in a handful of private laboratories and by the Federal Bureau of Investigation. According to Pilant (1992), the FBI cost was $60,000 for equipment alone. In the future, county or regional laboratories will undoubtedly adopt DNA testing.

If police management is to have the maximum use of the technical expertise of a regional laboratory, low-priority work needs to be screened out of the system. This means that police officers need some criminalistics training and additional evidence technicians. Sullivan and O'Brien eliminated some low-priority work by training local police officers in the techniques needed to identify marijuana and provided them with enough technical expertise so that they could be court witnesses and survive cross-examination. We would also suggest that middle management be trained to recognize evidence. Thus, investigators have to stay away from the shotgun approach where, for example, they might ask the laboratory to test for seminal stains where there is no suspect identified, analyze narcotics found on property where there are no suspects, or examine tool marks without submission of the suspected evidence (Sullivan and O'Brien, 1980: 232).

Evidence technicians are sworn police officers who have been specially trained in the handling and gathering of evidence. Evidence technicians are normally not responsible for protecting the crime scene. In the Detroit Police Department, "evidence technicians photograph and diagram the crime scene in addition to identifying, collecting, and transporting evidence; completing reports: and giving testimony" (National Advisory Commission, 1973: 196–297). Richard H. Fox, director of the Ventura County Criminalistics Laboratory and a fellow of the American Academy of Forensic Sciences, gives us some notions of what the evidence technicians should be able to do (1977: 469–70):

1. Determine items of evidentiary value.
2. Be proficient in the use of several pieces of camera equipment, including closeup photography, use various collection techniques for blood and fluids, and use silicone or plaster techniques on tire and shoe impressions.
3. Collect minute items of trace evidence, hair, fiber, thread.
4. Mark and recover various items of firearm evidence.
5. Collect and package evidence protecting it from contamination.
6. Lift latent fingerprints.
7. Examine deceased persons, charting and photographing wounds, and lifting fingerprints from partially decomposed or mutilated bodies.
8. Examine bodies of living persons for foreign material, fingernail scrapings, and so on.
9. Prepare a crime-scene sketch.
10. Prepare detailed reports to maintain further a chain of custody.
11. Give expert court testimony.

In deciding how to screen cases for processing as evidence, a time management system needs to be created for laboratory personnel. Sullivan and O'Brien suggest an ordering of priorities that should prove useful (1980: 237):

Recommended Priority System

Priority 1	Police emergency case
Priority 2	Death investigation, in-jail narcotic case (no bail), narcotic case (buy-sale-burst)
Priority 3	Crime against persons, possession (any drug other than marijuana)
Priority 4	Crimes against property, in-jail case (with additional charges)
Priority 5	Prints only, marijuana only, controlled bugs, other low-priority cases

Priority 5 would have 10 days as target day and 30 days as a deadline for chemistry work; all other units would have 30 days as a target date and 45 days as a deadline date.

The Detroit Police Department gives a five-week evidence-technician course consisting of 200 hours (National Advisory Commission, 1973: 297) that includes:

Photography	40 hours
Latent prints	20 hours
Homicide	16 hours
Drug identification	16 hours
Cast technicians	16 hours
Trace evidence	15 hours
Robbery and breaking and entering	10 hours
Firearms	8 hours
Handling of evidence	8 hours
Report writing	6 hours
Law (as related to evidence)	2 hours

Every police agency should have at least one well-trained evidence technician available for every shift of patrol duty. Larger departments should have a team of evidence technicians. This is an efficient use of personnel and saves the use of expensive laboratory time while winning cases because of good evidence and good continuity. With a modest but realistic investment in training and additional equipment, police managers can gain a great deal of respect from the legislature and community because of their efficient use of evidence technicians.

COMPUTERS AND FINGERPRINTS

Computerized fingerprint identification systems such as Automatic Fingerprint Identifications System (AFIS) have made it possible for latent fingerprints to be matched with a suspect's prints in minutes. Until this development, a latent fingerprint (print lifted from a person or object at a crime scene) had to be matched visually with a ten-print set of prints taken from a person. This old process often took days. Identification officers are playing a greater role in investigations because of this. Before, detectives needed a suspect which is now being done on cold searches.

Many states, such as Virginia and New York, have begun state-wide programs, which has created management issues such as coordination of equipment procurement, procedures for data entry, and operation protocols. The FBI is in the early stages of implementing a new image-based identification system which can meet projected increases.

As presented by the Bureau of Justice Statistics on new technologies (1993), computer equipment can scan impressions and automatically extract and digitize identifying characteristics in detail, enabling the computer to distinguish a single fingerprint from millions of file prints that have been similarly scanned and stored in digital form in the computer's memory.

Even the taking of fingerprints is changing. "Live-scan" is a new technology that eliminates the need for rolling ink onto a pad. Instead, the subject's uninked fingers are rolled onto a scanning pad attached to a live scan device that captures an image of the prints. If the quality of the prints is good, then copies can be electronically transmitted to state repositories and other agencies for storage or analysis via "card scan" technology. AFIS is expensive; the cost can run in the millions of dollars depending on agencies participating and complexity. In all, AFIS programs have led to the greater use of prints and increasing identification of suspects. As the technology improves, there will be a great decline in the use of standard fingerprint cards for analysis and transmission to other agencies.

▶ ANCILLARY PUBLIC SAFETY SERVICES

There are many services provided by American police departments that fall into the heading of public safety. These include the following:

1. *Emergency Mobilization.* A response plan is required in times of natural disaster or special community needs. These situations can range from a parade that shuts down traffic for five hours, to a riot or earthquake that immobilizes the community for days. An emergency plan includes resources that can be used for events, as procedures that define chain-of-command and coordination responsibilities. The critical piece of this plan for police operation is calling-in internal personnel and acquiring radios, vehicles, and other equipment. A police department's emergency mobilization plan may be just one part of a county- or state-wide emergency action plan. Many plans include the use of civilians or auxiliary police who can do the following:
   - Assist regular forces at crowd-control scenes (sports events, parades, concerts, fires).
   - Assume routine or inside jobs to allow for the release of regular officers to street duty for riot control, concentrated investigation activities, or hostage situations needing additional personnel.
   - Augment the regular forces by providing for a second person in a car on patrol, or working with the Neighborhood Watch programs.

2. *Animal Control.* A recent Bureau of Justice Statistics survey on Local Police Departments (1996) found that almost one-half of the departments in its sample were responsible for animal control. This includes enforcing local ordinances related to pets, and capturing or destroying wild animals that are a nuisance.

3. *Emergency Medical Services.* The same survey reported that 20 percent of local police departments in the sample were the primary

provider of emergency medical services. This means that officers are trained and equipped not only for police situations but also for emergency first-response procedures such as heart attacks, accidents, broken limbs, and so on.

➤ CONCLUSION

The major auxiliary functions of police organizations were analyzed. As we noted, auxiliary services direct and supply resources to those units or individuals that provide police services to the community. Central to auxiliary services is communications, insofar as all units or divisions of the police organization must have access to this service. Reviewing main needs and capabilities, we pointed out that technology is rapidly advancing in this area. Many departments, however, have difficulty in purchasing updated equipment simply because of their limited size and resources. We emphasized the pooling of resources through the formation of a mobile radio district. Interagency competition and political considerations, however, are main stumbling blocks in adopting such a program. Our discussion in the communications area also included personnel. Of all the services provided by the police organization, communications is one in which personnel competency is a crucial factor.

Police organizations, like many others, seem to operate by paper; therefore, the efficient recording and flow of paperwork is essential. As with communications, computerized technology for recordkeeping and word processing continues to advance. The silicon-chip revolution is bringing down the cost of small computer systems so as to make these advances accessible to all departments.

In this chapter, we included a discussion on security, sealing, purging, and public access to police records. Current procedures related to the Freedom of Information Act (1974) and updated regulations pertaining to records were presented. An issue that will continue to be addressed in the future is the citizen's right to privacy and access to personal information versus the police's need for accurate data on criminal suspects.

Although often overlooked, the property section has responsibilities involving inventory control of physical property, evidence, and found property. Maintaining the security of evidence as it is delivered from the crime scene may appear to be a mundane task, but it is of crucial importance to the investigative process. Because of the rising cost of police vehicles, equipment, and fuel, we recommended that many departments experiment with compact-size patrol cars. In most departments, a patrol vehicle is operated 24 hours a day under less than optimum conditions.

Physical plant considerations were also presented in this chapter. Our discussion included issues related to security, facilities, morale, location, and emergency power needs. The temporary detention facility, or lockup, was discussed in some detail because of general concern over jail suicides and other incidents. We briefly touched upon the licensing section, which may or may not be under the control of the municipal police in many communities.

As with other technology, smaller agencies have difficulty both in procuring and fiscally defending the need for a crime laboratory of any meaningful size. Crime laboratories are, therefore, found in most larger municipal and state police agencies and serve many departments on a regional basis. The main operations of a crime laboratory include chemical and biological analysis of evidence, firearms, tool marks and document examinations, latent fingerprint identification, and the collection and processing of crime-scene photography. In our general discussion of laboratory operations, we noted that there is a definite need for procedures to screen cases for processing. The capabilities of laboratory personnel were also discussed in terms of applying scientific know-how to law enforcement operations.

Computerization has streamlined crime-laboratory services ranging from routine recordkeeping to management systems for death cases, accident reconstruction, criminal profiling, and photography reconstruction and storage.

We concluded the chapter with a review of various ancillary services that relate to the public safety function.

QUESTIONS FOR REVIEW

1. What functions usually come under the organizational heading of auxiliary services?

2. What capabilities must communications units provide? What limitations are placed upon many agencies in obtaining updated technology in this area?

3. Consolidation has been proposed by the authors as a means of solving police communications inferiority. What are some hindrances to this solution?

4. Why are communications personnel often referred to as "key people" in police operations?

5. List the main categories of police records. How is the computer proving to be a useful tool for these tasks?

6. What are some general guidelines related to public access of police records? What types of records are not governed by public access regulations (for example, the Freedom of Information Act)?

7. What kinds of data may be released about an individual who was not convicted of a crime?

8. What are the main duties of the property section? How does this section assist in the continuity of evidence?

9. Why is it said that police vehicles are exposed to the "worst" road and driving conditions? Why is preventive maintenance important?

10. What general items must be considered in designing or maintaining a police station?

11. List the main functions of a crime laboratory.

12. Outline the flow of evidence involving the crime laboratory. Why is case screening an important procedure?

13. What are five duties of crime-scene technicians?

KEY TERMS

AFIS

civil defense officers

criminalistics

DNA

emergency plan

forensic science

Freedom of Information Act

MRD

PCP

purging, sealing

records

temporary detention facility

BIBLIOGRAPHY

BUREAU OF JUSTICE STATISTICS, *Local Police Departments, 1993*. Washington, D.C.: U.S. Department of Justice, 1996.

BUREAU OF JUSTICE STATISTICS, *Use and Management of Criminal History Record Information*. Washington, D.C.: U.S. Department of Justice, 1993.

COLTON, KENT W., *Police Computer Technology*. Lexington, Mass.: Lexington Books, 1978.

FOX, RICHARD, H., "Criminalistics," In Bernard L. Garmire, ed., *Local Government Police Management*, pp. 457–74. Washington, D.C.: International City Management Association, 1977.

BASHINSKI, JAN S. and JOSEPH L. PETERSON, "Forensic Science," in *Local Government Police Management* (3rd ed.). Washington: International Management Association, 1991.

HAYDEN, TRUDY, and JACK NOVIK, *Your Rights to Privacy*. New York: Avon Books and American Civil Liberties Union, 1980.

LYNCH, LAWRENCE, "Interview with Vincent D. Jimno, Chief of Police, City of Escondido." Escondido Police Department, Escondido, California, March 21, 1988.

_____. "Interview with George F. Suttle, Captain, Carlsbad Police Department." Carlsbad Police Department, Carlsbad, California, May 16, 1988b.

NATIONAL ADVISORY COMMISSION ON CRIMINAL JUSTICE STANDARDS AND GOALS, *Police*, Washington, D.C.: U.S. Government Printing Office, 1973.

New York State Department of Criminal Justice Services, "Regulations for Criminal Justice Data." Albany, NY: 1990.

Peterson, Joseph L., *Use of Forensic Evidence by the Police and Courts*, Washington, D.C.: National Institute of Justice, 1987.

Pliant, Lois, "Spotlight on...Equipping a Forensics Lab," *Police Chief*, 59, no. 9 (September 1992), pp. 36–47.

Ruegg, Rosalie, "Life-Cycle Cost Evaluation of the Personal Patrol Car Program," *Journal of Police Science and Administration*. 3, no. 3 (September 1975), pp. 290–98.

Serrill, Michael S., "Forensic Scenes: Overburdened, Underutilized," *Police Magazine* (January 1978), pp. 21–30.

Sullivan, Robert C. and Kevin O'Brien, "A Systems Approach to Crime Laboratory Management," *Public Management*, 8, no. 2 (June 1980), pp. 225–38.

11

Human Resource Management

The objective of police recruitment and selection is to find qualified candidates for law enforcement positions in terms of their talents, ethics, drive, and emotional stability. Patrick Murphy, the former commissioner of police for the New York City Police Department and director of the Police Foundation, has pointed out the importance of the recruitment selection process as follows (Stahl and Staufenberger, 1974: 12):

> No challenge in policing is greater than the management and administration of personnel. The successful use of innovative patrol strategies, better investigative techniques, improved community relations programs and advanced technological hardware, all depend on the proper selection, training and utilization of police personnel.

The socioeconomic and political demands and realities of the 1990s show the need for diversity in the recruitment and selection process. This entails employing modern selection processes currently utilized by private industry where the candidate is matched with the appropriate job. This matching process, as applied to law enforcement, will be discussed throughout this chapter.

PERSONNEL: THE MAJOR COST

Law enforcement is a labor-intensive service industry, where 80 to 90 percent of agency budgets are devoted to personnel costs. Paradoxically, most managers do not realize the investment they have in terms of their human capital: police officers. Just a few of the expenses involve testing, oral interviews, background checks, uniforms and equipment, and the police academy program. As a rule, it takes about a year and a half before the *police recruit* becomes a *police officer* who then makes a working contribution to the agency and community.

Another important variable that has entered the discussion of police personnel is the high number of qualified applicants seeking police careers. Before the 1970s, many departments were begging for applicants, and many positions went unfilled. Today, there is a larger police labor pool due to a number of factors that range from the state of the U.S. economy to the increased prestige of the police career, a by-product of criminal justice education and media glorification.

POLICE CIVIL SERVICE SELECTION: HISTORICAL BACKGROUND

Figure 11–1 (next page) illustrates the police personnel selection process used in many states. The chief criterion in this selection process resides with those portions overseen by state civil service—written test, physical agility examinations, and physical requirements. Candidates who complete a written examination and physical agility test and measure up to the physical requirements are then placed in either a pool or a rank-order certification list prepared by the Civil Service Commission. States with a rank-order process continue to follow the **rule of 3**, whereby one of the first three candidates on the list is chosen while the other two candidates are returned to the pool for the next ranking of three. This method of selection may seem outmoded, but it is still viewed by many as a reform measure when compared with practices that existed in the nineteenth century.

PUBLIC SERVICE EMPLOYMENT

In the early days of the Republic, government service was looked upon as a duty reserved for those of aristocratic background. The change of presidential administrations, however, heralded a new break from tradition in that all presidential appointees were replaced by those of the new victor. This was the

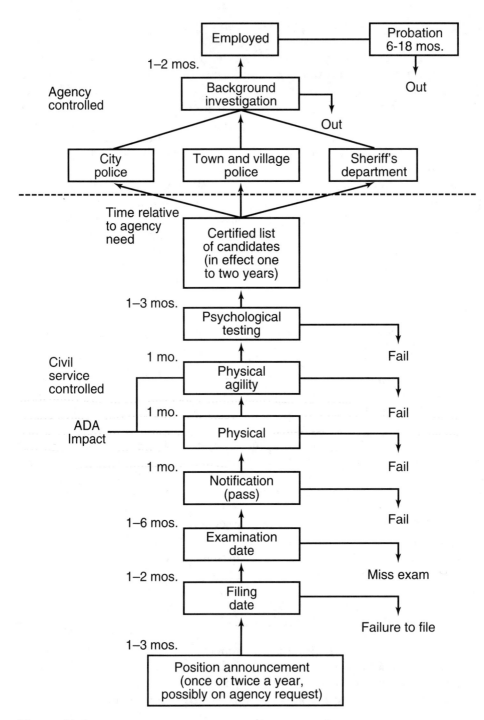

Figure 11-1
Personnel Selection Process.

beginning of the **spoils system** (doling out positions for political support) that became firmly entrenched by 1830. The practice soon spread to all municipalities on the state and local level. This process affected early police organizations, which often underwent a complete personnel turnover after the victory of the out-of-office party.

In the early days of American policing, there were no requirements for becoming a police officer except having the right connections and being willing to fight to protect yourself. Sadly enough, most police officers were no more than political hacks who received their positions solely by a payment to a public official in return for the position. Many times in urban areas, a local gangster chieftain might have some say as to who would enforce the law in the community. A career in policing, moreover, was seen as an avenue of economic improvement by each wave of immigrants to the United States in the early nineteenth century. Police jobs, which were not often sought after by the native middle-class population, were readily dispensed by the political machine to immigrants in return for votes and support.

Due to the negative effects of the spoils system such as mismanagement and bribery, a reform movement for personnel selection was under way by the beginning of the 1880s. In 1883, Congress passed the **Pendleton Act** for a majority of federal positions. This law sought to ban political patronage as the sole criterion for personnel selection and retained on the rate a system whereby employees would be selected and retained on the basis of open competition according to experience and ability. Moreover, the new law sought to protect employees against arbitrary discharge or discrimination, especially from discrimination based on political influences. In that same year, New York and other states enacted similar provisions. The assassination of President Garfield in 1881 by a disgruntled office seeker had focused public attention on the problems with the spoils system and helped to speed up enactment of Pendleton-style legislation in other states.

The passage of civil service statutes did not result in overnight reform. In his history of American policing, Robert Fogelson (1977) showed that civil service reform was stymied by the political machines that existed in most urban communities. He states (p. 110): "The machine politicians proved to be formidable opponents. When they dominated city hall, which was most of the time, they could usually prevail on the authorities to sidetrack, postpone, or vote down the reform schemes. Even when the reformers took over, the politicians generally counted on their cronies in the police forces, prosecutor's officers, local courts and other agencies to undo any inopportune changes."

From the nineteenth century to today, political interferences in American policing has not disappeared, even in states that have civil service requirements. Moreover, many municipalities and states still do not provide civil service protection to police officers. For example, county sheriff's departments in many states are often not regulated by any civil service guidelines; often, police selection is strictly a matter of political patronage.

Police employment in civil service-regulated states does not necessarily bring great monetary benefits, but it does provide (1) job security, (2) a pension, and (3) generous vacation and personal days off. The Great Depression from 1929 through the 1930s underscored the security of public employment as millions of workers were laid off by private industry. As the range of government services has grown since World War II, the number of workers has likewise risen, making government on the federal, state, and local level this nation's number one employer.

However, some new factors have altered the traditional notion of government service:

1. In many states, and on the federal level, wages and benefits have matched those provided by private industry. This has made government service further attractive when coupled with pensions, retirements, and time off.

2. As the number and range of government services has increased, taxes have also risen. In this decade, a number of taxpayer revolts may affect the number of workers in public service.

3. Researchers are undecided as to whether or not this will affect the number of government services since budget surpluses were obtained in previous years, thus stalling layoffs. The notion of government employment being secure has been altered by the financial dilemmas faced in many municipalities. This has forced the laying off of police, firefighters, and other public-service workers.

While these general trends have all affected police administration, one other movement has had a striking effect on selection and promotion, namely, Equal Employment Opportunity legislation.

EQUAL EMPLOYMENT OPPORTUNITY

Although the Fifth, Thirteenth, and Fourteenth Amendments to the U.S. Constitution provide the basis for due process, government has been slow to adopt a strict interpretation of these amendments, especially with regard to employment of blacks, Latinos, and women. Both the Thirteenth and the Fourteenth Amendments gave Congress the right to enact legislation to enforce the provision of law, which resulted in civil rights legislation in 1866 and 1871 on the issue of employment discrimination. Presidents Roosevelt (1941) and Kennedy (1961) issued presidential executive orders for fair employment of minority groups, which have had an impact in industries on government-related contracts. The 1961 order by Kennedy was significant in that it imposed the first requirement for affirmative action in government employment—mainly that each agency had to plan and implement a program to ensure that employment practices were nondiscriminatory in application, and set out methods by which the effects of past discriminatory employment practices could be corrected. This executive order was updated by President Johnson (1965) and President Nixon (1971), who made affirmative action an important area for all government service (Territo and others, 1977: 21–22).

But the real boom to affirmative action resided not with executive orders but with the passage of the Civil Rights Act of 1964, which had a number of titles dealing with various facets of discrimination. The significant legislation for personnel practices was found in **Title VII**, which provided that [Public Law 92–261, Section 703(a)]

> It shall be unlawful employment practice for an employer (1) to fail or refuse to hire, or discharge any individual or otherwise to discriminate against any individual with respect to his compensation, terms, conditions, or privileges of employment, because of such individual's race, color, religion, sex, or national origin; (2) to limit, segregate, or classify his employees or applicants for employment in any way which would deprive or tend to deprive any individual of employment opportunity or otherwise adversely affect his status as an employee because of such individual's race, color, religion, sex, or national origin.

Title VII was directed at employers with more than 25 persons, labor organizations with more than 25 members, and private employment agencies. Title VII was further upgraded two years later to include coverage of both private and public employment agencies, including those on the state and local level employing 15 or more people. The amendment to Title VII also established the **Equal Employment Opportunity Commission (EEOC)** as a regulatory agency to oversee compliance with Title VII. It is the EEOC to which many complaints on police hiring practices are directed.

Many other federal agencies are also involved in forcing compliance with Title VII: the Department of Justice, the Department of Labor, the U.S. Civil Service Commission, and the U.S. Civil Rights Commission. But one agency that was an important factor in reducing or forcing the issue of discriminatory practices was the Law Enforcement Assistance Administration (LEAA).

LEAA was founded in 1968 as a result of the Omnibus Crime Control and Safe Streets Act of 1968 and terminated April 15, 1982. With the budget totaling billions of dollars, LEAA was able to provide grants-in-aid for all operating agencies and researchers of criminal justice to study problems with the U.S. criminal justice system, and to present solutions to these problems.

 AFFIRMATIVE ACTION

Affirmative action is a concept applied to personnel administration in which an employer takes positive steps to expand employment opportunities of nonwhite persons and women. These steps include addressing and abolishing past discriminatory employment practices, increased solicitation of minority and women applicants from different hiring pools, and the setting of goals for the hiring or promotion of under-represented persons and women in the organization.

The statutory language and political intent of initial Title VII legislation did not include preferential treatment for nonwhites and women for employment and promotion considerations over white candidates (Glazer, 1975;Territo and others, 1977; Fallon and Weiler, 1985). Since 1964, however, federal and state case law, EEOC administrative rulings, and police agency employment practices have determined that the statistical imbalances between the number of nonwhites represented in an organization and the determined labor pool constitute a prima facie case for discrimination. Remedies to address imbalances have included quota systems and preferential treatment for nonwhites and women in employee selection.

Despite strong political and legal opposition by private-sector and public-sector labor unions and aggrieved individuals, these remedies have been constitutionally upheld.The Supreme Court in 1979 upheld the use of a voluntary quota system for selecting black candidates for a training program over the objections of an unsuccessful white applicant who claimed that he had been the victim of discrimination (*United Steel Workers v. Weber*, 443 U.S. 193). In his majority opinion, Justice Brennan wrote that the intent of Title VII was to improve the economic plight of nonwhites through the use of preferred selection systems.

Before the Weber case, the use of quotas and preferential treatment had received judicial approval through a number of Supreme Court cases and EEOC rulings under the **disparate impact theory**. In the 1971 case, *Griggs v. Duke Power Company* (401 U.S. 424), the Court ruled that employment tests and practices which exclude a disproportionate number of nonwhites and women may be discriminatory regardless of whether there was intent by an employer to discriminate. If a situation of disparate impact exists, the employer must demonstrate that such tests and practices relate to a business necessity and the demands of the position. Disparate impact is any case where a civil service test, for example, admits more white male employees to the occupation than minorities or women, even if the white applicants have higher civil service scores on the test than those of the minority or female candidates.This legal reasoning raises complaints of *reverse discrimination* and the use of quotas when using civil service tests for the admission of new candidates for employment.

Disparate impact was applied to police departments because of their failure to recruit nonwhites and women in comparison to a statistical representation of these minorities in a designated community. Disparate impact formed the basis for court orders and consent decrees by which police agencies had to remedy the historical effects of discrimination through quotas.Agencies, under court orders, were forced to review their hiring and testing procedures in the light of the principle of disparate impact. In the case of consent decrees between police agency employers and federal or state courts, there was no admittance of intentional discrimination on the part of the employing agency.

When representation in a police agency matches minority representation in a defined community labor pool, affirmative action is said to be successful

(Hochstedler, 1984). Quotas and preferred hiring have also had a backlash effect because many qualified whites have complained that they were not considered for employment simply because of race. In police circles, this practice is know as *dipping* and in public policy discussion regarding quotas, it is often called *reverse discrimination*. In a review of the affirmative action policies in 15 departments, Hochstedler (1984) points out that there is no substantial body of research that addresses reverse discrimination.

Fallon and Weiler (1985) note that the term *reverse discrimination* is subject to difficult legal and moral dimensions involving judicially mandated quotas prescribed at the end of a law suit or the outcome of a so-called "voluntary" affirmative action program. Fallon and Weiler (1985) prefer the term "*affirmative discrimination*," which they borrowed from Glazer's (1975) discussion on the development of quotas and preferential treatment since the enactment of Title VII legislation. Affirmative discrimination denotes three areas of action (Fallon and Weiler, 1985: 3):

1. The use of racial preferences to prescribe the selection of candidates who otherwise appear less qualified than rival candidates.
2. The use of preferences for candidates who have not proven that they were the victims of past discrimination.
3. The use of targets and goals to determine the number of nonwhite candidates to be hired on the basis of race.

Reverse discrimination related to employment was the basis of many law suits and public policy debates with regard to voluntary and court-mandated affirmative action plans and consent decrees. The federal government since 1978 has altered considerably its policy on racial imbalances. The Reagan and Bush administrations, for example, did not seem to feel that affirmative action should be used to remedy racial imbalances.

Although individuals as well as under-represented groups have pressed for the use of the quota system, there have been no substantial changes in judicial interpretation. In 1984, in the case of *Firefighters Local Union No 1784 v. Carl W. Stotts* (104 S. Ct. 2576), the U.S. Supreme Court ruled that a bona fide seniority system's layoff provisions could not be altered by court order to protect the gains of minorities. The suit was filed by Stotts, a Memphis, Tennessee firefighter who opposed that city's plan to lay off black firefighters because of fiscal problems. The city's plan to use the last-hired-first-fired seniority rule would have had an adverse effect on black personnel who had been hired under the terms of a 1980 consent decree. The dispute involved a clash between black firefighters under a consent decree and white workers with seniority rights hired under an existing collective bargaining agreement (Fallon and Weiler, 1985). The court overturned the District Court and Appeals Court that the last-hired-first-fired was discriminatory. In effect, the U.S. Supreme Court has said that the *principle of last-hired-first-fired is not discriminatory*.

Disparate impact theory, however, was challenged in an 1989 Supreme Court ruling *Ward Packing v. Atonio* (49 FEP 1519). Filipino and native Alaskan cannery workers employed at several companies charged discrimination on the basis of statistics because the majority of skilled jobs were filled by whites. Because of the unique seasonal nature of the work and the make-up of both the skilled and unskilled workforce, the court ruled that statistical imbalances alone could not be used to prove disparate impact discrimination. Instead, it had to be shown that the imbalance occurred because of the application of a particular employment practice. The court also added that it was the plaintiff's responsibility to prove discrimination instead of the company having to defend its practices. This ruling led to others of similar vein which appeared to halt statistical imbalance lawsuits. However, the 1991 Civil Rights Act restored disparate impact premises so that "neutral employment practices" which resulted in discrimination could continue to be challenged. Since 1990, federal and state court rulings regarding affirmative action discrimination cases have been very specifically applied to the employment practices and existing affirmative action plans of an agency or municipality.

Dramatic changes in affirmative action as a public policy occurred in 1995. The landmark case involving affirmative action was *Adarand Constructors v. Pena* (132 L. Eo.2 158) which involved a lawsuit filed by a construction company. The company was the low bidder for a public works project and it contested the work being awarded to an Hispanic-owned company. The main contractor for the project in turn, received a monetary award by the Federal government for furthering an affirmative action plan. The Supreme Court struck down the awarding of the contract, ruling that affirmative action plans that created racial discrimination must meet a strict scrutiny test according to the following guidelines:

- There must be a compelling reason why a program was put in place.
- The plan must be temporary with a definite end in sight.

 # THE END OF AFFIRMATIVE ACTION?

At the same time that the Adarand case was being argued, the California Board of Regents in 1995 dismantled its affirmative action-based programs, arguing that the set-aside programs in college admissions are discriminatory. In another closely-watched higher education case, the U.S. Court of Appeals for the Fifth Circuit (Texas, Louisiana, and Mississippi) in 1994 found that admissions procedures at the University of Texas that promoted racial and ethnic diversity were improper (*Hopwood v. Texas*, 861 F. Supp. 551). On July 1, 1996 the Supreme Court announced that it would not review the decision. Although the ruling only applies to institutions of higher education in these states, it has prompted many colleges and universities to review their admissions standards and procedures.

For policing, many agencies have ended their quota programs for recruitment and promotion, pointing out that the workforce was representative of the resident population. McWhirter (1996) argued that most state and federal government affirmative action programs created in the 1970s and 1980s that create quotas or set-aside programs will not stand this strict scrutiny test. Commenting on the political realities of the Adarand decision, Eastland (1996: 19–20) stated that in sending the case back to the lower courts for review under strict scrutiny, the Court signaled that preferential treatment is undergoing strict political scrutiny as well. Affirmative action, however, as a governmental policy is not going to dissolve completely. Many police agencies have readjusted their programs to consider affirmative action as a way to conduct proactive recruitment for underrepresented populations in the workforce, and to review employment hiring practices that may be discriminatory.

As a social policy, affirmative action continues to have a profound impact in many areas of human resource management, college admissions, and the awarding of contracts. Based on our experiences and observations in classroom discussions and agency personnel hirings over the last two decades, we can say the following about affirmative action:

- It created deep divisions in American society in that many white persons could not understand why preferential treatment and quota programs were fair.

- It allowed women and persons of various races access to police organizations that hitherto were not representative of their communities. As Bergmann states, the job market in many occupations remains stacked against African Americans and women. (1996: 19).

- It challenged formal and informal methods of discrimination that prevented women, African Americans, Latinos, Asians, and other groups from becoming police officers.

 ## THE ROLE OF THE POLICE PERSONNEL OFFICER

Based on the constraints and controversies arising from personnel practices, the director of personnel and his or her staff hold key positions in determining employment practices and promotion qualifications. Although their judgments are based, in part, on the myriad court cases and legislation stemming from affirmative action and civil service rulings, their decisions will have a profound effect upon the level of quality personnel in a department.

In the small agency, the chief police administrator, normally the police chief, performs most of the tasks of a personnel department in a larger agency. In some small agencies, the political unit, be it county, town, or village, has a personnel office that handles staffing for all municipal offices.

The personnel officer in agencies of all sizes has the potential to serve the department in a number of useful roles. He or she can develop performance evaluation systems for both the general officer and for supervisory personnel. Personnel policy statements are best developed by a professionally trained and educated personnel officer. In some agencies, the personnel officer serves as management representative during contract negotiations with police employee groups and also during grievance proceedings.

 ## PERSONNEL SELECTION: ISSUES AND CONCERNS

Before 1965, the police personnel selection process generally consisted of a written examination, a physical agility test, a physical, and perhaps an oral interview. Based on these criteria, a list was established of successful candidates, and the police administrator picked new officers from this list. Various aspects of this process are continually under attack and revision because of the emergence of affirmative action. We will now review the police personnel selection process, especially those areas affected by Title VII.

WRITTEN TESTS

The civil service procedures of the nineteenth century incorporated the extensive use of written tests as a chief criterion of selection. These tests were usually comprised of multiple-choice questions related to the position being sought. But according to Schacter (1979: 86), "traditional written examinations do not measure many of the skills and competencies which effective police work requires. In fact, a written test of this nature cannot really assess the entire range of skills and situations that are related to job competency." On this issue, she comments further that

> Generic traits are necessary for effective performance in almost any professional or managerial position and include the ability to communicate orally with sensitivity and a sense of authority, to make decisions, to work with many different types of others, and to solve problems under stress and within severe constraints of time and resources.

The affirmative action movement of the 1970s has resulted in an increasingly bitter attack on written civil service testing for a wide variety of reasons. The major arguments center on the following issues:

1. The relationship between the test and the job (often called the attitude/behavior relationship in research literature on testing).
2. Content validity of the testing instrument.
3. Reliability of test items.

AGE

The normal age for application ranges from age 21 to 29, although some agencies will accept recruits as young as 18. This lower age has been the subject of much controversy since many police administrators feel that this lower age limit will recruit police officers who lack mature judgment. At this time no research data are generally available to document anything concerning this controversy. Although age requirements are published and adhered to in most cases, there are an increasing number of age requirements.

Exceptions to the higher age limit are given to wartime veterans. The intent is to be able to recruit qualified future officers from the military without penalizing their years of military service from the maximum age limit. For example, if the veteran is age 32 and has 10 years service in the military, he is qualified to enter a department with a maximum age limit for recruitment of 29 years of age. State civil service limits the number of veteran years that can be subtracted. In the past, especially during the early part of this century, former military men were considered prime candidates for the police department. At present, veterans' preference and exceptions are resented by many younger recruits who lack military service.

Why are there age limits? One reason is related to the physical requirements that are supposed to be justified in terms of the rigors of the job, which, in turn, are related to physical requirements.

Another major reason for the age requirement is the lifetime of work of the police officer compared with retirement and training costs. This is an especially crucial point when considering the 20-year and 25-year retirement programs. This means that the best and most experienced officers are often lost at the peak of their use to the department and only to receive half-pay for not working. Surprisingly, police agencies with these policies allow their best people to go at a time when private business would consider them to be in their prime productive years.

The Age Discrimination in Employment Act of 1974 extended coverage of age discrimination to state and local police agencies, and many state constitutions have developed antidiscrimination policies concerning age. There have been a number of cases throughout the nation concerning age discrimination by police departments, and these police agencies have had mixed results in defending their policies. At the moment, the trend seems to be a breakdown of the upper age requirement unless there is specific state legislation empowering the civil service department to set an upper age limit.

PHYSICAL FITNESS

Physical fitness concerns the health of the individual officer and is a measure of the physiological readiness to perform critical physical tasks when required. Physical fitness has been demonstrated to be a bona fide occupational qualification.

Historically, police officers have been expected to be physically fit. Preservice selection and training academy programs generally have some component for physical training and testing. The type of agility tests and courses vary from department to department. The types of tests commonly employed include running, an obstacle course, climbing ropes, barbell pushups, chinups, scaling walls, and climbing through tubes. What is lacking in these tests, however, is applicability to the job of police officer.

To address job relatedness, a testing regimen being adopted by many departments was developed by the Institute for Aerobics Research of Dallas, Texas. Based on national scores and a review of physical agility needs for the police officer, the Cooper Method tests for four competencies (Institute: 1990):

1. *Aerobic Power.* A 1.5 mile run is scored to measure cardiovascular endurance or aerobic power. The run can be conducted on a treadmill or correlated to a 12-minute distance run.

2. *Flexibility.* A sit-and-reach test serves as an important measure of hip and back flexibility. *Flexibility* is defined as the range of possible movements in a joint or group of joints. These joints can be tested to determine their functional ability through a full range or motion indicated by the sit-and-reach test.

3. *Maximum strength.* This is defined as the amount of tension a muscle can exhibit in one maximal contraction. The one-repetition maximum bench press correlates well with total body strength.

4. *Muscular endurance.* The sit-up (with knees bent) is used to determine a person's endurance effort.

Scores obtained from a national sample are used to determine fitness and are measured according to percentiles according to the person's age and gender. For example, in Rhode Island, entry-level officers are expected to attain the 40th percentile for each activity and attain the 50th percentile before graduating from the training academy. Table 11–1 shows the breakdown of scores for police officer candidates in New York state.

Because of the Americans with Disabilities Act (ADA), physical tests have come under greater scrutiny. Departments are required to address the following questions regarding their standards:

1. The relationship between the standard and the job performed by officers.

2. The relationship between the standard and training required for the basic academy and advanced schools.

3. The applicability of standards to all members of the department.

As Swanson and Hale point out (1975: 183–88), EEOC guidelines state that police agencies may not maintain minimum height requirements unless they can be proved to be job related. Based on the phrase *job related*, many police

TABLE 11–1
MEDICAL AND PHYSICAL FITNESS STANDARDS AND PROCEDURES FOR POLICE OFFICER CANDIDATES

Sit-up	Muscular Endurance: The score indicated below is the number of bent-leg sit-ups performed in one minute.
Flex	Flexibility: The "sit and reach" test measures the range of motion of the lower back and hamstrings. This portion involves stretching out to touch the toes and beyond with extended arms from the sitting position. The score is in inches reached in a yardstick with the 15" mark being at the toes.
Bench	Absolute Strength: One (1) repetition maximum bench press using Dynamic Variable Resistance (DVR) protocol. The score indicated below is a ratio of weight pressed divided by body weight.
1.5 Mile Run	Cardiovascular Capacity: The score indicated below is calculated in minutes:seconds.

	TEST			
AGE: MALE	SIT-UP	FLEX	BENCH	1.5 MILE RUN
20–29	38	16.5	.99	12:51
30–39	35	15.5	.88	13:36
40–49	29	14.3	.80	14:29
50–59	24	13.3	.71	15:26
60+	19	12.5	.66	16:43
AGE: FEMALE				
20–29	32	19.3	.59	15:26
30–39	25	18.3	.53	15:57
40–49	20	17.3	.50	16:58
50–59	14	16.8	.44	17:54
60+	6	15.5	.43	18:44

Source: Institute for Aerobics Research, Dallas, Texas: 1990.

agencies have had to embark on studies to determine the relationship between height and job performance. At this time, most studies have been inconclusive or contradictory.

Related to this issue is the reality that most departments do not enforce any physical standards on their officers once the officer has passed recruit training. By the end of a five-year period, many officers have exceeded recruit weight requirements and many must wear glasses. Sadly, many seasoned officers cannot run a mile. Should all officers that do not meet the rigid physical entering requirements be fired? Do you disqualify an officer because he or she becomes obese, develops flat feet or poor vision, or has heart problems?

Because of the protection afforded by civil service and union contracts, physically unqualified officers are able to retain their police jobs. Others go on permanent disability due to injuries that may have been avoided if the officer had been in top physical shape. As a result, many departments are initiating formal programs involving physical reconditioning and mandatory medical checkups. Some have gone so far as to issue "Fat Albert" letters to officers with unchecked obesity problems. Utilizing informal group relationships, other departments are able to utilize peer pressure as an incentive for the officer to keep in physical shape.

Traditional physical-fitness standards related to vision are also being contested. Until this decade, most departments required police recruits to have vision corrected to 20/20 and be free of color blindness. The theory behind these standards is that officers must be able to identify suspects, vehicles, and other items at a reasonable distance, to function without glasses in serious situations, and to correctly identify the color of objects such as vehicles. A review of vision standards by Holden (1993) shows that these reasons cannot be supported by agency data or empirical research. A national review of vision standards by the author shows a wide range of variance ranging from the traditional 20/20 corrected standard to no standards. He concludes that most standards are merely supported by what-if scenarios.

There is still another aspect to this issue. In the future, we may see different physical requirements being specified for different categories of police jobs. It may be that officers on patrol must meet one standard and older officers assigned to administrative tasks must meet a different standard. There may come a time when all officers in a department will be physically certified in terms of the jobs they will be allowed to do within the department.

Americans with Disabilities Act (ADA)

The Americans with Disabilities Act (PL 101-336) which became fully effective in July of 1992, prohibits discrimination against disabled people in employment, public services, transportation, public accommodations, and telecommunications. According to O'Connor (1991), the law makes a very broad interpretation of a disability: any impairment limiting a major life activity. Disability for this statute includes sight, hearing, suffering with a disease such as AIDS (Acquired Immune Deficiency Syndrome), and disfigurement which does not result in an actual impairment. Persons who feel that they have been discriminated against on the basis of a disability may file complaints with the EEOC.

Title I of the ADA applies to all areas of police employment such as testing, hiring, assignments, evaluations and disciplinary actions, training, promotion, sick leave, and termination. The immediate impact of ADA on police already has been felt in preemployment processes such as physical medical tests. A department that disqualifies a person because of a disability must show why the rejection is job related and consistent with business necessity. Furthermore, the agency must be able to demonstrate that it cannot make a reasonable accommodation to enable the individual to perform the essential job functions or that the accommodation would impose an undue hardship. The concept of *reasonable accom-*

modation is quite broad. It ranges the employer making physical adaptations to the work environment to changing policies and work practices.

Returning to our civil service selection chart in Figure 11-1 (page 270), it is important to note that qualified candidates cannot be screened out because of their disability before their actual ability to do a job is evaluated. Thus, police employers have to make a tentative job offer before medical testing is undertaken.

The ADA has prompted a review of preemployment police medical and physical agility standards in terms of those factors necessary for performing the essential elements of the job. Relatedly each department or state regulatory agency such as civil service must define the minimum physical agility requirements necessary. A person who is disqualified on the basis of a disability such as impaired hearing or loss of a limb, can seek a challenge to see if a reasonable accommodation can be made.

Alcoholics and recovered drug abusers are also included as disabled under this act. Certain cynics have charged that the ADA could force a department to hire a recovered drug abuser. Other observers point out that ADA does not impact on character investigations nor does it impact on physical agility tests. Thus a substance abuser could be disqualified because he or she disobeyed the law in conducting his or her drug use.

Thus, ADA has resulted in large numbers of unsuccessful candidates filing lawsuits addressing normally held medical and agility standards related to police employment. For example, in *Joyce v. Suffolk County* (5 AD Cases 935), the court rejected a candidate's contention that he was a disabled person within the definition of ADA because he failed eyesight and blood pressure requirements for the position of police officer. These conditions, the court ruled, might render him unfit for the position but they in no way constitute a major impairment limiting major life activity. This case and others demonstrated that the department must be able to define the essential functions of the job and, on a case-by-case basis, determine if the person's conditions constitute a disability within the legal definition of ADA. It should be noted that assignment and staffing practices will be taken into consideration to ascertain if a reasonable accommodation can be made.

The main intent of ADA is to combat discrimination against persons who are disabled, by attacking commonly-held notions related to the disability and matching the disability with the essential functions of the job. As reviewed by Webster (1996: 12–13) ADA cases involving law enforcement operations have mainly been involved with disabilities such as back disorders and job-related injuries. Two of the sample cases used in her analysis include:

> *Santos v. Port Authority of New York and New Jersey*, No. 94 Civ. 8427, 1995. After an officer injured his foot, he sought permanent administrative duty assignment. Even though the plaintiff had been placed on light duty, the court ruled in favor of the police department, stating that the officer could no longer perform the essential functions of the position of police officer. As stated in the ruling,… "very use of that term suggests a position whose essential function

include far more rigorous activities than the clerical duties plaintiff has been performing."

Ethridge v. Alabama (860 F. Supp. 808 M. D. Ala. 1994). The defendant sued on the basis of discrimination after he was terminated from his job for failing to complete mandated firearms training. The court ruled in favor of the police department, stating that the required training was essential for the position of police officer.

essential functions

What are the essential functions of a police officer position? Based on a job analysis, essential functions include arrest and detention of suspects, controlling civil disorder, collecting and preserving evidence, conducting a crime scene search, operating a motor vehicle, and using physical force. Under these general headings, there are a number of essential tasks that must be performed. For example, under the heading of "Using Physical Force" we have the following essential tasks:

1. Break up fights between two or more persons
2. Carry by yourself an immobile child
3. Pull person out of a vehicle to effect rescue
4. Subdue an attacking person
5. Use weaponless defense tactics
6. Subdue person resisting arrest
7. Disarm violent armed suspect
8. Pull person out of vehicle who is resisting arrest
9. Search for a person in a darkened building or environment
10. Strike person with baton.

Equipment that a police officer must use to perform these essential tasks are: baton, flashlight, flexicuffs, and handcuffs.

THE BACKGROUND INVESTIGATION

After a candidate has passed the written and physical portions of the selection process, a background investigation is conducted by the agency. The objective is to obtain information relating to the candidate's suitability (or nonsuitability) for police employment. Due to the mobility of today's population, the background investigation is a long-term process that is expensive and eventually may cover a variety of locations in many states. Informal relationships among police agencies are tapped for this facet of police personnel selection, since it is economically impossible for investigators to check every location.

The thoroughness of the background investigation varies from agency to agency. In some cases, it is perfunctory; in other cases, it is meticulous. Based on the candidate's application, each place of residence (usually within a ten-year period) and the immediate neighborhood are checked. Neighbors and landlords are asked questions related to the candidate's character that cover a wide range of topics (for example, the number of parties held while the candidate lived in the premises; drinking habits; driving habits; relations with spouse, girlfriend, boyfriend, and so on. Former and present employers are also questioned as to honesty and work habits. Other areas that are also reviewed are educational and military history.

But the most important piece of information that investigators wish to learn is that of a criminal history, especially incidents that were never addressed by the candidate on an employment application. As a routine practice, information as to a possible criminal record is obtained from criminal computer banks maintained by federal, state, and local law enforcement agencies. A copy of the candidate's fingerprints is also sent to the FBI and state criminal justice records for verification as to possible criminal record. During the background investigation, police investigators also wish to know of offenses for which the candidate was arrested that may not be classified as crimes, such as public intoxication, disorderly conduct, harassment, and various violations of local municipal ordinances.

Related to the check for criminal history is the driving record. As most police agencies have access to data on all aspects related to motor vehicle operation and registration in just about every state through a computer terminal in the police station, this information is readily obtained. An important issue that comes to light with regard to background checks is that these investigations are another method of "weeding out." Having excessive traffic tickets is a common reason for rejection as is falsification of any information.

RESIDENCY

Many departments give preference to citizens who live within the boundaries of the local police jurisdiction. This is handled in a number of ways. In one approach, only citizens with prior residency in the local agency jurisdiction are eligible for police employment. Prior residency varies from a few weeks to many months. In other jurisdictions, residency is required only after employment. Others give a preference to prior residents on the hiring list; this means that local residents will be hired before the residents of any other jurisdiction will be considered. One of the authors' students who placed fourth on a local civil service police examination discovered he had been placed sixty-fourth on the list when the examiners found out that he lived about a mile outside the city limits. He hadn't been aware of these residency preferences when he took the examination but he was certainly aware of them after the civil service lists were published.

Residency areas vary widely. They can be limited to municipality in question or extended to contiguous counties or throughout the state. Some departments, for example those in Houston and Los Angeles, have nationwide recruitment programs with no prior residency requirements. They are looking for the best talent, nationwide, for their departments.

The issue of residency is related to the questions of (1) merit and talent versus (2) the need of local knowledge and adherence to local customs that local citizens would have and (3) the wish to give preference in the spending of tax dollars to those who provide those tax dollars. Reform-minded police managers, especially those in the larger departments, prefer talented and meritorious candidates regardless of place of residence. Local conservative politicians appeal to home rule and local pride in establishing rigid residency requirements. If police departments are to upgrade their personnel, rigid residency requirements will have to be abolished since these requirements limit the talent pool from which potential officers can be drawn.

PSYCHOLOGICAL TESTING

Basically, standardized psychological tests called *psychometrics* are used only by large departments. Andrew Crosby, who directed an IACP project on the police application selection tests, grouped the qualities that were being examined in the psychological assessment of police (1979: 215):

1. Personality, character, temperament, interests, and motivation
2. General aptitude—including "intelligence quotients," aptitude batteries, and tests to predict performance in areas such as "verbal" and "quantitative"
3. Special aptitudes—e.g., clerical, spatial relations, or fluency of ideas
4. Achievement—measures of how well an individual has learned to perform, for example, in typing of languages
5. Other constructed measures—these may be useful in predicting behavior and, on this basis, can be considered a parallel category

An example is the biographical inventory measure by which an individual is evaluated in terms of marital status, work history, and so on. One of the problems in developing, administering, and using these tests is the need for an agreement on the characteristics of a good police officer.

An extensive psychological study of patrol officers in relation to an evaluation of field performance by police management personnel was done in the Chicago Police Department in 1968. This study gave a description of the kind of personality that operates most successfully, and that is easy for police administrators to agree with (Baehr et. al., 1968: 230):

> The desirable response is one of cooperation and an active endeavor to solve the problem rather than withdrawal from the situation, undue competitiveness in attempting to resolve it by outdoing others or an expression of hostility towards it. In the area of temperament and personality functioning, the desirable attributes are

those which make for control of purely impulsive and emotional responses and for a "work" rather than a "social" orientation. Other important characteristics would be personal self-confidence, resistance to stress and a realistic rather than a subjective and feeling-oriented approach to life.

Basically, personnel managers who use psychometric testing and clinical evaluation in assessing police recruits are looking for a stable personality that is flexible enough to adjust to the stress situations in police work along with the complex peer relations. Police managers are especially concerned with having some idea as to whether that particular recruit is apt to "break" in a stress situation sometime in the future. If that is, in fact, a major concern, then the authors would recommend that personnel managers in police departments create a series of stress interviews to use in selecting recruits. One problem with this type of testing is that researchers have barely scratched the surface in testing the predictability of these tests in police performance. However, we do have an extensive research literature on industrial and business personality profile testing and have excellent empirical evidence in terms of predictability of performance and standardized group scores.

Crosby's article and others indicate a range of 10 to 20 percent rejection of recruits based on psychological testing. Following are the reasons why a group was rejected in a clinical appraisal program (Crosby, 1979: 226):

Psychotic disorders	20%
Chronic brain disorders	5
Personality trait disturbances	32
Sociopathic personality disturbances	29
Psychoneurotic disorders	4
Personality pattern disturbances	10
Total	100%

Basically, psychological testing is useful in weeding out psychotic and potentially dangerous human beings. In the example, one out of five people interviewed was rejected.

Most professionals agree that psychological testing is useful only for rejecting the truly abnormal. In that gray area encompassing normal-neurotic-deviant, different kinds of judgments need to be made to be fair to the recruits.

What is rather scary is that most departments and practically all smaller police departments use no psychological screening for recruits. If, say, even 10 percent can be rejected for potentially psychotic behavior, then what we have created by not using this technique is a group of unguided missiles with great potential for harm. Industry and businesses have found these techniques to be useful and spend millions of dollars a year to employ them. Business would not go to this expense unless there was clear-cut evidence of these tests being useful in judging future performance. It is now time for law enforcement to catch up with the private sector by using personnel-evaluation techniques of proven value.

The basic problem in this area is that police managers themselves need to learn about and understand the limits and usefulness of psychological testing. Until we have in-service training in this area for the top police management in large and small departments, the tests will not be used. Thus police management, through ignorance, will be rejecting an important management tool that has proven its use in the private sector.

LATERAL ENTRY

Lateral entry allows recruitment for various levels in a police agency. It allows for mobility in that an officer can transfer at a rank above recruit and below such elected or politically appointed positions as chief, sheriff, and deputy chief. This means that a sergeant in one agency may be able to transfer laterally to another police agency, keeping his or her rank.

Of course, lateral entry is almost nonexistent. Mobility comes only to the lowest and highest levels of policing. In relation to the entry-level positions, it is normally a termination of one job and an entry into another job. It is lateral entry at the bottom and difficult to distinguish from simple job mobility. This may mean an upgrading of the officer from a local police job to a more prestigious county, state, or federal law enforcement occupation. This is a simple case of upward mobility rather than lateral entry.

At the top level, we see chiefs moving from agency to agency. Sometimes it is to a larger and more prestigious department; for example, when Chief Patrick Murphy moved from the head of the Syracuse, New York, Police Department to chief of the Washington D.C., Police Department. When he became chief of Detroit, it was a lateral move. His subsequent move to police commissioner of New York City, his old department, was obviously a move upward.

In smaller communities, state civil service commissions have created a civil service position of chief. The net result is normally freezing the chief in his position and reducing mobility. In fact, some small communities have it in their police charter that the chief must come from the ranks, regardless of qualifications. This indeed reduces mobility.

There are a number of real restrictions on the creation of a lateral entry system: (1) nonuniform retirement systems, (2) differences in pay scales for the same positions, (3) residency requirements, (4) nonuniform training for different levels of staffing, and (5) differences in civil service requirements for the same management level. Generally, in many of these cases, it would take a major adjustment by local management and the police benevolent association's personnel policies, and in some cases change in local and state laws to implement a lateral-entry personnel system.

The Pros and Cons of Lateral Entry

Lateral entry can affect morale in a department as police officers wait for someone to leave or die to assume a promotion. If the position is taken by an officer from the outside, it means that promotions from within may become even more limited. There would be pressure on smaller communities to raise their pay scales and retirement systems to compete with the large police agencies in the area. Local government would not support lateral entry, normally, because of the fear of having to pay these costs.

It is common knowledge that police unions oppose the concept of lateral entry. Why? It would seem to be in the best interests of the police officer to be able to upgrade himself or herself in a move to another agency. However, police benevolent associations take another point of view. Traditionally, unions have been concerned with job security, and this is a legitimate concern in a changing economy. Thus union contracts, both public and private, provide for seniority systems and a formal grievance system that will protect employees from being taken advantage of by management. The opposition to lateral entry is found in this tradition. Lateral entry is seen as a direct attack on the seniority system and the ability of the union to offer secure tenure under civil service to public employees.

Management may also worry about having to take qualified personnel into their agency. Supervisory examinations are largely pencil-and-paper civil service tests, often created and administered by a central state agency. In states where central agencies do not control this examination, there is a lack of uniformity, and management in one agency may not agree with the criteria used for promotion by another agency. Even where centralized criteria and examinations exist within a state, there is a problem of relying too much on a pencil-and-paper test for reviewing supervisory skills, especially when that officer may live and work in a community completely different from the one into which he or she wishes to enter laterally. When we talk about lateral entry across state lines, the problems become compounded. Crossing national lines, even in the 1990s, will remain an unsolved problem.

Arguments in favor of lateral entry are those for the merit system of employing personnel. The most talented police officers in the nation would compete for the best supervisory and management slots. In terms of efficiency, it is being able to appoint the best person for the best job; in terms of a free market, lateral entry is the only justified concept. Restrictions create a limited market for police talent on the supervisory and management level, and this restrictive movement normally means that the local departments will not have the best talent for their supervisory and management positions. Finally, local police services will have to become more competitive because they are competing for promotion on a statewide and a nationwide basis.

POLYGRAPH TESTING

A **polygraph** is an instrument that is used to measure physiological responses to questions. Three variables—breathing, blood pressure, and amount of perspiration—are monitored as a subject is introduced to stimuli by way of specific questions; for example, "Have you smoked marijuana in the last five years?"

Today the polygraph is increasingly being used by law enforcement agencies as a preemployment screening device as well as an investigatory tool. The objective in utilizing the polygraph for police personnel selection is to uncover those aspects of a person's character that would be deemed undesirable for a career in law enforcement. These include excessive drinking, gambling, immoral sexual conduct, and criminal behavior that might not be uncovered during a background investigation. Police agencies that use the polygraph for their personnel selection point to the high number of applicants who are disqualified based on information obtained during the course of the polygraph test. Also, by publicizing the use of the polygraph for police selection, many agencies feel that this tends to deter candidates who would ultimately be found unsuitable.

Many important questions emerge on the use of the polygraph for selection purposes. First, the polygraphist must be well trained. This involves a rigorous course of some 600 hours followed by refresher seminars to keep him or her abreast of new trends. Then, the department has to establish criteria that would disqualify a candidate; that is, determine what past or present behavior is unsuitable for police work. For example, should candidate Jones be disqualified because he smoked marijuana five years ago while in college? If Jones admits to stealing while he was a juvenile, what type of stolen property will result in his disqualification? a car? a fountain pen?

In essence, the use of the polygraph is based upon the subjective judgments of the polygraphist and the overall policies of the department.

THE INTERVIEW

Traditionally, the candidate is either required or invited to have an interview with the chief of police regarding his or her candidacy for employment. In states where civil service prevails, this interview may be perfunctory or an important portion of the process, if the department is able to select from a pool or a certified list of candidates. The purpose of the interview is for the administrator to meet the candidate and ask questions to determine if the candidate would be able to become a good police officer and an asset to the department.

Many departments have turned the interview into a stressful group process, whereby the candidate meets with three to six interviewers from the department, the community, or the department and community combined. Difficult questions are asked ranging from personal philosophy to judgment in police situations, and the candidate's responses are measured accordingly. This process gives the department something that no multiple-choice tests can ever give—the ability to examine the potential officer in a stressful situation, for in the interview room, the candidate is required to make immediate judgments on the questions presented.

In reviewing group interview questions from a variety of sources, here are examples of some basic questions:

1. What unique skills, strengths, and abilities will you bring to the department?
2. What do you expect from a supervisor?

3. What kind of call would be distasteful to you (or most stressful)?

4. Suppose that while you are on patrol, you receive a call to go to a residence and are informed that a baby is crying. There is a babysitter inside the residence, but no one comes to the door. What do you do?

The candidate is judged not only on his or her responses but also on his or her ability to communicate and to make judgments.

Interviews for candidate-selection purposes range from structured questions that require somewhat specific type of knowledge or responses to interviews where there may be a few structured questions, but the interrogators are allowed to free associate and probe the candidate's replies.

COLLEGE EDUCATION REQUIREMENTS

Of the many programs created by the Law Enforcement Assistance Administration, some that will endure are the college criminal justice programs that were created in response to the mandate of the President's Commission on Law Enforcement and Administration of Justice that all police officers should possess college degrees. In the 1970s a trend began for police departments and civil service commissions to raise educational requirements from the traditional high school diploma to two or four years of college study with a major in criminal justice or a related field.

While this would appear to be a step toward creating a professional police force and attracting candidates who are able to think, write, and articulate in addressing the social problems as they affect the community, many police administrators and college educators question the value of a college education as it relates to police work. Detractors or those neutral to the idea point out that the realities of the police role (making arrests, seeing people at their worst) may nullify the value of classroom study (Weiner, 1976). Furthering this controversy, the National Advisory Commission on Higher Education of Police Officers (1979) concluded that many criminal-justice college programs were no more than extensions of the police training academy staffed by ex-police officers who offered "how to" types of courses (scoffed at as "Handcuffs 101") rather than courses related to important social and police managerial issues. Others have contended that college cannot really teach common sense and that many college graduates do not know how to read and write well. Some college educators have replied that common sense is simply the sum total of the prejudices that one has developed over a lifetime. They also have argued that much of this "common sense" is not twenty years of professional growth, but that same rookie year repeated twenty times with all the mistakes integrated into a rigid approach to law enforcement.

Stepping back from this argument, many criminal justice educators and police professionals recommend that learning should be a combination of knowledge and experience. Those college and training programs that synthesize the combination are generally those most lauded by police administrators. It makes no sense to invent the wheel each year because the recruit was never given the knowledge of how wheels operate.

In a recent edition of a text on the role of the police, Radalet and Carter (1994: 152) cite research which suggests that higher education provides a number of benefits for law enforcement personnel. In addition to learning more about history, law, and ethics, which contributes to an officer's information base, higher education benefits include:

1. Developing greater empathy and tolerance for persons with different lifestyles and ideologies, which in turn helps with communication skills.

2. Helping officers make decisions and use discretion while handling individual cases, without direct supervision.

3. Permitting officers to be innovative and flexible while dealing with complex policing strategies such as problem-oriented or community policing.

4. Enabling officers to cope better with stress, resulting in more stable and reliable employees.

5. Helping officers communicate and respond to situations and service needs of the public in a civil manner.

THE ASSESSMENT CENTER

While most agencies have continued to utilize the various traditional steps just discussed for police personnel selection and wrestle with affirmative action complaints, others have adopted selection models from private industry. One that shows promise is the assessment center, a concept first used by the German and British military in World War II for selecting persons qualified to perform special missions. After the war, the idea caught on in private industry in the United States, and today, some federal and municipal law enforcement agencies are experimenting with or are using the assessment center concept.

At the assessment center, the candidate participates in a number of activities ranging from a structured interview to group simulation exercises. In the group exercise, the candidate must confront a problem that could be found on the job, such as intervening in a family fight. Trained police officers and psychologists are designated as assessors and rate the candidate in how well he or she performs the assigned tasks.

As Gavin and Hamilton conclude (1975), these exercises simulate on-the-job behavior in a way that could not be accomplished using traditional pen-and-paper tests. Moreover, a large amount of information can be obtained in a relatively short period of time. Although various methods are used, the exercises are constant for all candidates undergoing the process.

The assessment center concept is in use in police departments in such cities as Fort Collins, Colorado, and Fort Worth, Texas. The New York City Police

Department has been using the assessment process for promotional considerations for lieutenant and captain. In the Fort Collins process, candidates undergo the following three phases (Gavin and Hamilton, 1975: 172–76).

Phase I

A. Written examination
B. Verbal screening
C. Psychological testing

Phase II

A. Oral board interview, composed of a senior police officer, a psychologist, and a community representative, in which questions are asked concerning the candidate's background and motivations for entering police work.
B. Situational testing, in which the candidate is confronted with typical police situations (assessors watch the exercise behind a one-way mirror).
C. Leaderless group discussions, at which time the applicants are presented with a police-related topic. At the end of the discussion, the candidates present their conclusions. The assessors watch the discussions and rate the candidates on their participation.
D. Individual psychological interview.
E. Combining the data gathered from phases I and II and ranking the candidates.

Phase III

Based on successful completion of phases I and II, the candidates then undergo a polygraph examination, background check, physical examinations, and police/staff interviews.

The assessment center can be expensive or even unobtainable for smaller departments due to cost and geographical considerations.

RECRUITMENT TECHNIQUES

The basic considerations in recruiting are who you want to reach and the dollar cost per sworn-in recruit. The department needs to provide funds for travel for the recruitment team as well as funds for printing materials. Basically, the media messages should be produced by professionals for maximum impact. Professional organizations will be able to provide cost figures in terms of populations reached and numbers in those populations. The department needs to quiz new recruits in terms of how they found out about new positions and use this information in charting the recruitment cost experience.

Recruitment activities will come under increasing scrutiny as departments are mandated to diversify their personnel. The professionalizing of police departments is beginning to meet head to head with affirmative action plans, but this problem can be mitigated by a well-planned recruitment campaign that is not limited by locality.

TOWARD A RATIONAL MODEL OF POLICE SELECTION

The authors feel that the multistep traditional model has served its usefulness—in essence, the dictates of the 1883 Pendleton Act are still being employed as the chief criteria for selection. What we propose is a new model that attempts to include methodologies used for personnel selection both in private industry and by some law enforcement agencies in the United States.

In reviewing this chapter, it becomes obvious that the traditional civil service selection process is outmoded on two bases. First, we are no farther ahead than we ever were in abolishing certain personnel abuses that existed before 1870, especially those related to the influence on the police by the community political establishment. Although the wholesale firing of police officers after election day has ended, the outright spoils system that existed in the nineteenth century has been replaced by a system that we call *sophisticated patronage* in which party affiliation becomes a factor in who gets selected in a rule-of-3 situation. Moreover, not all police departments use civil service. In many states, and even in those states that have civil service, there are departments that are noncivil service that still use a selection process based on political influence and informal community relations (for example, "I am a friend of the chief and I have lived here all my life.").

Many police administrators, moreover, are fed up with civil service. Although there are many qualified candidates who wish to become police officers, these individuals are forced to put off career plans simply because they must take a pencil-and-paper test that may be scheduled only once a year. Frequently, too, the results of the test are not made known until months after the examination. When coupled with the other factors related to the selection process—interviews, background checks, polygraph examinations, and so on—it may take a year and a half from the time of the examination to eventual employment. Many departments have solved this dilemma by doing a large portion or the entire process excluding the background examination within a specific time frame of a week or days.

Police administrators who desire a specific candidate are still able to find loopholes to further the cause of sophisticated patronage. One department studied conducted its own selection process and hired a number of officers under the statute terms of provisional appointment. When the civil service test was held, the new officers, who had been on the job for a year, had to take the examination with other candidates. The results showed that some of the year-old appointees did not rank very high on the list. The administrator solved the dilemma by importing a residency requirement (again within the terms of the state law), which eventually eliminated all the applicants who had taken the examination except for the officers previously hired.

Another aspect of civil service is the termination of incompetent officers who are under the protection of civil service. Termination of police employment according to civil service procedures is a long and drawn-out process. In many cases, informal methods replace the formal method under the heading of *forced resignation* and *managerial harassment*.

Many police administrators and reformers are unhappy with civil service, and the rise of affirmative action in the 1970s has prompted the move for reform and a review of traditional civil service requirements. As a result, many departments have been forced by the courts and federal agencies to introduce reforms or quota systems. The use of a federally induced quota, while seen as an immediate solution, is viewed as an ineffective long-term remedy in terms of employee and agency dissatisfaction, charges of lower entry standards, "dipping," countersuits, and on-the-job harassment. Against this background, many researchers employed by police departments, colleges, or research institutions are attempting to upgrade the existing process by answering diverse legal and methodological questions related to job performance and specific portions of the process. To date, this has only resulted in the allocation of time and monetary resources to upgrade the status quo.

New Police Recruitment Selection Model

To address the issues presented, we propose a model for police recruit selection. This rational model for police selection is based on three premises:

1. There is a need for better designed entrance-level, pencil-and-paper tests. Present pencil-and-paper tests often fail to predict on-the-job performance or the potential of the candidate.

2. The responsibility for police personnel selection rests with each state in terms of allocating financial and human resources for this objective. Since 90 percent of the police departments in the United States are small agencies composed of 15 officers or less, it is obvious that most agencies cannot afford to maintain an ongoing professional selection process. At the same time, each police agency must abide by state requirements for the position of police officer.

3. The present civil service personnel in existing departments need to be retooled to perform ably in this proposed model. The present personnel must be retrained, acquiring (a) new skills and (b) new attitudes toward their roles as police officers. This entails the various tasks police officers perform.

To be considered for the position of police officer, based on this proposed model, a candidate should be able to fulfill the following requirements:

1. *Age.* Twenty-one years of age with no maximum limit is recommended. It is at age 22 that most people in the United States embark on careers. There is no set maximum age to give each department the flexibility that is needed to decide on what kinds of experience and skills are needed of potential employees. At the same time, those departments with 20-year retirement systems will have to adjust their pension systems for the older worker. This would be a proportionate pension system based on years of service to the retirement age.

2. *Education.* Each candidate, under this new model of policing, would have to possess a bachelor's degree from an accredited college or university. The bachelor's degree is the socially accepted norm for most professional careers. It is assumed that routine and clerical tasks would be performed by civilian employees and that police officers would serve as professional law enforcement officers. Thus the kind of education that allows one to deal with a large range of cultures and roles, and teaches one to write well, would be of value for this type of police officer. District attorneys have known for years that cases written up by college-educated police officers are better than are those written by officers without a college education. A college-educated police force of professionals whose job description is related to professional skills and knowledge will be a superior police force.

3. *Physical requirements.* Each candidate must be in good health and physical condition according to a national standard such as Cooper. Nevertheless, each department will have physical requirements for selecting officers to special units (for example, SWAT, hostage negotiating teams, bicycle patrol, and emergency services). Candidates must be free of any disease or physical ailments that would keep them disabled for long periods of time or prevent them from performing police duties.

After fulfilling these three basic requirements, the candidate would then report to a regional assessment center. Here the candidate would undergo a variety of testing currently in use by many police agencies. The testing would include a battery of psychological examinations.

Upon successful completion of the assessment center review, the candidate would then be eligible to attend the regionally operated police academy. The academy curriculum would include the basic tasks related to police work: firearms, crisis intervention, law, introduction to the criminal justice system, and physical conditioning. Candidates who fail tests or firearms requirements would be eliminated.

Upon completing the assessment-center and police-academy stages, the candidate would then be issued a certificate making him or her eligible to be a law enforcement officer for state and local agencies. The officer would be notified of available openings in the various departments and be required to notify the department of her or her interest in working for that agency. From this pool of applicants, the agency would select the police officers for its department. The selection process would be based on the desires of the department and the community.

Burbeck and Furnham (1985: 68) reviewed the research on police personnel selection over the last 20 years. They concluded that "very little has changed since 1965...." They reviewed the works on the structured interview and concluded that it has some predictive validity, while the research on the police personality has not come to any clear conclusion. They also reviewed the methodological problems with psychological evaluation and said that although there are major problems, "psychological testing may be useful for selecting out people suffering from some mental abnormality" but should be "complementary to other selection processes." They also urge police managers to do a better job analysis so that we know what we are looking for in future police officers, a solid proactive recommendation and one that needs to be acted upon.

McLaughlin and Bing (1987: 275) look at the future selection of police: "The future of police selection is obviously dependent upon political factors, perceived public need, legislation, and courtroom mandates." Good training and selection will always be with us no matter what the political mandates are and court cases may be. It is the responsibility of the proactive police manager to plan ahead and deal with these issues in a professional and objective manner.

 ## OTHER PERSONNEL ISSUES

SEXUAL HARASSMENT

The confirmation hearings for Supreme Court Justice Clarence Thomas in 1991 prompted renewed interest in the topic of sexual harassment, especially with regard to interpersonal relationships in the work place. Sexual harassment occurs when

1. The supervisor demands sexual consideration in exchange for job benefit.
2. An employee makes unwelcome sexual advances on another employee in the form of pressure for dates, stalking, love letters, and calls.
3. The activities or behavior by one or more employees creates a hostile work environment for the complainant regardless of the loss of economic or tangible job benefits. Situations in this manner could include pranks, jokes, and comments of a sexual nature.

Prohibitions against sexual harassment are not new. In the 1980s there were a number of federal and state court cases which concluded that sexual harassing activities violated EEOC guidelines and Title VII of the Civil Rights Act of 1964.

Sexual favors for job benefits is a very understandable concept for most employers and employees because of the quid pro quo that is involved for advancement or job assignments. The "hostile work environment" standard, however, is very complex and often depends on the pattern of behavior in the work environment. Employer liability with regard to fines also depends to what extent the employer knew or could have reasonably known and prevented the sexual harassing activity. There have been a number of noted cases where public and private companies have been fined by either state or federal courts for failing to stop the activity.

Since the Thomas confirmation hearings, most employers have reviewed their sexual harassment prohibition policies and the processes by which employees can make complaints and seek resolution of sexual harassing work situations. Many organizations have conducted training sessions for employees and supervisors to discuss the various aspects of sexual harassment and its negative effect on the mission of the department.

The crux of police department efforts against sexual harassment remain departmental disciplinary processes insofar as investigations, hearings, and sanctions must be meted out according to due process standards. In situations where the department fails to address sexual harassment complaints, the employee may go outside of the department realm and prepare a complaint through either a state or federal regulatory agency. Returning to our discussion about the police subculture in Chapter 2, policing remains a male-dominated occupation in many departments throughout the United States. While the number of women officers has increased in many large state and metropolitan departments, there are few or no women in small agencies. Regardless of agency size, sexual harassment and the "hostile work environment" remain a problem for male and female supervisors and agency heads because of the delicate, complex nature of interpersonal relationships. We suggest that sexual harassment is a problem that must be continually addressed through training seminars, roll-call training, departmental advisories, and efficient complaint/resolution procedures.

DRUG TESTING

Drug testing for police personnel became widely used by the mid-1980s as a response to the widespread use of illegal substances by citizens coupled by the dramatic rise of drug-related police corruption cases. Policymakers, legislators, and police administrators reasoned that the so-called war on drugs could not be waged by police officers using illegal substances. Aside from the negative effects on physiomotor skills, the use of illegal substances by police officers provides a wide range of moral and legal dilemmas regarding drug enforcement. Perhaps the most profound are those life-and-death implications for drug-enforcement officers who are compromised or threatened by fellow officers "bought" by drug dealers.

Despite widespread use, drug testing remains controversial among police officers and police unions because of the invasion of personal privacy and the legal consequences for personnel who test positive. Departments that have drug screening may use one or a combination of the following programs:

1. Random testing for all personnel on a routine basis.

2. Mandatory testing for all preemployment applicants.

3. Testing for pre-service and in-service officers based on reasonable suspicion that the person is using illegal substances. Reasonable suspicion may be based on (1) internal investigation in response to a complaint, (2) observation of behavior at work (for example, slurred speech, unsteady gait), or (3) long-term work patterns regarding sick time and attendance.

4. Testing of officers being considered for sensitive assignments such as narcotics enforcement, helicopter operations, explosives, and special weapons and tactics.

5. Voluntary testing by officers to show that they are above reproach.

The legal basis for drug screening is based on the Fourth and Fourteenth amendments regarding searches and procedural due process. As commented on in Connors (1989), by the end of the last decade, both the United States Supreme Court and higher state courts ruled on the legality of certain kinds of searches related to drug testing. The most noted case was *Skinner v. Railway Labor Executives Association* (109 S.Ct. 1402) when the Supreme Court in 1989 decided that drug testing undertaken for railroad workers after accidents and safety violations constituted a search within the confines of the Fourth Amendment. The Court reasoned that the need to regulate the conduct of employees for safety purposes was far greater than the need for individual privacy. The same logic was applied for drug screening for United States Customs officers assigned to law enforcement duties. In *National Treasury Employees Union v. VonRaab* (109 S.Ct. 1384), the Court also concluded in the same year that preventing the entry and promotion of drug users to sensitive positions outweighed the privacy interests in view of the physical and ethical demands related to the position. In both cases, the Court also discussed the deterrence value of drug screening; in each situation, employees had fair warning that the tests would be conducted.

Of note, the arguments set forth in Skinner and VonRaab appear much earlier in state court cases upholding drug screening. In *Caruso v. Ward* (–NY2d–) the New York Court of Appeals in 1988 upheld random, periodic drug screening for the New York City Police Department's Organized Crime Control Bureau. In its opinion, the court ruled that police officers, because of the nature of the position, have a reduced expectation of privacy especially in view of the background investigation conducted during the job-screening process. The New York court noted that employees were given fair warning that drug screening would be a condition of employment for members of this unit.

The upholding of drug testing in these cases does mean that testing for all personnel will be automatically upheld. In either a court or an administrative-hearing setting, the following key elements will be analyzed: the nature of the testing (random versus postincident), the preliminary notice given to employees who are to be tested, the laboratory procedures used and their validation, and the need for testing based on the particular functions of the job. According to the Bureau of Justice Statistics (1996: 6), in 1993 about one-fourth of all departments had drug testing programs for recruit and in-service officers. Mandatory testing for in-service personnel accounted for only three percent of the departments that were surveyed.

In 1988, the Police Executive Research Forum sampled police chiefs around the country. The following are the policies the chiefs favored:

- Drug testing if reasonable grounds existed to suspect an officer using drugs (87.7%)
- Drug screening of police applicants (76.4%)
- Regular drug testing of officers during probationary period (66 percent)
- Random drug testing of officers in "sensitive" positions (64.7%)

These policies would be subject to legal and union contract considerations. In order to have credibility with the public it is necessary to have specific alcohol and drug abuse policies which are enforced. Police unions would have drug and alcohol abuse policies geared toward rehabilitation, with sanctions as a last resort.

Drug Testing in Practice

The most common screening procedure used at this time is urine testing by way of the Enzyme Multiplied Immunoassay Technique (EMIT). In this procedure, a urine sample is analyzed from a single substance or a class of drugs or metabolites by separating the various enzymes. The procedure is inexpensive and, thus, widely used. The use of EMIT only suggests the presence of a substance, it does not show quantity and level of impairment. As Connor (1989: 165) suggests, there must be further testing and investigation through gas chromatography and mass spectrometry to address the problem of "false positives." Figure 11–2 shows drug-screening procedures for the Honolulu Police Department which incorporate the use of a second sample to corroborate tests that show positive. The key elements in screening procedures are the safeguards used in this testing including such variables as the quality of equipment, chain of custody of evidence, training of personnel administering the test, and the test-site procedures.

For in-service personnel who test positive in random or periodic testing programs, the next course of action by management involves interrogation and disciplinary action. Most police unions have at this time negotiated a series of

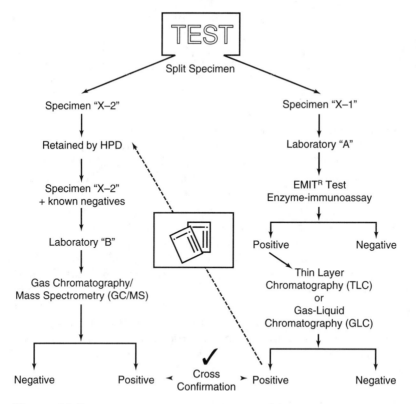

Figure 11-2
Honolulu Police Department drug testing methods.

steps to protect the interests of employees in situations when an employee has been ordered to submit to drug testing and related interrogation. These steps—representation by counsel, written notice of charges, reasonable privacy during urination, and second-opinion testing by the suspected employee— are generally in addition to any other rights negotiated by contract. To support administrators in situations where a complaint about drug use by an officer is based on the testimony of a confidential informant, language of the collective bargaining agreement often states that the employer does not have to reveal the name of a confidential informant.

Police executives generally agree that termination from employment is perhaps the only fitting way to deal with confirmed illegal drug users. As Connor (1989) points out, there are the legal aspects of the situations including possession of a controlled substance and association with known drug users. Some departments, in concert with their police unions, have started programs related to drug-abuse education and professional assistance for personnel who voluntarily declare that they have a substance-abuse problem. The success and employee acceptance of these programs varies because police officers will generally stay away from these programs if assistance offices are located in the police station and confidentiality is not insured. Some collective bargaining agreements declare that the officer will not be subject to drug screening if he or she voluntarily enters a rehabilitation program. Whether the officer is temporarily suspended or allowed to continue in another assignment varies from program to program.

This trend in drug screening and discipline will not drastically change in the future based on recent state court and administrative rulings that continue to uphold valid screening programs and disciplinary sanctions for drug abuse committed in both on-duty and off-duty situations. Further, a related federal policy for drug-free workplaces and schools was insured by the end of the last decade. In 1988 the Federal Drug Free Workplace Act was signed into law. It requires employers with federal contracts in excess of $25,000 to certify that they will provide a drug-free workplace through the following: (1) providing publications and education about drug awareness, (2) requiring notification to the employer by the employee if he or she is arrested for criminal violations occurring in the workplace, (3) requiring convicted employees to participate in a drug-abuse assistance or rehabilitation program, and (4) notifying employees of possible sanctions that might be taken against them by the company. The language and intent of the 1988 act was also applied in the Drug Free Schools Act which stipulates that financial aid can be withheld from students convicted of drug violations.

PUBLIC POLICE AND PRIVATE POLICE

Cunningham and Taylor (1984:2) estimated that 1.1 million persons are employed in private security, outnumbering public police by a hefty 2 to 1. While the expenditure for public police is an estimated $13.8 billion, private police expenditure is estimated at $21.7 billion (Cunningham and Taylor, 1984: 2). With the rapid growth of the private security sector, there have been much higher estimates of a 4 to 1 ratio or even a 5 to 1 ratio of private to public police. The growth of the public police force has stabilized, while private policing has been experiencing rapid growth. Two major issues of concern to police managers today are (1) the need for more active cooperation between public and private police, and (2) the employment of public police in the private sector.

Public police managers feel there is a need for licensing of private police as well as a need to upgrade the training of private police. Liability problems have arisen concerning the estimated 150,000 public police who moonlight with private jobs. According to Cunningham and Taylor (1984: 3), the areas of cooperation between the public and private sectors are many, including "hazardous materials movement, protection of dignitaries and executives, disaster management, traffic control, crowd control, measures to counter terrorism and economic crime investigation."

According to Albert Reiss, Jr. (1988: 9), there are three major models for the secondary employment of the public police officer:

1. The *officer contract model*, where each officer is a principal who independently contracts with an employer for a particular job....

2. The *union brokerage model*, [where] an officer's union or association brokers the employment for its members so that they need not search for their own job and negotiate pay....

3. The *department contract model*, the department is the principal agent for officers and contracts their secondary employment.

There are many variations of the officer contract model. For example, Arlington, Virginia restricts outside employment to the state of Virginia, county of Arlington, and the U.S. government. Cincinnati handles the billing and compensation of officers when the contracting party is the city; otherwise, it lets its officers contract on their own for employment.

According to Reiss, under the union brokerage model, the union sets conditions and pay of paid details and may bargain with the police department concerning status and condition of paid details. The Seattle Police Officers' Guild coordinates requests for off-duty employment, but the officers act as independent contractors. For special events held at the Seattle Center complex, off-duty officers "are employed by the complex's director of security and compensated by an outside accounting firm" (Reiss, 1988: 11).

The department contract model has three major features (Reiss, 1988: 11): "(1) contracts with employers for paid details; (2) assigns officers to details; and (3) pays the officers from reimbursements by employers." The Metro-Date, Florida Police Department contracts for all police-related work but "officers are allowed to contract independently for non-police related work on application for a specific job and under permit for that employment." Metro-Dade is unusual in that it subcontracts police services for private security. Boston, Colorado Springs, New Haven, and St. Petersburg operate primarily with the department contract model.

The three major issues that restrict employment of the public police are (1) potential conflict of interest, (2) threat to the dignity of police as an occupation, and (3) "an unacceptable risk of temporary or disabling injury that would limit their [the police officer's] return to regular duty" (Reiss, 1988: 11).

Most departments have rules and regulations and issue work permits for all outside employment. Departments place even more stringent restrictions when the public police officer is employed in uniform. Many departments and police unions also restrict the rate of compensation that can be earned; for example, demanding a minimum rate. They also restrict the type of employment and the amount of time spent on secondary employment, such as a maximum number of hours outside work per week. The exact times of employments—for example, working prior to coming on duty—is also an area of concern. These restrictions are normally enforced through the use of issuing or denying work permits to individual officers. All in all, the relationship between private and public police will continue to be a major concern of police managers in the public sector.

► STRESS MANAGEMENT

Police work is high stress, and managing that work can produce a great deal of stress. Stress itself can be good or bad. If it motivates you to complete a job and act in a responsible manner, "manageable" stress becomes a positive factor in organizational life. If it leads to avoidance of work, a feeling of being over-whelmed by events, it can become a strong negative force.

More and more studies are being written on the subject of police stress. The major issues relate to stress created by the organization and stress created by the individual. Organizational stress is created by lack of communication or even mis-communication. A lack of consistency may cause the line officer and his imme-diate superiors to think that they lack control over their jobs.

Individual stress is often created by a personality type attracted to police work that has been labeled *type A*. Type A personalities tend to overcommit them-selves to a wide variety of tasks and feel that they have to be doing something all the time. They feel that they must be in control of all situations affecting them. They often have insomnia but they also accomplish a great deal of what they set out to do.

This is in contrast to type B personalities who accomplish what they can, worry a bit about what they have control over, and do not worry about what they cannot control. If the job is not finished on one day, this individual feels that there are other days to finish the job. The type A personality, in contrast, would either finish the job in the time allotted or be overwhelmed by guilt. When stress management consultants do their task well, they are able to apply type A and type B personality profiles to individuals and work out specific exer-cises that strike a balance between the two personality types. This is a very real problem and can make or break a police organization. Mediation, posture and a variety of exercises are excellent tools that have been used to deal with stress and stressors. Remember that stress, itself, is not bad. It is uncontrolled stress that is destructive.

Stress-reduction techniques should be part of every in-service police train-ing program. However, all the techniques in the world will not change stress-pro-ducing situations. By the nature of their work, police officers are often confront-ed by dangerous situations. However, perceptions of violence and techniques to handle violence can reduce stress on individual officers. An officer must have enough training and experience to handle and control stress-producing situa-tions. That is why, for example, domestic-crisis-intervention training is so vital for the patrol officer, as is specific training for riot and crowd control, the handling of juveniles, and so on. The more skills an officer has, the less stress he or she will experience.

Organizational structures can produce or diminish stress. In plain English, this means police personnel need consistency of command, time for new orders to be assimilated, and a good feedback system that allows for modification of orders in terms of the needs of the line officer. Officers and managers, especially middle managers, need communication skills so that the line officer will feel that

(1) someone up there in management land is listening and (2) he or she has a real and responsible input into the orders that affect his or her everyday professional life. People need to feel in control of their lives. Capricious orders with no explanation destroy this feeling of control.

When you are drinking coffee with a number of police officers from different departments at 2:00 A.M. in the middle of a patrol assignment, what is the talk about? Is it about crime, forensics, or how to patrol more effectively? Not usually. The talk is normally about promotions, orders, personalities in the police force, and individual stories about police-related incidents. Good police managers know this and will take steps to assure line officers and supervisors some control over the affairs that dominate their lives.

Stress management is a major concern for police managers. A bibliography published in 1979 by the National Institute of Justice listed 113 bibliographical sources and 33 training films on police stress and stress management (Duncan, Brenner, and Kravitz, 1979). Police have to make instant life-and-death decisions, face violence, and yet are also stressed by boredom. Some stress-related factors in police work are (Kroes and Hurrell, 1975; Niederhoffer, 1974; Reiser, 1974; Terry, 1983; Stratton, 1984):

1. Shift work
2. A quasi-military structure
3. The need to repress emotions and keep psychological distance
4. Lack of promotions and very few lateral transfers
5. Having to live up to a media image of the supercop
6. Police cynicism
7. Frustration and lack of input into the police bureaucracy
8. Fear and danger (killing a citizen or having a fellow officer killed, especially your partner)
9. A sense of social isolation
10. Retirement
11. Excessive paperwork
12. Frustration with the judicial system
13. Impact of a profession stressing danger and imposing a paramilitary organization on the spouse and children

Police officers, despite the social solidarity of police, often do not trust each other. As Graf (1986: 184) quotes one officer, "I find it hard to confide with work associates because of pride and fear of gossip. I don't wish to show any signs of weakness as this may be detrimental to one's career." When there is a support system of fellow officers, stress is decreased but many officers do not use this system. Peer counseling has enjoyed some success (Klyver, 1983). Graf recommends increasing the officer's role in departmental decision making, hiring a psychological consultant for individual and group counseling, and training for coping skills. John Stratton, former director, Psychological Services, Los Angeles County Sheriff's Department, also gives many practical examples and suggestions in his book *Police Passages* (1984). These include counseling programs for spouses, police widows and widowers, officers who will be retiring, and the availability of a 24-hour crisis hot line for police officers.

Violanti (1983) showed that stress increases in what he calls the first two stages of a police career: 0 through 5 years, the alarm stage; and 6 through 13 years, the disenchantment stage. He recommends that programs on stress management should be focused on these years. He concludes with this hopeful note (Violanti, 1983: 216): "Despite strong pressures and the imbalanced nature of the police functions, officers managed in time to reduce stress." He felt that "individual perception is the most important factor in determining stress levels." Thus stress can be coped with both by the individual and by the police organization bringing in positive intervention strategies.

One approach that large departments can use and smaller departments can create on a regional level is what Robert Loo, the first chief psychologist of the Royal Canadian Mounted Police, calls his proactive approach to psychological services. He recommends the creation of a center which will have a career-cycle perceptive on providing psychological services, including (Loo, 1985: 134) "recruit selection, support of force training programs, the support of members in the workplace and pre-retirement services." In the past he felt that police agencies simply reacted to such problems as low morale, stress reactions, drug abuse by police personnel, and community/citizen complaints against police officers. He feels that this proactive approach will help police managers deal more adequately with these problems.

Family stress can be decreased by departmental intervention. At the training level, spouses and domestic partners should learn about the job and the stressors in the job, tour the police unit, and take part in a ride-along program. Emergency communication and debriefing procedures for critical incidents, along with counseling for families need to be available. Counseling and support groups need to be created with the support of the police administration. These can provide stress management workshops, social affairs, and volunteer opportunities.

Officers need to be physically fit and should have good eating and sleeping habits in order to reduce stress. Departments need to set up nutritional guidelines and physical fitness programs that are related to an officer's age, work area, and physical condition. Many departments consider this a frill. However, given the investment in training and work experience in the human capital of police officer and police supervisor, the approach should be considered essential to the job.

Anderson, Swenson and Clay in *Stress Management for Law Enforcement Officers* (1995) show four major factors that affect officers' negative attitudes toward their work. These are "(1) the particular stresses they face, (2) the extent to which the legal system backs them and rewards them with convictions for the good arrests, (3) their zone of stability, and (4) their support system." (Anderson, Swenson and Clay, 1995: 283)

The zone of a person's stability is "The range of stimulation (excitement, arousal) from the least to the most an individual can handle without signs of distress." (Anderson, Swenson and Clay, 1995: 17) A person operating below their zone of stability will be bored and uncomfortable; when operating above the zone of stability, will feel stressed and pressured. Good police managers need to know their own zone of stability and their subordinates' zones of stability so that there is enough good stress to keep people moving while the stress does not go beyond their comfort zones.

Supervisors, such as sergeants, lieutenants, or captains who are trained in supervision techniques are less stressed and create less stress for subordinates. This approach improves the morale of the whole police department. As one lieutenant and shift commander stated, "the daily stressors associated with management...can produce the same kind of stress reactions among supervisors...as a domestic disturbances call might provoke among line officers." (Standfest, 1996: 10) Training and stress management is just as important for supervisors and managers as any line officer.

Standfest has a four-stage approach:

1. *Assessment* This is where police executives learn which stressors are affecting their supervisors.

2. *Planning* The police executives need to remove the stressors in a cost-effective manner. Standfest says fundamental approaches such as repairing station houses and vehicles could reduce a great deal of stress at low cost.

3. *Action* Police executives need to carry out fully any plans and let the supervisors know what is going on.

4. *Follow-through* Police executives need to evaluate the action, making sure that the orders were fully carried out, and assess the outcomes.

Anderson, Swenson and Clay show the nature of police role stressors and role overload. To summarize these recommendations (1995: 130):

1. Clear and current policies and procedures concerning work tasks reduce police role ambiguity.

2. A consistent expectation by supervisors concerning their subordinates, along with a clear two-way feedback system, is essential.

3. Officers and supervisors need to have a high tolerance of ambiguity.

4. Active participation by all authority levels in decision making provides a system of mutual responsibility that continually relieves stress.

Supervisors can reduce stress by "(1) teaching the officers 'verbal judo'; that is, how to use words to control citizen's behavior; (2) showing the officers the laws that apply and when to use them; and (3) explaining the nature and characteristics of the particular public they serve." (Anderson, Swenson and Clay, 1995: 285)

This is exactly what proactive participatory management and proactive community policing do when they are working effectively.

EMPLOYEE ASSISTANCE PROGRAMS

During the past decade, police departments have learned the painful lesson that their employees have personal problems similar to the general population. This theme has been picked up by popular television shows which show police at their best and worst. From time to time police officers have to cope with marital problems, alcohol and drug dependency, children with delinquency and academic problems, job stress, and burnout. The reasons police officers have these problems are the same for any other occupation. What is different is the physically demanding task of adjusting to shift work and the mentally demanding task of seeing people at their worst or dying. One officer has a recurring nightmare about a drowning incident: "He comes to me at night when I sleep. Sometimes once or twice every week. His hand was above the water but my supervisor held on to me to prevent me from going in after him. The water was electrified—there was not one goddamn thing I could do to help."

Many departments, under their own initiative or through union pressure, have begun employee assistance programs (EAPs) to deal with these problems. Smaller agencies also participate through regional arrangements or with state or county sponsored programs. Generally, these programs are staffed by fellow police officers who receive training in counseling and referral. Larger departments have the services of professional counselors and psychologists.

When first started, many officers stayed away for fear of being labeled crybabies, cowards, or destined for the rubber gun squad. Confidentiality was and remains an issue, and many initial programs were doomed to failure when offices were located in central headquarters. Begrudgingly, police officers have accepted the value and need for these programs, and the stigma associated with going to EAP has somewhat declined.

The trauma associated with critical incidents such as shootings, mass disaster, and gruesome death has received special attention in training and operations policies. In one seminar attended by one of the authors, a panel of veteran police officers recounted the following post-trauma experiences to an academy of police recruits.

Killing a person who was trying to choke the officers.

Responding to a car accident in which the officer's daughter died.

Search and recovery operations after a drowning.

Being gunned down by an armed suspect.

An officer who terminates another human life goes through a number of physical and mental reactions that will never entirely go away (Myles, 1986). He or she will be questioned by investigators and his or her actions will be reviewed in grand jury proceedings, administrative hearings, and trial situations. There will also be pressures on the officer's family and children. Thus many departments have posttrauma policies (for example, supervisory reaction, rules on interrogation) and counseling to deal with these problems.

▶ CONCLUSION

Personnel is a major expense in law enforcement, taking up approximately 80 percent of an administrator's time. Once a candidate has completed probation, he or she stays on the job until retirement. The majority of police departments in the United States continue to have permanent appointment or tenure for officers, which means that the employee cannot be fired without a lengthy hearing process unless he or she has been arrested for a crime or has committed a series of grave mistakes. It is not surprising that police candidates are carefully evaluated during the probationary period, since the employee serves at the pleasure of the department and can often be terminated without a formal hearing.

The first step of police hiring remains the written test, which is either administered by the department or by state or local civil service units. This test measures the ability to understand written material and gives some indication of situational judgment. Oral interviews are commonly used and they are very important for assessing interpersonal skills. Ideally, we view the assessment center as particularly useful for candidate selection because of cost. Issues related to personnel section and administration were presented, such as college education requirements, physical agility and medical standards, background checks, age requirements, drug testing, residency requirements, and the use of polygraph testing. In the absence of national or state hiring standards, each issue must be evaluated according to local agency and state personnel practices and procedures.

Drug testing for new candidates has now become routine as a method of deterring drug users from becoming police officers. Recent court cases conclude that there is a public interest in deterring drug use by police officers. However, drug testing for in-service employees is subject to collective bargaining negotiations and court cases have ruled that testing cannot be applied to all classes of employees. Commenting on random testing, Webster and Brown (1989: 6) conclude that mandatory testing programs have been upheld when there is evidence of a drug problem in the department.

Since 1970 affirmative action legislation and related court cases and administrative rulings have had the most profound impact on police candidate selection through judicial review of hiring processes and criteria. Police hiring processes underwent critical scrutiny based on the nonrepresentation of women and minorities in the police workforce. Certain agencies were forced to hire and promote under consent decrees or quota systems as a means of creating a diverse workforce, which led to allegations of lowered standards and reverse discrimination by white male candidates and veteran police officers. Nevertheless, the trend in this decade is to end quota programs where statistical representation has been achieved.

The increase of women in the police workforce has forced all departments to review sexual harassment complaints and referral policies and training on this topic for all line and management personnel. From our experience, the most common complaints by women officers are related to hostile work environment situations which include pranks, jokes, and offensive comments.

The Americans With Disabilities Act (ADA) has had a profound impact on policing hiring. This law has already forced agencies to review medical standards and the actual duties performed by officers. At this time, many departments in the United States have precise medical and physical agility standards for candidates and police academy recruits but not for in-service personnel. Candidates disqualified because of eyesight, weight, or other standards will no doubt challenge their disqualification based on the relationship between the standard and its relationship to duties performed by in-service police officers. Court cases and administrative rulings will lead to medical-physical standards, which will apply to all in-service officers, a situation that will require periodic medical and physical agility retesting.

QUESTIONS FOR REVIEW

1. Compare and contrast police hiring practices in the nineteenth century with those of today.

2. What is the controversy surrounding affirmative action programs?

3. What are the benefits of the following personnel selection tools: polygraph, assessment center, interview, lateral entry? Also, give criticisms of each.

4. Explain why written tests have generated great controversy in police personnel selection.

5. Explain how ADA affects assignment decisions.

CLASS PROJECTS

1. Role play an interview. There should be no more than three or four interviewers. The interviewers may assume the following roles: a police personnel officer, a detective, a civilian who is head of a local civil rights group, and a patrol officer. One member of the class is asked to be the police candidate. As the interviewers ask their questions, the rest of the class should be rating the responses of the candidate. After the interview, the class members will discuss their reactions to the interview process, their assessment of the candidate, and various issues regarding interviews.

2. Define *affirmative action*. Since affirmative action plans are public documents, select at least three of the local police agency affirmative action plans and compare and contrast them to the materials in this chapter concerning police selection. How do you deal with the controversies surrounding the raising and lowering of standards: ethical, educational, physical, skills, knowledge, and so on?

KEY TERMS

ADA
affirmative action
assessment center
dipping
disparate impact theory
EEOC
equal employment opportunity
Fat Albert
Hostile work environment

lateral entry
Pendleton Act
polygraph
rule of 3
sexual harassment
spoils system
stress
Title VII

BIBLIOGRAPHY

Adarand Constructors v. Federico Pena, 132 L. Ed. 2d 158 (1995).

ANDERSON, WAYNE, DAVID SWENSON, and DANIEL CLAY, *Stress Management for Law Enforcement Officers*. Upper Saddle River, N.J.: Prentice Hall, 1995.

AYRES, R. M., and G. S. FLANAGAN, "Preventing Law Enforcement Stress: The Organization's Role." Washington, D.C.: U.S. Department of Justice, 1990.

BAEHR, M., J. E. FURCON, and E. C. FROEMAL, *Psychological Assessment of Patrolman Qualifications in Relation to Field Performance*. Chicago: Industrial Relations Center, University of Chicago, 1968.

BERGMANN, BARBARA R., *In Defense of Affirmative Action*. New York: Basic Books, 1996.

BUREAU OF JUSTICE STATISTICS LOCAL POLICE DEPARTMENTS, 1993. Washington, D.C.: United States.

CALDWELL, D. S., and E. W. DORLING, "Preventing Burnout in Police Organizations." *The Police Chief* (April, 1993), pp. 156–159.

GOODMAN, A. M., "A Model for Police Officer Burnout." *Journal of Business and Psychology* (May, 1990), pp. 85–99.

Joyce v. Suffolk County, 5 AD Cases 939.

KANNADY, G., "Developing Stress-Resistant Police Families." *The Police Chief* (August, 1993), pp. 21–26.

LEMANN, NICHOLAS, "Taking Affirmative Action Apart." *New York Times Magazine* (June 11, 1995), p. 40.

MacKinnon, Catherine A., "Sexual Harrassment: Its First Decade in Court." in Barbara Raffel Price and Natalie J. Sokoloff, eds., *The Criminal Justice System and Women*. New York: McGraw-Hill, Inc., 1995.

McWhirter, Darien A., *The End of Affirmative Action*, New York: Birch Lane, 1996.

Myles, Gregory, "Post Incident Trauma Seminar," Albany, N.Y.: New York State Police Academy, Summer 1986.

National Treasury Employees Union v. VonRaab, 109 S.Ct. 1384 (1989).

National Advisory Commission on Higher Education for Police Officers. *Proceedings of the National Symposium on Higher Education for Police Officers*. Washington, D.C.: Police Foundation, 1979.

O'Connor, Martin. *Brief Notes Regarding the ADA*. Suffolk County Police Department, Yapank, N.Y.: 1991.

Reiss, Albert J., Jr. *Private Employment of Public Police*. Washington D.C.: National Institute of Justice, 1988.

Robinson, John P., Robert Anthanasiou, and Kendra B. Head, *Measures of Occupational Attitudes and Occupational Characteristics*. Ann Arbor, Mich.: Institute for Social Research, 1969, pp. 276–80.

Santos v. Port Authority of New York and New Jersey, No. 94 Civ. 8427.

Schachter, Hindy Lauer, "Job Related Examinations for Police: Two Developments," *Journal of Police Science and Administration*. (March 1979), pp. 86–89.

Stahl, O. Glen, and Richard A. Staufenberger, eds., *Police Personnel Administration*. Washington, D.C.: Police Foundation, 1974.

Standfest, Steven R., "The Police Supervisors and Stress." *Law Enforcement Bulletin*, 65, no. 5 (May, 1996), pp. 7–10.

Swanson, Cheryl G. and Charles D. Hale, "A Question of Height Revisited: Assaults on Police." *Journal of Police Science and Administration*. (June 1975), pp. 183–88.

Territo, Leonard, C. R. Swanson, Jr. and Neil C. Chamelin, *The Police Personnel Selection Process*. Indianapolis, Ind.: Bobbs-Merrill, 1977.

Thomann, Thomas, and Tina M. Serritella, "Preventing Sexual Harrassment in Law Enforcement Agencies." *Police Chief* (September, 1994), pp. 31–38.

United States of America v. State of New York et al., 77 C.V. 343 (1979).

United Steel Workers v. Weber, 443 U.S. 193 (1979).

Wards Cover Packing Co. v. Atonio, 49 Fair Employment Practice 1520 (1989).

Webster, Barbara, and Jerrold Brown, *Mandatory and Random Drug Testing in the Honolulu Police Department*. Washington: National Institute of Justice, October 1989.

Webster, Stephanie, "The Future of ADA Litigation." *The Police Chief* (February 1996), 53, no. 2, pp. 12–14.

Weiner, Norman L., *The Role of the Police in Urban Society: Conflicts and Consequences*. Indianapolis, Ind.: Bobbs-Merrill, 1976.

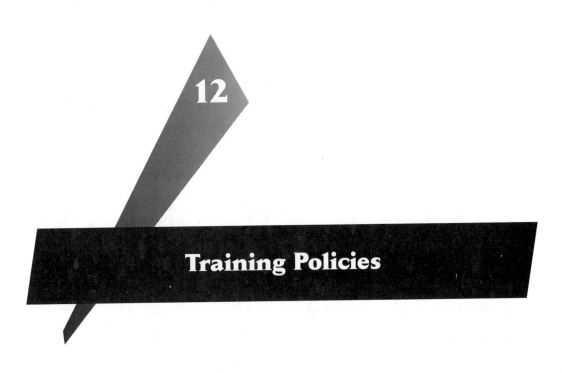

Training Policies

 HISTORICAL PERSPECTIVES

Modern police training has come a long way since the early days when a police officer might have been told the following (Sullivan, 1971: 250), as part of his training by veteran police officers:

> When you hit a suspect, hit him hard.
>
> When you tell someone something, tell him only once because once is enough.
>
> Do not trust anyone—not even your wife.

Herbert Jenkins, an Atlanta, Georgia police chief, described the full range of training when he entered the force in Atlanta (1970: 1):

> When I joined the Atlanta Police Department in the early thirties I was issued a badge, a revolver, blackjack, and Sam Browne belt, and sent out on patrol with a senior police officer. After one week of 'training' I was a full fledged policeman on my own.

As late as 1952, Charles Reith, the well-known writer on police history, was able to comment, "Ignorance of police duties is no handicap to a successful career as a policeman" (1975: 106-7). He went on to point out "in their handling

313

of criminals and armed gangsters, ignorance and a lack of training and under-standing are defined as being the causes of the frequency of police discomfiture." Although this was true of most departments in that era, in 1920, based upon personal visits to American police departments from 1915 to 1917, Raymond B. Fosdick related some outstanding examples of police training schools of that day (1969: 298–99):

> Probably the most ambitious police school at the present time is in Berkeley, California. Here the class, which meets one hour a day, takes three years to complete the courses included in the curriculum. The New York school involves two months of full-time instruction; in Chicago, Philadelphia, St. Louis, Detroit and Newark, the training period is four weeks; in Cleveland it is three. In Cincinnati and Louisville only part of the day is devoted to school work, the remainder being spent in the performance of regular duty.

The Berkeley police school had an extensive curriculum, including the following subjects over a three-year period: physics, chemistry, biology, physiology, anatomy, anthropology, criminal psychology, psychiatry, theoretical and applied criminology, police organization and administration, police practice and procedure, microbiology, microanalysis, public health, first aid, and elementary and criminal law. Interestingly, during this same period, in Milwaukee, police officers went to in-service training one night a week, all year long (Fosdick, 1969:299).

In 1970, one of the most extensive surveys on police training and the best information available today was published. It entailed a nationwide search where letters were sent to 360 agencies and 60 usable replies were received. Excluding Boston, which included extensive patrol operations in its 1,600 hours of training with 1,015 hours of its curriculum devoted to patrol and traffic training, the Chicago Police Department (1969 figures), with 1,085 hours of training, had the longest training period; Kalamazoo, Michigan—at 120 hours—having the shortest. In other words, the Chicago police recruit spent 27 40-hour weeks in training whereas the Kalamazoo recruit spent 3 weeks (McManus, 1970: 175, 183).

In 1993, the Bureau of Justice Statistics surveyed more than 12,000 municipal and county law enforcement agencies. They found that, on average, departments required 640 training hours of their new officer recruits including 425 classroom training hours and 215 field training hours (1993: 5).

GENERAL NEED FOR TRAINING

Lack of morale, surges of unnecessary grievances, and such factors as negative relations with citizen groups and minority communities all reflect a need for training. Officers who do not know how to handle situations are criticized by both police management, the press, and victims. They become the subject of bad publicity for the department and may even become the object of civil suits by citizens. If an officer deprives a citizen of his or her legal rights and civil liberties just because the officer is not trained properly, then citizens may have legal recourse to ask for indemnification for this loss.

This lack of judgment may not be the police officer's fault. It could be the fault of the department and the law. Two major causes may be:

1. Officers who have been on the force for less than a year may not have received any training, including training in the use of a deadly weapon. Most state laws let departments appoint officers and then give them a period of months for the officer to begin his or her training. Meanwhile, untrained and often dangerous personnel are on the streets wearing badges and guns.

2. Some departments provide no more training than the state's minimum requirements. These programs lack trained instructors and modern curricula. The newly trained officer may not know what to do when a hostage situation develops or a domestic crisis looks like it will become violent. Thus lives are lost because the department felt that training in domestic crisis intervention and hostage negotiation was a "frill."

These may not be the only reasons that an officer fails to respond in an effective and professional manner to stressful situations, but they are reasons that have been cited too often in the past. Many modern police administrators feel that lack of training should never exist because the department's reputation and citizen's lives are at stake. One mistake made by a poorly trained or untrained officer is one mistake too many.

Most states demand some minimum training standards. However, these standards normally deal with what has been called "nuts and bolts" training, dealing with a "how to" approach as to what are considered essential tasks. Such programs might include weapons training, report writing, basic criminal law, minor criminal investigations techniques including some crime scene control, and so on. Most of these standards either deal briefly or do not deal at all with human relations skills.

With officers spending the overwhelming majority of their time in contact with citizens, dealing with a multitude of social problems rather than direct crime-related activity, the lack of human relations training spells trouble for the police department on a daily basis.

COMMON DEFICIENCIES IN CURRENT TRAINING PROGRAMS

1. *Program content.* Police training curricula may not cover major areas of human relations and communication such as rape, internal communication, victim/witness control, basic communication with citizens, or adult and juvenile behavior.

2. *Quality control of instructors.* Instructors may be pulled from the field, but not know how to teach. Too often, "instructors" are

command and supervisory officers who relate stories about policing just to impress young recruits with their experience. Some modern police academies go to the opposite extreme bringing in a professor who talks about research on violence in families, for example, without ever relating this research to practical skills. The goal is to strike a balance between the common practice of using police instructors from the field and basing instruction on the findings of academicians. This is an area in which rank should *not* have its privileges. The best instructors are needed, regardless of rank. The chief of police is not necessarily a good instructor. The major question that must be asked of each instructor is: Can this instructor communicate effectively and serve as a role model for the recruits?

3. *Training facilities.* In the past, training has taken place in basements of jails, gyms, auditoriums, and so on. Most instruction is lecture style. Multimedia and small-group instruction, including role-playing activities, need to be made available for all instruction sessions. Isolated and secure facilities for multiple weapon training, including driving skid pans, are needed.

4. *Training equipment.* This is closely tied to the upgrading of facilities. Instructional technology and methodology should include the use of transparencies, VCR tapes, cassette training modules, movies, and so on. Demonstrations and hands-on work have to be an intimate part of the instruction. Basically, seven hours of lectures over five days equals 35 hours of boredom.

5. *Part-time training instructors and directors.* Training should be provided by full-time instructors with experts brought in part time from higher education and the field as part of an overall instructional program provided by the full-time staff.

6. *Full-time attendance.* Recruits should attend the academy full time with no other job-related duties. Part-time students and part-time work makes for tired officers and half-trained students who fall asleep during instruction.

7. *Training before exercising police power.* All recruits should be made employees of their respective police departments as recruits but not using full police powers until they graduate from the academy. This accomplishes two major goals of professional law enforcement: (1) it takes untrained officers off of the street, and (2) recruits do not have to unlearn any bad habits from the street. This assumes that there will be follow-up training.

8. *Follow-up evaluation.* Training should take place at planned intervals for two years after the recruit has graduated from the academy.

9. *Field training officers.* These are specially trained officers who are experienced and can evaluate the recruit's work in the field.

These goals and the solutions proposed to achieve them have been covered by many of the commissions that have developed training materials. Where this is the case, we will not repeat the materials in detail but simply note their recommendations.

WHERE AND WHEN IS BASIC TRAINING UNDERTAKEN?

When we discuss "the police academy" we are talking about the three main types of police academies in this country: agency, regional, and college-sponsored. Agency schools are generally found in large municipal areas or are established for the state police or highway patrol. They are staffed and operated by individual police departments and offer recruit training as well as a variety of in-service courses. Regional academies handle the training functions for both large and small departments located in a designated geographical area. Finally, there are training academies operated on the premises of post-secondary institutions, particularly community colleges. These college-sponsored academies allow a person to take police training and earn college credit. As will be discussed, the curriculum for an academy must follow a state mandate for police training that is overseen by a training agency. Regardless of training model, police agencies have two basic objectives:

1. Train the recruit in the skills necessary to perform the functions of a police officer.
2. Socialize the recruit into the police profession, and train for mastery of the insignias of the office—uniform, handgun, nightstick, shield—and, what former New York City Police Inspector Arthur Niederhoffer calls, "...the web of protocol and ceremony that characterizes any quasi-military hierarchy" (1969: 43).

The traditional model of recruit training consists of an officer being sent to the academy after appointment. Certain states, such as California and Minnesota, allow non-sworn officers to fulfill basic training as a requirement before appointment at their own time and expense. This certificate allows the candidate to seek employment in a local department for a specific period of time. Upon appointment, the candidate must then complete field training and probationary requirements related to the department's rules and practices. Not all agencies in these states embrace this model. For example, all recruits for the Los Angeles Police Department must complete that department's academy, regardless of past training and experience.

The obvious advantage to this pre-employment training model is that the appointing agency saves time and money for basic recruit training. Opponents of this practice, especially those in large departments, argue that the department would rather "train its own" in order to socialize and give basic skills according to department dictates. They also argue that police training should only be given to persons who have undergone a full background check as part of the police hiring process.

FIELD TRAINING FOR POLICE OFFICERS

Field training programs that use practical problems to train police officers on the streets of this nation have been advocated for a number of years. Michael S. McCampbell (1986) surveyed a random sample of 588 police departments throughout the nation concerning their use of field training. He found that 64 percent (183) of the responding departments used field training. Some major advantages of field training were a decrease in the number of civil liability complaints, the standardization of the training process, and better documentation of recruit performance.

San Jose, California had one of the first field training programs, which was established in 1972. It continues to serve as a model training program for other departments. In San Jose, "the Patrol Division administers the field training program: six-officer teams consisting entirely of **FTOs** [*field training officers*] and their sergeants conduct the training....The recruit normally spends four weeks with three different FTO's" (McCampbell, 1986: 4).

There are three phases to the San Jose training program:

> *Phase I*, for weeks 1 through 16, has 14 weeks of a standardized training academy; if the recruit passes, then there are two weeks of in-house classroom training.
>
> *Phase II*, for weeks 17 to 30, consists of (1) four weeks with one FTO, a district evaluation, then (2) four more weeks with a different FTO on another shift, another district evaluation, (3) four more weeks with another FTO on yet another shift, a district evaluation, and (4) a final two weeks with the original FTO that the recruit started with. There are daily observation reports by FTOs and weekly evaluation reports by supervisors. At the end of this stage, the recruit passes on to phase III, is given remedial training, or is dismissed from the force.
>
> *Phase III*, for weeks 31 to 52, starts with a solo beat outside the training district and biweekly evaluation report by the supervisors. At the end of 10 months there is a review board, and if the recruit is certified, he returns to the solo beat outside the training district. Then there are monthly evaluations by the supervisor. At the end of this period, the recruit is either certified as a permanent employee or phase III is extended.

Flagstaff, Arizona, a 59-officer department, has a unique approach where the recruit is assigned to the criminal-investigation section during the final week of field training. Largo, Florida requires the recruit to pass a series of interviews, including one in which the recruit is involved in role-playing different field situations.

McCampbell (1986: 6–7) has a series of recommendations to police managers who wish to use field training. They are:

> Chief executives should view the field training program as a normal part of the recruit selection process.
>
> Administrative control of the field training program in larger agencies should be assigned to the patrol function.
>
> All training in the field program should occur in a planned, organized sequence and be identified by clearly written policies.
>
> Agencies should perform a task analysis for the job of patrol officer and use the analysis as the basis for evaluating recruits.
>
> Agencies should use standardized evaluation guidelines to reduce FTO discretion.
>
> FTOs should give recruits a written evaluation every day.
>
> Each recruit should be assigned to several FTO's.
>
> The FTO's role as trainer and patrol officer should be well defined [to avoid conflict between the two roles].
>
> Agencies should conduct a job task analysis for the position of FTO.
>
> FTOs should receive at least 40 hours of training before they are allowed to assume their duties.
>
> Agencies should consider offering extra compensation to ensure that the most qualified personnel are attracted to and retained in the position of FTO.
>
> Field training programs should be evaluated at least annually.

Field training, if planned carefully, with special emphasis on having the most qualified officers as field training officers, can be an excellent way to train recruits, increase professionalism, and diminish police cynicism.

THE IMPORTANCE OF TRAINING TO POLICE MANAGERS

Police training is of paramount importance to both police supervisors and command personnel. Supervisors need to feel confident that their officers know the fundamentals of the job. They also have to be concerned that their officers develop skills in both the technical aspects of patrol operation and defensive tactics and in the area of human relations. On-the-job training of fundamental skills such as these becomes dangerous since police are often dealing with people in tense situations. With officers who lack fundamental skills, the supervisor has to worry about neglecting normal backup and administrative duties. A proper training program eliminates many of these worries.

If there are too many poorly trained individuals, command personnel cannot rely on the officers to carry out the commands because the officers do not know how to carry them out. Without trained personnel, investigations become error prone, paperwork becomes confused, and morale gets lower and lower as the officers become more frustrated with their own inadequacies.

Modern managers realize that training their forces in modern police methods over a long period of time is a capital investment for a department with high morale. It takes years to train a whole force fully, including in-service training. The investment pays off as morale rises and the officers realize that they can handle situations that were formerly unnerving. Confidence breeds confidence. Let us now examine the model programs that captured the imagination of professional law enforcement managers in the 1970s.

 # 1973 TASK FORCE ON POLICE RECOMMENDATIONS

In 1973 the National Advisory Commission on Criminal Justice Standards and Goals, Task Force on Police, published a volume of policy recommendations titled *Police*. The recommendations reflect the consensus of professional opinion from the more advanced police departments of the day and national agencies concerned with the training of police. This report sparked a great deal of discussion and some change in police training methods, curricula, and basic organization.

Because of its importance to the police professional, we will examine some highlights from its recommendations. *Preparatory training* is emphasized with the recommendation being a minimum of 400 hours of basic police training. Besides police subjects, law, psychology, and sociology as related to police-community relations are to be emphasized. Ongoing in-service training is mandated as is a minimum of four months of field training. In all, this is a rigorous but effective series of recommendations.

A recommended curriculum based on a variety of experiences from Dayton, Ohio; Oakland, California; Seattle, Washington; Chicago, Illinois; and Los Angeles, California would be

Introduction to criminal justice system	8%
Law	10
Human values and problems	22
Patrol and investigation procedures	33
Police proficiency	18
Administration	9

Training before promotion as a policy was likely to produce some self-confidence and better efficiency if an officer knew what to do on the job before promotion. It was also felt that middle management training programs should be integrated with college and business programs. (National Advisory Commission, 1973: 399).

In-service training was a significant part of the report, with a recommendation of a minimum of 40 hours per year up to and including captains. This was considered to be a routine, mandated procedure that would be a normal part of every police budget.

Instruction quality control with a certification for specific training subjects was mandated to ensure that training performance objectives would be met. This included an annual review of instructional materials along with the use of up-to-date audio-visual and computer-assisted instruction.

Police training academies and criminal justice training centers were mandated, with 1978 being the target date for the availability in every state of such training for every police officer in the state. In terms of quality control, there was state certification of the basic police training along with encouragement of the states for interagency cooperation. The authors of this text feel that regional police academies would make a major contribution to police professionalism and efficiency of training on the grounds that they would

1. Benefit from economies of scale. Classes should be large enough to justify more expensive and expert instructors along with the increased use of expensive media.

2. Justify salaries for an expert full-time staff and an organized, ongoing curriculum and evaluation of that curriculum. The instructors would be expected to keep up to date in their respective fields in order to retain their positions. Part-time instructors with no obligation to a full-time staff could become completely dated and no one would even know it.

3. Begin the fight against parochialism and localism in law enforcement. By being trained regionally, officers, at the start, would look at the big picture of crime fighting and act in a more professional manner.

4. Encourage the formation of professional relationships and friendships with officers outside of the local department at the start of an officer's career. This leads to more cooperation, especially on a regional basis, which becomes increasingly important as recruits rise in rank and begin to cooperate on fencing rings, white-collar crime, and regional relationships for crime problems.

Others may be added, but these will give you a start on why this is a significant approach for management to use in the creation of a training program.

▶ PROJECT STAR

Originally developed by the California Commission on Peace Officer Standards and Training in 1969, Project **STAR** (System and Training Analysis of Requirements for Criminal Justice Participants) eventually involved four states: California, Michigan, New Jersey, and Texas. Project STAR in its 1976 report (Smith, Pehlke, and Weller, 1976) relied on a systems approach emphasizing management by objectives and the breaking down of police behaviors into specific roles and tasks.

Project STAR identified 13 roles that were to be filled by 33 tasks. For example, a role would be "building respect for law and the criminal justice system," whereas related tasks might be "deterring crime," "interacting with other agencies," and "participating in community relations and educational programs." Using the standard behavioral objective format, performance objectives for each task may be stated in behavioral terms with a context and criterion of success.

For example, in the role titled "building respect," a performance objective would be (Smith, Pehlke, and Weller, 1976: 103) "avoid making unreasonable demands of citizens and other criminal justice personnel in terms of time and scheduling." The problems with these kind of objectives are the undefined terms; for example, *unreasonable*.

What STAR was trying to do, along with much of the educational community of the day, was to state the tasks that needed to be learned in such a way that they would be easily measured in empirical terms and evaluated. Let us review another example from Smith and others (1976: 107):

> Maintain self control when interacting with citizens or suspects as you carry out your required duties.
>
> Deter violation of the law and criminal activity through your continual interaction with people in the community.
>
> Maintain appropriate order among people as you discharge the responsibilities of your position.

As will be noted, these performance objectives lack the "punch" of the everyday reality of the street.

STAR recommends a sound liberal arts education along with specific skills and knowledge in criminal justice (Smith and others, 1976: xix):

> Further, *public* education recommendations were developed in areas such as law, the criminal justice system, human behavior and social relationships.

However, STAR did not wish to recommend a specific set of curricula (Smith and others, 1976: xix): "Finally, due to the independent nature of the educational system in the United States, no recommendations were made for specific curricula organization, prerequisites, detailed course outline, credit hours or credentials." Thus, the STAR approach is basically a humanistic, liberal arts, and behavioristic approach.

STAR RECOMMENDATIONS

It is recommended that participants earn at least the equivalent of an associate degree, and better yet, a bachelor's degree to have time to even generally cover the topics. Here are some of the general topics (Smith and others, 1976: 150-54):

Law

Criminal justice system description

Human behavior

Social relationships

Philosophy (ethics, logic, aesthetics)

Political science

Public administration

Economics

Science (physiology, chemistry, narcotics, research methodology, statistics)

Organization and management

Journalism

Speech

Constitutional law

Criminal law

Criminal procedures

General law

Alternatives to arrest

Techniques of crime control

Ethics

Criminal justice

The recommendations in management were:

Organizational theory, setting of goals and objectives, organizational alternative, planning and scheduling, systems analysis, resource acquisition and allocation, identifying and overcoming constraints, administrative behavior, information and system development, evaluation of achievement; general description of alternatives and methods for the criminal justice system to organize, set goals and objectives, plan and schedule, analyze requirements, acquire and allocate resources, manage cases and processes, identify and overcome restraints, provide leadership and supervision, develop and use information systems and evaluate achievement.

In an attempt to bring some of the latest thinking on management and human behavior into the police training curriculum, STAR lost sight of the fact that the police have to be trained in their jobs. In response to the very basic nuts and bolts training curricula, STAR managed to provide some excellent concepts that were widely discussed and *not adopted*. To the ordinary police trainer and even college-trained police training director, much of STAR was written in a strange systems language that was incomprehensible. One excellent contribution of STAR, however, was the list of instructional techniques that went well beyond the standup lecture approach.

CHANGES IN THE TRAINING CURRICULUM: 1952–PRESENT

In 1952, T. Frost did a survey of training curriculums in 33 police departments of various sizes around the country. This survey was then replicated by T. Frost and M. Seng in 1982 (Frost and Seng, 1984). They discovered that the entry-level training programs grew from an average of 342 hours in 1952 to an average of 633 hours in 1982. However, much of the content had not changed. The percentage of time devoted to military drill went down but was replaced by a rise in the time devoted to general physical fitness, while the time devoted to firearms training remained about the same. Table 12-1 is a comparison of the two curriculums in 13 subjects.

TABLE–12–1
COMPARISONS OF 1952 AND 1982 POLICE TRAINING CURRICULUMS—NATIONAL

SUBJECT	1952 RECOMMENDATIONS	1982 AVERAGE
Bombs and explosives	1	3.1
Coroner's duties	1	2.8
Discipline and deportment	4	4.7
Election duties	1	
Ethics	2	2.9
Graduation ceremonies	3	3.3
Human relations	4	25.3
Law enforcement as a profession	1	3.6
Moot court	4	5.5
Narcotics	4	10.4
Note taking	1	2.2
Public relations	3	3.3
Rules and regulations	12	5.4
Total hours	42	72.3

Source: Frost and Seng (1984).

Although much of the curriculum remained the same, the 1982 curriculum reflects an emphasis on human relations and narcotics with a decrease in time spent on rules and regulations. First aid remained in the curriculum, while traffic became covered under the more generalized topic of patrol duties. The authors feel that there was a striking change in the emphasis on constitutional issues and the rights of citizens.

As discussed earlier, the average length for a police recruit training program is 640 hours. Table 12-2 gives an overview of minimum training requirements for California law enforcement officers as presented by the Commission on Peace Officer Standards and Training (POST). This curriculum lists classes and the number of hours devoted to each topic.

TABLE 12–2

CONTENT AND MINIMUM HOURLY REQUIREMENTS—CALIFORNIA, 1996

DOMAIN NUMBER	DOMAIN DESCRIPTION	MINIMUM HOURS
01	History, Professionalism & Ethics	8 hours
02	Criminal Justice System	4 hours
03	Community Relations	12 hours
04	Victimology/Crisis Interventions	6 hours
05	Introduction to Criminal Law	6 hours
06	Crimes Against Property	10 hours
07	Crimes Against Persons	10 hours
08	General Criminal Statutes	4 hours
09	Crimes Against Children	6 hours
10	Sex Crimes	6 hours
11	Juvenile Law and Procedure	6 hours
12	Controlled Substances	12 hours
13	ABC Law	4 hours
14	Laws of Arrest	12 hours
15	Search & Seizure	12 hours
16	Presentation of Evidence	8 hours
17	Investigative Report Writing	40 hours
18	Vehicle Operations	24 hours
19	Use of Force	12 hours
20	Patrol Techniques	12 hours
21	Vehicle Pullovers	14 hours
22	Crimes In Progress	16 hours
23	Handling Disputes/Crowd Control	12 hours
24	Domestic Violence	8 hours
25	Unusual Occurrences	4 hours
26	Missing Persons	4 hours
27	Traffic Enforcement	22 hours
28	Traffic Accident Investigation	12 hours
29	Preliminary Investigation	42 hours
30	Custody	4 hours
31	Physical Fitness/Officer Stress	40 hours
32	Person Searches, Baton, etc.	60 hours
33	First Aid & CPR	21 hours
34	Firearms/Chemical Agents	72 hours
35	Information Systems	4 hours
36	Persons with Disabilities	6 hours
37	Gang Awareness	8 hours
38	Crimes Against the Justice System	4 hours
39	Weapons Violations	4 hours
40	Hazardous Materials	4 hours
41	Cultural Diversity/Discrimination	24 hours
	Minimum Instructional Hours	599 hours

The minimum number of hours allocated to testing in the Regular Basic Courses are shown below[1]

TABLE 12-2 (CONT'D)

TEST TYPE	HOURS
Scenario Tests	40 hours
POST-Constructed Knowledge Tests	25 hours
Total Minimum Required Hours	664 hours

[1]Time required for exercise testing, learning activities, and physical abilities testing is included in instructional time.
Source: California Commission on Peace Officer Standards and Training, 1996.

Nationally, most training programs can be divided according to the following areas:

Administrative procedures: includes quizzes, graduation, and instruction on note taking.

Administration of justice: includes history of law enforcement, police organization, probation, parole, and social services.

Basic law: includes constitutional law, offenses, criminal procedure, vehicle and traffic law, juvenile law and procedures, and civil liability.

Police procedures: includes patrol observation; crimes in progress; field notes; intoxication, mental illness; disorderly conduct; domestic violence; police communication; alcoholic beverage control; civil disorder; crowd and riot control; normal duties related to traffic enforcement including accidents and emergency vehicle operations; criminal investigation, including interviews and interrogations; control of evidence; and various kinds of cases, such as burglary, robbery, injury, sex crime, drugs, organized crime, arson, and gambling.

Police proficiency: includes normal firearm training, arrest techniques, emergency aid, courtroom testimony and demeanor, and bomb threats and bombs.

Community relations: includes psychology for police; minority groups; news media relationships; telephone courtesy; identification of community resources; victim/witness services; crime prevention, officer stress awareness; law enforcement family, and police ethics.

▶ TOPICAL ISSUES IN TRAINING

Here is an outline of some of the newer topics that have been covered in police training:

1. *Stress training.* The officer must know how to handle the normal job stress and how to handle stress in others. This is especially crucial for training supervisory personnel. They must remain calm so they can handle stress in the officers they are commanding. A number of techniques have been developed that work well with police personnel.

2. *Dealing with terrorist activity.* This is a more important topic in a metropolitan area, but terrorists can strike anywhere. Officers who may get these special assignments learn about letter bombs, security perimeters, and so on. However, in municipalities where terrorist activates are a possibility, officers must be able to recognize terrorist activities and techniques and know how to deal with them.

3. *Domestic crisis intervention.* Although a good many officers are injured in domestic fights, many departments neglect this area in their training curricula. Domestic fights are unpredictable and dangerous, and specific techniques have been developed to handle these tense situations.

4. *AIDS Awareness.* Concern regarding AIDS (Acquired Immune Deficiency Syndrome) and hepatitis B brought about safety regulations and training requirements from the Occupational Safety and Health Administration (OSHA) with regard to blood-borne **pathogens** (any microorganism or virus that can cause disease). Because police and other public safety personnel frequently come in contact with blood and other body fluids, the regulations call for agency control plans to limit direct exposure and to administer a vaccine for hepatitis B to affected employees. The regulations also call for training regarding measures one should take to prevent contamination. Stewart (1993) suggests the following topical outlines:
   • Means of Human Immunodeficiency Virus and Hepatitis B Virus transmission
   • Suggested personal prevention practices
   • Universal precaution strategies
   • Protective equipment
   • Specific workplace prevention practices
   • Exposure management and treatment procedures

5. *Domestic Violence Training.* One of the many legacies of the O. J. Simpson trial was renewed public policy discussion on domestic violence. Traditionally, domestic violence offenses occurred between married persons and involved such crimes as assault and harassment. In the vast majority of cases, the victim is a woman. Murder, which frequently occurs in these situations was usually not mentioned in earlier discussions of domestic violence.

   Previously, law enforcement and prosecution offices did not give these situations high priority or serious attention because they occurred behind closed doors, and the role of the wife was considered subservient to the husband. An instructor in one of the authors' basic recruit classes in 1973 called these situations "get in and get out calls," because complainants do not press charges the next day even if you make an arrest.

It was not until the early 1980s that this attitude changed. Research on violent crime and murder concluded that many cases were the result of domestic violence situations. The women's rights movement paid particular attention to the role of women in society and the "battered wife cycle." Presented in various ways, this cycle consists of stages that start with emotional abuse and then end up with serious physical assault. If, despite police intervention, the abuser and the victim make up, in many cases the cycle begins all over again. In response to this, many communities established 24-hour crisis hotlines and safe houses, where women with children can find refuge and obtain counseling. Police training programs include the topic of "Domestic Violence Calls" as part of their training especially because of the potential for serious physical injury against responding officers.

In the 1990s, many states changed their laws and arrest policies regarding domestic violence so that an officer could make an arrest for a petty offense, without witnessing the act, and without the express consent of the victim. In Florida, for example, a law enforcement officer in domestic violence situations may arrest the suspect and does not need to witness the abuse.

This pro-arrest policy is based on the theory that immediate intervention will stem the cycle of violence. Additionally, the definition of a domestic violence incident has been expanded by laws and police agency policies to include offense situations in which the persons have an intimate relationship and police intervention is requested (N.Y. State Office for the Prevention of Domestic Violence, 1995).

In addition to reviewing laws and departmental response policies regarding domestic violence, training programs include such topics as protecting yourself against injury, listening skills, preparation of special reports, investigation of domestic violence complaints, procedures for the arrest and detention of offenders, and victim assistance programs.

6. *Stalking*. Closely related to domestic violence incidents are stalking crimes. These are crimes of a person willfully, maliciously, and repeatedly following or harassing another person, and making a credible threat with the intention to place that person in reasonable fear of death or serious bodily injury. Recent examples of high-profile cases include the murder of actress Rebecca Shaffer, and the shooting of Robert Hoskins by a security guard as he attempted to break into Madonna's house. Stalkers are profiled as persons who are obsessed with someone, or erotomaniacs who believe that the target is "really in love" with them and will do anything to get the attention of the

victim. The stalking eventually may result in violent assault and murder against the victim if the stalker believes that he or she has been rejected. Stalkers may be former spouses or partners who have been spurned by the victim and arrested for domestic violence crimes, or criminal predators who follow people at random and eventually assault and kill them. Police training for stalking situations includes investigatory skills such as threat assessment, and denying access to the victim. Access denial can result from police interviewing the stalker or having the target change daily lifestyle habit (Williams et. al., 1996). Some cases may require 24-hour protection coupled with a manhunt to intercept the stalker.

7. *Tactical Operations.* This is usually an in-service training course for veteran officers to review basic academy topics as use of personal weapons, handcuffing techniques, high risk vehicle stops and building entry techniques. The focus here is not only on review but to encourage a partner-team approach in high risk situations. Courses of this nature include hands-on exercises, low light situations and even the use of blank or paint guns for realism.

8. *Diversity.* Cultural diversity is defined as having empathy towards other cultures and ways of life in order to explain why people feel that way they do. In the late 1980s, instruction in cultural sensitivity (sometimes called *cross-cultural training*) for officers was initiated to improve community relations and to reduce, in part, citizen or community complaints against police officers for either unwarranted use of force or arrest powers on underrepresented persons in the community. These issues are not new but a continuation of the historical animosity between the police and minority groups in the community. As discussed by Johnson (1992), the police represent the majority culture in a community and are often viewed as the defenders of the status quo or the ruling elites. Ideas, lifestyles, and persons outside the mainstream are often viewed by the police with distrust and vice versa. What happens, as recounted by Weaver (1993: 3) is a "clash between two icebergs" as typified in the following routine situation:

> A Nigerian cab driver runs a red light. An officer pulls him over in the next block, stopping the patrol car at least three car lengths behind the cab. Before the police officer can exit the patrol car, the cabbie gets out of his vehicle and approaches the officer. Talking rapidly in a high-pitched voice and making wild gestures, the cab driver appears to be out of control, or so the officer believes.
>
> As the officer steps from his car, he yells for the cab driver to stop, but the cabbie continues to walk toward the officer. When he is about 2 feet away, the officer orders the cabbie to step back and keep his hands to his sides. But the cab driver continues to

babble and advance toward the officer. He does not make eye contact and appears to be talking to the ground.

Finally, the officer commands the cab driver to place his hands on the patrol vehicle and spread his feet. What began as a routine stop for a traffic violation culminates in charges of disorderly conduct and resisting arrest.

According to Weaver (1992: 4), the situation escalates out of control because of a breakdown in non-verbal communication. While most Americans are socialized into staying in their vehicles, the cab driver felt that it was a sign of respect to exit his vehicle and not troubling the officer to leave his patrol car. As the driver approached the officer, the social safe distance between the two decreased and the driver ignored the "step back" command. The social distance for conversation in Nigeria is much closer than in the United States. In the mind of the officer, the lack of eye contact and the rapid, high-pitched voice denoted a person who was dangerous to the officer.

9. Closely related to the issue of diversity is bias or hate crime. **Bias crime** is an all-inclusive term that refers to criminal offenses committed against a person because of his or her race, religion, sexual preference, or ethnicity (Memorandum, 1989). Bias crimes are not new; however, such acts are at odds with current public policy which is in total support of the idea of a diverse American culture.

Police departments across the country have conducted training seminars and revised response policies to deal with bias crime. Training programs most typically deal with the "how to" of conducting criminal investigations and the sensitivity needed to deal with the victim and the community. Officers are also trained how to identify bias crimes, ranging from the obvious—a swastika painted on the side of a building or a cross burned on a lawn—to the not so obvious—a series of assaults that occur on the victims' religious holiday.

10. *American with Disabilities Act (ADA)*. As discussed in Chapter 11, the ADA requires police departments to provide services to persons with disabilities. Department policies and training must address ways for officers to deal with disabled persons (for example, a mugging victim who is blind or an arrestee who is mobility impaired and requires a wheelchair). Training programs also include responses to routine and emergency calls for services for disabled persons. Quite often, there are persons who are not immediately identified as disabled; for example, a diabetic suffering a seizure who appears to be a disorderly drunk, but is actually in need of insulin.

11. *Computer/Video Simulation Training*. In the past five years, computer-aided training has been applied to police training. Borrowing from earlier technologies for airline pilots and driver education, computer and video instruction was developed for firearms training. Through

video, students are presented with various street scenarios for which they must decide whether to shoot or not shoot. The instructor can observe and evaluate the proper draw, stance, and shooting technique of each trainee. The computer evaluates whether the plastic round hitting the video screen hit the suspect or an innocent bystander, and whether the officer fired within an appropriate time period. What is dynamic about this type of learning is the noise and realism.

12. *Interactive teleconferencing/cable TV.* Through satellite communications, many colleges, universities, and government agencies are able to sponsor teleconferences where participants can hear a presentation and phone in questions and comments. From the experience of the authors, a great deal of preparation is required and the audience attention span for a teleconference is about two hours. Teleconferencing is ideal for transmitting information to multiple sites, thus reducing the time and cost for travel and lodging.

Specific training for police departments is offered through the Law Enforcement Television Network (LETN), which offers a TV schedule of training programs and police information updates. The monthly cost for service varies by the number of people in the department. The majority of programs are good and geared to police audiences. Because the program content is directed at a national audience, there may be some differences with state and local laws and departmental policies. Departments that use LETN as a major format for in-serve training also use pretest and posttest exams to gauge the effectiveness of the programs.

There is also more specific training for specialized units such as SWAT (Special Weapons and Tactics) teams, major felony squads, regional arson investigation teams, and the like. Instruction includes courses in computer security and electronic surveillance as well as emergency vehicle handling, "routine" traffic stops, and crowd control.

Quite recently, one of the authors entered an amusement arcade and found customers pumping quarters into machines to play a game of shooting bandits in a Dodge City setting. While commonplace, as with other computer games these will soon be outdated with the release of the next generation of games, which will be based on virtual reality. Virtual reality is computer-generated, three-dimensional environment that engulfs the senses of sight, sound, and touch (Hormann: 1995, 8). For police training, the computer creates environments that are viewed by a trainee in a helmet. The trainee is also connected to the computer by a special glove that manipulates objects and deploys weapons. Unlike current computer-generated training, where one faces a screen and reacts, virtual reality allows the person to turn around, open doors, switch transmission gears, and perform other tasks while feeling the "action" as if he or she were in the scene.

Hormann points out that virtual reality is a cost-effective and safe training method for such courses as firearms, pursuit driving, and critical incidents. Law enforcement applications at this time are still underway and the technology is far from perfect. For example, there are costs to obtain the equipment and software programs, and the helmet apparatus is somewhat bulky. The computer, moreover, cannot generate images faster than the eye so a reaction called "simulator sickness" can result from trainee disorientation. However, these shortcomings are being addressed through further research and software design.

 # PHASE APPROACH TO TRAINING*

"All types of enterprises have responded to the need for skilled personnel by investing in training and development programs. Too often these programs involve what might be called the 'shotgun' approach." These observations by William Tracey are frequently applicable to police training programs. With the exception of basic recruit training programs, much of law enforcement training is haphazard at best. This is not to say that specific courses, seminars, or workshops lack quality. Indeed, most are very good. The problem is lack of goals, objectives, and coordination for the overall training program. In short, there is not enough planning.

Planning is a basic function of a manager. As the administrator of training, planning is no less important to the training director. Robert L. Craig identifies planning as "the key to optimum use of training manpower and resources." Planning answers the questions what, when, where, who, and by whom and allows us to avoid the common mistake of "training for training's sake."

The importance of planning the training program has even greater dimensions for today's training director. A 1978 survey of members of the American Society for Training and Development revealed several significant findings in this respect. Among them were the expansion of training and development programs and an increase in the time that training directors devote to management and administrative matters.

These findings are obviously applicable to law enforcement. During the last decade, the expansion of law enforcement training has been phenomenal. Added to the ever-increasing demands that are placed upon police officers are concerns for civil and vicarious liability.

Recognizing these factors, the Greensboro, North Carolina Police Department began the development of a framework for planning the training program. This led to a concept that was termed the **phase approach** to training. In essence, the department recognized that there are multiphases in the training and development of police officers, and a standard training program for each of these phases was established.

PHASE I—RECRUIT TRAINING

New officers enter the department in a trainee status and are given 560 hours of recruit training in the police basic introductory course. Upon successful com-

---

*The following discussion presents an advanced model of sophisticated training program from Wood (1980).

pletion of this course, new employees are promoted to sworn status as Police Officer I's. As Police Officer I's, they are assigned to a field training program under the supervision of a police squad leader, who serves as their training coach. When they have successfully completed the field training, the officers receive patrol duty assignments in one of the four field operations divisions.

PHASE II—INTERMEDIATE TRAINING

Upon assignment as patrol officers, Police Officer I's enter the second phase of their training and development. During this period of approximately one and a half years, the officer's training will consist primarily of on-the-job training within his or her assigned field division. This is supplemented with quarterly in-service training, consisting of eight-hour sessions based on the training needs of the department. In addition, shorter two-hour sessions are presented monthly during a roll-call training session.

PHASE III—ADVANCED TRAINING

After two years on the job, an officer is eligible for promotion to Police Officer II. This is accomplished by passing a written competency test comprised of questions concerning knowledge gained by the officer during phases I and II of his or her development.

In phase III, officers continue to receive quarterly in-service and monthly roll-call training. In addition, they receive advanced training through periodic seminars and workshops presented in developmental as well as performance oriented frameworks. The objective is to have as many officers as possible receive this type of training. Accordingly, assignments are made on the basis of seniority and are rotated so that each officer attends one seminar or workshop before a senior officer is assigned to a second one.

PHASE IV—DEVELOPMENTAL TRAINING

Police Officer II's are eligible to participate in two developmental programs—the career development program and the police squad leader program. Officers participating in the career development program receive a short-term (six to eight months) temporary assignment to one of the investigative or staff divisions. During this assignment, the officer receives approximately 30 days of orientation within his or her selected area, followed by supervised on-the-job training. The officer also attends seminars and workshops related to the specialty area. Both the Builford Technical Institute and the North Carolina Justice Academy offer the desired training in this area at little or no cost to the department.

Officers in the police squad leader program go through an established selection procedure and are promoted to police-squad-leader status. This promotion adds two important dimensions to the officer's responsibilities—he or she periodically serves as training coach for newly assigned officers and, when so designated, acts as the squad supervisor in the absence of the regularly assigned supervisor. These added job dimensions necessitate additional training for the officer, including officer coach training, instructor training, and introduction to supervision.

Participation in the police-squad-leader program is not a prerequisite for promotion to sergeant, and not all officers choose to participate. Many of the officers who do participate choose to withdraw after a period of time to accept assignments in other areas or to participate in the career development program. This is encouraged by both the low pay differential (5 percent) for a police squad leader and the desirability of other assignments. Participation in the program offers the officer an excellent opportunity to develop his or her supervisory skills.

PHASE V—SPECIALIST TRAINING

Officers assigned to specialized units, such as criminal investigation, vice/narcotics, youth, traffic, or training are provided seminars and workshops to develop their expertise in these areas. Primarily, external resources offering the needed training are used for these activities. These resources include the Northwestern University Traffic Institute, Southern Police Institute, FBI National Academy, and others. Refresher or advanced training in these areas may also be provided, depending upon the length of the officer's assignment, job performance, new developments in the specialized areas, or other factors. Officers in specialized assignments will also be assigned to quarterly in-service training sessions.

Phase V also encompasses officers who participate as members of special teams such as special response team, underwater recovery, or the bomb squad. Instructors at the academy also fall within the realm of the specialist training phase and are provided any additional training required for this function.

PHASE VI—SUPERVISORY TRAINING

Officers promoted to sergeant enter into the supervisory training phase. As soon as possible, all newly promoted sergeants are scheduled for a practical supervisors' course. In addition, they attend an in-house supervisory orientation program to familiarize themselves with specific departmental policies, programs, and procedures.

Following one year in a probationary status, sergeants are eligible for assignment to a basic administration course. At the present time the department uses two primary sources for this training—the Institute of Government in Chapel Hill, North Carolina and the North Carolina Governor's Highway Safety Program. Both offer a management-administration course consisting of approximately 200 hours of instruction.

In addition to these programs, the authors recommend the following model for first-line supervisory training. Police first-line supervisors, meaning sergeants and lieutenants, are usually the first managers to arrive at the scene of critical field situations. The first responders, that is, the officers who first respond to service calls, are normally the department's line officers. Routinely, these first-line supervisors also make decisions on a myriad of issues ranging from employee discipline to civil, that is, tort liability. In many departments, peer pressure becomes an important issue since a promotion means that the new supervisor is now directing the activities of fellow officers whom he or she worked and socialized with previously as an equal. It requires special skills and talents to make this transition from a line officer to a management-oriented supervisor. Unfortunately, in some agencies some police officers wearing stripes are not really functioning as supervisors. The paper-and-pencil tests used for promotion in most departments cannot predict command presence or the attainment of communication and decision-making skills under stress.

A first-line supervisory training course must provide the knowledge and skills needed by the supervisor to function effectively, efficiently, and professionally. The course needs to provide a framework to assist the new supervisor in developing strategies aimed at dealing with the supervisor's critical role in the department's operation. The model proposed is a two-week or four-week intensive program. Departments may vary in their requirements and demand a more extensive course of study.

This is seen as an *intensive residential program*, where the student prepares for each class with out-of-class readings and other homework assignments. The students will live and work together and, in addition to daytime classes, have additional evening classes. This training should be given prior to assuming the duties of a supervisor as part of a one-year civil service probationary period before certification as a supervisor. If the officer fails the training program, he or she will return to line officer status.

A Model First-Line Manager's (Supervisor's) Course*

The following program covers the major things a first-line supervisor needs to know and provides an opportunity for supervisors to practice skills and be critiqued in this new role. The major portion of the program is presented in the classroom with daily quizzes and weekly comprehensive examinations. Students will be expected to attend all classes, maintain an academic average of 70 or better for the daily quizzes, and achieve a score of 80 or better on the two comprehensive examinations.

The director of the program welcomes each student during an opening ceremony and informs them that they are supervising a mythical squad of line officers. Throughout the program the students will complete the following in-basket exercises with this mythical squad; (1) conducting briefings, (2) issuing orders, (3) planning events, (4) attending to routine administrative matters, and (5) dealing with a variety of personnel problems. The squad will exist only on paper; however, it will be as realistic as possible, consisting of a number of police officers who will be described in vivid detail. Assignments will be linked to daily class top-

---

*The model supervisory curriculum is adapted from the revised supervisor's curriculum being used in New York State by the Division for Local Police, Municipal Police Training Council, Albany, New York.

ics and the results will be graded on a pass/fail basis. All "fails" have to be repeated until they become passes.

1. *Registration and overview of the program.* This consists of a review of academic requirements of the program and an introduction to the details of the mythical squad.

2. *Role of supervisor and leadership skills.* This course presents the role of the supervisor in the formal and informal organization. Leadership concepts and styles are defined. Important concepts covered are delegation, command presence, span of control, and formal and informal organization.

3. *Wellness program (every morning).* These morning physical exercises will include running, aerobics, and team sports, along with physical examinations and counseling for any personal health problems.

4. *Supervisor communications and media relations.* The purpose of part of the course of study is for the student to recognize what effective communication channels are. Methods for clearing obstacles from existing written and oral channels are discussed. The program will use role play to demonstrate the effective flow of the communication's grid and then go on to deal with specific problems related to the print and electronic media, general communications, and the use of the computer-assisted communications.

5. *Civil liability.* This course will review major national and state tort law cases, with emphasis on the liability of supervisors who fail to supervise or train subordinates. Liability issues related to legally high-risk police operations, such as high-speed car chases and the use of deadly physical force, will also be reviewed. Included will be a review of defenses with regard to negligence, failure to perform, and the purview of indemnification under prevailing public officers' law.

6. *Evaluation, counseling, and discipline.* This part of the course will be composed of the following components: (a) review of existing collective bargaining contracts and departmental policies, (b) review of evaluation methods for employees by supervisors, (c) progressive discipline based on departmental policies, (d) state common law, (e) techniques for dealing with problem employees, (f) conducting successful counseling sessions, (g) the role of the supervisor in documenting employee problems, and (h) preparation for administrative hearings. Preclass readings will consist of collective bargaining agreements, along with departmental policies relating to discipline and grievances.

7. *Intermediate law.* This portion of the course of study will review the rights of individuals in relation to (a) victim/witness rights, (b) employee rights, and (c) juvenile rights. The rights of the accused will be analyzed through the case study method, along with a review of

changes in the penal law, criminal procedure law, and search-and-seizure issues.

8. *Crime prevention and community relations.* The student will be expected to develop specific crime-prevention and citizen-cooperation programs. Techniques for improving good cooperation from citizens in all areas will be discussed.

9. *Stress management.* Major stressors will be identified for supervisors and subordinates. Stress reduction techniques will be practiced.

10. *Incident and critical-incident management.* As front-line administrators, supervisors in their capacity as lieutenants and sergeants must immediately take command of crime scenes. Other incidents such as demonstrations and parade details need to be planned for. The differences between an *incident* (a parade) and a *critical incident* (a homicide) are discussed, including the issue of the prioritization of incidents.

    In dealing with critical incidents such as the use of deadly physical force, physical injury/death, hostage negotiations, and environmental safety accidents, emphasis is placed on protecting the crime scene and protecting personnel. Patrol operations related to the supervision of crimes in progress and sensitive crimes such as sexual assault and child abuse will also be reviewed.

11. *Personnel issues.* This section of the course develops an awareness and ability to deal effectively with a wide range of employee issues and problems: sexual harassment, substance abuse, burnout, and prejudice.

12. *Use of deadly physical force.* The first part of this training deals with legal issues, while the second portion presents defense tactics such as the proper techniques for handcuffing, take-downs, use of the baton, and use of mace.

13. *Report review.* This part of the course analyzes how to review reports of crime incidents, legal papers, and summonses. It also offers corrective techniques.

14. *Supervisor as trainer.* Supervisors train recruits and veteran officers. The focus of this portion of the course is to have the supervisor identify training needs for his or her subordinates through observing firsthand, reviewing reports, and identifying the need for remediation.

    Only first-rate instructors drawn from the field and from higher education institutions should be used. Each instructor needs to use a variety of classroom techniques which go beyond the normal lecture/discussion (for example, role playing). Hand-held VCR camcorders provide an opportunity for electronic feedback for many of the exercises in the course of study. Many state police and regional academies have introduced computerized work-board simulations where a miniature town is created and supervisors deploy resources as conditions change.

PHASE VII—MANAGEMENT TRAINING

Promotion to lieutenant marks the next phase of an officer's development. At this level, the officer functions primarily in a management capacity, and newly promoted lieutenants are scheduled for training in this area. Their initial training consists of either a three-month police administration course at the University of Louisville Southern Police Institute or the three-month traffic police administration training program offered by Northwestern University Traffic Institute. After attaining the rank of captain, one is eligible to apply to the FBI National Academy for continued management training.

In addition to these major programs, officers who are lieutenants, captains, or majors may participate in a variety of seminars, workshops, and retraining conferences to keep them abreast of changes and new developments in the field of law enforcement.

Using this framework allows the department to anticipate the bulk of its training needs and plan accordingly; yet there is flexibility. Specific programs in any phase can be changed to meet the changing needs of the department. Entire phases can be deleted or others added. The concept is not intended as a rigid structure to be religiously followed; instead, it is a tool to be used in the planning process.

The authors are aware that *police executive courses* are needed. Despite the fact that law enforcement is an expensive business in terms of the impact that equipment and personnel costs have on the community, few police command officers have had the benefit and experience of executive police training. Police command officers are personnel in policymaking positions, such as chiefs, deputy chiefs, majors, captains, and directors of public safety. It is difficult to come to closure on the necessary training needed for a good police executive. Certain chiefs would even say that executives have the benefit of both experience as well as graduate education in administration, criminal justice, business, and law.

There are a number of individual courses that are offered throughout the country on a departmental or regional basis. The National Academy sponsored by the Federal Bureau of Investigation offers advanced-level courses to police executives at Quantico, Virginia. Such topics as public administration, budgeting, forensic management, and critical incident management are covered. To qualify for this course of study, a candidate must apply to the FBI and be sponsored by the employing police agency. This is also a self-selected program, where either the student or his agency must assume the travel and living costs. It is the closest program to the police-college model that exists in many European countries which offers required programs to command officials. Many departments use attendance at this program as a means of selecting future executives. Smaller departments sponsor the chief or assistant chief as a way to obtain formal management education.

Not all police executives will have the opportunity to attend the National Academy. What, then, is the prerequisite formal training one needs in order to be a proactive police executive?

The police executive course, offered by the Southwestern Law Enforcement Institute located at the University of Texas, Dallas, offers the following topics for police executives:

Introduction to public administration with an emphasis on organizational theory

Statistics for public policy analysis

An introductory course in the use of computers

Communication skills with an emphasis on public speaking and organizational writing

Research methods with an emphasis on those common to police policy analysis

Command-level courses in critical incident management, with an emphasis on planning

An introductory course in accounting and budgeting followed by an elective in public budgeting

History of American policing through a review of the great books on policing, major police figures, and social trends affecting police administration

Human resource management, including crucial personnel topics such as exercising discipline procedures and stress management

Civil law with emphasis on liability

Using the phase-approach-to-training concepts provides a number of benefits to the department. First, it helps to ensure that officers have the skills and knowledge to perform at each level of their development in the department. Second, the concept ensures that the officers continue career development on a timely basis. Third, officers know what they can expect from the department in the area of training and development—this can be very beneficial to officers' morale. Fourth, it provides for a fair and equitable system in which every officer receives approximately the same level of training. In addition to being a positive morale factor, this is also beneficial in administering the department's affirmative action plan. Fifth, the phase approach to training aids in the coordination and planning of the department's overall training program and helps to avoid many of the common pitfalls in administering the program.

 CIVIL LIABILITY AND TRAINING

The early 1980s established that municipalities can be held liable for a police officer's negligence and intentional wrongdoing. During the Reconstruction period of the Civil War, Congress provided citizen access to the federal courts when their constitutional rights under the Thirteenth and Fourteenth Amendments had been infringed upon. The Sovereign Immunity doctrine stated that governments could not be sued. This was the first step in chipping away at this legal doctrine. State and local governments became civil defendants when citizens sought monetary awards and injunctive or declaratory relief based on allegations of unconstitutional acts.

These torts defined civil wrongs which resulted in lawsuits by the party being harmed. Currently, a majority of torts against state officials are filed under *42 Section 1983* of the *United States Code* (USC), which forbids any deprivation of constitutional rights by public officials acting in their official capacity or "under color of state law." In cases involving federal officials, these actions are begun under the Bill of Rights and are known as *Biven's action* (Silver, 1988).

The landmark decision was a 1978 case involving a requirement for pregnant employees to take unpaid leaves of absence before medically necessary. In *Monell v. Department of Social Services* (436 U.S. 658), the Supreme Court ruled that governments could be sued directly in addition to the individual officer when the government is held responsible for injuries inflicted under the auspices of official policy in violation of Section 1983 USC. Local governments were also held liable for the attorney's fees of a successful complainant. There have been further developments in federal and state court cases which held municipalities liable for action by employees and their supervisors who are directly involved in such incidents. The interpretation of what is official policy has ranged from written standards of a police department all the way to a series of unwritten practices over time.

Training has become an important legal issue in tort actions involving negligence and nonfeasance. Legally, training is an affirmative duty of police administrators. Liability exists in failure to train a police officer or training a police officer in a negligent fashion. In tort actions, directly or indirectly related to training, questions will be asked regarding state minimum standards regarding training and the scope of duties performed by the trained or untrained employee. Certification of instructors and even lesson plans used in training have become legal issues. A few examples of the complex tort issues raised are:

> *Turpin v. Mallet, 619 F. 2d 1961 (1980).* The court found that the plaintiffs had cause for action since the police agency failed to properly hire, train, and supervise a police officer who had kicked a pregnant woman.

> *Sager v. City of Woodland Park, 543 F. Supp. 282 (1982).* This is an example that is often used in police training liability discussions. A film used in a police academy training session in Colorado showed how not to do something in a felony stop. A police officer who had been to this training academy, while attempting to handcuff a suspect, shot and killed the suspect. The burden of responsibility shifted from the municipality to the regional police academy conducting the training.

Roman v. City of Richmond, 570 F. Supp. 1554 (1983). $1,500,000 was awarded in a wrongful-death case for failure to properly hire, train, and supervise and for allowing unconstitutional policy to exist in the harassment of black residents.

Oklahoma City v. Tuttle, 105 S.Ct. 2427 (1985). A single incident of police misconduct did not, in and of itself, prove a policy of inadequate police training or supervision in holding a municipality liable. Where the policy itself is not unconstitutional, there is a need for more proof than a single incident to establish requisite fault and the causal connection between "policy" and constitutional deprivation.

Tennessee v. Garner, 105 S.Ct. 1694 (1985). The U.S. Supreme Court held that the use of deadly force to prevent the escape of a fleeing, unarmed burglary suspect constituted an unreasonable seizure in violation of the Fourth Amendment. Review was conducted of departmental operational training policies related to the use of deadly force in these situations.

Voutour v. Vitale, 761 F. 2nd 812 (1985). The police department was found liable for wrongful shooting involving procedures that were supposed to be taught at a six-week training program. A 30-minute training film at roll call was substituted for the regular training.

Kibbe v. City of Springfield, 777 F. 2d 801 (1985). Reviewing the actions of officers involved in a high-speed chase that resulted in the death of the fleeing suspect, the First Circuit Court of Appeals found that the involved police officers were inadequately trained and that departmental policies on high-speed pursuits and alternatives to pursuits contributed to the death of the suspect. During the course of this event, there were three separate shooting incidents involving 10 officers. A kidnap victim was also present in the suspect vehicle during the pursuit. The city of Springfield argued that civil rights liability litigation was not appropriate litigation for the actions of the officers. The Supreme Court dismissed the case as being improvidently granted.

City of Canton v. Harris, 489 U.S. 378 (1989). The Court ruled that the policy and custom of a police department need not be unconstitutional on its face. Under limited circumstances, a failure to train may create municipal liability when there is deliberate indifference to the rights of citizens especially in recurrent situations which involve potential damage to citizens' constitutional rights.

Since the Harris case, plaintiffs in Section 1983 tort actions have attempted to prove "deliberate indifference" with regard to training or nontraining of officers. Reviewing several post-Harris cases, Silver (1993: 8-226. -7) cites the following examples of what might be considered departmental deliberate indifference regarding constitutional rights:

1. Contemporary standards of relevant law enforcement duties not being incorporated into departmental regulations
2. No in-service training
3. No command training for new supervisors
4. No operational guidelines
5. Haphazard and infrequent discipline
6. Ignoring requests for training by officers

Interestingly enough, failure to train in canine use of force or to monitor the use of dogs has resulted in training-related tort actions. In *Kerr v. City of West Palm Beach*, 875 F. 2d 1546, (11 Cir. 1989) the deliberate-indifference standard was used in a complaint against the department for failure to issue operational guidelines and conduct training for its canine unit.

This is only a small sample of cases that have raised issues regarding training in tort actions. Proactive police managers need to realize that their police agencies, municipalities, and even individual employees may be sued and that issues in relation to training may very well be raised.

Following is a basic checklist that police managers should use in order to prevent such tort actions:

1. Do not allow untrained officers to perform any field police duties! *Untrained officer* may be defined as any officer who has not successfully completed basic school and field training.
2. Training academies need to keep accurate records, including (a) lesson plans, (b) attendance of all students, (c) instructor qualifications, (d) test scores, (e) all handout materials given to students, and (f) all films and videos shown students. In addition, it might be a good idea in skill-related courses, such as the use of the baton, to videotape the student in order to document the students' proficiency in the skill area.
3. Official departmental policies should be reflected in training. For example, the use of deadly physical force should be presented within the context of a course of instruction on deadly physical force.
4. Lesson plans, policies, and instructional techniques need to be reviewed and updated. A saying for instructors that comes especially true in tort cases is: "Do not laminate your lesson plans, for they will probably become obsolete next year!"

▶ CONCLUSION

In the future, training will continue to play a key role in law enforcement. However, as we have seen, the training will become increasingly sophisticated. Law enforcement is attracting more and more college graduates. Human relations skills including such topics as stress management will continue to be emphasized and become a larger part of the curriculum. At the same time police training officials will attempt to fill in the technological gap with the use of the microprocessor revolution in communication. Word processors are starting to become part of the everyday life of some innovative departments. Knowledge of communication has always been a significant need in training and will continue to be so.

One of the key innovations that has affected training around the country has been field training. When carefully planned out with adequately trained and well-selected field training officers, field training can combine theory and practice and have a significant impact on new police officers.

Civil liability is becoming an increasingly significant issue for both line officers and police managers. Solid, professional, documented training remains one of the best protections for civil liability.

More training is also needed for police executives as well as supervisory personnel. Major corporations provide hundreds of thousands of dollars for training their major executives, while police agencies are just starting to create training programs in this vital area.

Hopefully, we will also see more in-service training for middle management personnel. Newly promoted officers, especially, need to develop new knowledge along with personnel, management, and administrative skills. A curriculum providing the technological and human relations skills to operate in a modern police department will take commitment on the part of a proactive management. Personnel can anticipate events that they have been trained to recognize as familiar situations. A truly proactive department will synthesize planning and training so that line officers and police supervisors will have a positive, plan-ahead perspective of their respective roles in the police organization.

QUESTIONS FOR REVIEW

1. Why is there a need for improvement in police training?
2. List four common deficiencies in many current training programs.
3. Why is training of crucial importance to police managers?
4. Outline the main recommendations for training as posted by the 1973 task force report.
5. Why does the regional-training concept offer many remedies to small police agencies?
6. What are the major components of Project STAR? What are the strengths and weaknesses of this program?
7. Explain the importance of the following training topics: crisis intervention, first aid, firearms training, ethics, domestic violence, and stress management.

CLASS PROJECTS

1. Depending on size, the class is divided into a number of task forces. The instructor will ask each task force to review the curriculum of a police academy either in the area or the state. (If possible, the task force should visit the academy.) Compare and contrast the curriculum in terms of recommendations made by either the authors, the task force report, or Project STAR.

2. Devise your own training curriculum so that (a) everything that you think is relevant for police work is covered, and (b) the course can take place in a maximum of 16 weeks. Compare this training curriculum with a local training curriculum and tell why you may or may not differ with the total local model.

3. Design a community policing training curriculum.

KEY TERMS

bias crime
blood-borne pathogens
civil liability
diversity
domestic crisis intervention
field training
FTO

phase approach
planning
stalking
STAR
SWAT
virtual reality

BIBLIOGRAPHY

BARD, MORTON, and BERNARD BERKOWITZ, In S.I. Cohn, ed., *Law Enforcement and Technology*. Baltimore: Port City Press, 1969.

Canton v. Harris, 489 U.S. 378 (1989)

DUNNETTE, MARVIN D., and STEPHAN J. MOTOWIDLE, *Police Selection and Career Assessment*. Washington, D.C.: U.S. Government Printing Office, November 1976.

FOSDICK, RAYMOND B., *American Police Systems*. Montclair, N.J.: Patterson Smith, 1920, reprinted 1969.

FROST, THOMAS M., and MAGNUS J. SENG, "Police Entry Level Curriculum: A Thirty Year Perspective," *Journal of Police Science and Administration*. 12, no. 1 (1984), pp. 251-59.

HORMANN, JEFFREY S., "Virtual Reality: The Future of Law Enforcement Training." *FBI Law Enforcement Bulletin*, 64, no. 7, July 1995, pp. 7-9.

JENKINS, HERBERT, *Keeping the Peace: A Police Chief Looks at His Job*. New York: Harper & Row, 1970.

JOHNSON, ROBER, *Cultural Diversity*. Albany, N.Y.: Human Resources Training, 1992.

Kerr v. City of West Palm Beach, 875 F 2d 1546.

Kibbe v. City of Springfield, 777 F. 2d 801 (1985).

MATTHEWS, ROBERT A., and LLOYD W. ROWLAND, *How to Recognize and Handle Abnormal People: A Manual for Police Officers* (5th ed.). Arlington, Va.: Mental Health Association, 1978.

MCCAMPBELL, MICHAEL S., *Field Training for Police Officers: State of the Art*. Washington, D.C.: National Institute of Justice, 1986.

MCMANUS, GEORGE P., *Police Training and Performance Study*. Washington, D.C.: U.S. Government Printing Office and Law Enforcement Assistance Administration, 1970.

"Memorandum on Handling Bias Related Incidents." Albany, N.Y.: Office of University Public Safety, State University of New York, 1988.

Monell v. Department of Social Services, 436 U.S. 658 (1978).

NATIONAL ADVISORY COMMISSION ON CRIMINAL JUSTICE STANDARDS AND GOALS, *Police*. Washington, D.C.: U.S. Government Printing Office, 1973.

NEIDERHOFFER, ARTUR, *Behind the Shield: The Police in Urban Society*. Garden City, N.Y.: Doubleday, 1969.

NEW YORK STATE BUREAU FOR MUNICIPAL POLICE, *A Guide to the Police Officers Basic Training Course*. Albany, N.Y.: Division of Criminal Justice Services, Bureau for Municipal Police, Municipal Police Training Council, 1986.

NEW YORK STATE OFFICER FOR THE PREVENTION OF DOMESTIC VIOLENCE, "Domestic Violence Incident Policy: Model Law Enforcement Policy Language," (July, 1995).

Oklahoma City v. Tuttle, 105 S.Ct. 2427 (1985).

REITH, CHARLES, *The Blind Eye of History*. Montclair, N.J.: Patterson Smith, 1952, reprinted 1975.

Roman v. City of Richmond, 570 F. Supp. 1554 (1983).

Sager v. City of Woodland Park, 543 F. Supp. 282 (1982).

SILVER, ISIDORE, *Police Civil Liability*. New York: Matthew Bender, 1993.

SMITH, CHARLES P., DONALD E. PEHLKE, and CHARLES D. WELLER, *Project STAR: Police Officer Role Training Program*. Cincinnati, Ohio: Anderson, 1976.

STEWART, JERRY D., "Bloodborne Diseases: Developing a Training Curriculum," *FBI Law Enforcement Bulletin*, May 1993, 62, no. 5, pp. 11–15.

SULLIVAN, JOHN L., *Introduction to Police Science*. New York: McGraw-Hill, 1971.

Tennessee v. Garner, 105 S.Ct. 1694 (1985).

Turpin v. Mallet, 619 F. 2d 1961 (1980).

VanZandt, Clinton R., "Stalkers: Their Threat to Our Nation's College Campuses." Paper presented to the International Association of Campus Law Enforcement Administrators, Charleston, S.C., 1996.

Voutour v. Vitale, 761 F. 2d 812 (1985).

Weaver, Gary, "Cultural Diversity," *FBI Law Enforcement Bulletin*, 61, no. 9 (1992), pp. 1–7.

Williams, Willie L., John Lane, and Michael A. Zona, "Stalking: Successful Intervention Strategies." *The Police Chief*, 53, no. 2 (1996), pp. 24–26.

Wood, Daniel E., "Phase Approach to Training," *FBI Law Enforcement Bulletin*, 49, no. 5 (May 1980), pp. 13–15.

13

Proactive Planning: Operational and Fiscal

Proactive police management is the result of effective planning. Police management teams need to develop the necessary control to manage future events and anticipate future action. This control is developed through the planning function that draws upon a solid, empirical research data base produced by quality research. Police planners need to develop contingencies based upon documented and known facts with conservative *extrapolation* indexes. **Extrapolation** is the ability to forecast future events based upon trends that exist in current situations. The **forecast** is usually stated in terms of probabilities; for example, a 95 percent probability that a burglary will occur in a certain four-block area during the midnight shift. There is also **macroforecasting**—the attempt to give probability curves and indexes to large-scale events. One example would be an 80 percent probability that police manpower needs will increase during a major national disaster, therefore demanding an increased manpower budget and certain types of reorganization of the police structure to meet this demand.

 PLANNING DEFINED

O. W. Wilson, one of the best-known police administrators to consider planning essential to the police function, gives the following definition to *planning* (1952: 3):

a process of developing a method of procedure or an arrangement of parts intended to facilitate the achievement of a defined objective.

Wilson is specific in his view of the planning process in that he is looking at implementing procedures that are aimed at well-defined objectives that are largely operational. This means that planning is not a series of abstract, analytical notions but rather a blueprint for immediate, practical use.

Hudzik and others, in their overview of personnel planning (1981: 133), reinforce this approach with their three-pronged definition of *planning*:

> First, there is recognition that planning is future oriented, that it somehow links present actions to future conditions. Second, there is either implicit or explicit mention of a conscious process of gathering information in support of such assertions about cause and effect. And third, there seems to be agreement that planning is action oriented, primarily intended to affect the real world of things rather than simply the world of ideas.

They reinforce this last point by quoting a 1979 report of the National Academy of Public Administration, which states that "planning differs from academic analysis, which mainly seeks understanding, in that planning aims toward getting something done." That is what this chapter is all about—the creation of a solid planning base so that there can be a proactive police approach to getting that "something done."

Souryal quotes Yehezkel Dror on planning in terms of a succinct definition and then elaborates upon it (Souryal, 1977: 280): "The process of preparing a set of decisions for action in the future directed at achieving goals by optimal means." This is an activity-oriented definition with the emphasis on using efficient methods of achieving the goals sought. Planning is seen as a continuing activity concerned with a set of interdependent parts, where a number of alternate choices are developed in relation to future events. Besides the concept of optimization of means to achieve goals, another major contribution of this approach is the concept of developing alternate means of reaching the desired goals. Too often, police planning units tend to look for a single answer to a problem when the good management choice is to decide among an equal number of viable alternative means and be able to switch from one choice to another depending upon events. Here, *flexibility* is a key word, but an organized flexibility with clearly spelled out parameters in terms of real choices.

Another major distinction is that between normative and instrumental planning. **Instrumental planning** occurs when choices are created in terms of the means of obtaining goals that have been stated and given. Normally, the goals, under instrumental planning, are not questioned. **Normative planning** occurs when the goals to be chosen are considered part of the planning process. Thus planning, under normative planning, is clearly linked to public policy analysis and the creation and implementation of public police policy. Police agencies have no problem, in most cases, with the setting of certain public policy in relation to organizational goals. However, some managers consider this type of broad police-policy goal setting as part of the political process, and many feel that this should be left in the hands of local legislators and political executives such as mayors and county executives. However, if a police manager is to deal with future events and have an understanding and feel for controlling these events, normative planning must be part of his or her particular management style. A forward-planning chief police executive must be able to develop policy alternatives and not feel locked into given policy goals and a constricted set of policy alternatives.

 ## SIGNIFICANCE OF PLANNING

People talk about intuitive knowledge and hunches and often use such knowledge to achieve results. In some cases, this approach may seem reasonable, especially when decisions have to be made in the absence of essential data. However, if police management is going to operate at optimal efficiency, something more than hunches is necessary. Good police managers wish to operate in an organized and efficient manner and eliminate as many errors as possible. This does not mean that the **intuitive approach** should be eliminated, but, rather, that the intuitive approach needs to be channeled and controlled. One of the major thrusts of proactive police management is to have an alert, rational, and efficient organization with the known purpose of controlling unknown variables and creating a reasonable base for future action.

A major objective of planning is to create consistency over time, so that day-to-day police operations are uniform. Policies need to be made known to all the officers in the organization, and thus they need to be written and understood easily. Moreover, these policies must be applied in an even-handed manner to police personnel, citizens, and situations.

Police deal on a daily basis with many volatile situations, and officers need a secure base from which to operate if they are to reduce their feelings of stress in relation to the organization. Consistent and forward-looking planning accomplishes reduced organizational stress for individual police officers as well as for managers and administrators and lets individuals in the organization know that policies will not change abruptly. A secure organizational base will provide the stability needed to make wise policy decisions and ensure fairness and equity.

Planning also helps to define organizational roles for all ranks in the police department and the formal relationships between these roles. Since roles are often considered simply a pattern of expected behaviors, this will also reduce police-officer and manager stress by creating a stable base of role expectations. It lets each individual holding the various ranks and positions know, within reason, what is expected of him or her in that police organizational role. Police administrators often need to have the parameters of their jobs defined. This is done through organizational charts and standard operating procedures.

A well-organized planning staff that works closely with management can help administrators and officers understand the limits of each position in the organization. It will also anticipate the need for advanced training and positive two-way communication whenever there is a need to change the parameters of the various roles in the police organizational structure. For example, from time to time, training officers take on additional duties in relation to recruitment, especially in the area of affirmative action. Traditional departments without a planning component would simply have an order written and assign the additional duties to the head of the training sections. A proactive, planning-oriented department would call the officers in to discuss the additional duties with members of the management team. A plan of action would be formulated with the planning unit, and any additional training that would be needed would begin before the officers had to take on the additional duties.

▶ NEED FOR PLANNING OFFICER(S) OR A PLANNING UNIT

Whether there is a planning officer or a separate planning unit naturally depends upon the size of the department. Whatever the case, every department, regardless of its size, needs a specific location in the organizational chart in which the planning-function activities will be carried out. For the sake of brevity, we will speak of the planning unit with the realization that in smaller departments this planning unit will most likely consist of a single officer who would be doing the bulk of the planning and research work of the department.

Basically, the planning unit provides staff services to the proactive police management team in five vital areas:

1. Dissemination of information
2. Preparation of orders
3. Long-range planning of departmental procedures
4. Development of legal and statistical information
5. Provision of specific and general assistance in the decision-making process

These services are performed in terms of the three basic functions of planning and research in any police department:

1. *Records and reports.* Maintain statistical records, rules, and regulations of the department; design, formulate, modify, and, when necessary, eliminate departmental forms.
2. *Data and fiscal analysis.* Assist in budget preparation both internally and for presentation to external funding sources such as political executives and legislatures; provide trend analysis of crime statistics

for both managerial planning and the line officer's daily needs; prepare annual report, etc.

3. *Legal.* Interpret recent court decisions for use by staff and line officers; assist in departmental hearings, provide information and data base needed for future criminal justice legislation, provide copies of new laws that affect operations and prepare explanations and analysis of new laws, using ordinary and understandable English rather than legal jargon; provide explanations of new technical legal jargon that affects planning and operational activity.

With the exception of keeping some records and reporting data to the Uniform Crime Report system, many of these needs are not met in many medium-sized and smaller departments. However, they are vital to both the short-range and long-range health of any police organization. Positive, effective management includes an information machine that digests enormous amounts of data into summarized and analyzed forms. Thus, the planning unit provides such uniform and timely information for the proactive management team.

 ## STEPS IN THE PLANNING PROCESS

As in the development of any process, certain factors or conditions need to be determined to follow through logically to a successful conclusion. In the planning process, the following steps have been identified.

1. *Recognition and analysis of the problem: specifying the need for a plan.* This is one of the most difficult steps in the planning process. There is a need to make sure that the problem really exists and is one that is relevant to the police organization. Is this a problem that is unique and simply needs to be dealt with on an ad hoc basis or will there be a continuing need to deal with this problem in terms of future organizational activity? Planning resources should be targeted on problems that are relevant and significant to the police organization.

   Ultimately, the problem needs to be defined so that it can be resolved through the use of empirical data. General questions of ethics or metaphysical notions cannot be resolved by planning units. Also, the problem needs to be stated in such a way that it can be resolved with the tools and resources that the planning unit has available. Specifics are also needed in terms of the resolution of problems and the creation of specific plans. For example, rather than an increase or decrease in crime rate in general as a problem, planning units should specify a narrower scope; for example, the decrease in burglaries in a specific area of the police jurisdiction.

2. *Formulation of a detailed set of objectives.* This goal-setting activity should be formulated in specific empirical terms, that is, be stated so that the data gathered are either directly or potentially verifiable through the five senses—seeing, hearing, feeling (touch), smelling, or tasting. A context for the verification has to be identified, that is, a laboratory procedure, gathering of statistical data, interviews, and so on. Also a standard of goal attainment needs to be stated. Rather than simply a reduction in property crime, it would be better to state that there should be a 5 percent reduction in robberies in certain geographical locations within a specified time period. Internally, planning could propose a 10 percent reduction in personnel grievances against middle management. However stated, the goals, or behavioral objectives, must be (a) specific; (b) obtainable, that is, possible; (c) empirical; and (d) related to general goals of the police organization.

3. *Gathering data.* Literally anything can be called data: gun shots and noises, gossip, scientific experiments, even people crossing the street. The major test of the data gatherer is that of considering what is significant (relevant) data, in relation to the problem to be solved. If you have too fine a net used to gather data, your time is wasted and your files are filled with irrelevancies. If the mesh of your data-gathering net is too large, then significant facts may slip through and be lost to the investigation.

   Data gathering is not simply looking at random events and choosing facts with little or no judgment. There is a need for a crude but effective cost-benefit flow chart at this stage of the problem-solving planning process. For some data, cost is literally not a factor. In the solution of homicides, for example, both the police and the public are willing to sustain high costs. Data are collected that might be considered irrelevant in less important cases, on the off chance that something might be there that would lead to solving the crime. In a highly publicized multiple murder, for example, the data net is fine indeed, and costs are generally not even considered. All we need do is remember the summer of 1981 and the approach to multiple murders in Atlanta, Georgia; when the state of Georgia was finding the costs of the investigations too high, the federal government was willing to contribute monies and personnel to the investigation.

   Increased availability of computer-generated information has stressed a need for personnel trained in analysis and the ability to make sound judgments concerning relevance. A major problem in current practices is not the lack of data but rather existence of too much information. The secret of success is the ability to have enough analytical skills to use the significant data you have to solve the planning problem while discarding, or better yet, *not* gathering the irrelevant data.

4. *Planning the attack.* This is where highly organized analytical skills come into focus. Technical data, for example, need to be digested,

interpreted, and refashioned in such a manner that they become useful to planners and management. This might include the reorganization of statistical and evaluative data in clear English. Thus, conclusions can be drawn that can be used to organize and identify the plans of attack.

The plan of attack needs to have enough specifics that it makes sense to both line officers and supervisors. Orders have to be drawn and definite action commitments have to be made in terms of specific timetables. Definite procedural orders are needed so that line personnel will know what they have to do to implement the attack plan. A brief example of personnel procedural orders follows:

Orders Implementing Administrative Assistant to Chief

1.10 General Duties

Assistant shall report directly to the chief of police and his or her duty hours, vacation, and days off schedule shall be as designated by the chief of police. He or she will be responsible for the enforcement of all departmental rules and regulations, orders, procedures, discipline, and efficiency of members within his or her assigned jurisdiction. He or she shall be commanding officer of the Administrative Staff Unit, which shall consist of the following areas:

1.20 Research and Planning

1. Research and study recommendations for the coordination of the activities of all units of the department.
2. Have staff supervise orders, forms, and procedures to prevent duplication or conflict with rules, regulations, and procedures of the department or orders of the chief of police.
3. Review department rules, orders, and procedures and recommend amendments thereto as required.
4. Provide ongoing research on crime control data.

1.30 Personnel

1. Investigate recruits and civilian personnel prior to employment with the department.
2. Maintain personnel records on all members of the department.
3. Provide statistical data concerning personnel records as required.

1.40 Training

1. Coordinate recruit and in-service training with Police Academy and other training or academic programs.
2. Conduct roll-call training within the department.
3. Conduct firearms training and practice sessions for members on a regular basis.

1.50 Intelligence

1. Maintain records of activities of persons and organizations to assist the department in fulfilling its obligation of service to the community.

1.60 Internal Investigation

1. Maintain a record of complaints against the department and individual officers. Conduct an investigation in cooperation with the appropriate commanding officer into the facts of the complaint. Record the results to be filed with chief of police and individual officer's personnel folder.

1.70 Records and Orders

1. Maintain an order system of communication within the department.
2. Provide staff assistance to desk officer in preparation, distribution, and retention of departmental records.

This example was taken from a planning study of a police department of around 35 sworn personnel. The plan was designed to develop a unit that would take care of administrative detail and provide planning continuity for the police chief. The unit could have consisted of anywhere from 1 to 3 persons. The chief would decide which ones would be civilians and which ones would be uniformed.

5. *Attainment of the agreement of those involved in the plans: obtaining concurrences.* In the military, obtaining concurrences means obtaining the agreement of those who are to be involved with the operationalization of the plan. In some cases, it would be valuable to obtain specific input from line officers. The obtaining of concurrences is an attempt to have the officers and agencies involved agree at an early stage on the details of how the plan is going to be carried out. If this is done, positive cooperation is more likely to occur. The reason for this positive feeling is that officers who are consulted concerning the implementation of plans will feel that they are part of the team and have something personal at stake in the success of the plan. In addition, involved officers are less likely to place obstacles in the way of implementing the plan.

A further practical reason for obtaining concurrence is the need to receive input from those who are most familiar with the field work necessary to operationalize a plan. Without such input, necessary details may be missed. Concurrence should also mean that those carrying out the plan will have a better understanding for the need of the plan and its success. They will be able to anticipate problems and obstacles to implementation because of prior consultation. Involvement of this kind, in basic management decisions, normally increases morale among all levels of personnel.

6. *Evaluation.* Needless to say, unless the plan is actually made operational and there is a means of evaluating its success, much time and effort will have been wasted. Unfortunately, many good plans fail to reach the operational stage for a variety of reasons (for example, administrative change, change of priorities, lack of budgetary support, internal conflict).

▶ TYPES OF PLANS

Planning, doing, and controlling are three phases of the management process. Total planning helps to ensure success of both the doing and controlling. It is essential that planning be well thought out. In that regard, we have divided our discussion into long-range administrative/management plans, fiscal plans, and short-range operational/tactical plans.

LONG-RANGE ADMINISTRATIVE/MANAGEMENT PLANS

These are plans that concern the basic structure of the police organization. They are the responsibility of the jurisdictional officials who created the agency and the responsibility of the department head who is charged with its daily operation. It is at this level that the policies governing the departmental activities are formulated. *Policy* is defined as a may-do activity as opposed to lower-level procedures which usually are detailed and presented as must-do activities. Special emphasis is placed on interfacing and overlapping areas of authority. Following are central issues to be considered in formulating these types of long-range plans:

1. *Decentralization versus centralization.* One of the most difficult tasks facing the long-range planner is determining at what level in the organization structure the administrator is willing to allow subordinates to make decisions. This fundamental management decision focuses on how much control there should be for central management versus how much for line supervisors. Although this planning problem has often been considered in terms of internal organizational concerns, there is a wider arena in which this problem should be considered. The major question is, how much does either organizational mode speed up the optimal delivery of services to the citizen? Another issue is, how much change in terms of authority roles can be sustained by personnel in the organization while keeping morale high? Larger police organizations tend to shift their emphasis in terms of centralized authority in a number of ways and rather sharply in terms of time needed for organizational change.

So much time may be spent centralizing or decentralizing authority, that the major missions of the police organizations are lost in the organizational shuffle. Although these types of plans should be examined quite carefully and implemented rather infrequently, there are times when these types of plans need to be implemented. The management team should not hesitate to bring about needed organizational change when it is justified in terms of operational efficiency and the goals of the organization.

2. *Changes in basic organizational planning.* This can include the centralization-versus-decentralization issue, but is much broader in concept. It could mean, for example, a shift in where the major investigations take place—in the detective division or among a team of field police officers. This includes a basic change in the authority relationships and functions of the different units of the police organization. A hard look at current organizational practices is taken in conjunction with the planning unit. Developing authority relationships are examined in the light of the need for an efficient department. Optimization of general administrative and managerial practices in conjunction with effective leadership styles is also examined. The question to be asked is: Do these relationships optimize the effective administration of the police organization, or is there a more effective mode of organization that should be implemented?

3. *Long-range personnel deployment planning.* This includes hiring, firing, grievance procedures, fringe-benefits negotiation and implementation, along with effective use and maintenance of the tools of the trade such as vehicles, armaments, mobile communications, and so on. In a service organization such as law enforcement, where up to 90 percent of the budget may be devoted to personnel and the servicing of personnel, effective planning in this area may have a serious impact on the police organization. Budgets have to be related to the optimizing of individual morale and efficiency and this has to be related to the overall operations.

4. *Planning training needs and requirements.* In the budget-cutting process that police budgets experience at the hand of legislatures, training is often considered a luxury item by politicians. They often fail to see the relationship between effective training and effective operations in the field. When training monies are cut and a plan is being implemented, there may not be enough of a budget to train personnel in implementing the plan. Personnel might need new skills, a possible change in some attitudes and perceptions, and some new knowledge in order to facilitate the implementation of certain plans. When personnel are not able to acquire these effective tools for planning implementation, then plans fail, not because the plan was bad, but because the training budget was cut.

Without the implementation of the training function as part of the overall planning process, management may need to implement training in the middle of a plan and with less than adequate training personnel. What happens in such a situation is that the plan limps along at higher cost and with lower morale.

The training plan should be implemented prior to and concurrent with the general plan of attack. Police managers have to educate legislators to the notion that effective training is essential to solid management planning. Training is not a luxury, but essential to every budget. Training needs to be written in as essential to any change in organizational structure and in the implementation of new plans.

FISCAL PLANNING

Fiscal planning, which should be a continuous departmental activity, requires the department to be able to project a number of fiscal futures, pick one of these futures, add on the normal contingency plans, and live within this budget. If this is not done, the department will not have the resources when it needs them and politicians and legislatures will end up specifying the needs of the department. Every department develops an annual budget to deal with its specific needs. What is needed is long-range fiscal planning projecting beyond the immediate needs of the annual budget. Solid fiscal planning is always a part of long-range planning.

The fiscal plan is normally prepared from one to three years in advance and often becomes one of the few bridges between old and new police administrations. Although these budgets may be modified and changed within limits by new administrations, most new administrations live with the old budgets until they can prepare their new budgets with their own priorities. Good fiscal planning can help to improve police operations and delivery of services to a community in a more effective manner.

Most administrators lack training in fiscal planning. The normal approach of police administrators who lack budgetary skills or access to personnel who do have these skills is simply to add 10 percent to the old budget when they submit their new line budget and hope for the best. When these administrators run out of fiscal resources, they depend on crisis management to deal with the situations, often approaching the local government for more resources. This type of approach is no longer feasible in an era of fiscal constraint. Police administrators have to either become more sophisticated concerning the budget process or be able to hire the experts needed. Of course, the top administrators are going to have to understand the fiscal experts that they hire or they will not understand their own budgets.

TYPES OF BUDGETS

Most budgets can be broken down into three types:

1. Line-item budgeting
2. Planned program budgeting system (PPBS)
3. Zero-based budgeting (ZBB)

Most other types of budgets that are referred to in public management and police management texts are variations on these three approaches.

The approaches to budgeting under these systems include the following: (Lewis, 1978: 229):

1. Open-end budgeting
2. Fixed-ceiling budgeting
3. Work measurement and unit costing
4. Increase-decrease analysis
5. Priority listings
6. Item-by-item control

In an *open-end budget*, the manager submitting the budget attempts to justify the fiscal request in terms of services performed with few or no guidelines. In a *fixed-ceiling budget*, an executive or legislative body gives the police agency a dollar amount that it will fund and then tells the police management team to create a budget and justify it in terms of the given dollar ceiling. *Work measurement* or *unit costing* is more sophisticated and is often used with PPBS or zero-based budgeting where each service performed by a police department is given a dollar value in terms of the cost of that service and then is justified for budgetary purposes.

In *increase-decrease analysis*, the funding body or executive in control asks for justifications in the police budget only where there is an increase or decrease in a budget request compared with the prior year's requests. In *priority listing*, the police management team lists budget items in order from most important to least important. This is especially useful to a local legislature that is interested in cutting the police budget. Finally, in *item-by-item control*, often called *line-item control*, the executive or funding body exercises control in terms of approval of specific fiscal decisions concerning certain line items in the budget during the fiscal year. The funding body actually exercises a veto over certain police management decisions concerning the spending of funds during the fiscal year. This last approach makes it difficult to exercise management control over the fiscal policies of a police department. It should only be done in times of fiscal emergencies or fiscal chaos.

Whatever approach is used for the budgeting process, certain principles must be observed by every police manager:

1. The focus should be on future as well as on present problems.
2. Budgeting should be considered as one aspect of the overall planning process.
3. Budgets should be created in terms of an overall philosophy of law enforcement, thereby enabling management to set general goals for the law enforcement agency.
4. Specific, attainable, and measurable objectives need to be set if the overall goals are to be met.

Keeping these principles in mind makes it easier to take a look at the different kind of budgets; many different approaches and types of budgets will fulfill these principles, but, some types and approaches will work better than others.

Line-Item Budgeting

This is the most widely used approach because (1) it is simplest to construct, and (2) it is easily understandable by people who might lack fiscal expertise and training. The line-item budget simply makes a list of all personnel in terms of rank and salary. This personnel list normally makes up 85 to 90 percent of the budget. Equipment, including such items as desks, laboratory equipment, and so on, are listed with their costs. Next, fixed charges—heat, light, gas for buildings, gasoline for vehicles, pensions and other fringe benefits—are listed with their costs. Most of these items are normally given as totals under these or similar categories. A sample line-item budget is shown in Table 13–1.

TABLE 13–1
BASIC SCHOOL COSTS

		95/96 24 STUDENTS	96/97 30 STUDENTS
.01	Director ($900/week)	$13,500	$14,400
.02	Temp service for adm. assistance	3,000	3,500
.03	Books/equip	900	900
.04	Recruit lodging	26,520	25,200
.05	Instructors lodging	3,600	3,800
.06	Food	15,600	19,000
.07	Phys. Ed. Uniforms	900	900
.08	PE Instructor cost	4,000	4,200
.10	Travel for instructors	3,000	3,800
.14	Bus rental for crime-prevention program	400	
.20	Emergency Vehicle Operations Course	400	
.21	Emergency Vehicle Operations Course equipment	400	350
.22	Defensive Driving Course training	350	345
.23	Psychological testing	1,500	1,200
.30	Classroom rental	3,250	4,825
.31	Honorariums for nonpolice personnel	800	800
.40	Telephone charges	120	300
.45	Miscellaneous	400	400
.50	Awards		500
.60	Composite Class picture		500
	Total	$78,640	$84,920

The line-item budget is normally passed from police administrator to police administrator and fiscal year to fiscal year with additional costs and requests simply added to the appropriate category. Some administrators may simply increase the requests by 10 percent over the last fiscal year when creating a new budget. Thus, this type of incremental budget often

1. Lacks details of the specific costs of each operation.
2. Does not relate costs to general goals and specific objectives.
3. Lacks fiscal planning capability justification.

As a result, this is one of the hardest budgets to defend before a legislative body that is interested in cutting costs. It is also one of the easiest budgets to cut. Because of the broad categories involved, legislative bodies and fiscally hard-pressed executives may simply tell the police manager to cut the budget by an overall percentage or eliminate certain categories. Since these budgets generally do not relate budget items to specific services performed for a community, it makes it difficult to justify the costs. Because of the nature of this budget, it is difficult for a police executive to say whether an increase or decrease in categories of the budget will lead to a *significant* increase or decrease in what the police executive considers a needed police service for the local community. Thus what a police manager gains in the advantage of the ease of preparation of the line-item budget may be lost when it is cost-cutting time for the local legislature.

Planned Program Budgeting System (PPBS)

This is a more difficult budget to formulate because it demands an analysis of the organizational structure of the police agency and the individual units of the agency. In social science, this is a structural-functional approach. The planning unit or officer draws up an organizational chart of the agency showing the authority relationships. This is the structure part. Then the function of each unit is described, much in the same manner as the civil service would describe the services to be performed in a standard job description. This is the function part.

Once you know how the units relate to each other and what function each unit is supposed to perform in the law enforcement organization, it is possible to set specific objectives for each unit in the light of the overall goals of the organization. These objectives are created in conjunction with middle management and supervisors in charge of each unit. The objectives are expected to be attainable and measurable, and all have to be justified in practical, empirical terms and related to all fiscal requests. The distribution of personnel and materials is identified with each planning unit or subsystem in the organization, and each unit is related to the structure of the total police organization to create the overall fiscal justification for the services that the police organization performs. This is a planning-oriented budget.

This approach, according to Schick, has produced convergence of three developments in public policy analysis (1978: 59):

1. Economic analysis—macro and micro—has had an increasing part in the shaping of fiscal and budgetary policy.
2. The development of new informational and decisional technologies has enlarged the applicability of objective analysis to policy making.
3. There has been a gradual convergence of planning and budgetary processes.

According to our approach to planning, the planning and fiscal analysis functions of management are brought together. In the 1990s, in an era of fiscal constraint, the two processes will be even more closely related as fiscal matters become more important. The successful police manager of the future will be able to relate budgeting and planning on a daily basis as well as for the purposes of overall planning.

PPBS is basically a performance budgeting system in which management examines how the police organization and its different units perform, that is, function. Catherine Seckler-Hudson has given us a useful checklist of questions that police managers should be able to answer if they are creating an effective performance-based budget. She feels that all public agency budgets should be in conformance with a central public policy. She has given us this list of questions that such a budget should answer (Seckler-Hudson, 1978: 88):

Appraising a Performance Budget System: A Yardstick

Are there well-defined work programs and activities with a careful definition of their costs?

Is there a system of work measurement and the use of performance standards?

Does administrative reporting include reporting on a functional basis?

Are records kept in terms of functional activities accomplished?

Are cost accounting and accrual accounting methods used where applicable?

Is there provision for continuous management analysis and improvement including a system of internal auditing?

Are expenditures divided into appropriate major categories?

Is the appropriation structure in terms of programs and activities to be achieved?

If the answers to all of these questions are yes, then the police agency will have a modern fiscal management structure that should be able to stand up to the scrutiny of any audit or legislative body. It is also obvious from this list of questions that the budget is not simply an annual affair. With the yes answers, budgeting becomes another planning tool for the management team to implement proactive planning and management.

Because budgeting is being justified in terms of the programs in the department that are being undertaken, a justification for each program or service that is performed is a normal part of the budgetary process. Management can take a look at this justification and relate it to the costs incurred and monies asked for. Then management decisions are made based on what management feels the service itself and the quality and level of services that is being performed is worth in terms of cost. This makes the ongoing fiscal management of the law enforcement agency part of the evaluative process that should continually be active in any professionally managed police agency.

The review process needed to create and justify a PPBS budget gives the top police administrators a unique opportunity to examine waste and duplication and thus plan for the optimal utilization of resources. This process also allows the police manager to place responsibility on appropriate supervisors and middle managers. Thus, personnel are held accountable for both fiscal and operational matters. This accountability makes personnel and unit leaders sensitive to the optimum use of scarce resources, thus generating an awareness of what fiscal responsibility means operationally. Requisitions have to be justified and justified even more so if they exceed the original requests developed by the PPBS system.

The process of justifying fiscal items in terms of the service performed to the department and the community makes a PPBS budget harder to cut. There are objectives for each budget item, and these objectives lead to the delivery of needed police services. If a legislator wishes to cut this budget, he or she has to justify his or her budget cut in terms of the acceptance of a lower level of police service delivered to the community by a specific unit of the police agency.

Zero-Based Budgeting (ZBB)

The zero-based budgeting approach creates and justifies an entirely new budget each year; there is no reliance on precedent and incremental planning from previous years. The object is to force agency planners and administrators to create new justifications for every expenditure, thereby providing a comprehensive fiscal analysis of every unit of the agency in relation to (1) a justification for the very existence of the unit and the services it provides and (2) the relationship between the justification of the services provided and the cost of these services. The originators of this approach helped both to encourage comprehensive planning and to eliminate waste and inefficiency. As Wildavsky and Hammond state (1978: 243):

> The major purpose of the zero-based budget was to examine all programs at the same time and from the ground up to discover programs continuing through inertia or design that did not warrant being continued at all or at their present level of expenditure.

Monies saved by this analysis would then be used for programs of a higher priority than the ones defined as redundant or would simply be a means of reducing expenditure for the total budget.

Zero-based budgeting is part of a long tradition of comprehensive fiscal planning that fiscal experts have tried to have public agencies adopt for many decades. In 1940, V.O. Key, Jr., defined a *completed budget* (1978: 20): "The completed budgetary document (although the budget-maker may be quite unaware of it) represents a judgment upon how scarce means should be allocated to bring a maximum return in social utility." This point needs to be emphasized when looking at any fiscal process. Because there are never enough resources to meet all demands, which is true of all public agencies including law enforcement, the basic decision to be made is how to allocate these resources. This allocation, after all the fiscal experts have completed their budgets, may, in the end, be a political decision.

However, zero-based budgeting has met full force one of the major points that V.O. Key, Jr., made in his classic 1940 article (1978: 20):

> Whether a particular agency is utilizing and plans to utilize its resources with the maximum efficiency is of great importance, but this approach leaves untouched a more fundamental problem. If it is assumed that the agency is operating at maximum efficiency, the question remains whether the function is worth carrying out at all, or whether it should be carried out on a reduced or enlarged scale, with resulting transfers of funds to or from other activities of greater or lesser social utility.

This, in fact, is the basis behind zero-based budgeting, whether a function should be carried out at all is the real question. Also, a standard approach of zero-based budgeting is to ask the different units what kind of services they would provide at different funding levels (for example, a 90 percent funding level or a 70 percent funding level). This allows policymakers to cut their budgets in a logical manner with a reasonable awareness of the specific consequences of the budget cuts in the delivery of services by various units of the police agency.

Criticisms and Contributions of PPBS and ZBB

The major contribution of PPBS is that the budget became a management tool of analysis for the overall picture and for an analysis of each unit. On the other hand, ZBB asks a fundamental question of each unit: How do you justify your existence in terms of services performed? ZBB also encourages managers to develop a comprehensive picture of their fiscal process rather than rely on the line-item approach of incremental additions to an already existing budget. Both are excellent tools of analysis, and the kinds of reports that are expected of unit managers make these managers more analytical in justifying their existence in terms of performance. Thus, another major contribution of these approaches is to force police managers and administrators from the lowest supervisor to the police chief or commissioner to think in terms of the utility of services performed. Performance-based budgets means that unit police managers have to be responsible for justifying the use of scarce resources in terms of the performance of the police personnel under their command. As daily fiscal controls are built into department operations through the increased use of computer technology, it will become absolutely vital that professional police managers become aware of these various budgetary approaches.

The criticisms of PPBS and ZBB are basically the same: both tend to create unneeded paperwork and both use too much jargon that is often unrelated to the actual job being done. In other words, the implementation of a jargon-laden abstract system may confuse even competent police supervisors, administrators, and managers.

In addition, the definition of *social utility* and the setting of priorities of police services is, more often than not, a political decision. Consider the saying, "People get the level of service they want." Law enforcement is a public service and the public should have some say in the overall priorities of its public institutions, including police service. In a well-ordered democracy this often takes place at the budgetary level in terms of appropriations. A professional police department that is run objectively without political interference will reflect the needs and values of the community. Therefore, police managers should have to defend their budgets in terms of the definition of social utility that makes sense for their individual communities. Elected officials need to respond to this definition of social utility in a responsible manner so that (1) there is no political interference with professionally managed law enforcement agencies, (2) adequate funding will provide services in the area of public safety and emergency police services, and (3) the public will have a representatives to set priorities in terms of services delivered the public.

SUPPLEMENTING THE POLICE BUDGET

The most successful strategies for law enforcement agencies to raise money outside the normal budget have been *donation programs* and *forfeiture*. Another strategy, the charging of *user fees* directly for police services (for example, special patrols, copying of accident reports) is the least effective way and creates a great deal of resentment among citizens. However, the Miami, Florida Police Department was able to raise $3 million in a two-year period by aggressively charging user fees.

Donation drives often generate free positive publicity for police agencies. A private fund drive in Chicago, for example, raised $1.5 million for equipping the patrol force with body armor, with the result that within a few months, four police officers' lives had been saved by their vests. New York City has its New York City Police Foundation, which regularly raises over $1 million each year to be spent on such items as health screening, scholarships, mounted patrol, automation of records, training, and rewards (Stellwagen and Wylie, 1985). These examples illustrate the two major approaches to this type of fund raising: special-issue campaigns and ongoing foundations.

If the donation approach is going to work, it must be run and controlled by police managers rather than by using professional fund raisers. Professional fund raisers are very commercial, often taking a large percentage of the gross (up to 90 percent) for overpriced services; in some cases they have been indicted and convicted of illegal activity in the area of fund raising. Donation programs can work, but only when they are controlled by police management and are part of a community effort.

Of great interest to police managers around the nation is the **forfeiture** approach, where goods and monies gained illegally are forfeited to the police department. Departments have seized such items as cars, airplanes, and yachts; one department even obtained a computer. The Atlanta, Georgia police department broke up a 10-county high-tech gambling operation. Through the use of forfeiture, they confiscated the gambler's minicomputer, and now use it to keep track of radio usage, gasoline consumption and the hourly activities of the officers.

The most successful forfeiture operations involve drug cases on the coast of Florida, in part because Florida in 1980 enacted one of the broadest state forfeiture laws in the country. The Florida Contraband Forfeiture Act allows for the forfeiture of any "instrumentality" used in the commission of any felony. Under this system police departments get to keep everything they confiscate, and can hire their own lawyers for the civil proceedings. In addition, local governments cannot reduce the police budget because of forfeiture income. The Fort Lauderdale Police Department in a two-year period seized 20 vessels, $1.4 million in cash, 89 vehicles, and two airplanes, with the total forfeiture amounting to over $3.3 million. In a three-year period the amount came up to $5.5 million. Even the Delray Beach Police Department, a small department, in one year confiscated a $24,000 Formula boat, $240,000 in cash, a Mercedes-Benz, and a Cadillac.

If forfeiture is going to hurt the criminal element while helping the police department, it has to be planned carefully. First, the chief needs to be familiar with forfeiture laws in that jurisdiction. Many laws are needlessly complex, limit the monies that can go to the police department, or place all monies in a general fund. Second, the chief needs to protect the detectives from getting involved in entrapment and/or criminal soliciting. Third, there are costs involved: lawyers, storage, upkeep of property, advertising, and the selling of confiscated items. Finally, drug dealers are becoming more sophisticated and are keeping large loans attached to their property to protect themselves from the forfeiture laws. Forfeiture can work and has worked on the coast of Florida, but once again, good police management means proactive planning.

The *imposition of fines* may prove useful and are much like user fees. Many departments, especially those in rich suburbs, have had to impose fines for false alarms coming from burglar alarms. Responding to false alarms is a waste of police time. In Danbury, Connecticut, a survey revealed that 12 percent of the police service calls were due to burglar alarms, but only 0.01 percent of the alarms were due to any criminal activity. Los Angeles did a survey and found that there was a 97.9 percent false alarm rate in 1983, which cost the department nearly $100,000 in police officers' time (Stellwagen and Wylie, 1985: 60).

Miami, Florida has a sliding scale with a yearly fee of $25; if there are no false alarms, subsequent yearly renewals are free. Each user is given five free false alarms and then the following fee system is imposed (Stellwagen and Wylie, 1985: 60–61):

$25 for false alarms 6 through 8

$50 and a letter from the alarm service saying that the system works for false alarm 9, with number 10 being free

$100 for false alarm 11, with number 12 being free

$250 and police inspection for false alarm 13, with numbers 14 and 15 being free

$350 for false alarm 16, with numbers 17 through 19 being free

$500 for each subsequent false alarm

Miami collected $270,000 in permit charges and false-alarm fees for 1983. The object is to reduce the false-alarm rate by making those people who create the unnecessary work pay for it.

There is also the fable of the boy who cried "wolf" when there was no wolf. With these many false alarms crying "wolf," police officers may be less than alert when the alarms and the burglars actually get together.

Finally, the IRS gives a finder's fee to people who turn in tax evaders. The city of Atlanta found that they were able to turn in tax evaders in terms of investigation of racketeers. Atlanta has an arrangement whereby the finder fees are to be paid to the city through the comptroller for Atlanta.

Throughout the country, police budgets are becoming pinched. This section points out some strategies that police managers may use to supplement their police budget while doing a great deal of good for their departments.

SHORT-RANGE PLANS

Up to this point we have been examining planning as a long-range endeavor. Of the types discussed, fiscal planning comes closest to short-range planning in that immediate needs in the fiscal year are normally analyzed in terms of function and performance. However, for long-range planning to work, specific objectives and even orders need to be created to carry out the plan. Long-range plans also need feedback-evaluation systems that can be used to modify the plan as it is operationally carried out.

Operational Plan

Long-range planning, including fiscal planning, sets the basic principles and the context for short-range operational planning. To carry out any planning, specific procedures have to be drawn up and implemented. Operational plans control the day-to-day activity of the police organization in a uniform manner. Specific procedures have to be created to carry out police duties in a predictable manner so that there can be accountability and consistency.

1. *The duty manual.* The major example of an operational plan, although many police chief executives do not realize it is an operational plan, is the standard police duty manual. The duty manual creates standard operation procedures for the department, including job descriptions and authority relationships. Specifics such as procedures concerning the use of deadly force may be a combination of law and operational procedures created in a standard order by the police agency. However, the list

of operational procedures includes virtually every operation of the police agency (patrol procedure, evidence flow, civil emergencies, line-up procedures, etc.). Although often codified in a duty manual, operational procedures are changed according to condition. Thus, the duty manual is supplemented by both temporary operating procedures (TOPs) and standard operating procedures (SOPs). If these two supplementary procedures are in place, they may become part of the duty manual. However, one problem with this type of procedure is in keeping the SOPs and TOPs to a minimum so that the duty manual is a useful document. Another problem is to have the duty manual be comprehensive enough to cover operations but not so bulky that it loses its utility.

2. *Patrol planning.* Another major example of an operational plan and one that dominates a department is a **patrol allocation plan**. The overwhelming majority of resources in a police agency are devoted to patrol. Table 13–2 shows the general trends that have occurred in patrol planning through a comparison of traditional and recent plans. Items in the traditional categories really require no planning; the chief simply divides the patrol force into three shifts and maps out patrol zones based on the geography of the municipality and some personal rule of thumb. Plans reviewed by Levine and McEwen (1985: 9) involve obtaining activity data. Patrol personnel and vehicles are allocated according to calls for service which include both service and crime incident responses.

TABLE 13–2
TRENDS IN PATROL PLANNING

TRADITIONAL	RECENT
Equal staffing on three shifts	Staffing proportional to work load
	Overlapping shifts for extra coverage during peak demand periods
Little emphasis on scheduling	Overlapping and delayed shifts implemented
	Development of models to guide scheduling decisions
Enough patrol units available to provide an immediate mobile response to all calls for service	Enough patrol units available to provide an immediate mobile response to emergency calls for service
	Diverting calls for service to telephone reporting units, queuing calls for delayed response, setting appointments for taking reports, referring calls to other agencies
Time not spent on calls for service largely devoted to unstructured, random patrol (preventive patrol)	Non call-for-service time spent on both routine patrol and directed patrol
	Directed patrol assignments planned in response to problems identified through crime analysis
Minimal analysis of patrol operations	Increased use of data processing for analysis
	Routine monitoring of reports generated for management
	Recognition of the integrated relationship of patrol with other police functions and inclusion of representatives from such functions in decisions that affect patrol

Source: Levine and McEwen (1985: 9).

There are a number of patrol planning models that are used in the United States. One developed by the International Chiefs of Police Association and used in New York and elsewhere involves measuring calls for service to determine the amount of patrol posts and staff needed to fill these posts. This is done according to the following steps:

1. The total calls for service for each tour of duty are obtained for one year (12 months).

2. The 12-month total is multiplied by the average time required to respond to a call for service and complete the preliminary investigation. This provides the number of hours per year spent in handling calls for service. Previous studies show that the average time required to investigate adequately at the preliminary level by members of a patrol force is 45 minutes (.75 hours).

3. The hours per year in calls for service is multiplied by 3. This is a "buffer" factor to account for the time spent on preventative patrol, inspectional services, vehicle servicing, and personal needs. This gives total patrol hours.

4. The total hours are divided by 2,920, the number of hours necessary to staff one post on one 8-hour shift for one year (8 hours x 365 = 2,920). The quotient equals the minimum number of patrol posts needed for the particular tour of duty (McDougall, 1992: 15).

The above model was used to review staffing for a small police department located in upstate New York. The first step was to determine the number of patrol posts, which is outlined in Table 13–3.

TABLE 13–3
DETERMINING PATROL POSTS FOR A POLICE DEPARTMENT

SHIFT HOURS	ACTUAL CALLS FOR SERVICE
7 A.M.–3 P.M.	2,781
3 P.M.–11 P.M.	3,810
11 P.M.–7 A.M.	2,336

Next these numbers were multiplied by .75 to get the average time expended by officers on a call over the year.

SHIFT HOURS	APPROXIMATE TIME EXPENDED
7 A.M.–3 P.M.	2,085.75
3 P.M.–11 P.M.	2,857.5
11 P.M.–7 A.M.	1,752

These figures are converted to include a buffer and time for routine patrol activity (× 3).

SHIFT HOURS	PROJECTED TIME EXPENDED
7 a.m.–3 p.m.	6,257.25 hours/year
3 p.m.–11 p.m.	8,572.5 hours/year
11 p.m.–7 a.m.	5,256 hours/year

TABLE 13-3 (CONT'D)

These numbers are then divided by 2,920 (the total hours needed to fill an eight-hour post for one year 365 × 8 = 2,920).

SHIFT HOURS	POST NEEDED
7 a.m.–3 p.m.	2.14
3 p.m.–11 p.m.	2.93
11 p.m.–7 a.m.	1.80

Source: McDougall (1992: 17).

Once posts have been determined, the next step is to obtain the number of personnel to staff these posts. Because of regular days off, sick days, holidays, personal leave and other factors, an assignment availability factor must be determined. This is obtained by subtracting the number of "average hours off" from 2,920 hours, which is the total number of hours needed to cover a shift. For this police department, Table 13-4 calculates the assignment/availability factor.

TABLE 13-4
DETERMINING ASSIGNMENT/AVAILABILITY FACTOR

FACTOR	NUMBER OF DAYS × 8	=	HOURS OFF
Reg. Days Off	104.62	=	836.96
Vacation	27.41	=	219.28
Personal Leave	4.95	=	39.60
Sick/Injury	15.84	=	126.72
Holidays	12.00	=	96.00
Court Time	1.60	=	12.80
Training	11.81	=	94.48
Other	0.84	=	6.72
Total	179.07		1,432.56 Average Hours Off

HOURS IN STAFF-YEAR		AVERAGE HOURS OFF		HOURS AVAILABLE
2,920	−	1,432.56	=	1,487.44

TOTAL HOURS IN A STAFF-YEAR		HOURS AVAILABLE		ASSIGNMENT/AVAILABILITY FACTOR
2,920	÷	1,487.44	=	1.96

Source: McDougall (1992: 17).

The figure of 1,432.56 is the number of hours an officer is away from duty each year. This is subtracted from 2,920 hours to produce an hours available figure of 1,487.44. An assignment/availability factor is obtained by dividing the available hours figure of 1,432.56 hours into 2,920 hours which creates a factor of 1.96, the number of personnel needed to fill each post. Table 13–5 applied this factor to determine staffing for this department, which was found to need 14 people.

TABLE 13–5
RECOMMENDED STAFFING FOR A SMALL POLICE DEPARTMENT

POST	7 A.M.–3 P.M.	3 P.M.–11 P.M.	11 P.M.–7 A.M.	RAW SCORE	STAFF NEEDED
Chief*	1.00			1.00	1
Lieutenant*		1.00	1.00	2.00	2
Post #1	1.96	1.96	1.96	5.88	6
Post #2	1.96	1.96		3.92	4
Secretary	1.00			1.00	1
				Total =	14

*Supervisory ranks are given a value of 1.00.
Source: McDougall (1992: 18).

The Myth of Rapid Response

Although response time is part of the planning model, a word of caution must be exercised. Police managers have often felt that if their response was 2 minutes or less to service calls, this was a mark of an efficient department. The opposite may well be true. A 2-minute response to every service call may mean that the patrol force is not properly distributed. Response is important to emergencies and crimes in progress. For most other service calls, the 2-minute response is normally irrelevant.

There were a number of studies critical of response time in the 1970s (Meyer, 1976; Bercal, 1970; Maxfield, 1979; Reiss, 1971). Less than 20 percent of service calls are related to criminal matters with emergency calls accounting for less than 15 percent of the service calls. Even in relation to crime, normally too much time elapses from the time the crime is committed and when police are called. Cohen and McEwen (1984: 4) report that "research (Farmer, 1981; Spelman and Brown, 1981) showed that police response time had no effect on the chances of on-scene arrest in 70 to 85 percent of serious crime cases." Are citizens dissatisfied with slower response time? The answer is that citizens are dissatisfied only if they expect rapid response time. However, "if callers were told to expect a delay, their satisfaction did not significantly decrease if response time was slower" (Cohen and McEwen, 1984: 4).

Response time may be helpful for emergencies and a few cases of crimes in progress; overall, departments should be careful not to place too much emphasis on providing rapid response for all service calls. Complaint clerks who take calls for service and dispatchers who dispatch the vehicles need specialized training. This includes training in telephone courtesy, screening, and referrals to other agencies. All agencies need to use a priority classification dispatching system.

The operational plans serve as control mechanisms for management by providing guidelines for employees, both civilian and uniformed. Operational plans give supervisors a means of evaluating personnel in relation to specific duties that are clearly defined and in writing. Evaluation and discipline can only take place in the light of written guidelines that both supervisory personnel and line officers understand. They have to be clearly stated, unambiguous in content, and practical enough to be carried out on a daily basis. They also have to have internal consistency and be in line with the long-range goals of the department, including the philosophy of social utility and law enforcement that is demanded by the community in which the police agency is located.

CONTINGENCY PLANS

These are plans that are made for specific events and occurrences but are not part of the daily duties of the police department personnel. This type of planning demands some specific detail in terms of procedures, but because of changing conditions in the field, it often demands more flexibility than do other types of planning. There are two major types of contingency plans:

1. *Tactical plans*, which are plans for major events, such as crowd control at athletic events and VIP escorts.
2. *Emergency plans*, which are plans for general situations with the specifics to be inserted when the emergency occurs. When done in conjunction with other agencies, this type of planning is often termed *planning for emergency mobilizations*.

Tactical plans are formulated based on what is expected to take place. A recurrent event is one that is expected to happen again; however, the time and place of the event may not be known. Tactical plans are made for mundane events (parades, political rallies) as well as for natural disasters (blizzards, floods).

Emergencies come and go, and no one can predict when they will strike. However, contingency plans offer a general framework for action with the specifics to be inserted when the emergency occurs. Emergency planning has been considered by some police managers as a type of tactical plan for unusual occurrences and crisis situations.

EMERGENCY MOBILIZATIONS

These include the police reaction to natural disasters, riots, civilian disorders, terrorism, and episodes that normally come under the hearing of civil defense. The police agency has to be organized to become part of an overall plan for mobilization of all government and private assistance organizations. This generally calls for specific contingency planning that every department and municipality should do. The National Advisory Commission on Criminal Justice Standards and Goals has outlined what should be included in such planning (1976: 44-45):

1. The steps to be taken so as to proclaim, or cause to be proclaimed, a state of emergency and the executive and administrative consequences of such a proclamation.

2. Publication and diffusion of the proclamation and its consequences to the general public.

3. Emergency lines of responsibility among the various components of civil authority and relationships with other Federal, State, and local authorities.

4. Any alternative locations, facilities, and modes of operation as an authority.

5. The safeguarding of existing communications systems and the developing of secure alternative systems.

6. Rumor control and maintenance of effective communication with the public.

7. The protection and continuance of vital community services.

8. Clarification of the powers of governmental personnel who are taken hostage or otherwise incapacitated from acting as required by law.

9. The safeguarding of vital archives and documentation.

10. Any measures of public relief for victims of crime involving civil disorder, terrorism, and similar acts of extraordinary violence, and others whose lives have been disrupted.

This is basically a planning function followed by training. The planning unit of every department working closely with top management should develop standard mutual assistance pacts with other police agencies with specific areas of responsibilities being set out. This is not limited to natural disasters such as blizzards, fires, and so on, but can also include political demonstrations and rock concerts. Management must have enough contingency planning so that if and when disaster strikes, the police will be prepared and trained for mobilization and will exercise direct leadership.

The National Advisory Commission also makes the following recommendation that cannot be ignored by any police department if contingency planning is to be effective (1976: 221): "In general, one principle should govern all planning for such emergency command patterns; wherever feasible, the source of operational direction should be the designated emergency field commander from the agency with primary law enforcement responsibility in the jurisdiction where the incident is located or centered." The exception is "when one cooperating agency—even though it does not have primary responsibility—has an overwhelming advantage in size or expertise over another." Even where a large number of cooperating agencies exist, overall command has to be established and information has to be shared. Mutual aid agreements should include local, county, and state police, and the National Guard.

For this system to operate effectively, there must be annual training and field exercises. The field exercises are especially important for the long-term coordination of communication and the sharing of intelligence.

Police Response to Special Populations: Networking

Police have been called in for assistance in areas such as the public inebriate, the mentally ill, and the homeless. However, these are not police problems but problems that really demand a human-services solution. Deinstitutionalization of the mentally ill and the inebriate have left many of these people on the street, often without adequate housing. It makes sense for police to use the human-service-agency network when it is available. However, this cannot be done at random. Police managers need to do the following (Finn and Sullivan, 1987: 6):

1. Develop a formal agreement to collaborate—preferably a written document that commits each group to the partnership.
2. Describe the specific activities in the agreements that each party in the network will undertake.
3. Sooner or later involve every important agency and facility that provides emergency services to the target population.
4. Make sure that the arrangements benefit every participant.

Los Angeles has created a special relationship with the County Department of Mental Health, while the Boston Police work with the Pine Street Inn, which serves 3,000 to 4,000 homeless each year, and San Diego has a 7-minute drop-off for public inebriates at an inebriate reception center. The sheriff in Washtenaw County, Michigan has developed a two-tier approach to assisting the mentally ill. The executive directors of the sheriff's department, community mental health department, community services agency, county planning department, department of social services, public health department, and the United Way formed a *policy team*. At the same time midlevel managers from these agencies formed an *operational team* to oversee day-to-day operations.

These are just a few examples where police agency networking can go from just one agency to multiple agency agreements. The benefits of the approach are many, as shown in Table 13–6.

TABLE 13–6
BENEFITS FROM NETWORKING

FOR LAW ENFORCEMENT	FOR THE SOCIAL SERVICE SYSTEM
Saves time: reduces or eliminates need to: Stabilize the situation at the scene. "Shop" for an available facility. Wait at the facility. Book the individual. Make repeat runs for the same individual. Testify in court.	*Saves time:* reduces or eliminates need to: Evaluate, treat, or transfer inappropriate referrals.
Reduces danger, because: Trained staff take over volatile situations. Social workers warn officers about potentially dangerous cases. Officers receive training in handling problem persons.	*Reduces danger*, because: Officers come quickly to help in situations involving violence in the facility or in a home.
Increases job satisfaction, because: Fewer repeat cases are handled. Feedback on case results is provided. Positive relationships with social service workers develop. Homicides involving problem persons and jail suicides are reduced. Municipal police department working relationships improve with jail officials concerned about overcrowding. Dispositions are available that are more appropriate than jail or doing nothing.	*Improves job performance*, because: Clients are referred to facilities that have treated them before. Trained officers testify at commitment hearings. Agency's image in the community improves. Positive relationships develop with law enforcement officers. Client contact with criminal justice system is reduced.

FOR LOCAL GOVERNMENT OFFICIALS

Increases political support, because:
Constituents are pleased to see a serious community problem addressed.
Business people are pleased to have the downtown made more attractive to customers.
Embarrassing incidents are less likely to occur.

Prevents political crises and unexpected expenses, because:
Chances of a law suit are reduced.
Jail overcrowding is alleviated.

Source: Finn and Sullivan (1987: 7).

 # CONCLUSION

Planning is an important tool for proactive police managers so that they can anticipate events and, in some sense, respond. A number of definitions were offered regarding planning, which, in essence, consists of developing a method to achieve organizational goals.

As we noted, all police agencies, consciously or unconsciously, engage in planning. Planning is useful to the police organization in that it operationalizes rational decision-making procedures for organizational policies. It also assists in defining organizational roles for all members of the agency. Whether there is a formal planning unit or one officer or manager assigned to the planning task, planning involves disseminating information, and assisting in the managerial decision-making process.

The planning process for our purposes consists of six functions, namely (1) recognition and analysis of a problem, (2) setting objectives, (3) gathering data, (4) making a plan of attack, (5) attaining agreement of those involved in the plan, and (6) evaluation. Various types of plans were discussed.

Specific attention was devoted to fiscal planning. Three widely used budgets—line-item, PPBS, and zero-based—were presented, and their strengths and weaknesses were analyzed.

The chapter examined some innovations in the planning process: (1) procedures to supplement the police budget, including donation programs, forfeiture, user fees, and the imposition of fines; (2) a model for patrol planning: automated resource allocation; and (3) responses to special populations such as the mentally ill, the homeless, and the public inebriate through networking with social service agencies.

We also looked at the myth of rapid response. This example showed the need to plan with specific goals in mind and not waste limited resources on responding to all service calls within 2 minutes. Rapid response should be limited to crime in progress and emergencies. While the chapter emphasized long-range planning, we included short-range, contingency, and emergency mobilization planning, as they are also important to all police agencies.

The economic realities of the 1990s demand responsible fiscal and contingency planning. Expertise, anticipation of events, evaluation, and the responsible supervision of personnel are the traits that will characterize police managers of the future.

QUESTIONS FOR REVIEW

1. What are the benefits of planning for police organization?
2. List the duties of a planning officer or a planning unit.
3. What are the main steps of the planning process?
4. Discuss three types of plans.
5. What are the differences between long-range and short-range planning?
6. Why is budgeting the important part of the managerial process?
7. What are the main attributes of emergency mobilizations?

CLASS PROJECTS

1. Police budgets are public documents. Obtain from a department an operating budget for the past fiscal year, and answer the following questions:

   a. What portion of the budget is devoted to personnel costs (e.g., salaries, benefits, overtime), equipment, training, and miscellaneous items?

   b. What is the fiscal year for this department?

   c. Is this budget document representative of line-item, PPBS, or ZBB fiscal planning?

   d. If possible, try to determine whether this budget represents an increase or decrease in police costs when compared with the budget for the year before. If a large increase or decrease is noted, in what areas did they occur? What do you suspect are the reasons for the increase or decrease?

2. The police department of your community has asked your class to help with the planning of a Fourth of July parade. According to the mayor, this will be the "biggest parade ever." With consideration of geographical variables in your community, prepare a plan to provide police coverage for this parade. Your instructor will supply the needed additional information (proposed number of marchers, units, general route). Your plan must take into account all factors related to police operations during the event and the costs for such coverage. Follow the guidelines in this chapter.

KEY TERMS

budgets
centralization
contingency plans
decentralization
emergency mobilization
evaluation
forfeiture
intuitive approach
instrumental planning

line-item budgeting
networking
normative planning
operational plans
patrol allocation plan
planning
PPBS
zero-based budgeting

BIBLIOGRAPHY

BERCAL, THOMAS E., "Calls for Police Assistance: Consumer Demands for Public Service." *American Behavioral Scientist*, 13, no. 5/6 (May/June 1970). pp. 681-91.

COHEN, MARCIA, and J. THOMAS MCEWEN, "Handling Calls for Service: Alternatives to Traditional Policing," *NIJ Reports*, no. 187 (1984), pp. 4-8.

FARMER, MICHAEL T., ed., *Differential Police Response Strategies.* Washington, D.C.: Police Executive Research Forum, 1981.

FINN, PETER, and MONIQUE SULLIVAN, *Police Response to Special Populations.* Washington, D.C.: National Institute of Justice, 1987.

GAZELL, JAMES A., "O. W. Wilson's Essential Legacy for Police Administrators," *Journal of Police Science and Administration*, 2, no. 4 (December 1974), pp. 365-75.

_____. "William H. Parker, Police Professionalism and the Public: An Assessment." *Journal of Police Science and Administration*, 4, no. 1 (March 1976), pp. 28-37.

HUDZIK, JOHN K. and others, *Criminal Justice Manpower Planning: An Overview.* Washington, D.C.: U.S. Government Printing Office, 1981.

KEY, V. O., JR., "The Lack of Budgetary Theory," in Albert C. Hyde and Jay M. Shafritz, eds., *Government Budgeting: Theory, Process, Politics.* Oak Park, Ill.: Moore, 1978, pp. 35-38.

LARSON, RICHARD C., and MICHAEL F. CAHN, *Synthesizing and Extending the Results of Police Patrol Studies.* Washington, D.C.: U.S. Department of Justice, 1985.

LEVINE, MARGARET J., and J. THOMAS MCEWEN, *Patrol Deployment.* Washington, D.C.: U.S. Department of Justice, 1985.

LEWIS, VERNE B., "Toward a Theory of Budgeting," in Albert C. Hyde and Jay M. Shafritz, eds., *Government Budgeting: Theory, Process, Politics.* Oak Park, Ill.: Moore, 1978, pp. 221-35.

LYNCH, LAWRENCE, *Fulton Police Department: A Management Study.* Syracuse, N.Y.: Privately Printed, 1976.

MAGEE, JOHN F., "Decision Trees for Decision Making," in *Business Classics: Fifteen Key Concepts for Managerial Success.* Cambridge, Mass.: Harvard University Press, 1975, pp. 83-95.

MAXFIELD, MICHAEL G., *Discretion and the Delivery of Police Services: Demand, Client Characteristics and Street Level Bureaucrats in Two Cities.* Ann Arbor, Mich.: University Microfilms, 1979.

MCDOUGALL, THEODORE E., *A Study of Police Operations at the SUNY Cobleskill Campus.* Albany, N.Y.: Bureau for Municipal Police, 1992.

MEYER, JOHN C., "Empirical Analysis of Police Service Tasks: Antecedent for Management Planning," *Journal of Police Science and Administration*, 4, no. 3 (1976), pp. 264-73.

NATIONAL ADVISORY COMMITTEE ON CRIMINAL JUSTICE STANDARDS AND GOALS. *Disorders and Terrorism.* Washington, D.C.: U.S. Government Printing Office. 1976.

NIGRO, FELIX A., and LLOYD G. NIGRO, *Modern Public Administration* (4th ed.). New York: Harper & Row, 1977.

REISS, ALBERT J., JR., *The Police and the Public*. New Haven, Conn.: Yale University Press, 1971.

SCHICK, ALLEN, "The Road to PPB: The Stages of Budget Reform." in Albert C. Hyde and Jay M. Shafritz, eds., *Government Budgeting, Theory, Process, Politics*. Oak Park, Ill.: Moore, 1978, pp. 47-65.

SECKLER-HUDSON, CATHERINE, "Performance Budgeting in Government." In Albert C. Hyde and Jay M. Shafritz, eds., *Government Budgeting: Theory, Process, Politics*. Oak Park, Ill.: Moore, 1978, pp. 80-93.

SOURYAL, S.S., *Police Administration and Management*. St. Paul, Minn.: West, 1977.

SPELMAN, WILLIAM, and DALE K. BROWN, *Calling the Police: Citizen Reporting of Serious Crime*. Washington, D.C.: Police Executive Research Forum, 1981.

STELLWAGEN, LINDSEY D., and KIMBERLY A. WYLIE, *Strategies for Supplementing the Police Budget*. Washington, D.C.: National Institute of Justice, 1985.

TAYLOR, GRAEME M., "Introduction to Zero-Based Budgeting." in Albert C. Hyde and Jay M. Shafritz, eds., *Government Budgeting: Theory, Process, Politics*. Oak Park, Ill.: Moore, 1978, pp. 284-92.

WILDAVSKY, AARON, and ARTHUR HAMMOND, "Comprehensive Versus Incremental Budgeting," in Albert C. Hyde and Jay M. Shafritz, eds., *Government Budgeting: Theory, Process, Politics*. Oak Park, Ill.: Moore, 1978, pp. 236-51.

WILSON, O.W., *Police Administration*. New York: McGraw-Hill, 1952.

14

Collective Bargaining and Police Management

The emergence of police unions has had a major influence on police operations and basic management decisions. Unionism has led to

- The use of job actions to attain goals after negotiations have stalemated.
- The increasing atmosphere of police activism reflected not only at the bargaining table but in outside political lobbying over various issues affecting police services to the community.
- The wide variety of items found in labor contracts that were once deemed areas of management decision.

In this chapter, we examine the development of police unionism and its effect on the police manager. Specific attention is given to collective bargaining, for this is one of the most important managerial processes affecting the police organization today.

 COLLECTIVE BARGAINING DEFINED

According to Bowers (1973: 6), **collective bargaining** is the process by which representatives of labor and management negotiate wages and working conditions for a given employment entity. For both the public and private labor sectors, bargaining is chiefly an economic enterprise in which two sides negotiate over how much money management will give employees for their work. For the private labor sector, collective bargaining is termed a bilateral process in that management and the union representing the employee unit are the two factions that determine the increases that will be given to union members.

In the public sector, politics enters the situation as a third force. The addition of this third factor leads to what is termed a *multilateral labor relationship*; that is, more than two parties are involved. For example, in the preparation of a departmental budget, the budget planner must obtain information from a number of sources before presenting the final proposal. Moreover, in government there are many persons who must have their say to protect their own self-interests. In the case of public labor unions, the chief effect is on the range and cost of services provided to the community. The length of time that these public managers remain in their positions is often determined by how effectively and economically these services are provided to the community.

Other interest groups also enter into the collective bargaining relationship. In 1978 in Annapolis, Maryland after negotiations had broken down between the city and the Fraternal Order of Police, union members of the department drove unwashed patrol cars and held up traffic by driving at a rate of 10 miles per hour during rush hour while their spouses picketed in front of the police station. These actions finally forced the city to agree to a 5 percent pay hike. The labor negotiations were thus expanded not only to the political administration but also to spouses and public pressure. In other negotiations, outside actors entering into the situation may include the judiciary, the governor, and the civil service commission, as well as the management of the police department. Nevertheless, politics remain an important factor in the multilateral relationship between the police union and municipal or state management.

The strong political influence on collective bargaining of the municipality or state becomes particularly apparent around election time. This was highlighted in a study of a county election in which the candidate for district attorney made a concerted effort to receive endorsements based on his position of law and order from every police benevolent association in the county. The endorsements received were used in public relations and in a media campaign to other voters.

 HISTORY OF POLICE UNIONISM

In 1919, the **Boston Police Department** went on strike in an attempt to increase officers' wages. Although other police departments had used the strike tactic as a means of protest, the Boston strike gained nationwide attention, in large part because of the looting, robberies, and general disorder that occurred after it was apparent that there were no patrolmen on the streets. Massachusetts governor Calvin Coolidge eventually ordered the state guard into Boston to police the city and replace the striking officers with auxiliaries.

Observers of the Boston police strike (Gammage and Sachs, 1972; Juris and Feuille, 1973) agree that the actions taken by state authorities in quelling the strike retarded the development of unionism in American police forces for the next 50 years. Prior to 1919, many metropolitan police departments had formed social clubs to serve as liaison between the officers and the municipality for the purpose of improving wages and conditions of employment. In Boston, an invitation had already been tendered to the Boston Social Club by the American Federation of Labor to join the national organization. This invitation was soon withdrawn after the strike. The wave of public support toward Massachusetts authorities in their blanket dismissal of the strikers signaled to other budding police labor unions that union militancy would not receive support either from the public or national labor organizations.

Police unionism in the United States remained dormant until the 1960s, although a few police benevolent associations did join national labor groups for public employees. This general trend held not only for police officers but also for all public employees. That is, in the public sector between 1920 and 1950, unionism was opposed by both public management and their employees. While wage scales for public employees generally lagged those of private workers, significant benefits were earned by government workers in the form of job security via civil service and a generous system of vacation and personal leave.

After World War II, three main developments altered this trend:

1. An expansion of government services coupled by an increase of government employees.

2. A continued policy by the federal government that supported the right of public and private workers to unionize and bargain collectively. For the public sector, this culminated in 1962 with President Kennedy's signing of Executive Order 10988, which allowed most federal employees to organize unions and bargain collectively. Further refinements of Executive Order 10988 were signed by Presidents Johnson, Nixon, and Ford.

3. A significant decline of union membership in the private sector. This trend forced many private union organizations to look for new membership, readily available in the public sector.

It became apparent to many public employees that there was no reason why they should not receive salaries and conditions of employment similar to those earned by their private counterparts in an affluent society. Unions, which were at one time spurned by public employees, were now welcomed as a means by which to achieve employee demands. Private and public union organizations welcomed these new members with open arms to boost sagging union membership. Lobbying efforts were initiated by these union organizations to have cities and states enact comprehensive collective-bargaining statutes modeled on the existing federal statutes enacted by the federal government as well as certain cities and states. Starting in the late 1950s, such statutes were enacted by New York City (1956), Wisconsin (1959), and New York State (1967) (Juris and Feuille, 1973).

It is not surprising that the trend to unionize by public employees was readily accepted by many police officers at this time. These officers felt that they were underpaid and the frequent object of public abuse and criticism for a variety of social problems, particularly, the rise in crime. While low pay became the chief determinant for the rise of police unions, an equally significant factor arose from poor personnel practices that were commonplace in many police organizations. According to Juris and Feuille (1973: 21), practices often cited as a source of contention were:

> Lack of internal civil and constitutional rights for officers being investigated for misfeasance and malfeasance.
>
> Lack of a functional grievance procedure.
>
> Being called to duty and held on standby or called to court, for no compensation.
>
> Having to lose a day's pay as penalties for rule infractions.
>
> No premium pay for overtime work.
>
> Being transferred from one shift or job to another with little or no advance warning.
>
> Physical and verbal intimidation and degradation by superior officers.

This demand for higher wages and improved working conditions can also be traced to the influx of younger officers, many with college degrees, who balked at a militaristic bureaucracy that demanded blind obedience. Moreover, the militancy that is often attached to police unionism should come as no surprise. This attitude reflected the mood of the 1960s in which protest and activism were the main tactics of generally all social change groups, ranging from students to minority groups. It is no wonder that many police union groups became particularly adept at protest tactics (calling in with "blue flu," wearing sneakers while in uniform, not shaving, engaging in street protests) by simply borrowing such methods from groups that they had fought against.

 POLICE UNIONS TODAY

Most police unions in the United States today are local organizations that may or may not be affiliated with a national parent organizational. The reason for this local orientation is that wages, benefits, and conditions of employment, including promotions, are heavily dependent upon local economic and political conditions. The police department is the arm of local government. Unlike multinational corporations with their strong national and even international unions, those who control the destinies of the nation's police are clearly tied to the local community, and in police matters, their concerns end at the community boundary.

However, police unions affiliated with national groups have received valuable assistance during negotiations and work actions by obtaining outside consultants. The national unions have developed strong campaigns to interest local police in national union affiliation. However, the response has been mixed nationally because of the strong community control over law enforcement.

State legislation on public unions has performed a significant role in the type of unions that have developed in law enforcement. The state legislation on collective bargaining can be divided into two major categories:

1. Those states that have comprehensive statutes that allow police officers to bargain collectively in some manner.

2. Those states that make it illegal for police to form a union and absolutely forbid union membership to police officers.

The general rule in both these cases is that states, in the light of the 1919 Boston strike, generally forbid police to strike.

States that do not allow bargaining by police and firefighters usually allow state agencies and municipalities to "meet and confer" with police representatives to discuss employees' issues and grievances. Despite the existence of no-bargaining statutes, many officers have joined national unions in a first step at organizing.

More and more police officers have formed benevolent organizations for social and athletic purposes. Eventually, the organization takes on many, if not most, of the characteristics of a union, and these no-union state laws are either being tested or ignored. In general, nonunion states provide some form of binding arbitration. One of the major problems with these binding-arbitration clauses is that the final decision on the contract is made (1) not by a neutral party or (2) not on an equal bargaining basis, but instead by those who are the ultimate "bosses" of the police departments, the local and state legislatures. In effect, management has great impact on the binding arbitration machinery.

In states that have comprehensive collective bargaining statutes, such as New York, Ohio, California, Wisconsin, Michigan, and New Jersey, the members of each police department are allowed to form a union. The key element for union formation resides in the union being the only recognized body to negotiate with the employer followed by the right for the union to collect dues. In certain states, such as New York, legislation allows for the **agency shop** where the union collects dues from all employees, members and nonmembership alike. The rationale is that all employees should share the cost of negotiating contracts with the employer.

A second important element in the establishment of the union is the question of the categories of employees that will be represented, otherwise known as the **community of interest**. For example, in the New York City Police Department, separate union groups represent patrol officers, supervisors, and middle managers. The community-of-interest question was complicated recently when detectives formed their own organization breaking away from the Police Benevolent Association. In other cities such as Utica, New York, all members of the department, including the chief of police, are represented by one union. In some cases, especially in smaller departments, this presents problems since the chief and his or her friends may be able to control the union and, of course, control the collective bargaining process.

Although one union is recognized as the sole representative for collective bargaining, each state law allows for a designated time period when a rival organization may solicit petitions and, if receiving a certain percentage of votes, conduct elections to contest representation. This is an important aspect for police unions that wish to become affiliated with national groups when consensus does not exist in the union membership for such a move.

Finally, states with comprehensive statutes provide a series of mechanisms to deal with disputes that cannot be resolved during the course of collective bargaining or the administration of the contract. The following are mechanisms used to avoid strikes:

> *Mediation:* a noncoercive process in which a neutral third party studies the issues in dispute between the two parties. This mediator works behind the scenes with the parties and attempts to act as a go-between in settling the dispute.
>
> *Fact finding:* another noncoercive procedure by which a third party gathers evidence from the two parties and then offers a solution. The recommendations may be publicly released in an effort to have community pressure enter into the settling of the dispute.
>
> *Arbitration:* as opposed to fact finding and mediation, a third-party process in which an official body or representative of a state arbitration board studies the issues in dispute and then makes a ruling. This decision may then be binding upon both parties, depending upon statute.

These three processes are used to settle disputes between labor and management during the course of collective bargaining when an impasse occurs.

For police and fire unions, binding arbitration is often used as a method to forestall a strike. Arbitration can also be used to settle grievances that arise during the administration of the union contract. Basically, a **grievance** occurs when either management or the union feels that the contract has been violated in some way. Grievances can also arise from a violation of the rules and regulations involving employee health, safety, physical facilities, materials, or equipment. Consider the following example of a grievance procedure:

1. A time limit of ten working days is set as a limit in which a grievance may be filed after an officer becomes aware of the event constituting the alleged grievance.

2. Informal discussion usually marks the next step. Here the employee presents his or her claim promptly to the immediate supervisor on an informal verbal basis and both parties attempt to solve the situation.

3. If the grievance is not resolved in the informal stage, and the employee wishes to continue into the grievance, a written notice is forwarded to a higher command officer. Again, a time limitation is set between the final determination made by the supervisor and the filing of written notice.

4. Within a specific period of time, the ranking supervisor must process the grievance and schedule a hearing. At the hearing, the employee presents written and oral statements on his or her position.

5. Within a specific time frame, the command officer answers in writing his or her course of action on the grievance.

6. If the grievance is still not adjusted at the command-officer level, the grievance is filed with the head of the agency. In some departments, the sheriff or the chief of police has the final say as to the determination of the grievance. In states that have comprehensive collective bargaining statutes, the grievance is handled by a public employee-relations board.

A fifth method of conflict resolution is through litigation. As Juris and Feuille point out (1973: 91), litigation is perhaps one of the strongest methods by which unions make their greatest gains. Since the courts are the traditional forum for solving disputes between public agencies, many unions, especially those in large metropolitan jurisdictions or affiliated with national organizations, have a battery of attorneys on the payroll. Litigation sponsored by police unions has produced various noteworthy cases involving drug testing, discipline, and off-duty employment.

MAJOR POLICE UNION ORGANIZATIONS

The trend in policing today appears to be increased unionization especially in those states that as yet do not allow police officers to form unions. Nonunion police departments are the rule rather than the exception in the South and the Midwest, whereas unions are especially strong in the Northeast and on the West Coast as states in those areas have comprehensive collective bargaining statutes.

There is also the additional trend for many local police unions to affiliate with national groups to strengthen their bargaining position and increase union benefits to members. The main national union groups are:

> *International Union of Police Associations:* founded in 1953, grew in membership to 150 departments representing 150,000 police officers. In December 1978, this organization split apart after a decision was made to affiliate with the American Federation of Labor–Congress of Industrial Organizations (AFL–CIO). Many departments were opposed to the higher dues and the greater percentage of this money that went directly to the national organizations. Today there are two groups that have been created from the old IUPA organizational structure. The International Conference of Police

Associations continues to be affiliated with the AFL–CIO, while the National Association of Police Officers is composed of those police unions that opposed the merger. Despite their organizational rivalries, both groups consider themselves national professional bodies and seek to create a national police union.

Fraternal Order of Police: although it is the oldest police organization in the United States, the FOP is basically a professional organization that emphasizes collective bargaining in some areas or exists mainly as a social organization in others. Each lodge is independent of control from the national organization. The FOP claims to have 100,000 members representing 9,000 police organizations.

International Brotherhood of Police Officers: founded in Rhode Island in 1969, the emphasis of the IBPO is strictly on collective bargaining. The national organization sends advisors to the local organizations during collective bargaining negotiations.

International Brotherhood of Teamsters: a private union that was quick to see the potential for government workers to increase membership. Estimates of police officer membership range as high as 15,000. Many police union officials (and management as well) distrust the Teamsters due to its long history of organized crime influence and mismanagement of pension funds via low-interest or no-interest loans to gangsters. Nevertheless, the Teamsters are aggressive in seeking public-sector membership and are presently in recruitment and organization drives in those Southern states that forbid police to form unions.

Black Officer Associations: these have been formed in police departments that have a high percentage of minority officers as well as a record of prejudice and discrimination against these officers in terms of recruitment, promotions, or job assignments. Examples of these associations are the Guardians in New York City and Hartford, Connecticut; the Afro-American Patrolmen's League of Chicago; and the Oakland, California Black Officer's Association. These associations usually remain apart from the union structure of their departments and attempt to settle differences between their members and management by direct negotiations and political lobbying.

American Federation of State, County, and Municipal Employees: affiliated with the American Federation of Labor, this union for public employees was founded in 1936. AFSCME was the first organization to make serious attempts to enroll public employees in the decades before the rise of union membership in 1960.

The long-term organizational goal for many of these groups is the creation of a national police union. This appeared to be a real possibility in the 1970s with the large increases in membership and activism associated with police unions.

The decentralization of American police, the state of the economy, and the changing nature of American unionism makes a national union less likely in the 1990s.

Police wages and benefits are tied directly to local tax rates and political processes. As the industrial base economy has changed from one based on sales to one based on the transfer of information, general union membership has declined. The old Northeast–Midwest industrial belt has suffered the closing of plants and the migration of workers to the sun belt as global corporations have taken over the production of essential goods. As wages, benefits, and company policies become based on participatory management, workers may increasingly shun unions.

The national industrial labor union model once sought by many police unions today may be outmoded. What is more likely, as a trend, is the creation of statewide police lobby groups, since state laws and economic policies have a greater impact on the locally based municipal police. A lobby group is created for the purpose of influencing state legislation favorable to the interest of the union (lobbying). Trends of this nature have occurred in New York, Wisconsin, and Texas.

MANAGEMENT RIGHTS AND COLLECTIVE BARGAINING: A DILEMMA

The most crucial factor facing the police administrator—managing the agency—arises from the emergence of collective bargaining and police unionism. Union contracts today contain a variety of clauses affecting police operations. For example, the union contract may specify that two troopers must be assigned to patrol vehicles during the midnight watch. Decisions of this nature would appear to be the prerogative of management. Yet there are two general reasons why such clauses appear in union contracts.

First, the police management role in collective bargaining in the 1960s was generally characterized as either negligent or nonexistent. Due to the multilateral nature of the process, negotiations often were carried on by a member of the state or municipal personnel office who may or may not have advised the police agency affected by the outcome of the contract. On the other side of the table, union negotiators were generally better prepared to argue their demands, strengthening their position with the use of outside consultants for expertise on issues and tactics.

Second, not all infringements on managerial prerogative occurred by the collective bargaining process. In some case, police departments were forced to comply with union demands via binding arbitration rulings through grievances or court litigation. In Cleveland, an arbitrator ruled that officers assigned to patrol a high-crime housing project would have to patrol in pairs since many of these projects were "snakepits" in terms of "patrolmen taking a probable hazard" in policing these areas (Anon., 1979a: 21).

Arbitration and legal rulings such as the one in Cleveland have forced many law enforcement administrators to undertake participatory management in the formulation of policy within their agencies. In many cases, grievance and litigation proceedings may be avoided in having union input as a part of the policy decision-making process. On the other hand, militant unions may harass management through their use of grievances at every turn of the corner.

The first step in "making the rules" with union infringement on managerial rights lies with the management rights clause in the contract. A model clause prepared by the National League of Cities states (Rynecki, Cairns, and Carnes, 1978: 7):

> The parties agree that all subjects not specifically listed here are retained by the city, and the union further agrees to waive its rights to grieve concerning the contemplation, approval, application, implementation or adoption of any management rights, whether heretofore listed, regardless of the frequency of exercise.

In simple terms, this contract language states that management has certain rights that may not be grieved by the union even if such rights are not exercised on a frequent basis. According to the International Association of Chiefs of Police, such rights include the right to (1977: 80–81):

1. Establish departmental rules and procedures.
2. Schedule overtime work as required in the manner most advantageous to the employer.
3. Discipline and discharge for cause.
4. Lay off employees if the need arises.
5. Transfer employees and transfer governmental operations.
6. Consolidate the operations of two or more departments and to reorganize the operations within a department.

Nevertheless, the union should be consulted on important matters affecting the operations of the department simply because it is good administrative procedure. The existence of a management-rights clause is not the final solution in the ability to manage without union interference. Unpopular decisions still may be the basis for a lawsuit or for resistance by personnel. Yet there remains the need for such a clause as it is the first line of defense if a decision is grieved and reaches arbitration. Management can point to this clause as part of the contractual agreement.

 ## THE COLLECTIVE BARGAINING PROCESS

The goals and objectives of police management and labor in the collective bargaining process are similar although they may differ somewhat in detail and substance and substantially in the means to obtain these goals.

Management	*Labor*
1. Provide fair and adequate pay for all employees including a reasonable and competitive compensation package for management.	1. Provide fair and adequate pay for all employees in the bargaining unit along with a solid fringe benefit package.
2. Maintain managerial efficiency producing an efficiently run police department.	2. Respect police officers as individuals and as a group along with an efficiently-run police department.
3. Preserve the public interest in policing the community.	3. Preserve the public interest in policing the community.
4. Have employees identify with managerial and departmental objectives, along with a positive esprit de corps and high morale.	4. Have a positive esprit de corps, with high morale and the creation of departmental objectives that are mutually beneficial to both the department and the sworn officers.
5. Have adequately trained officers that respond in a professionally-oriented manner to management's needs, objectives, and specific orders.	5. Have adequately trained officers who have good working conditions and who respond in a professional manner to the reasonable requests of officers by management personnel.

These objectives are complex because police personnel relations are complex and often not as clear as this chart would indicate (Klotz, 1978).

The language of the goals for management and labor differs along with some of the content of this language. The matter of definition becomes paramount in having good management-employee relations. The municipality setting wages and fringe benefits may differ considerably in what it considers adequate and fair pay and may well be below what the union considers fair and adequate and even below what management considers fair and adequate. The same holds true for (1) conditions and benefits of employment, (2) reasonable orders or requests, (3) mutually beneficial objectives, and (4) an efficiently run department. A major problem is the existence of three groups—(1) police management, (2) sworn officers and other police department members of the bargaining unit, and (3) municipal politicians and governmental officials—using differing definitions.

Although bargaining has been likened to horse trading, certain preparations must be made before the horse trading begins. Effective use of the collective bargaining process means that the police management team has an organization that collects data and does extensive homework on a year-round basis. The basic issues that are normally reviewed are (Klotz, 1978):

1. A review of prior contracts with key administrative personnel to see what items are in need of being updated or revised. Special attention should be given to items that have poor language or have been the source of problems or grievances with the union.

2. A review of current union agreements with other area police agencies and agencies of similar size and problems. This should be looked at in terms of remaining competitive in the market, keeping the officer's morale high, and the ability to make reasonable offers in the light of union demands.

3. Collection and analysis of economic data concerning what the municipality can afford to pay and is willing to pay given political and economic realities. This could include informal discussions with local decision-making leaders concerning what they feel is a reasonable increase in wages and benefits.

4. A thorough study and analysis of arbitration decisions awarded under the current contract or awarded to police unions.

5. Checking out rumors informally as to what are items important to the union and members of the bargaining unit and areas of dispute that might be unknown to management. By checking informally before bargaining is begun, management may make compromises and settlement possible before either party takes a solid position.

The next step in the bargaining preparation is the selection of the bargaining team. The key person of this team is the chief **negotiator** who has the authority and prestige to represent the department with credibility. The negotiator has to be able to have frank discussions with the chief concerning all issues, especially those deemed undesirable or contrary to management's best interest. He or she also has to enjoy the chief's confidence. Assisting the chief negotiator are other members of the team who generally provide two major services: (1) information retrieval and research and (2) expertise in areas with which the chief negotiator might not be familiar.

In small police agencies with limited budgets and personnel, the chief often takes an active role in the bargaining process. While it is imperative that police management be represented at the bargaining table, it is *not* recommended that the chief become his or her own negotiator. By becoming personally involved in the bargaining process, the chief may foster future morale and personal repercussions that would be detrimental to management. For example, if the chief is seen as not supporting his or her people on the issue of higher wages, this could be a blow to morale.

Some municipalities have been hiring professional negotiators, and most have found them well worth the expense. These negotiators are familiar with the labor laws and the expenses of such items as health and dental insurance. They have gone through the process thousands of times and are familiar with the rituals and customs of collective bargaining in relation to the membership, government, and the press. National unions often send professional negotiators to unions in the field when a contract is about to end. Since literally millions of dollars and the basic welfare of the department are involved, the negotiating process is really no place for amateurs.

CONTRACT ADMINISTRATION

The signing of the contract is only the continuance of the collective bargaining relationship. The contract reflects new guidelines between the employer and the union that will be subject to future review by both sides. The most important aspect of administering the contract involves the dissemination of information to all members of the agency on policies, programs, and equipment affected by the new agreement. Those items affected by the contract will still have to be worked out between management and union representatives. For example, while the contract may specify that all officers will receive a new caliber of weapon, the actual issuance of the weapon will not occur overnight.

Between the signing of the new contract and the initiation of negotiations for the next round of negotiations, a chief portion of contract administration by union and management involves handling and monitoring formal and informal deviances arising from situations and interpretations not covered in the existing document. The most effective manner in which to work out these disputes is to have one person or office administering the contract and keeping records concerning these differences or disagreements. What often happens is that over the life of the contract, these differences become agenda items for the new contract negotiations. Unresolved issues often become agenda items during the next round of bargaining or may become major grievance items. Naturally, these issues can be summarized as follows:

Seniority

Seniority, meaning the number of years or days that an officer has served, remains the cornerstone of collective bargaining agreements for such items as shift and special detail assignments. Grievances that arise over this issue are, in fact, very complicated in terms of the calculation of seniority time. For example, depending on the locality, "time on the job" may begin the first day the person walks through the front door, after graduation from the training academy, or after the probationary period. From the management view, seniority is a hindrance in terms of assigning the best person to the best job, and seniority often interferes with the administration of the daily operation of the agency.

Grievance Procedure

The reasons and guidelines for a grievance procedure have been discussed in detail. Grievances can arise from disputes over administration of the contract relating to wages as well as benefits and conditions of employment. Conditions of employment pose an open-ended arena for grievances. Police officers in states with comprehensive collective bargaining statutes can grieve anything and everything and they do! A review of a typical batch of grievances in one large state agency for one six-month period includes:

• Lack of interior or writing-light replacement bulbs in patrol vehicles.

- Administration of first aid to a person suspected of having AIDS.
- Transporting of prisoners by only one officer in an uncaged vehicle.
- An officer responding to fires and going inside to locate the cause of the alarm before the arrival of fire-service personnel.
- Not being allowed to wear leatherlike athletic shoes in place of the prescribed leather shoes.
- The presence of rats in a locker room.

The reader, no doubt, will ask why these items could not have been settled by open, face-to-face communication. The reality is that mundane and seemingly simple issues should be worked out either through informal communication or formal labor management meetings. Although necessary and important, formal grievances take time and bruise egos in terms of win-lose-or-draw outcomes between management and labor. Most of these issues could and should be worked out with direct and frank discussion.

Improper Labor Practices

Known in the field as an **IP**, an **improper practice** occurs when an employer does one or more of the following:

- Interferes, restrains, or coerces employees into forming or joining a labor union.
- Dominates or interferes with the formation or administration of a labor union.
- Discriminates against any employee for the purpose of encouraging or discouraging membership or activity in the union.
- Refuses to negotiate in good faith with the recognized or state-certified representatives of the union.
- Assigns work performed by union employees to nonunion employees.

Charges of improper practices can also be alleged against employees for similar reasons: (1) failure to negotiate in good faith with management, and (2) interfering, restraining, or coercing fellow employees from exercising their rights as union members: for example, seeking new representation from another labor organization. In most cases, IP complaints are handled at the local administrative level up to a final resolution at a state employee relations hearing.

Charges of improper practices by both labor and management often occur when contract negotiations reach a stalemate. They also seem to arise when officers of a department begin to organize a union under prevailing legislative guidelines. Invariably, in these situations, there are outright or implied threats by command personnel or the civilian administration about abolishing jobs, cutting back on existing benefits, and sometimes, abolishing the entire department! It is best in these situations for police and civilian administrators to back off before it is too late. When previously nonunionized police officers desire to form a union, it normally means that there are serious, unresolved problems relating to wages, benefits, and conditions of employment. Time and effort will be better served by administrators in taking a training course on "collective bargaining and contract administration" rather than dirtying the arena with threats, lawsuits, counterlawsuits, and so on.

Another rich area for improper-practice complaints involves instances when management attempts to hire or use outside consultants or employees for work that is normally done by police union members. Two common IP complaints are the use of civilians for dispatching or for writing parking tickets. The basis for these complaints is the contention that management is discriminating against union employees by having civilians do the jobs of sworn officers.

Discipline Procedures

In states with comprehensive collective bargaining statutes, disciplinary procedures invariably appear in the collective bargaining agreement. (The specifics of disciplinary procedure, such as the concept of progressive discipline and the range of sanctions, are analyzed in Chapter 9.) Contract language often defines the process by which discipline is imposed in terms of written charges, the parameters for interrogation, and union representation during interrogation.

Contracts often have prohibitions against the use of chemical or polygraph tests unless voluntarily agreed to by the suspect employee. Employees may also demand a review by an outside arbitrator on the punishment that the agency has imposed or seeks to impose. As with improper-practice complaints, employee-discipline procedures follow a grievance-type process involving a local hearing and then review of the charges and punishment by a state labor relations board. The desire by the employee to dispute either the notice of discipline and/or the punishment must be made within specified periods.

Union contracts vary with regard to representation of members by union-paid attorneys for charges filed by other police agencies and civilians. With some contracts, the union defends all officers against charges, while in other jurisdictions, paid-for legal defense is optional or nonexistent. As discussed in Chapter 9, the police administrator must know by heart the rules and conditions for discipline that appear in the union contract and the relevant civil service law. The police manager needs to follow the common law that evolves through the administration of a contract or contracts over time. Although many say that every case is different, state arbitrators have dismissed charges due to

1. Lack of proper and complete investigations and proper documentation.
2. Too severe punishment in relation to the offense (for example, suspension for failing to wear the uniform).
3. Lack of just cause in initiating discipline (for example, a personality clash rather than a legitimate issue).

Thus, a labor agreement is not a static document but, rather, changes as the organizational needs change. Also, conditions change and fringe benefits are looked at differently from one year to the next. One general rule: It is easy to add a benefit to a contract but extremely difficult to take one away, even if the benefit proves too costly.

FAIR LABOR STANDARDS ACT

An important element in the collective bargaining relationship is the payment of money for work performed. The Fair Labor Standards Act (FLSA) passed by Congress in the 1930s proscribes that employees must be paid overtime at a rate of one and one-half times the regular wage rate for over 40 hours of work. For many years, state work practices exempted law enforcement agencies, because operational needs required personnel to work shifts that would fill 24 hours without any gaps. However, in 1986 this concept was judicially tested in *Garcia v. San Antonio Metropolitan Transit Authority* (29 U.S.C. Sections 201–262); the Supreme Court ruled that FLSA was applicable to state and local law enforcement agencies.

Since that time, police unions and employers have addressed a number of complicated issues related to the law, either through labor/management processors or lawsuits. Law enforcement officers must be compensated for overtime, with either pay or compensatory time off, at a rate of not less than one and one-half hours for each hour over 43 hours per week, or 171 hours for a 28-day work period. The notion of work performed includes all activities that provide a benefit to the employer, such as pre-shift briefing, finishing reports from the previous tour, and travel to and from training courses. The rules for overtime apply to investigators, who may work for days on one case. When the FLSA is violated, law enforcement officers may sue for back wages, attorney fees, and punitive damages.

There are exceptions to these standards. As McCormack discusses (1995: 29), the FLSA does not cover law enforcement agencies that employ fewer than five officers within a workweek. Elected officials, such as the sheriff, or volunteers or management officials who are paid on a yearly salary are FLSA exempt. Those who are attending a training academy may not be covered because they are not considered regular employees. The issue of who is an exempted employee is always problematic for law enforcement managers who hold command rank. For example, if the manager can have hourly wages deducted based on a fine imposed by the department, then he or she is not FLSA exempt.

> ## THE POLICE STRIKE

Even though most states prohibit strikes or work slowdowns by police, in 1979 police **strikes** (stoppages of work) of one or more days occurred in the following areas: Cleveland, Ohio; Newark, New Jersey; Huntsville, Alabama; Los Angeles,

Monterey County, and Santa Monica, California; Toledo, Ohio, Salt Lake City, Utah; and Hawaii. In many other cities job actions resulted in **blue flu** (not reporting to work for alleged sickness), slowdowns, smashing of squad-car windows, and the initiation of "Fear City" campaigns over police cutbacks. In Newark, after the City Council discussed police layoffs, visitors were given literature stating that the city was a dangerous place in which to be.

There have been fewer police strikes and job actions in the 1980s and 90s compared with the 1970s. A major reason for this is the economics of local municipalities that have suffered decreased tax revenue along with cutbacks in federal and state aid. In the light of the many austerity budgets, there has been a new tendency for many police unions to cooperate with administrative and legislative leaders and managers in order to retain job security.

What has arisen in many contracts is the concept of givebacks, where the union gives back certain benefits negotiated and won in the past. There have also been many cases where unions have agreed to wage freezes or to work free for a specific number of days in order to continue job security.

While the Boston police strike remains an important event for historical purposes, a strike in Montreal in 1969 should be considered. Soon after it was realized that police were not on the streets, there was a rash of robberies and looting in the central area of the city. The absence of police led many observers to conclude that perhaps there was some validity to "the thin blue line" philosophy in that the police are the last defense against total anarchy. For the strikes cited in 1979, however, in all cases, contingency plans had been prepared, which included patrolling the city by outside police agencies, state troopers, and, at times, the National Guard.

Even though most contracts and state statutes forbid strikes by police and firefighters, it is important that all agencies have prepared plans to maintain essential police services. Most police agencies rely on outside assistance and the use of supervisors and nonstriking officers to fill this need. While services are being maintained, it may become the duty of the chief to be the mediator between the striking union and the political administration. As Burpo states, "the issues precipitating the strike are usually economic and cannot be unilaterally resolved by the chief, therefore the chief becomes the go-between" (1977: 416).

The use of a court **injunction** is a mechanism that is often used in halting a strike. Because of the no-strike clauses in labor contracts and state legislation, the injunction forces the officers back to work under the threat of contempt of court. In some strikes, court injunctions have been successful and strikers have returned to work under threat of jail or huge fines levied against the union treasury.

After the dust has settled and the police officers return to work, there are the follow-up issues of disciplinary proceedings against the strikers. There are no precise answers to this dilemma simply because each strike has different variables. However, a no-penalty or no-punishment clause in some contracts helps to stop petty punishments that serve only to damage morale and undermine employee-employer relations. A general rule that might be applied is that punishments do not deter future strikes and do a great deal of damage to the organization in terms of creating resentment among the employees.

➤ CONCLUSION

Collective bargaining is an important process for law enforcement agencies throughout the nation. Professionals who manage police departments see it as a step toward easing some of the strain between employees and employer, as written contracts help to eliminate misunderstandings. A fair grievance procedure, one that is fair both to management and labor, if used as intended, can settle disputes before they worsen. Disputes settled at the informal stage of the grievance procedure can help a department grow and adapt to changing times and conditions. However, disputes that go through the formal machinery assure all officers that they can have their day before a neutral hearing officer.

In all, collective bargaining is seen as a generally powerful force in upgrading police agencies. However, contracts do give management less flexibility in exercising the necessary authority to administer an agency. This problem will be met when management is willing to use the civil service and/or contract machinery to fire undesirable employees. Many managers feel that it is not worth the trouble; however, inaction means that the department will have to live with that undesirable employee for many years.

One new concept concerns givebacks; that is, returning or giving up certain benefits that have been previously earned at the bargaining table; for example, agreeing to give up uniform cleaning. This stems from the dire economic state in which many municipalities find themselves due to rising inflation and a declining tax base.

Overall, there is nothing that has dramatically changed with collective bargaining and police over the past twenty years. The majority of officers in states where collective bargaining is allowed belong to local police unions that focus on the terms and conditions of employment for their city, town, or county members. The idea of a national police union for all officers remains abstract.

Nationally, unionism in the private sector appears to be declining due to (1) the transformation of a manufacturing economy into a service economy; (2) growth of economies in nonunionized states, particularly in the South; (3) competition by companies with unions in granting job security, benefits, and a say in company operations without employees paying union dues. Citing Department of Labor statistics, Flipczak (1993) states that union membership in the United States dropped from around 30 percent of the workforce in 1970 to a low of 16 percent in 1992. In the public sector, the reverse is true, particularly in states with a long tradition in collective bargaining. The battles over management rights, wages, and conditions of employment continue to be waged at bargaining sessions and in grievance proceedings.

The concepts of work teams, quality circles, and partnering challenge the traditional adversarial relationship in collective bargaining. Consider this example:

> A worker has a problem and files a grievance through the formal process set up by his union. Management stalls the grievance procedure by failing to respond until the last possible minute at every step in the process. These delays can drag out a grievance for a year or even two. Then along comes the company's new teamwork program. All sorts of things can be discussed in team meetings, and the disgruntled employee discovers that he can get his problem solved in about 15 minutes. The team starts to look like a racing sloop next to the rusty barge of the union system. Soon the worker is wondering why he pays union dues when the company's team concept seems to work so much better. (Flipczak: 1993, 27)

Although the resolution of the problem seems nice, the worker may forget that the union also deals with wages, benefits, and safe working conditions outside of this team concept. Is unionism dormant in policing for the future? Hardly. However, certain benefits and outdated work rules appear to be doomed because of a public perception that certain rules stifle productivity and competition.

QUESTIONS FOR REVIEW

1. What are the major issues surrounding the rise of collective bargaining for police in the United States?

2. Define the following terms: *blue flu, arbitration*, and *management rights*.

3. Identify four major national police unions in the United States. Why are many local police unions reluctant to join national organizations?

4. Define *collective bargaining*. How does public-sector collective bargaining differ from that found in the private sector?

5. Explain the significance of the following strikes: Boston (1919) and Montreal (1969).

6. Give three reasons why police should have the right to strike. Give three reasons why police should not have the right to strike. Give one reason why you choose one side or the other.

7. List what you feel are the major issues in collective bargaining for police today and why.

CLASS PROJECT

The city of Jonesville will be negotiating a contract with the newly formed Jonesville Police Benevolent Association. At present, the overall conditions of employment for Jonesville officers are as follows:

1. Salaries are $20,000 for patrol officers, $25,000 for sergeants, and $27,000 for lieutenants. All personnel receive a $500 pay increase every two years.
2. The following holidays are allowed: July 4, Christmas, Thanksgiving, and Memorial Day.
3. There is one week of paid vacation for all personnel.
4. All officers must contribute toward their own pension fund.
5. All officers receive major health and dental care benefits from the city.
6. Uniforms are provided except for leather and handguns.
7. There is no pay for overtime or call-in time.
8. All grievances are handled by the chief of police.

JONESVILLE—GENERAL BACKGROUND OF AREA

This city is located anywhere in the United States. As with many American cities, Jonesville is showing a deficit, in this case $2 million, for this fiscal year. There is talk of layoffs for municipal workers. General unemployment for the area runs roughly 6 percent.

GAME PLAN

The class will be divided into two teams. One team will represent the Jonesville Police Benevolent Association; the other, the city of Jonesville. We suggest that teams be limited to eight persons each. Each team must select a chief negotiator. The chief negotiator will then assign each member specific research tasks. For example, one team member might be assigned to research the costs of pension programs for municipal employees; another member would deal with the issue of salaries, and so on.

ROLES OF NEGOTIATORS

The instructor will assign various team members to play specific roles. During one role-play session, one of the authors had the following characters:

For Jonesville PBA

Bill Griffith—recently elected as chief negotiator. Bill has promised to "bring home the bacon" and improve working conditions.

Wayne Freeman—a veteran patrol officer who sees this whole process as "chicken s—t" stuff. Freeman advocates the use of blue flu and strikes.

Linda Tomley—the first female officer in the department. Officer Tomley wants such things as lockers for female personnel and paid time during pregnancies.

Jack Smith—presently serves as public relations officer for the PBA. Among other things, he feels that the PBA should go "national" and get some clout to improve salaries and working conditions.

For City of Jonesville

Bill White—recently hired as director of personnel for the city. This is his first job since graduating from the School of Labor Relations, State University. White has promised the mayor and the city council to "kick ass and take names" when it comes to increasing personnel costs for any group of city employees. White hopes to make a name for himself here in Jonesville before moving on to a larger city.

Susan Brown—deputy director of personnel relations. She has great concern for the role of women and minorities in city personnel practices. Brown also handles complaints filed against city workers including the police. She feels that too many members of the police department are overpaid and are unfit to be police officers.

James Castle—city councilman who is assigned to the Public Safety Committee. Castle received an endorsement from the PBA in the last election. He is known as a "cop lover" by other politicians.

OBJECTIVES

The Jonesville PBA must try to improve its present wages, benefits, and other conditions of employment. The city of Jonesville must attempt to keep the status quo lest it plunge itself deeper into debt.

PLAYING THE GAME

Both sides must organize and prepare themselves for the bargaining session. Review this chapter and follow the processes presented by the authors. Enough time must be allowed to complete the game, but your instructor will impose some time constraints. In one bargaining session, the class spent over 40 hours and still was at an impasse before the role play was terminated.

KEY TERMS

agency shop
arbitration
blue flu
Boston Police strike
collective bargaining
community of interest
grievance procedure

improper practice
injunction
lobbying
mediation
negotiator
seniority

BIBLIOGRAPHY

ANON., "Bargaining Preparations for the Negotiator," *Police Law Reporter*, Vol. 5 (1978), pp. 10–13.

ANON., "Labor Notes," *Police Magazine* (July 1979a), p. 21.

ANON., *The Law Officer* (August/September 1979b), p. 1.

BOPP, WILLIAM J., "The Detroit Police Revolt." In William J. Bopp, ed., *The Police Rebellion*. Springfield, Ill.: Charles C.Thomas, 1971, pp. 162–72.

BOWERS, M.H., "Contemporary Police Employee Organizations and the Labor Relations Process," in *Crucial Issues in Police Labor Relations*. Gaithersburg, Md.: International Association of Chiefs of Police, 1973.

BURPO, J.H., "The Legal and Management Aspects of Police Strikes," In R.Ayres and T. Wheelen, eds., *Collective Bargaining in the Public Sector*. Gaithersburg, Md.: International Association of Chiefs of Police, 1977.

FLIPCZAK, BOB, "Unions in the 90s: Cooperation or Capitulation?" *Training* (May 1993), pp. 25–34.

FALLON, DENNY, "Police Labor in the 80's," *The National Centurion: A Police Lifestyle Magazine*, II, no. 5 (June 1984), pp. 38–45.

GAMMAGE, A.Z., and S.L. SACHS, *Police Unions*. Springfield, Ill.: Charles C.Thomas, 1972.

INTERNATIONAL ASSOCIATION OF CHIEFS OF POLICE, *Crucial Issues in Police Labor Relations*. Gaithersburg, Md.: The Association, 1977.

JURIS, H.A., and P. FEUILLE, *Police Unionism: Power and Impact in Public Sector Bargaining*. Lexington, Mass.: D.C. Heath, 1973.

KLOTZ, R., "Ground Rules," *Police Law Reporter*, Vol. 5 (1978), pp. 13–16.

MCCORMACK, WILLIAM U., "Law Enforcement and the Fair Labor Standards Act," *FBI Law Enforcement Bulletin*, 5, vol. 64 (May, 1995), pp. 28–32.

RYNECKI, STEVEN, D.A. CAIRNS, and D.J. CARNES, *Police Collective Bargaining Agreements: A National Management Survey*. Washington, D.C.: National League of Cities, 1978.

The Future Is Proactive Police Management

A SCENARIO FOR THE NEAR FUTURE

Captain Ryan Ortega put on his virtual helmet as his command vehicle came to a stop. His partner, Mary Fung Kan, looked at the swirling crowds. Stealth helicopters transmitted clear pictures of the housing project directly to Ortega's helmet. The computer screen in the car was alive with probability curves of potential crimes and disturbances in the ten-block area surrounding the car. Lieutenant Kan was doing an asset array, including undercover assets and firepower potential, on her laptop. Ortega opened the command channel, which included a digitalized encrypted line to the community police section headquarters.

Captain Ortega calls the sergeant for the community policing unit in the area and requests information on the causes for the gathering. According to Sergeant Anthony Smith, a rumor has started that the project is scheduled to be closed because of the collapse of federal and state housing funds. The project, which used to be a brick city in the 1990s, was turned into a neighborhood with townhouses, trees, and gardens. The majority of the population here is over 50 years old. According to the rumor, everyone will be forced to move and the area will be turned into a manufacturing site owned by a multinational corporation. What has sparked this event is that private police officials from the Euro-Pacific and Space Transportation Company have been doing crime prevention surveys to see if the area can become a repair station for earth and space transport ships.

Smith requests Ortega to contact the mayor's office and ask representatives to come and talk to the crowd. "The organizers have promised not to hurt the public community police officers but they will take out property owned by Euro-Pacific that is in the area," Smith reports.

The information is transmitted directly to the executive team at headquarters and becomes part of a database for the district community policing team. A riot is forming. Riot control dispersal experts are called in while the burglary prevention team secures the majority of apartments in the projects. A notification via the 3-D video goes to a computer-generated address list in the neighborhood, overriding all other broadcasts.

All of these events and actions have been anticipated by the central police agency planning team, who work out of the regional planning, hiring, training, and laboratory center. The metropolitan department had just been given high marks for training/education, community involvement, and police service per 100,000 population. The rapid response team was one of the department's highlights.

 ## ANTICIPATING THE PROACTIVE POLICE UNIVERSE

How did we get here? The list of trends and the police response is fairly obvious:

- Scarce resources, growth of inexpensive technology, instant communication, and concentration of lower class populations in the city.

- Changes in population demographics depending on section of the country. The middle class continues to leave the city in the west and east, while in other areas urban life is very desirable.

- Career equality regardless of gender, race, and ethnicity.

- Decline in the overall crime rate but increasing concern for violent felony offenses committed by juveniles with weapons. Great concern and emergency planning for technical crimes such as disruptions in electricity and communications links by terrorists.

- Increasing power of multinational corporations, many of which are based in the United States, competition, and cooperation from the private police establishment largely controlled by these same corporations. Target hardening and executive protection become major concerns.

- Increasing professionalization of the public and private police. Concern about community involvement in crime defense tactics and public police matters. Private police remain isolated from the community.

THE PROACTIVE POLICE RESPONSE

This is a series of strategies that include cost-effective concentration of administration, human resources, laboratory services, corruption and police brutality intervention, and training services for police departments. It includes:

- Deployment of community policing, including giving more authority to remote unit supervisors; human service/communication training for officers, supervisors, and police managers.

- Proactive planning to anticipate planned and unplanned events, including critical incident and hot spot management; centralized rapid-response teams with maximum firepower and human relations experts organized for instant deployment.

- Greater dependence on private police, auxiliary police, and community volunteers; major corporation private police begin to have more and more public police powers.

- Major police executives are highly educated, professionalized and move from major police department to department throughout the country.

All of this is the extrapolation of current trends. This is done by becoming thoroughly familiar with current police management data, policies, and concepts. Ours is a rapidly changing society. Adults from the WWII and Korean War generations can still remember a childhood without electricity. The car became important to policing in the 1920s, before television. Anomalies exist. As we did in the last century, we still use horses for effective crowd control. Computers only became available to the general public during the last two generations.

The global world is here to stay with instant communication and rapid transportation. The pace of change for the post-industrial generation is staggering. This is a scenario for America and other industrial and post-industrial countries. The overwhelming majority of the world's population live in preindustrial conditions, with some advanced products and communications. Proactive policing is addressed to the post-industrial American community. However, we must never forget that policing is global and both private and public. That globe is shrinking everyday. The overlooked power and authority of private police is growing all over the globe.

The human condition will always be with us despite the rapid changes. Law enforcement is still a human service agency, a people agency. Let us examine how we plan proactively to involve the community in the future. Of course, the realistic view is that the future is now.

What does the future hold for law enforcement managers? Given current trends, it is expected that police departments may be changed or organized along the lines presented in this chapter by the year 2001. We believe that this will result in effective policing given the socioeconomic, political, and technological realities of the future. The major thrust for change will be the demands made by cost-conscious municipal governments to continue to provide the wide array of police services demanded by citizens.

▶ POLICE DEPARTMENT CONSIDERATIONS

This abundance of forces is the historical result of our federal system of government and the wish of local communities to have control over their police. These realities of a democratic republic produce common problems of concurrent jurisdiction and duplication of effort. While citizens in cities can generally identify their police department, citizens of the many townships across the country have two or more options when they need the police. The selection includes the state police, town police, county sheriff's department, or village police. As a result, there exist these organizational realities in American policing today:

1. Active competition between police organizations for calls, resources, and, at times, personnel.

2. De facto spheres of influence arranged by formal and informal agreements between agencies. For instance, while the state police have statewide jurisdiction, many will normally not answer calls in a village that has a police department; the village police, in the same light, will not go outside municipal limits except in pursuit of an offender.

3. Informal relationships, usually based upon how well certain officers or agency heads get along, determine the distribution of intelligence information, assistance to other departments during emergencies, and the success or failure of interagency projects.

Some economists and social scientists might argue that this is healthy since it allows for competition, selection, and other market variables used by consumers for private-sector products. Some feel that police services can be provided by private contractors as long as the legal questions and cost-for-services formulas are worked out.

The number of law enforcement organizations would undoubtedly continue to increase were it not for the recent sharp demand for cost-effective police services. As municipal and police managers dealing with annual budgets know, costs for police personnel, equipment, and buildings have escalated in the last decade. Most of the funding is derived from taxation, and taxpayers are generally angry over the prospect of future tax increases at the federal, state, or local level. Political officeholders know that if taxes escalate in their communities, they will be out of jobs. The message to "hold down costs" has been relayed to all municipal department heads. This includes police commanders, who are told that their jobs will be jeopardized if they cannot balance their budgets. And so the story goes all over the country.

This financial crisis has reached new proportions created in part by policies on the federal level, which have slashed aid to state and local municipalities as a means of halting inflation. Some municipalities need these federal subsidies so as not to go bankrupt.

When funding is tight, vehicles are overhauled rather than replaced, plant maintenance and rehabilitation are deferred, and wage and benefit increases are forestalled either by contract or by mutual agreement. All in all, proactive police managers of the future will have to offer police services in an effective and economical way; that is, they will be required by their citizenry and elected officials to "do more with less." State and federal governments may have to respond with "creative" ways of raising money for policing. For example, we may see a tax on certain services, such as responding to home or building alarms in private businesses. Already, parking fines are returned either directly or indirectly to police budgets; other forms of revenue may be generated outside of the tax structure.

 ## THE JURISDICTIONAL DILEMMA

The existence of too many police departments results in duplication of services for many areas in the United States. Many argue for this, especially small-town politicians and police chiefs, who use the home rule argument to keep this jumbled, inefficient system intact. We predicted in our first edition that many municipalities would merge their police department with other governmental units or abolish the department outright. This has not occurred mainly because of home rule.

Many area schools have been closed or merged because of the decline in the numbers of children that have to be educated. When such an action is announced, there is often community protest and some delay, but usually the change is effected. Police departments are now subject to similar action, but there are some alternatives available for communities that wish to retain their local police. One common way is to share centralized services; for example, computerized recordkeeping, communications, vehicle acquisition and repair, supplies, equipment, and even laboratory and training facilities. In many instances, this type of sharing results in an upgrade of the present system of equipment currently in use by the local department.

A trend that we see increasing is police consolidation as when two or more departments are disbanded and merged into an area or county metropolitan police department. Departments that have undergone this process include those in Nassau and Suffolk counties in New York; Riley County, Kentucky; Jacksonville, Florida, and Toronto, Ontario. While this may sound easy, consolidation can be a very arduous process.

While there is potential for increasing police efficiency by reducing duplication of effort, consolidation does not always result in economy. From the outset, it can be expensive. Officer and command officials of previously existing departments are given new pay raises based on the highest wage scale paid in one of the "older" departments. New equipment has to be purchased on a mass scale for distinctive uniforms, vehicles, and weapons. New station houses have to be rented, purchased, or constructed. Aside from implementation, there are some other long-term managerial ramifications. Regarding the collective bargaining issue, smaller police unions are eliminated and reformed into one or more powerful union(s) because of increased membership. Former chiefs of police are "demoted" to ranking administrative officers. New organizational charts and duties have to be prepared. Interestingly enough, departmental subculture is revised with the creation of a consolidated police force, which results in new patrol zones, shifts, and duty assignments. But for lower-ranking administrators and patrol officers, consolidation presents all kinds of opportunities for professional and career advancement.

What this all means is that the concept of consolidation can be feasible where there are high concentrations of people or businesses that create a single socioeconomic municipality. Consolidation, moreover, may reflect another trend whereby municipalities merge as political entities resulting in a merger of police, fire, and other public services.

Another form of consolidation is combining police and fire departments. This has met with mixed success. Generally, it works best with small departments within a limited geographic area. For example, communities that have consolidated are: Clifton, New Jersey, population 90,000; Flagstaff, Arizona, population 26,000; El Dorado, Kansas, population 13,000; Glencoe, Illinois, population 10,000; and the largest population and area, Sunnyvale, California, 106,000 with 22 square miles of jurisdiction. According to Rubin (1984: 225), the cities of Peoria, Lincoln, and St. Petersburg adopted public safety programs combining fire and police and later abandoned them. In all cases Rubin concludes (Rubin, 1984: 226): "Labor-management cooperation is imperative."

Consolidation of fire and police services has been around the United States since 1911 and may work in some fairly small-population communities. There has been both partial and full consolidation. It is a difficult process with many legal, personnel, and organizational problems, but it is tempting to mayors and city managers hoping for cost savings. Cost savings may or may not come about and any fire/police consolidation should be carefully thought through, especially in terms of analyzing the different missions of police and fire departments.

Many communities in the United States contract for police services from another municipality. The basic considerations in determining contractual services are

1. Statutory provisions related to contract agreements.
2. Formulas to be used in charging for such services as patrol, traffic, criminal investigations, and so on.
3. Planning and resolving various issues that come with normal policing (for example, interruption of services, liability, physical plant needs, personnel requirements).
4. Determining performance criteria for continuance of the contract (for example, lower crime rate, citizen satisfaction with services).

Throughout the 1970s, a number of feasibility studies were undertaken by the Law Enforcement Assistance Administration and private firms on the issue of contractual services. Many of these organizations' recommendations have been implemented. According to the National Sheriff's Association, there are the following types of contractual arrangements:

City to city. Police service is provided by one city to another.

County to city or county to region. Perhaps the most common contractual arrangement in the United States occurs when a county sheriff or police department provides police services to municipalities in the county on a shared-expense or contributory-expense arrangement. Such situations exist in Cook County, Illinois; Los Angeles County, Orange County, and Riverside, California; Decatur County, Iowa; Brown County, Wisconsin; and Penellas County, Florida.

Resident officer program. Small towns that do not have a police department may contract for one or more full-time police officers from the state police or county sheriff's department. Expenses paid for these officers by the township are usually one-half the total cost of each person. In some cases, the officer(s) receive a bonus if they reside in the contractual area.

 ## TECHNOLOGY

If anything, the technological revolution continues to revise traditional police practices. Even the smallest of departments have embraced microcomputing systems and workstations. We see no end in sight to the various adaptations that can be accomplished. Nevertheless, police managers have to be informed consumers of this new technology.

Although managers are not expected to know how to tear apart a computer terminal system, they should know the strengths and weaknesses of implementing a computerized records system for a department or division. They need to know about basic programming to experiment with new methodologies that deal with budgets, crime trends, personnel records, and so on. The same is true for other forms of technology, such as video units, which can be used for long-term surveillance on target areas, thereby freeing personnel for other duties.

Ironically, a best seller in police circles is *PC's for Dummies* (Gookin and Kathboar, 1992) which is a tongue-in-cheek presentation on computer lingo for the nontechnical person. Relatedly, the paperless-police-department trend discussed earlier will continue to expand as equipment costs are reduced. Mobil data terminals, computer-aided dispatching, and other programs will be standardized for police jurisdictions by the year 2000.

As we talk about technology and policing, however, we must not lose sight of the need for greater interaction between citizens and their police officers. One program that has assisted in this endeavor is bicycle patrol (some might say a rather low-tech program), which on college campuses and in densely populated areas has received high marks for increasing visibility and officer-citizen interaction.

Patrol methods may change dramatically from the preventive brand that is employed today. It is now possible for every patrol vehicle to be equipped with a miniature computer-augmented mobile radio that relays an automatic signal back to the communications center giving the location of the vehicle on an electronic map of the metropolitan area. Computerized crime analysis also permits this map to be keyed to show a great variety of characteristics to facilitate planning. Some of these are

1. Street and map response time grid.

2. Modus operandi grid related to demographic characteristics and time of crime commitment.

3. Time, place, and nature of crimes shown by number and color for easy identification. Listings of burglaries, robberies, traffic deaths, juvenile crimes, and other grids would be available at the punch of a button.

4. Demographic vehicles: density, distribution, and vital statistics of population.

5. Trend-analysis grids for traffic control, civilian disasters, and energy blackouts would be available for planners if a disaster or traffic stoppage occurred.

Reflecting the state of the art for cable television, all homes and businesses can be linked to a central dispatch system in a police-approved, computer-based, remote linkage system. This would combine burglar and fire alarms operating through land lines and cable television circuits.

 PERSONNEL PRACTICES

Given the current trends in positive personnel selection, it is possible that we may see the following:

1. College degrees on an associate or baccalaureate level demanded of all recruits.

2. Men and women being assigned to all facets of the police mission on an equal basis and promoted to speciality units and command and supervisory positions.

3. The police-recruit selection process placing less emphasis on pencil-and-paper tests, with more emphasis on testing by role play, interview, aptitude, and other assessment-center methods.

More lateral entry between police departments on a state and national level would increase the pool of available candidates for line, staff, and managerial positions. If this becomes a reality, there will be renewed emphasis on the quality selection of police managers since the available pool will increase competition.

While running the risk of criticism for being too general, it can be said that the "typical police chief" of today generally

> Is 45 to 52 years of age.
>
> Has worked through the ranks of the department.
>
> Has had little experience in either public or private administration prior to appointment or selection as chief. Training consisted of some police academy seminars and learning by the ropes. Formal education is limited to high school augmented by courses taken at the local community college.
>
> Was selected as chief by written civil service examination or political appointment, or was elected.

With the organizational and milieus changes that we see occurring in American policing, it comes as no surprise that the credentials of future managers will also be undergoing some change. Reflecting current trends in patrol-officer selection, police managers of the future will also be the products of advanced managerial training and higher education. In the future the selection of police managers will correspond to that already practiced by many private-sector enterprises for executive talent. Psychological testing, role plays involving managerial problems, and oral review boards will be the rule for selection rather than the exception. This cadre of police executives will be highly mobile, in that a police executive could be "chief" at a number of departments during a law enforcement career, with minor or extended excursions into industry and teaching.

Selection for supervisors and administrative staff members will also reflect some changes. Again, less reliance will be placed on pencil-and-paper tests and years of experience. Requirements for future segments might be:

> A master's degree in administration or a related field.
>
> Three years of experience in police patrol or investigations.
>
> Successful completion of the state-certified training academy for police patrol officers and supervisors. Some states may be issuing licenses by this time that have to be renewed on a timely basis.

Individuals who show administrative talent would be "tracked" into a departmental executive development program that would provide a rational combination of in-class training and field exposure to all facets of the police mission for future executives.

 **CONCLUSION**

PROACTIVE COMMUNITY POLICING IN THE 21ST CENTURY

In a society of scarce resources, the police departments need to plan carefully a cost-efficient use of police resources targeting the most pressing community problems as perceived by the community. As corporate and private police become more evident, new legislation concerning professionalization of these forces will take place. Public and private police will work together using legally enforceable contracts. Increasingly, some police services will be contracted out.

The extensive use of technology makes this possible. The educated line officer will take on more responsibilities, using community enforcement as a major approach to street and neighborhood crime. Training in communication, use of technological services, and collective behavior will become most important to the proactive police officer, manager, and supervisor.

As more responsibility for anticipating events and taking proactive action is embraced by every level of command, morale will improve. Communities will take back their neighborhoods with the help of their proactive police department.

PROACTIVE RURAL POLICING

Meanwhile rural communities will become less isolated as the internet and communications systems link these with the worldwide network of work/communications. Rural police will have to adapt to the standards of the proactive police departments in metropolitan areas. Regional academies and services for rural agencies will upgrade the professionalism of these police officers. Their enlightened communities will also demand a higher level of community policing.

Rural communities have existed in the United States since its early years as an agricultural society. Police were already part of these communities even before the idea of community policing had been formed. The sense of community that urban areas are searching for was established in small town America. Since police, in these areas, are considered part of a greater community, it is a fairly simple step to establish the proactive community policing of the 21st century.

Technology will provide a vast communication network; distance and weather are no longer barriers to instant communication. Virtual communities have already been established. These virtual communities will welcome a professionalized proactive community police force.

THE PROACTIVE COMMUNITY POLICING MANAGEMENT MODEL

It will take time to establish proactive community police norms as part of police culture. Police still cherish their social isolation and their perception of public hostility. Reality and political pressure will play an important part in the transformation of the traditional police department into the technologically aware, proactive, professional police force of the future. Since the creation of the London Metropolitan Police Department in 1829, police culture has had to solidify its present subculture. It will take time and a great deal of effort to transform our police forces into a paradigm. However, it will happen. The new generation of police officers, supervisors, and managers who are reading this textbook will make it happen. But it won't be easy.

This is a consultative management model demanded by the new generation of professional police line officers and supervisors. They are college-educated and think proactive. These police managers are taking their place in police departments throughout the nation. The educated police officers and supervisors will demand more responsibility and autonomy. The promise of present and future technology, along with an attitude change brought about by the proactive community police model, will make this possible.

The major characteristics of proactive community police management are:

1. Participatory management with more responsibility and autonomy given to supervisors in the field.

2. Centralized rapid response for critical incidents and emergencies.

3. Community sets the agenda for proactive policing in every neighborhood, town, village, and community center.

4. A proactive preventive attitude and policy base. Police managers, supervisors, and line officers will be working with the community to prevent and contain crime, property theft and damage, and community violence.

5. Proactive, planned, and limited patrolling. The split force will have a section responding to 911 calls, and a section for planning, hot spot targeting, community policing, and so on.

6. Forecasting of events will take place in every part of every department, from a centralized planning unity to an individual team of officers making plans with a community neighborhood. Planning will be central to the proactive community police department.

7. Training and education will take place side by side. After thorough background checks and testing (including psychological testing), the college-educated police officer will enter a highly professional training program. This program will emphasize police ethics, community involvement, technological and communication expertise, and human service skills, along with the traditional subjects. Inservice and clinical training will persist throughout an officer's career, including supervisory and management training at promotion. Human resources will include stress management for all levels and their families, from line officers to major managers.

8. This will be a "smart" police force that will use technology extensively, but the educated proactive police manager will use technology as

a tool and never let technology drive policy. Human beings will be in charge of technology that will be used extensively in a community-oriented human service department.

9. This proactive department will use planning and technology to reduce crime and solve crimes for their communities. Cases will be solved using solid investigative work and the latest techniques, including DNA identification and forensic testing. Departments will employ or contract with their own lawyers to make cases prosecutable and to protect them against unreasonable plea bargains.

QUESTIONS FOR REVIEW

1. Agree or disagree with the societal changes for the 21st century. Add two changes to the list.

2. Is the proactive police response realistic, or so much science fiction?

3. State the pros and cons of police consolidation. Predict what you think will happen in the future, and why.

4. What would you add to personnel practices, and why?

5. Analyze the characteristics of the proactive community police model and state why you think it will or will not work.

KEY TERMS

centralized rapid response
community policing
consolidation
consultative management

home rule
proactive
proactive management model
technology

BIBLIOGRAPHY

AMERICAN BAR ASSOCIATION, PROJECT ON STANDARDS FOR CRIMINAL JUSTICE, *Standards Relating to the Urban Police Function*. Chicago: The Association, 1972.

BAEHR, M., J.E. FURCON, and E.C. FROEMAL, *Psychological Assessment of Patrolman Qualifications in Relation to Field Performance*. Chicago: Industrial Relations Center, University of Chicago, 1968.

BANTON, MICHAEL, *The Policeman in the Community*. New York: Basic Books, 1964.

BARD, MORTON, *Training Police as Specialists in Family Crisis Intervention.* Washington, D.C.: U.S. Government Printing Office, 1970.

BITTNER, EGON, *The Functions of the Police in Modern Society.* Chevy Chase, Md.: National Institute of Mental Health, 1970.

BLOCH, PETER B., and DAVID SPECHT, *Neighborhood Team Policing.* Washington, D.C.: U.S. Government Printing Office, 1973.

COHEN, B., and J. CHAIKEN, *Police Background Characteristics and Performance: Summary Report.* New York: Rand Institute, 1972.

COHN, ALVIN, ed., *The Future of Policing.* Beverly Hills, Calif.: Sage, 1978.

CRANK, JOHN, "The Community-Policing Movement of the Twenty-First Century: What We Have Learned," in John Klofas and Stan Stojkoic, *Crime and Justice in the Year 2010.* New York: Wadsworth Publishing Company, 1995, pp. 107–127.

CRUSE, DANIEL, and JESSE RUBIN, *Determinants of Police Behavior.* Washington, D.C.: U.S. Government Printing Office, 1973.

CUMMING, ELAINE, IAN CUMMING, and LAURA EDELL, "Policeman as Philosopher, Guide and Friend," *Social Problems,* 12 (Winter 1965), pp. 276–86.

DORAN, R.A., *Feasibility Study of Regionalized Police Services for the Barrington (Ill.) Area.* Chicago: Illinois Law Enforcement Commission, 1974.

DUNCAN, J.T. SKIP, ROBERT N. BRENNER, and MARJORIE KRAVITZ, *Police Stress: A Selected Bibliography.* Washington, D.C.: National Institute of Law Enforcement and Criminal Justice, 1979.

DUNNETTE, M.D., and S.J. MOTOWILDE, *Police Selection and Career Assessment.* Washington, D.C.: U.S. Government Printing Office, 1975.

EASTMAN, G.D., and S.G. CHAPMAN, *Short of Merger: Countrywide Police Resources Pooling.* Lexington, Mass.: D.C. Health, 1976.

EDGAR, JAMES M., MARVIN MARCUS, ROBERT J. WHEATON, and ROBERT C. HICOX, *Team Policing: A Selected Bibliography.* Washington, D.C.: U.S. Government Printing Office, 1976.

FOGELSON, ROBERT M., *Big City Police.* Cambridge, Mass.: Harvard University Press, 1977.

GAY, WILLIAM G. H. TALMADGE DAY, and JANE P. WOODWARD, *Phase I Summary Report: Neighborhood Team Policing.* Washington, D.C.: U.S. Government Printing Office, 1977.

GOOKIN, DAN, and ANDY RATHBONE, *PC's for Dummies.* San Mateo: IDG Books, 1992.

HELLER, N.B., *What Law Enforcement Can Gain from Computer Designed Work Schedules.* Washington, D.C.: U.S. Government Printing Office, 1974.

KELLING, GEORGE, and MARK H. MOORE, "The Evolving Strategy of Policing," in Victor Kappler, *The Police and Society.* Prospect Heights, Ill.: Waveland Press, 1995, pp. 3–28.

KLOFAS, JOHN, and STAN STOJKOIC, *Crime and Justice in the Year 2010*. New York: Wadsworth Publishing Company, 1995.

KOEPSELL, T.W., R.H. TERPSTRA, and L.E. STREETER, *Consolidation of Police Services Case Study: Executive Summary*. Falls Church, Va.: Koepsell-Girard and Associates, 1973.

MCDONALD, THOMAS D., ROBERT A. WOOD, and MELISSA A. PFLUG, *Rural Criminal Justice*. Salem, Wis.: Shieffield Publishing Company, 1996.

MEHAY, S.L., *Evaluating the Performance of a Governmental Structure: The Case of Contract Law Enforcement*. Los Angeles: University of California Institute of Government and Public Affairs, 1974.

MELCHIONNE, THERESA M., "The Changing Role of Policewomen," *The Police Journal* (October 1974), pp. 340–58.

NORRGARD, DAVID L., *Regional Law Enforcement*. Chicago: Public Administration Service, 1969.

RUBIN, RICHARD, "Consolidation of the Police and Fire Services." *Journal of Police Science and Administration*, 12, no. 2 (1984), pp. 58–69.

SOHN, R.L., R.D. KENNEDY, and E.A. GARCIA, *Multicommunity Command and Control Systems in Law Enforcement: An Introductory Planning Guide*. Pasadena, Calif.: Institute of Technology Jet Propulsion Laboratory, 1976.

STEPHENS, GENE, "Crime in Cyberspace: The Digital Underworld." in Edward Cornish, ed., *Exploring Your Future*. Washington, D.C.: World Future Society, 1996.

STRECHER, VICTOR G., "Revising the Histories and Futures of Policing," in Victor Kappler, *The Police and Society*. Prospect Heights, Ill.: Waveland Press, 1995, pp. 83–94.

Index

Automatic vehicle monitoring (AVM), 131–32

Auxiliary functions, 241–65
emergency mobilization services, 263–64
communications, 242–45
communications personnel, 243–45
crime laboratory, 257–262
license section, 262
personal patrol car program (PCP), 253–54
physical plant maintenance, 254–56
property section and operations, 249–51
records, 245–49
computers and, 246
public access to, 247–49
security and storage, 247–48
temporary detention facility, 256–57
vehicle maintenance and selection, 251–53

B

Background investigations for personnel selection, 284–85
Behavioral management model, 10–11
Bias crime, 330
Bike patrol, 194–95
Black officers, 34–36
Blake and Mouton's managerial grid, 98–100
Boston Police Strike, 380–81
Budgets, 319–24
line-item budgeting, 359–60
performance budgeting system (PPBS), 359–62
supplementing, 364–66
zero-based budgeting (ZBB), 362–63
Bureaucracy, traditional concept of, 4, 57–58
Max Weber, concepts of, 57–58

C

Canal City case study, 39–41
Career criminals, 175–78
Caruso v. Ward, 299
Case screening: criminal investigations, 170–71
Chain communication/chain-of-command, 110
Charismatic authority, concept of, 78–79
City of Canton v. Harris, 342
Civilian personnel, consideration for 50–51
Civil liability and training, 340–43
Civil service, 50, 269–72
Collective bargaining, 379–97
definition of, 379–80
discipline procedures, 393–94
grievance procedure, 391–92
history of, 280–82
improper labor practices, 392–93
major police union organizations, 386–87
management rights and, 387–88
police strikes, 394–96
process of, 388
College education requirements for personnel, 291–92
Commission on Accreditation for Law Enforcement Agencies, 59–60
Communications, operation of, 242–45
Communication, management theory related to, 108–12
assumptions in, 107
chain of command, 110
feedback, 103, 105
Johari window, 114
obstacles to, 112
over-generalization, 110
operational communications, 116–18
effectively organized directives, 118–19
proactive communications model, 123–25
typical model of, 108

Total quality management, 84–86
Tort actions (*See* Civil liberty and training)
Traditional management model, 3–4
Traditional vs. community policing, 202–03
Training, 313–32
    basic training, 317–18
    civil liability and, 340–43
    common deficiencies in, 315–16
    curriculum, 324–26
    executive training,
    field training programs, 318–319
    importance of, 319–20
    management training, 338–40
    phase approach to, 338
    Project Star, 321–23
    supervisors' course, 335–38
    Task Force on Police recommendations, 320–21
    topical issues in, 327–32
Trauma, associated with critical incidents, 308–09
Typologies of officers, 33–39

U

Union brokerage model, for off-duty work, 303
Unionism in policing, 341–43 (*See also* Collective bargaining)
Union rules for disciplinary actions, 303
United Steel Workers v. Weber, 274

V

Vehicle maintenance, 251–54
Vice, as line function, 149–53

Victimless crimes, 149–50
Violence, perception of, 22–24
Virtual reality training, 331–32
Vocational subculture
    characteristics of, 17–24
Vollmer, August, 5–6
Von Raab v. National Treasury Employees Union, 299
Voutour v. Vitale, 341

W

Ward Packing v. Atone, 276
Weber, Max, 57
    concept of modern bureaucracy, 57–59
Who communicates with whom, 106–08
Wilson, O. W., 5–6
Wincanton Case Study, 31–32
Women police officers, 36–39
Work community, effect on police bureaucracy, 25–26
Written civil service tests, 278–79
Written communications, 116–23

Y

"Y" Communication, 112
Youth services, 153–63 (*See also* Juvenile aid)

Z

Zero-based budgeting (ZBB), 362–63